Mastering Emotions

AMERICA IN THE NINETEENTH CENTURY

Series editors: Brian DeLay, Steven Hahn, Amy Dru Stanley

America in the Nineteenth Century proposes a rigorous rethinking of this most formative period in U.S. history. Books in the series will be wide-ranging and eclectic, with an interest in politics at all levels, culture and capitalism, race and slavery, law, gender, and the environment, and regional and transnational history. The series aims to expand the scope of nineteenth-century historiography by bringing classic questions into dialogue with innovative perspectives, approaches, and methodologies.

Mastering Emotions

Feelings, Power, and Slavery in the United States

Erin Austin Dwyer

PENN

UNIVERSITY OF PENNSYLVANIA PRESS

PHILADELPHIA

Published by
University of Pennsylvania Press
Philadelphia, Pennsylvania 19104-4112
www.upenn.edu/pennpress

Printed in the United States of America on acid-free paper
10 9 8 7 6 5 4 3 2 1

Library of Congress Cataloging-in-Publication Data
Names: Dwyer, Erin Austin, author.
Title: Mastering emotions : feelings, power, and slavery in the United
States / Erin Austin Dwyer.
Other titles: America in the nineteenth century.
Description: 1st edition. | Philadelphia : University of Pennsylvania
Press, [2021] | Series: America in the nineteenth century | Includes
bibliographical references and index.
Identifiers: LCCN 2021012062 | ISBN 9780812253399 (hardcover)
Subjects: LCSH: Slavery—Social aspects—Southern States—History—
19th century. | Emotions—Social aspects—United States—History—19th century. |
Power (Social sciences)—United States—History—19th century. | Slaves—Southern
States—Social conditions—19th century. | Slaveholders—Southern States—
Social conditions—19th century. | Southern States—Social conditions—
19th century. | Southern States—Race relations—History—19th century.
Classification: LCC E443 .D97 2021 | DDC 306.3/620973—dc23
LC record available at https://lccn.loc.gov/2021012062]

To those who found their families in freedom,
and to those who never stopped looking.

Need I pause to show how this system of servitude . . . is interwoven with our entire social fabric? That these slaves form parts of our households? . . . Must I pause to show how it has fashioned our modes of life, and determined all our habits of thought and feeling?

—Benjamin Palmer, New Orleans, Thanksgiving 1860

CONTENTS

INTRODUCTION

The Emotional Politics of Slavery

As an enslaved man in the antebellum South, Charles Ball was keenly aware that being fluent in the verbal and physical language of emotions was a critical survival skill. The narratives of formerly enslaved people reveal a widespread belief that reading, performing, and masking emotions could help them navigate the power-laden affective relations between enslaved people and members of the plantocracy. When several slaveholders interrogated the enslaved man about how his owner treated him, Ball recalled in his narrative that he grew flushed as his anger bubbled to the surface, but he knew he could not express that feeling. Instead he "forced a sort of smile" upon his face. Writing primarily for White, Northern, abolitionist readers, Ball explained that "a slave is often afraid to . . . divulge all he feels" and must never "manifest feelings of resentment"; rather, they should feign less threatening and more marketable emotions like "humility."[1] His description of the rapid succession of physical and emotional responses that he experienced while being questioned hints at how cognizant enslaved people were that counterfeit feelings had to be summoned immediately, and fully embodied, in order to adequately cloak their true sentiments. The speed with which he quashed his initial disdain speaks to how adept enslaved people became at this routine. Nevertheless, Ball made clear that it was no small feat to enact a feeling on command. Compelled to display emotions that were at odds with how he felt, the best he could muster was the simulacrum of a grin, a rictus of false joy that was all too familiar for enslaved people.

In a period steeped in sentimental culture, the ability to restrain one's emotions was considered a key component of self-control and character for middle-class and upper-middle-class Americans. One Southern woman of the planter class wrote in verse about emotional management:

The passions are a numerous crowd
Imperious positive and loud . . .
If they grow wild and rave
They are thy masters, thou their slaves.[2]

In the poet's view, failure to contain "wild" or excessive "passions" rendered a person enslaved by their own emotions. The metaphor of being enslaved by unruly emotions appeared in everything from magazine columns to advice books for young people, with one 1842 etiquette guide for men warning that "the passions are . . . excellent servants, but dreadful masters; and whoever is under their dominion, will have [to] obey their dictates."[3] Thus ambitious members of the planter class were counseled to make their feelings their subordinates, lest those sentiments come to rule them.

In the antebellum South, a society in which the master-slave relationship structured all other social dynamics, slaveholders and enslaved people were not merely using the language of emotional mastery in a figurative sense.[4] Nor did it suffice to simply achieve self-government. Rather, antebellum etiquette books, diaries, agricultural journals, and slave narratives indicate a popular understanding that one must exercise emotional self-mastery to effectively dominate other people. For slaveholders this meant suppressing some sentiments in order to be viewed as respectable members of the planter class. Examining how people strived to master their own emotions while exerting control over the feelings of others underscores how important emotions were to maintaining, negotiating, and challenging slave society. Studying the double standard of affective censorship for enslaved people and slaveholders exposes how closely freedom of emotional expression was linked to one's status as free or enslaved.

The desire for complete self-mastery was critical to the development of the affective norms and expectations of the antebellum South for members of the slaveocracy, enslaved people, and free Black people, albeit for different reasons. Notions of emotional mastery dictated which feelings were to be personified or tamped down, and in what situations. In order to maintain the affective norms of the antebellum South, slaveholders and enslaved people were required to repress emotions, including rage, jealousy, and sadness, and to feign others, all while paying close attention to the feelings of the people around them. Planter periodicals like *DeBow's Review*, *Southern Planter*, and *American Cotton Planter* advocated for emotional restraint as a plantation management strategy, urging slaveholders to quell their feelings, especially anger, particularly when disciplining enslaved people.[5] Slaveholders who were unable to govern their own emotions risked public scrutiny as well as the potential loss of capital, status, and reputation. For enslaved people the stakes of failing to fake or censor their feelings were even higher. Enslaved women and men like Charles Ball learned from a young age that if they were unable or unwilling to camouflage certain emotions and perform others, they risked the whip, the auction block, or even death.

* * *

In the antebellum South, felt and expressed emotions were fundamentally constructed by the institution of slavery and by enslaved people. The writings of enslaved people and slaveholders, as well as those of proslavery authors and abolitionists, demonstrate that in the antebellum South feelings were a currency of power in master-slave relationships. Such sources show that emotions were central to how members of the slaveocracy legally, politically, and culturally perpetuated slavery, as they wielded feelings like love, terror, and jealousy to maintain and justify the institution. Enslaved people also strategically employed feelings at times, selectively performing devotion, loyalty, or fear in order to avoid punishment, seek benefits, survive, or even resist enslavement.

The daily negotiations and contestations that occurred between slaveholders and enslaved people, through and about feelings, in conjunction with larger debates about race, freedom, and affective norms, are the basis of the emotional politics of slavery. Though conflicts over slavery and emotions in the antebellum and postwar South had a profound impact on policy, including manumission laws, Black Codes, and Jim Crow-era legislation and contracts, this definition of emotional politics is predicated on the idea that power flows in multiple directions, rather than resting solely in the domain of "high politics" or electoral politics. By analyzing the interactions between slaveholders and enslaved people, and between former slaveholders and free Black people, one can see how power operates through emotions and how before and after the Civil War Black Southerners and elite White Southerners deliberately deployed feelings or sought to compel them.

Though slavery is a subject wrought with emotion, historians of emotion have neglected antebellum American slavery and racial politics more generally. Meanwhile, scholarship on slavery has often addressed affective relations among the slaveholding class and among enslaved communities, but without considering the complex emotional interactions and power plays taking place between the two groups, or the legacy of those racialized affective practices and expectations.[6] Even histories centered on master-slave relations have traditionally been written from the perspective of the master, accepting proslavery propaganda that these relations were mutually affectionate and that paternalism was a reality rather than an inherently violent ideal. By peering more deeply into the hearts of slaveholders than those of enslaved people, such works fail to explore how emotions functioned in the realm of vastly unequal power that existed between slaveholders and enslaved people.[7] The history of emotion has focused on how feelings are collectively learned and socialized, but by combining that field with the history of slavery *Mastering Emotions* illustrates that the affective norms of slavery were not produced in a unidirectional fashion by elites; rather, they were forged by enslaved people and slaveholders together in the crucible of slavery.[8]

The affective norms of slavery that emerged in the antebellum period were based on a philosophy of racialized emotional difference: a White supremacist belief that people experienced emotions differently depending on their race. Thomas Jefferson's famed *Notes on the State of Virginia* explored the idea that race was both externally visible and internally legible. He catalogued what he perceived as physical disparities between the races, including skin pigmentation, which he surmised might stem from differing amounts of "bile, or . . . some other secretion," before enumerating differences in hair texture and perspiration. But Jefferson also hypothesized that race was more than skin (or bile) deep, positing that Black people did not feel emotions like love the same way White people did. He claimed that men of African descent were "more ardent after their female: but love seems with them to be more an eager desire, than a tender delicate mixture of sentiment and sensation," implying that Black people experienced lust rather than the nuanced "mixture of sentiment" felt by White people. Jefferson also asserted that Black people's sorrow was more muted and temporary, observing that "their griefs are transient."[9]

Jefferson's writing provides a glimpse of how racialized theories about emotions could be used to justify slavery, particularly in his discussion of Black people's limited feelings of "grief" and love. Contending that Black people's sorrows were short-lived, and that they felt physical lust in lieu of "tender" love, could easily be used to rationalize raping enslaved people, selling enslaved family members, and prohibiting legal marriage for enslaved couples.[10] In this way, White supremacist musings about racialized emotional differences took cruel, concrete form on plantations and on auction blocks. Henry Box Brown remembered that when his wife and children were being sold and he begged to be bought with them, their buyer was unmoved, advising Brown to "get another wife . . . so [he] need not trouble [himself] about that one." Nor was that slaveholder an anomaly; Brown noted that among slaveholders it was a "common expression . . . that 'niggers have no feelings.'"[11]

Arguments about racialized emotional difference, and slaveholder practices based on those White supremacist ideas, became more frequent in the sentiment-obsessed antebellum period as debates over slavery intensified. Other members of the planter class dismissed the emotional capacity of Black people, and they justified selling enslaved children in particular by comparing the familial bonds of enslaved people to those of animals. For example, Lewis Hayden's owner, a Presbyterian minister, announced from his "pulpit that there was no more harm in separating a family of slaves than a litter of pigs."[12] It is impossible to say how wide an audience the minister reached, but Hayden's story suggests that ideas about the animal nature of Black emotions circulated beyond proslavery literature and impacted countless enslaved families.

Confronted with White supremacist propaganda that stated that Black people felt emotions less intensely, or lacked familial affection altogether, formerly enslaved people and abolitionists responded with their own ideas about the relationship between emotional difference and slavery in order to oppose the institution and repudiate proslavery arguments. However, while proslavery authors accentuated how emotions differed by race, authors of slave narratives attested that emotional difference was instead tied to slave status. Slave narratives implicitly discredited claims of emotional inferiority with descriptions of falling in love, close-knit families, and the heartbreak of being torn away from loved ones. Some more explicitly rejected the idea that race determined their feelings; Charles Ball declared that "there is no difference between the feelings of the different races of men."[13] Josiah Henson also scoffed at proslavery theories that Black people were inherently emotionally limited, decrying the separation of enslaved families, vowing that familial "affections . . . are as strong in the African as in the European."[14]

To refute beliefs that they possessed limited or animalistic feelings based on race, authors of slave narratives argued that enslaved people in fact felt emotions more acutely, having experienced profound sentiments that were unknowable by those who had never been enslaved. This became a recurring trope in slave narratives, with Henry Bibb averring that "no one can imagine my feelings . . . but he who has himself been a slave" and with Harriet Jacobs confessing "reader, if you have never been a slave you cannot imagine the acute sensation of suffering at my heart."[15] The idea that any emotional differences were rooted in the conditions of slavery, and thus were not biological or fixed, jeopardized proslavery ideology and individual slaveholders, as it meant that emancipated enslaved people expected the same affective rights that free people enjoyed, including the ability to exercise a full range of feelings without restriction or censorship.

Many antebellum slaveholders may have balked at the notion that their emotions and affective practices were based on slavery and constructed by enslaved people, but they would have agreed that feelings were worthy of study. This would not have been the general consensus a century earlier. The emotional politics of antebellum slavery and an ensuing set of specific affective norms had developed at the turn of the nineteenth century due to four factors: the end of the international slave trade, the rise of sentimentalism, the growth of organized abolitionist and proslavery movements, and the western expansion of slavery. After the United States closed the international slave trade in 1808, slaveowners could no longer legally turn to the international slave market to increase their labor pool.[16] Though slaveholders vehemently denied engaging in "slave breeding," sources from enslaved people document how slaveholders compelled enslaved people to reproduce through rewarding new mothers, punishing infertile women, and rape.[17] Slaveholders bolstered these practices by promoting theories about racialized emotional and physical differences, including conjecturing that giving birth was easier for women of African descent and that Black mothers did not feel maternal bonds like White mothers did, all of which justified selling enslaved family members.[18]

The second factor shaping views on emotions in the antebellum period was the popularity of sentimentalism.[19] Sentimental novels, poetry, theater, and art modeled how contemporary American audiences should feel and express emotions. Beyond serving as templates, these cultural portrayals of emotions also highlight that people in the first half of the nineteenth century were preoccupied with how the people around them felt, whether those sentiments were sincere, and how emotions could be made visible. This meant that slaveholders and formerly enslaved people were encouraged to ponder feelings, their own and those of others, and to describe them in effusive detail. As a result, there is a greater set of firsthand accounts about the emotional lives of individuals in the nineteenth century than there were for slaveholders and enslaved people from the seventeenth or eighteenth centuries, and people had more motives to articulate, explain, and feign feelings.[20]

Third, the affective power dynamics of slavery were fundamentally shaped by the abolitionist movement and the attendant proslavery backlash. As the American abolitionist movement became more mainstream, there were increasing numbers of antislavery publishers, newspapers, and meetings that provided formerly enslaved people with forums for discussing their time in bondage. This in turn spawned a vocal proslavery movement that sought to repudiate their ideological enemy with the same rhetorical tools, producing romanticized texts that reconfigured master-slave relationships as mutually affectionate to counter sentimental slave narratives depicting the heartbreak of bondage.[21] Sentimental proslavery literature proliferated markedly after Harriet Beecher Stowe published *Uncle Tom's Cabin* in 1852, as slaveholders scrambled to critique her antislavery novel and to outdo her florid descriptions with their own maudlin defenses of slavery.[22] Against a broader backdrop of industrialization and class tensions, defenders of slavery honed their emotional arguments not only in response to abolitionists, but also in opposition to free labor as a system, in no small part by claiming that enslaved people were happier than free workers. Finally, if increasingly organized abolitionist and proslavery movements gave each side an adversary, and if sentimentalism gave the argument a vocabulary, the western expansion of slavery following the Mexican War raised the stakes of the debate for all involved.[23]

Because of these multiple, intersecting factors, emotions in the early nineteenth century were given tremendous weight, and it was believed that one could, in the words of Charles Ball, actually have "died of grief."[24] As such, slaveholders and enslaved people aimed to provoke, perform, or conceal emotions for a variety of purposes. First and foremost, emotions served as barometers. For slaveholders in particular, enslaved people's feelings were a metric of productivity and one's reputation as a master, were portents of possible danger, and held monetary value.[25] For enslaved people emotions and affective performances functioned as social capital in negotiations with slaveholders, as survival mechanisms, and as a possible avenue to freedom. Because emotions were so loaded, mastery of emotions was paramount for enslaved people and slaveholders, though their motives differed. Members of the planter class had to enact or repress some sentiments for the sake of propriety, in order to be seen as competent slaveholders. For enslaved people, complying with affective norms could be a matter of life or death, as enslaved people who failed to abide by those norms could be verbally or physically reprimanded, sold, or even killed.[26]

In an era in which affective control was akin to domination, and lack of emotional restraint was perceived as disempowering, slaveholders sought solace in the belief that feelings were legible on the face and body. Many turned to phrenology and physiognomy, the study of the skull and face, in an effort to decipher enslaved people's feelings and intentions. Throughout the antebellum South, reading faces helped both enslaved people and slaveholders navigate their daily interactions. Slaveholders often inspected enslaved people's facial expressions in the hopes of understanding what they thought or felt, scrutinizing any emotions that might be at odds with their words or actions. Sources including scientific texts and agricultural journals promoted surveillance as a key component of emotional mastery. The authors posited that with constant vigilance slaveholders and overseers could identify any "discontented" enslaved people who might be lowering worker productivity and suss out who was "sulky and dissatisfied" and therefore, it was theorized, more likely to run away.[27] In her diary, actress Fanny Kemble repeatedly alleged that she could discern enslaved people's authentic feelings based on her time on her husband's plantations. She boasted about being able to read enslaved people's true desires and bragged that she could easily read in a cook's face that she was lying because the enslaved person's deceit was "child-like, and transparent."[28] Kemble's confidence in her abilities indicates that slaveholders were equally certain that they could read enslaved people's body language and facial cues and that enslaved people were incapable of fully masking their emotions.

Enslaved people believed that their emotions were readily discernible, as evidenced by their widespread concerns that they had affective tells. In his narrative Josiah Henson related being so worried that his face would divulge his intentions and feelings that even after he decided against murdering several slave traders he was consumed by "fear" that his companions would "detect it" in his face.[29] His fear was not unfounded; Frederick Douglass corroborated that escape plans of would-be fugitive slaves had been uncovered before because slaveholders monitored enslaved people "with skilled and practiced eyes" so as "to read, with great accuracy, the state of mind and heart of the slave, through his sable face."[30] According to Douglass, when slaveholders peered questioningly into enslaved people's faces, they checked for "unusual sobriety . . . sullenness and indifference," seeking "any mood" that appeared atypical.[31] If Douglass was correct, then slaveholders needed to observe enslaved people's emotions over time in order to recognize what feelings were "unusual" or out of place.

Reading emotions from facial features was a critical survival skill for enslaved people as well. From the vivid descriptions in slave narratives of slaveholders' emotional states, it is evident that enslaved people were constantly scanning their owners' faces to decode their feelings.[32] The ability to differentiate emotions was incredibly useful to enslaved people awaiting sale. Ball encountered one potential buyer that he would not soon forget as he swore that he "never saw a human countenance that expressed more of the evil passions of the heart than did that of this man." Ball added that the slaveholder's language "corresponded with his physiognomy," confirming his reading of the man, as the customer's speech dripped with "profanity . . . and his eyes" betrayed a well of inner "cruel[ty]."[33] Ball's scathing portrait of the potential purchaser showcases Ball's trust in the power of physiognomy to externally reveal internal qualities, and that he believed such information would help him appraise, and perhaps appeal to, would-be buyers.[34]

Enslaved people also had to be attentive to subtle fluctuations in their owners' moods, because slaveholders' feelings could have significant impacts on the people whom they enslaved. Another passage from Kemble's diary illuminates how enslaved people perceived and reacted to slaveholders' feelings and exemplifies how sources from the planter class provide insights into how and when enslaved people performed emotions. Almost four thousand miles from her London home, isolated on her husband's remote Georgia plantation during the winter of 1839, Kemble took to her journal to chronicle her loneliness, her quandaries about slavery, and her increasing quarrels with her husband. In doing so, she left a record of more than her own mixed feelings about her predicament; she exposed how she felt about enslaved people and how she thought they felt about her, as she detailed how emotional politics played out on those plantations. This was apparent as Kemble remembered a fishing trip with an enslaved man named Jack, who had become a sort of companion and guide for her. She noted that while unsuccessfully trawling for fish, she "was absorbed in many sad and serious considerations," until, as she stated, "after I know not how long . . . without the shadow of a nibble, I was recalled to . . . my ill success by Jack's sudden observation, 'Missis, fishing berry good fun when um fish bite.' This settled the fishing for that morning." As they paddled home Jack changed the subject by asking her about England and by telling her about Mr. Butler's other plantations, which they would soon visit. Jack praised the St. Simon's plantation in particular, and Kemble remarked that "he appeared very glad that we were going," and she in turn "was very glad to hear, that it was a beautiful place for riding."[35] This passage delineates the nuanced emotional negotiations taking place between enslaved people and slaveholders each day. Based off Kemble's recollection it is clear that Jack perceived that Kemble was unhappy and decided to subtly address the matter. Regardless of whether the "many sad and serious considerations" that "absorbed" her were about her time in Georgia, her ambivalence about slavery, her husband, or the lack of fish, Jack could tell that she was upset. He proceeded to try to console her by letting her know that fishing could be "good fun" when one had more luck, insinuating that he knew she was sad. His subsequent questions about her past could be construed as an attempt to dispel her gloom by provoking thoughts of her homeland and of happier times. This could also be why he extolled the virtues of the plantation they planned to visit. Perhaps he hoped to comfort her because they had become friendly during their almost daily boating trips.[36] Or perhaps he recognized how he might benefit in the long run from any efforts to remain in her favor.

Interestingly, Kemble's diary entry hints that she was reading his emotions as well. First, she pointed out that "he appeared very glad" about traveling to St. Simon's. Her perception of his feelings subtly shaped her own as she used identical language to describe his emotional state and to acknowledge that she was "very glad" that she could indulge her beloved hobby of riding on the island. Judging from the passing mention of her "sad and serious" thoughts, the overall tone of the entry, and the fact that she ended the paragraph on a note of hopeful anticipation about St. Simon's, Jack's emotional efforts were successful. Of course, it is unclear if Jack was as "glad" as he "appeared" in speaking of St. Simon's, or if he was adopting the familiar role of "happy slave" in order to alleviate the somber feeling that had settled over the boat. As a person born into slavery, he no doubt knew that how a slaveholder felt could have far-reaching implications for his emotional and physical state, and that feigning happiness could potentially sway her toward contentment.

* * *

In the last thirty years pioneers in the history of emotions have demonstrated the critical role feelings play in society and established a theoretical framework for understanding emotions as a category of analysis. Scholars in the burgeoning field contend that emotions are not simply individual, physiological responses; rather, feelings are also socially constructed and historically and culturally contingent.[37] In spite of the excellent scholarship arising from the emotional turn in history, historians of slavery have been slow to embrace those theories. Some of the hesitance to probe into the affective dimensions of slavery stems from general trends in how earlier scholars treated the emotions of slave society, with the pendulum swinging from depictions of enslaved people as contented to portrayals of enslaved people as wholly defined by trauma.[38] The pathologizing histories of that era, combined with the influence of the Civil Rights and Black Power movements, gave rise to a generation of historians who dismissed claims of absolute emotional effacement for enslaved people, emphasizing instead the invaluable support provided by loving enslaved families and slave communities. However, these works did little to explore how emotions could be used strategically outside of the family, how affective norms were learned and opposed, and what relationships existed between the feelings and emotional practices of enslaved people and those who enslaved them.[39] *Mastering Emotions* tackles the emotional power dynamics between enslaved people and slaveholders, detailing the ways that slaveholders and enslaved people mobilized emotions in their daily encounters, identifying how enslaved people and free Black people resisted the emotional politics of slavery, and discussing efforts by White elites to reestablish racialized affective norms during Reconstruction and Jim Crow.[40]

Mastering Emotions relies on a variety of primary sources, including slave narratives, diaries, plantation account books, and letters, in order to reconstruct the emotional lives of enslaved people and slaveholders. By viewing emotions as both an analytical tool and a site of contestation between the dispossessed and those who seek to dominate them, this study examines the power dynamics, performances, and competing agendas that appear throughout these records. Even seemingly dispassionate legal documents like slave sales, court records, and wills disclose that members of the planter class used enslaved people to express affection, as enslaved people were often given as gifts to children, brides in particular, in documents that framed the sales as acts of love rather than solely commercial transactions.

There are more challenges when one tries to glean the affective experiences of enslaved people from primary sources, as teaching enslaved people to read or write was prohibited in slave states. Because enslaved people were legally barred from recording their own lives, letters, court testimony, travelogues and other sources from slaveholders, and slave narratives by formerly enslaved authors all offer a window into the thoughts and feelings of enslaved people and free Black people.[41] Of course, slave narratives were written by the fortunate few who managed to escape bondage.[42] Edited and printed by abolitionist publishers and peddled to largely White audiences, slave narratives written before Emancipation were consciously abolitionist texts written with the express goal of provoking antislavery readers' sympathy. Historians long discounted slave narratives in part because they were seen as politically biased, but as Charles T. Davis and Henry Louis Gates, Jr., observe in the introduction to *The Slave's Narrative*, "No written text is a transparent rendering of 'historical reality,' be that text composed by master or slave."[43]

Like all forms of literature, slave narratives had their own formulas and genre rules that were familiar to their target audience. It is important for historians to read critically and be transparent about how sentimentalism influenced proslavery and antislavery texts. Read in isolation, a formerly enslaved author reminiscing about the heartrending moment when their mother tenderly explained that they could someday be sold might be portraying the story to appeal to sentimental readers. But taken alongside other slave narratives, the fact remains that many enslaved families had such discussions, while other relatives tried to keep enslaved children blissfully unaware of the cruel fates that might await them.[44] By identifying where slave narratives overlap and diverge, it becomes evident that they are simultaneously historical documents, abolitionist pamphlets, literary works, and individual memoirs.[45]

While formerly enslaved authors were knowingly shaping their texts through an antislavery lens, their accounts are nevertheless corroborated by none other than slaveholders themselves. Formerly enslaved people wrote about slaveowners' perception that enslaved people's emotions were less nuanced, that feelings were a means and a motive for punishing enslaved people, that holidays could be used as an affective release valve, and that trust was both fundamental and difficult to forge, and all of that was substantiated by slaveholders in their own letters, account books, journals, and sentimental memoirs. To read slave narratives alongside documents from slaveholders is to see the same types of daily interactions that played out in homes, fields, and slave markets throughout the South from multiple perspectives. As Walter Johnson advises, scholars should therefore use these documents in "juxtaposition . . . to authenticate as well as interrogate one another."[46]

Scrutinizing texts by slaveholders and enslaved people side by side is also vital to seeing the emotional landscape of the antebellum South in its entirety, because what proslavery authors and planters wrote in defense of the institution did not always reflect their daily practices as slaveholders. For example, the recollections of formerly enslaved people reiterate how frequently and brutally slaveholders and overseers ignored counsel about avoiding emotions while disciplining.[47] Though articles on plantation management, etiquette books, and social pressure might discourage masters from punishing enslaved people in a fit of passion, the law recognized that this occurred nevertheless, sometimes fatally. To that end, South Carolina passed a law in 1821 stating that murdering an enslaved person "in sudden heat and passion is the same as manslaughter," and thus not a felony like premeditated murder.[48] Because many planters and overseers did not follow the advice laid out in agricultural journals, it is important to read sources against one another to identify the schism between prescribed feelings and actual emotional practices. Contemporary newspapers and journals, proslavery and antislavery writing, and other forms of prescriptive literature enable historians to compare what slaveholders and enslaved people were advised to do or feel, including suppressing anger, jealousy, or sorrow, with their actual emotional behavior, which was harder to circumscribe.

There is also the question of how to determine the feelings of people who are long dead. Even when writing letters to loved ones or recording thoughts in a private journal, antebellum authors might be performing an idealized self, based on cultural cues and prevailing affective norms. That does not mean that one cannot gain insights from such sources, or that these texts are not capturing authentically felt emotions. Letters and diaries from that era were still meant to be sincere and were intended for an audience of intimates.[49] One cannot know how people genuinely felt in the antebellum South any more than one can know how another person genuinely feels in the present. Instead, using a variety of sources sheds light on the rhetoric used to discuss feelings, what feelings were expected, and what ulterior motives people had to feign specific emotions. Rather than making assumptions about what people felt, or simply highlighting the language of emotions, the study delves into what people thought emotions could actually accomplish.

Emancipation triggered a seismic shift in the emotional landscape of the antebellum South, with long-lasting impacts. The debate over how to emotionally maintain slavery may have been rendered moot with the end of the Civil War, but the conflict over whether or not the emotional strictures governing the South would be based on race or free status had serious connotations, particularly for free Black people. Just as enslaved people chafed against the emotional restrictions of slavery, many free Black people resisted the affective norms imposed during Reconstruction and Jim Crow. Nevertheless, the postwar rise of legal and extralegal attempts to affectively control free Black people underscored the commitment of elite White Southerners in particular to preserving the legacy and the power dynamics of the emotional politics of slavery, by any means necessary.

CHAPTER 1

"To Change Their Sentiments"

In his epistolary proslavery book-cum-memoir, *Black Diamonds*, Edward Pollard interwove the personal and the polemical in order to defend the institution of slavery. Pollard described traveling the world as a young man, writing effusively about encountering an enslaved man again upon returning to the South. Pollard did not know the enslaved man but recalled that the man "looked like *home*." He described it as follows: "I looked at him with my face aglow, and my eyelids touched with tears. How he reminded me of my home—of days gone by . . . 'when I was a boy.'"[1] For Pollard the mere sight of an enslaved person, even a complete stranger, inundated him with simultaneous feelings of joy and homesickness. Throughout Pollard's work, it is evident that enslaved people were the building blocks of Pollard's emotional life, as they shaped his understanding of happiness, love, and sorrow and formed the scaffolding of his memories and very identity. No doubt trying to prove that slavery was rooted in mutual affection and paternalism, Pollard also revealed that enslaved people were so important to his emotional sense of self that the simple act of seeing an enslaved man again transported him to his own childhood.[2] This scene of an enslaved man unleashing a flood of nostalgia for a planter highlights the extent to which slaveholders' emotions were created by and through enslaved people.

Many historians of emotions as well as psychologists have argued that emotions are not just individually felt but are collectively constructed and historically contingent.[3] Yet all too often historians of emotion, in particular those who attribute collective emotions to cultural and social influences, focus solely on how elites shape affective norms, without attention to the ways that dispossessed people and subcultures contribute to or construct those feelings and emotional practices. Even historians who study the lives of slaveholders have downplayed the role of enslaved people in the affective lives of the planter class, contending that physical proximity did not breed intimacy or shared emotional rituals between slaveholders and enslaved people.[4] But sources from formerly enslaved authors and slaveholders offer insights into the variety of ways that enslaved women and men were central to the feelings and emotional practices of the people who owned them.

Slave narratives reveal that enslaved people were acutely aware of the effect they could have on slaveholders' emotions, whether they were intentionally trying to evoke certain feelings or not. One of Elizabeth Keckley's owners was married to a woman whom Keckley described as being of "humble" origins. Because of that class background, Keckley believed the woman to be "morbidly sensitive" about the enslaved woman, convinced that Keckley "regarded her with contemptuous feelings because she was of poor parentage." Keckley does not say if she possessed "contemptuous feelings" for the woman, but it did not matter. Despite doing "the work of three servants" Keckley was constantly criticized and "regarded with distrust."[5] Whether Keckley was disdainful of her mistress or not, Keckley's very existence made her mistress feel shame and class anxiety. Keckley was also forced to endure the ramifications of her unintentional emotional influence, as she was viewed as untrustworthy and was heaped with scorn and skepticism.

Some enslaved people deliberately tried to influence their owners' feelings. Henry Bibb explained that in his enslaved community it was commonly believed that if one chewed on a "bitter root . . . and spit towards their masters when they are angry with their slaves" it would dispel their owner's anger at the expectorating enslaved person. After an escape attempt Bibb feared that a whipping was imminent, so a friend advised Bibb to visit a "conjurer" who would sell him a charm that could stave off beatings. The conjurer sold him a powder, instructing Bibb that if his owner threatened to whip him he should "sprinkle it about [the] master" to "prevent him." The apotropaic concoction worked so well that Bibb returned for more and began scattering the enchanted "dust" in his owners' bedroom so they had more exposure to it. Bibb intended it to function as a "love powder, to change their sentiments of anger, to those of love," toward him. Despite these plans, Bibb's conjuring campaign ended prematurely after the substance reduced his owners to coughing and sneezing, leading Bibb to worry that they would discover his "dangerous experiments upon them."[6] If they thought Bibb was trying to poison them that would surely warrant an even more severe sentence, so he gave up his attempts to bewitch his owners.

In his narrative Bibb seemed abashed about this anecdote, dismissing his actions as superstitious, but the passage reveals a great deal about how enslaved people viewed the emotional politics of slavery. Like Keckley, Bibb both feared his owners' anger and recognized the power he had to impact how slaveholders felt. Even if only briefly, Bibb believed that he had "change[d] their sentiments" through the aid of conjuring and had transformed their anger into affection to avert a beating. Of course, this fleeting moment of affective victory was swiftly replaced by fear of an even harsher punishment than the one he originally hoped to avoid. The incident hints both at how much enslaved people were willing to risk in order to influence their owners' emotions and at how much power slaveholders' feelings had over enslaved people's fates.

While slaveholders like Pollard did not always explicitly acknowledge the ways that their closest relationships and feelings were based on enslaved people, documents written by enslaved people and slaveholders tell another story. As Presbyterian minister Benjamin Palmer observed in a sermon just weeks after the 1860 election, "Need I pause to show how this system of servitude . . . is interwoven with our entire social fabric? . . . Must I pause to show how it has fashioned our modes of life, and determined all our habits of thought and feeling?"[7]

When writing letters, wills, slave sale documents, or diaries, slaveholders demonstrated that the emotions and affective practices of the antebellum South were fundamentally conditioned upon and constructed by enslaved people. From the ways that slaveholding families bonded and fought, to how they marked occasions from marriage to death, enslaved people had a profound effect on slaveholders' relationships and feelings, creating sentiments like jealousy, pride, shame, and, in particular, fear. At times this was an unintentional process, as enslaved people were unwillingly incorporated into the lives of the people that owned them. At other times enslaved people deliberately made and unmade relationships, influencing the emotions of slaveholders as a form of self-defense or resistance. This chapter details how enslaved people forged the bonds between slaveholding spouses, lovers, siblings, parents, and children, and how enslaved people unmade these bonds, knowingly mining veins of family tension in order to obtain benefits, avoid punishments, or escape slavery. Finally, the chapter outlines the role of enslaved people in provoking specific feelings like envy, pride, and dread, and how gossip was used to teach and enforce the boundaries of appropriate emotions.

Making Family Ties

One important way that enslaved people constructed slaveholders' emotions was by forging the intergenerational affective relations that knit planter families together. In an article from *DeBow's Review*, an agricultural journal popular among Southern planters, the author, Dr. McTyeire, elucidated how enslaved people helped form those bonds, claiming that older enslaved people were "heirloom[s]" to be "cherished" with "tenderness" because they may have "laid the foundations of the families' wealth . . . bore your father in his arms, and went afield with your grandfather when he was starting in life."[8] The implication was that enslaved people not only produced heritable "wealth" but also generated family ties and could even embody the memory of beloved ancestors. One's father or grandfather might be dead, but that intimate relationship was preserved, made manifest through an enslaved person who had cared for that grandfather, father, and son, and might wait on future generations. James Henry Hammond used similar language when describing a thoroughly romanticized and supposedly reciprocal affective relationship between master and slave, reminiscing about enslaved people "who served his father, and rocked his cradle," shared in their owner's "griefs" as well as the celebration of holidays, and "whose hearty and affectionate greetings never fail to welcome" their owner.[9] Like Dr. McTyeire, Hammond blurred the lines between emotions about enslaved people and sentiments about family, revealing in the process the extent to which enslaved people shaped how he felt. Writing in proslavery journals and books, authors like McTyeire and Hammond claimed paternalism in order to defend the institution against its critics, but they also proved how thoroughly planters wove enslaved people into their own emotional lives and their feelings about home and family.[10]

Slaveholders did more than idealize the enslaved people who cared for their families for generations; members of the planter class also used enslaved people to cement intergenerational bonds by gifting enslaved people to relatives, typically when celebrating a specific rite of passage.[11] In an 1816 Virginia court case over a contested will that included gifting enslaved people, one lawyer observed that "the advancement of children is most frequently in negroes; and a bequest or gift of negroes is generally made as an advancement for the better establishing the child in life."[12] This suggests that the true affective power of an enslaved person lay not in how they tied a slaveholder to their ancestors, but in the promise of financial security and "advancement" that the enslaved person represented for subsequent generations of slaveowners. As a result, members of the planter class often gave enslaved people to slaveholding children to provide economic and emotional succor on the path to adulthood.

In 1819 John Perkins contracted a slave sale as a present to his sister's children. The bill of sale noted that "in consideration of his natural love and affection which the said John Perkins hath and bearth" for the four children, he sold them six enslaved people for the modest sum of five dollars. If it was not already clear from this dramatically low price and the language of "love and affection" that this was a gift, the bill went on to say that the sale of the slaves was intended to help fund the children's "schooling and support."[13] This was no mere economic transaction spelled out in boilerplate wording: this was a slave sale couched as an uncle's act of love for his nieces and nephews. Perkins's hopes for the children's stable financial future and education were embodied as six people, six individuals who harbored their own hopes and dreams of a different future.[14]

Because gifting an enslaved person to a child was more than a commercial calculation, sale documents provide a glimpse of the nostalgia, love, pride, and loss that slaveholding parents experienced when commemorating a momentous event in a child's life. A slave sale from November 1, 1837, announced, "My son Doct. W. Thomas Brent being on the eve of leaving me" in order to move to Louisiana, "I have this day given to him . . . two boys named Aaron aged about 22 years and William aged about 16 years," signed by George Brent.[15] George Brent might be comforted to know that his son Thomas would be tended to as he established a medical practice in Louisiana, but George still expressed his anguish in the document by dramatically describing his son's move as "leaving" him. While George Brent conveyed that he was taking his son's choice to move personally, there are no records showing how Aaron and William felt about this major change in their own young lives.

Marriages were another rite of passage of the slaveholding family marked by gifts of enslaved people. Documents from the antebellum South frequently reference slaveholding parents giving enslaved people as wedding presents, typically as part of the bride's dowry.[16] As William Craft explained in his narrative of his escape with his wife, Ellen, such a gift could be a loaded one for a young couple, larded with ulterior motives and meanings. Craft noted that Ellen's father was her White owner, a fact so evident that the slaveholder's wife was "annoyed" at how often Ellen was "mistaken for a child of the family," leading the slave mistress to give one of her daughters the eleven-year-old Ellen "as a wedding present."[17] The gift of an enslaved young woman in particular was a promise of financial security for newlyweds, since any children Ellen had in the future would multiply their estate and wealth. Giving a daughter an enslaved person from the family plantation also ensured that the new bride would have at least one familiar face in her new household. But making a present of the bride's own half-sister could also be construed as a none-too-subtle warning about the infidelity and heartache that awaited many slaveholding wives.

Perhaps because of enslaved people's prominence in constructing slaveholders' rituals and familial ties, as children of the planter class grew up, enslaved people continued to shape their relationships with their parents, even after those parents had passed. For many slaveholders, enslaved people served as a vehicle for remembering the dearly departed. In 1847 Louisiana slaveowner Phillip Moore petitioned to free a woman named Henrietta who had belonged to his late mother. Moore was explicit in court documents that manumitting Henrietta was his mother's "dying wish," evidently convinced that no contract or law could be more legally binding than a deathbed request. Carrying out her supposed "wish" was a way to honor his mother, and invoking her last words in court helped see her desires to fruition.[18] Rather than being manumitted, other enslaved people became a living memorial to a slaveholder's dead parents. Before Henry Box Brown's owner died, the slaveholder gave his son William "a special charge . . . to take good care of [Brown]." William demonstrated the extent to which he sought to respect his father's wishes when Brown "overheard him telling the overseer that his father had raised me—that I was a smart boy and that he must never whip me."[19] This shows how the philosophy of paternalism was learned: William's father conceived of himself as a kind slaveholder who "had raised" Brown like he was family. Through his deathbed request the slaveholder passed on to his son the gauzy fantasy that he had been a benevolent slaveowner and that William would be too. Unlike Phillip Moore's mother, Brown's owner had left no explicit instructions about manumitting him. Quite the contrary, "tak[ing] good care" of an enslaved person could be broadly interpreted. It is notable that William not only tried to mitigate punishment for Brown, but also invoked his father's affections for Brown in order to do so. Brown thus served as a dead father's best intentions incarnate, and any time William went out of his way to help Brown, the slaveholder would be reminded of his father and of the promise he was keeping.

For Pollard, memories of and feelings for enslaved people were ineluctably intertwined with those he had for his dead parents. After an enslaved woman named Marie passed away he claimed that she "numbered . . . among those whom, with love-lit eyes, I can so often see beckoning to me from Heaven," in a celestial entourage that included his "beloved parents," several siblings, and many of the other "dear, old, familiar blacks of my boy's home." His dream of a welcoming, integrated afterlife could be read as platitudes about enslaved people being viewed as family, nothing more than a performance of paternalism, were it not for how often he blended his affection for enslaved people with the memory of his departed parents. In another nostalgic passage Pollard remarked that during his travels he often thought of an enslaved man named George in the "garden, with its . . . cherry-trees, and the gentle mounds in the corner, that saddest, sweetest spot . . . the parental graves!"[20] In this stream-of-consciousness description, Pollard revealed how his mind correlated an enslaved man, the garden at his childhood home, and his dead parents, welding them into a chain of linked associations. He could not reminisce about an enslaved person without recalling the deaths of family members; his jaunts down memory lane always took a turn through the slave quarters.

Making Courtship and Marriage

Given the critical function they had in concretizing the familial relations of slaveholders, it is little wonder that enslaved people also shaped the courtship process and marriages of members of the planter class. The first step for many elite Southern White men who wished to compete in the marriage market was to become economically independent, by inheriting wealth or establishing a career, in order to prove to the parents of any would-be brides that they were financially secure.[21] Owning enslaved people was the best evidence of one's solvency and thus one's potential as a suitor. The opposite was also true: it was well known in the antebellum South that prospective in-laws did not look favorably upon nonslaveholding men. While enslaved, Charles Ball overheard a South Carolina man declare that his daughters would "never marry any but gentlemen of the first character," nor would they commit the unpardonable transgression of one local girl "who ran away with a Georgia cracker . . . who had not a *nigger* in the world." In the father's view "gentlem[a]n" status was synonymous with both "character" and class, and it could not be conferred upon a man who did not own even a single enslaved person. In the rigidly structured, patriarchal, slave South it was almost impossible to be considered husband material if one was not already a slaveholder; it was an exceptional occasion, worthy of remark by Ball, when a planter's daughter who "was esteemed a great beauty" married a man without any property or slaves.[22]

White Southern bachelors understood the role slaveholding played in making them eligible for marriage. While traveling through Mississippi in the 1850s, Frederick Law Olmsted met a young man who confided to him, "I have now but one servant; if I should marry, I should be obliged to buy three more," which he hazarded would cost him "at least three thousand dollars."[23] The man knew that his very ability to marry was determined not just by being a slaveholder but by the number of people he could afford to purchase. This suggests that a bachelor could get by with only one enslaved person, but to support a wife and family he felt "obliged" to enslave at least four people. This belief was pervasive enough that simply buying an enslaved person could be viewed as a sign that a single man was interested in marriage. In the marketplace of romance, even offering to buy an enslaved person was a way to evince marital intentions. When Moses Grandy was trying to buy his freedom for six hundred dollars, his owner protested that a Captain Cormack had offered a thousand dollars for Grandy. Grandy suspected that Cormack was disingenuous, responding that the Captain overbid because "he is courting Miss Patsey, and he did it to make himself look big." Rather than correct him, Grandy's owners "laughed . . . knowing that [Grandy] spoke the truth" about Cormack's ulterior motives.[24] Clearly enslaved people and slaveholders knew that a suitor might highlight his wealth, eligibility, and desire to marry by emphasizing that he planned to purchase enslaved people and would pay dearly for them.

Enslaved people were more than proof that a suitor was ready for marriage; they were sometimes integral to the rituals of courtship themselves. To ensure a bride's chastity, young women of the planter class could not be alone with a suitor: a family member had to be present when a man came calling. But according to historian Catherine Clinton, if no relative were available then "a female slave is seated on the rug at the door" to supervise. One slaveholder even confessed to drugging the enslaved chaperone with laudanum in order to covertly steal a kiss from his intended.[25] Thus enslaved people could provide security for a groom's finances and a bride's propriety, without which a wedding among members of the planter class could not take place. Enslaved women's bodies were also more directly exploited in order to forge bonds between slaveholding families and couples, as Sella Martin testified when describing his mother Winnifred's experience in bondage. Winnifred's owner was a woman whose sole heir was her nephew, Mr. Martin. As such the aunt was emotionally and financially invested in seeing Mr. Martin wedded well. Her wishes paid off, as Mr. Martin was eventually betrothed to a much younger woman "of wealth and position," necessitating a long engagement until the girl was old enough to marry. Concerned that the union "not be thwarted by her nephew forming attachments elsewhere" the aunt "encouraged, and finally secured a relationship between Mr. Martin" and the enslaved woman until the marriage could take place.[26] The aunt did not care that the "relationship" was predicated on her nephew repeatedly sexually assaulting Winnifred. Nor was the aunt concerned that any "relationship" between Mr. Martin and Winnifred might threaten his future marriage. Her only goal was wedding her heir to a suitable woman, even if that marriage was "secured" by the rape of an enslaved woman.

Enslaved people were highly cognizant of how profoundly their owners' relationships could impact their own lives. In one unique case an enslaved woman accompanied a slaveholding couple on their honeymoon to the North, including a stop in Niagara Falls, which enabled her to escape to freedom in Canada.[27] For most enslaved people the effects of slaveholders' marriages were more mundane, though no less deeply felt. Charles Ball readily acknowledged that when his owner's daughter married it "had a most material influence upon [his] fortunes, and changed the whole tenor of [his] existence" as Ball was among the enslaved people given to the young couple. Ball recalled that he "was much pleased with the appearance and manners" of his new owner, and he was surprised to find that both wife and husband were "kind" and trusting.[28] Ball was fortunate that the "change" wrought by the marriage was not negative for him. But many enslaved people dreaded the nuptials of a slaveholder's daughter, since the new husband was often a stranger and therefore unpredictable. James Pennington noted that an enslaved person who was inherited by a member of the family they had known since childhood was at least "acquainted with his character, bad as it may be," but if they were given to a daughter upon her marriage "the young mistress brings her slaves a new, and sometimes an unknown master."[29]

Since a marriage could dramatically shape their experience in bondage, some enslaved people tried to actively encourage or discourage certain matches. For them such romantic machinations were a matter of survival. In an 1838 letter to her mother, Elizabeth Keckley closed by writing, "tell Miss Elizabeth that I wish she would make haste and get married, for mistress says that I belong to her when she gets married."[30] Keckley knew that if her owner married she would join her in the young bride's new home. The enslaved woman clearly wanted to leave her current situation enough to encourage Elizabeth's marriage to any possible beau, so she tried to involve her mother in her schemes. Other enslaved people tried to vocally dissuade their owners from marrying, worried about how a particular match might affect them. Levi Douglass and James Wright recalled that a man named Simmons, whom they believed to be "of no very reputable character," was courting their owner, Mary Douglass. Concerned for what the marriage might portend for them, the enslaved men "ventured to ask their mistress not to marry this Simmons," confiding in her that "they feared his cruel treatment." Their gamble did not pay off; she married Simmons anyway, and as soon as he assumed the role of their owner "their situation was materially changed for the worse." Once Simmons learned that Douglass and Wright had opposed the marriage, he sought "to punish their audacity" by selling the men "to the far south."[31] Though Mary Douglass did not heed their advice it is telling that the two men were willing to risk so much to avoid a lifetime with Simmons as their legal owner. That Simmons sought revenge against the enslaved men suggests that he took their actions personally, perhaps recognizing what he could have lost if their gambit had succeeded.

Enslaved people also served as vehicles for displaying affection throughout the course of slaveholders' marriages. In his 1801 will Pierre Metoyer requested that an enslaved woman named Marie Suzanne take care of his wife and their youngest son until his wife's death, or for "as long as" the two women were "content with each other."[32] In this way Marie Suzanne embodied the emotional bonds of the Metoyer family, as a caretaker for Metoyer's wife and son. Because he intended Marie Suzanne's "services" to continue after his death, she became a manifestation of his own memory and love for his family. In vowing that Marie Suzanne would take care of his wife after his own death, Metoyer was making the enslaved woman into a postmortem valentine, a proxy for the care he could no longer give.

Unmaking Families

Enslaved people were integral in adhering the bonds of slaveholding families, but sources indicate that the enslaved did not just make slaveholders' relationships, they could unmake them. In the antebellum South, familial strife, including sibling rivalry, and arguments between parents and children, or husbands and wives, often played out through enslaved people. One case of sisterly enmity pitted affective claims to enslaved people against legal ones. On Valentine's Day of 1856 Evelina Prescott wrote to her father to express her dismay that some enslaved children she had received in the partition of a relative's estate had actually been intended for her sister. Prescott protested the decision, citing the affection that she and her children felt for the two enslaved boys, George and Spencer. Evelina lamented that her family would be stung by the "pang of separation" if they lost the boys, noting that she had "nursed" George "with [her] own milk" and that her "children were so much attached" to Spencer.[33] Evelina's plea highlights the complicated relationships that existed both within slaveholding families and between slaveholders and enslaved people. While Evelina purported to want to keep the children because of how "attached" they had become to the entire family, she seemed equally concerned with the power struggle with her sister, the supposed owner of George and Spencer. The letter had a juvenile quality, as she wrote "sister says I must send her slaves to her," and given that Evelina was involving her father in the matter at all. She begrudgingly agreed to accept her father's judgment on the situation, but she asked him to remember that she "was never so fortunate as her" sister. Perhaps the Prescotts really did feel heartbroken over any possible "separation" from the enslaved boys. Based on the bitter tone of the letter it is also possible that after years of accumulating perceived grievances, Evelina wanted to undermine her sister, both financially and in the eyes of their father. Records do not show if Evelina's father was swayed by her arguments, but the letter is a record of how enslaved people could divide sisters even as they purportedly knit together the Prescott family.

Enslaved people were often casualties of slaveholding family fights. Frederick Douglass saw this firsthand after his owner loaned Douglass to his own brother, Hugh Auld. Douglass had become accustomed to Auld's household when "a misunderstanding took place between" the brothers. Douglass claimed that "as a means of punishing his brother" his owner took Douglass back, forcing the enslaved man to undergo "another most painful separation."[34] The Prescott and Auld feuds illustrate that in intrafamily disputes enslaved people could be the source of a squabble, or a weapon deployed to wage the affective war. And it demonstrates once again that when battles were being fought over and through enslaved people, the emotions of enslaved people were inexorably shaped as well. Because of a disagreement between slaveholding brothers, Douglass was forced to face yet another "painful separation" from people he had grown close to.

Some enslaved people sought to take advantage of the fissures that riddled planter families. By doing so they could mete out revenge against an owner without ever lifting a finger or attracting blame. This is evident in the ways that people enslaved at the Pollard plantation learned to exacerbate sibling rivalries between Edward and his older brother Dick. Pollard recalled that as a child the brothers "were perpetually at fisticuffs," coming to blows over everything and anything. Pollard claimed that if he bickered with his brother some enslaved people would "egg [them] on to fight each other," which they did "in the most passionate manner." Not content merely to pit brother against brother to watch them skirmish, the enslaved spectators were also in league with their mother, Pollard swore. He noted that whenever enslaved people caught the brothers brawling they "informed upon" the bellicose boys, who were promptly caned for their infractions. Pollard confessed that the emotional repercussions for coming to blows with one another were far worse than the corporeal punishment. For the Pollard brothers "what was more painful to the proud and angry spirit of each" was that they "were made to kiss each other" while their mother "in vain" spoke to them "lessons of brotherly love." These "lessons" seemingly failed, as Pollard noted that the brothers "hated each other thoroughly."[35] Enslaved people on that plantation perceived their "hate" and sought to exploit it, first by encouraging the boys to fight one another, then by "inform[ing]" upon them to their mother. The enslaved people who tattled on the brothers may have been strategically trying to stay in the good graces of Mrs. Pollard. Or they may have wanted to take revenge on two members of the planter class who might someday own them, exerting the limited power they had to ensure that the boys received not one but two whippings, followed by the affective punishment of a forced reconciliation.

Enslaved people were also a source of strife in relationships between parents and children, typically between slaveholding fathers and sons. According to the formerly enslaved James W. C. Pennington some of this stemmed from the young men's anxieties about how they compared to their fathers as slaveowners. He contended that many young slaveholders developed complexes about competing with their fathers, and "the young master not being able to own as many slaves as his father," he generally worked the few people he enslaved "more severely."[36] Arguments also arose between father and son about the proper treatment and punishment of enslaved people. Jacob Stroyer witnessed such an issue when an enslaved man named Jim stole a pig from Stroyer's owner. Jim was caught, and the owner's son whipped him before tying a "cured middling of hog . . . around his neck." Jim was forced to wear the meat day and night, even while he worked in the fields in the sweltering heat, until he was found dead, the rotting hog flesh still hanging from his body. Stroyer explained that the slaveholder "was very angry at his son," blaming the reckless young man for Jim's death, and the son was told to leave his home and "never to return." From Stroyer's account it appeared that the loss of a valuable enslaved person in such a fashion was unforgivable, grounds for being disowned and ostracized. According to Stroyer, the father's actions "grieved" the son a great deal, as he worked to "regain his father's affection."[37] It is not clear if the father was most displeased by the financial loss of Jim's death or by his son's overzealous disciplinary methods. Either way, the enslaved man's punishment and subsequent death were considered grave-enough infractions for the father to cut financial and emotional ties to his son.

Some discord in slaveholding homes stemmed from concerns about the family's reputation, indicating that enslaved people made and unmade family relationships, and they were a building block of slaveholders' sense of pride and shame. A letter from Charles Batchelor to his mother revealed just how much enslaved people and slaveowning shaped his relations with his father and his sense of self-worth. Batchelor wrote to his mother in the winter of 1860 from the Military Institute of Kentucky, to proclaim that he "felt really vexed" about enslaved people his father had bought, an acquisition that Batchelor thought was unwise. According to the letter, his father had only recently emerged from debt, and Batchelor expressed shock and anger that his father would buy more slaves and "plunge . . . blindly into debt again." Batchelor declared that this irresponsible purchase was "enough to make [him] repent the day" his birth gave him his father's "name." He bemoaned the fact that he was applying himself diligently at school "in order to make [himself] worthy," only to see his father act so impulsively that it supposedly made Batchelor contemplate "abandon[ing his] course to glory." He condemned what he viewed as his father's "extravagance" not only because the man owed his son money, but because Batchelor clearly staked his own self-respect and capacity for future "glory" to his family's success as slaveholders and purchasers.[38] Beyond his concerns about his family's financial future, the young man was more anxious about the potential damage to the more invaluable asset, his family "name."

Sources reveal that differing philosophies about how to treat enslaved people also led to protracted hostilities between slaveholding husbands and wives in the antebellum South. Some of these disputes combined tensions about enslaved people with preexisting frictions between in-laws and extended family. Priscilla "Mittie" Munnikhuysen frequently complained in her diary about the way that her father-in-law ran the Louisiana plantation where she lived with her husband, Howard. In 1861 she wrote, "I feel sad—more whipping going on. One poor old man the sufferer of man's passion. Thank God my husband is not so heartless." She continued to articulate her hatred for her harsh father-in-law, concluding by declaring "I wish he was not Howard's father."[39] The whipping of the old enslaved man was knotted up with the tangle of feelings she had about her husband, her father-in-law, slavery, individual enslaved people, and her ambivalence about moving from Maryland to Louisiana to marry Howard. Munnikhuysen often wrote about her opposition to slavery, but in the passage above she conflated her own sorrow with the suffering of the enslaved man, all while blaming her father-in-law's cruel treatment of enslaved people on his "passion." From her diary entries it is impossible to tell where her political distaste for her father-in-law as a slaveholder ended and her personal enmity for her husband's father began. Nevertheless, her lamentations suggest that how slaveholders felt about enslaved people like the old man could create flashpoints for family conflict, including debates over what emotions were appropriate to feel about enslaved people.

Based on their frequent appearances in her diary, such events were more than a reminder of her disdain for slavery, or for her father-in-law; they were potential nodes for engaging issues with her husband. When the plantation's enslaved overseer Nace treated a runaway slave cruelly, seemingly at her father-in-law's behest, Howard objected to the fugitive's treatment. But Mittie stirred up more drama, informing Howard "loud enough for his father to hear" that she believed her father-in-law "thinks more of Nace than any one of his children" and was more apt to listen to the overseer than to his own kin. She was concerned enough about the influence Nace had over her father-in-law that she told Howard that if he was content "to have a black master over [him] it is more than [she was] willing to have."[40] This heated exchange speaks volumes about the ways that the emotional politics of slavery shaped planter family relations. Since Munnikhuysen was clearly intending to be heard by her husband as well as her father-in-law, it is difficult to discern whether she was proud of her husband for standing up to his father or whether she thought his actions were insufficient and proof that he was permitting himself to be cowed by his father and Nace. Though Mittie was opposed to chattel slavery, she was not without her own share of White supremacist sentiments, judging from the way she derided her husband about having a "black master." Her suggestion that he was allowing himself to be mastered by another man, and a Black man at that, was calculated to provoke her husband's anger and to emasculate him. Maybe this was a constant source of tension with her husband, as her journal entries allude that the two often fought about slavery in general and his father's practices in particular. Or perhaps Howard speaking out about the runaway helped the couple bond over their shared anger at his father.

As Mittie Munnikhuysen's writings show, the treatment of enslaved people could be a major point of contention between married couples of the planter class, especially when one spouse had antislavery leanings. Fanny Kemble's own diary offers glimpses of how her feelings about slavery and enslaved people became inextricably tied to both her own emotions and her relationship with her husband, Mr. Butler. She recalled having "a long and painful conversation" with Butler about an enslaved woman whom Kemble believed was unfairly flogged. Kemble confided that arguing with her husband made her feel "perfect agonies of distress for the slaves, whose position is utterly hopeless; for myself, whose intervention on their behalf sometimes seems to me worse than useless; for Mr. Butler, whose share in this horrible system fills me by turns with indignation and pity."[41]

Her plaintive entry suggests that her feelings about her husband could not be teased apart from her sentiments about enslaved people. It is impossible to say if she was empathizing with enslaved people or projecting, but it is notable that Kemble used similar language to describe the effect of her emotional state and those of the enslaved people, noting that their "position" was "hopeless" while hers was "worse than useless." Toward her slaveholder husband, however, she felt a mixture of anger and "pity." Such tempestuous quarrels were nonexistent when they were newlyweds living in Philadelphia, but her diary shows how cracks in their relationship emerged and widened after the couple moved to the slave South.

Just as enslaved people used the Pollards' sibling rivalry to their advantage, some enslaved people sought to deliberately manipulate the feelings and intrafamily conflict of slaveowners, often as a survival tactic. In his narrative of being captured and enslaved Solomon Northup detailed his efforts to emotionally subvert his owner's family. In attempting to protect an enslaved woman named Patsey from sexual assault, Northup incurred the anger of his drunken, concupiscent owner, Mr. Epps. When Mr. Epps tried to exact revenge by pulling a knife on Northup, Northup evaded danger by running to Mrs. Epps and telling her what her husband had done. Northup saw that Mrs. Epps was "possessed of the devil, jealousy," toward Patsey, and he knew that when Mrs. Epps was angry Mr. Epps often became compliant, "ready to gratify any whim" his wife had. Northup claimed that after he informed her the slave mistress became enraged at both her husband and Patsey. Meanwhile Mr. Epps, who could easily guess that Northup was disclosing his lascivious behavior to his wife, was duly chastened. In strategically seeking out Mrs. Epps in order to provoke her anger and envy, Northup was able to stave off an attack on Patsey and himself, while also causing strain on the Eppses' marriage.[42] It may only have been a temporary reprieve from violence for Patsey and Northup, but he was savvy, turning the incident into an opportunity to drive a wedge between Mr. Epps and his wife, transforming his owner's rage into Mrs. Epps's heartache. In this way enslaved people like Northup could, at times, exploit disputes between slaveholding husbands and wives, parents and children, or siblings in order to gain a short-lived benefit or to actively undermine a slaveholding family.

Making Emotions

As Northup's story about the Epps family demonstrates, enslaved people weaved and unraveled the affective bonds of slaveholding families, and they forged specific emotions for slaveowners, including jealousy, pride, shame, and fear. Mrs. Epps was no anomaly; sexual violence committed by slaveholders was such a defining feature of antebellum slavery that the jealous slave mistress was a stock figure in slave narratives and histories of slavery alike.[43] Such wives might have been the first to concede that enslaved women were the source of their envy. The heartache and anger of learning that a husband was sexually assaulting an enslaved woman were so ubiquitous that wealthy planter Mary Chesnut expressed surprise in her diary that the subject was not featured in *Uncle Tom's Cabin*, observing "Mrs. Stowe did not hit the sorest spot. She makes Legree a bachelor." Chesnut wrote about the novel's unmarried villain and discussed how other women of the planter class ignored their husbands' flagrant infidelity, all while nursing fears that her own husband had a sexual relationship with an enslaved woman she referred to as "Rachel."[44] According to Harriet Jacobs, "white daughters" of the planter class were inculcated in jealousy from a young age, taught that such feelings were triggered by enslaved women, as the constant refrain of their childhood was "their parents quarrelling about some female slave." Naturally the daughters became "curious" about the source of their parents' strife, and before long "they learn the cause": that their father had sexually assaulted an enslaved woman. Steeped in their mothers' envy and convinced that full culpability fell on enslaved women alone, young White women's conceptions of jealousy were passed down from one generation to the next, inseparable from their perceptions of enslaved women.[45]

The figure of the jealous slave mistress was more prominent in proslavery and antislavery literature, but male slaveholders also grappled with the emotion, and they blamed it on enslaved women as well. Louisa Piquet's owner was almost fifty and "gray headed" when he bought her to serve as both concubine and caretaker so that he could "end his days with [her]." Piquet was therefore forced to share her owner's bed and to endure his chronic mistrust. She explained that if she took too long to open the door when he came calling in the night he would suspiciously search her room, "under the bed, and in the wardrobe" and then ask her why she did not let him in more quickly. She believed that his age was "the reason he was always so jealous."[46] Piquet's recollections suggest that her owner might have been insecure about aging, or her potential feelings for him, or he may have been afraid that she would run away and he would be left to "end his days" alone. But these feelings were externalized as envy and distrust that was blamed on Piquet and whatever imaginary nocturnal paramours she was hiding beneath her bed.

Jealousy about enslaved people was commonplace in the antebellum South, but that did not mean people of the planter class deemed it an acceptable emotion. If antebellum etiquette books dictated the proper ways to express emotions, gossip and rumors helped police affective norms by highlighting when people had transgressive feelings. Gossip effectively chided its subject for committing an emotional infraction, while also defining for the listener what was affectively appropriate or inappropriate.[47] Olmsted saw how much airing dirty laundry revealed about affective boundaries when he was told about a Louisiana planter who was acquitted after attacking an enslaved man "in an anger of jealousy," believing that the man was courting an enslaved woman that the slaveholder desired for himself. Like so many elite, White Southern men, the slaveowner faced no criminal charges for "mutilate[ing]" the enslaved man, but the slaveholding community still "believe[d] he was guilty, and ought to have been punished" for "being jealous of the boy."[48] The gossip's wording suggests that the envious slaveholder's peers thought that his true crime was not injuring an enslaved man he owned, it was giving sway to jealousy. Each telling of the story damaged the slaveholder's reputation locally and provided the gossip's audience with a cautionary tale: envy was an unsuitable emotion for members of the planter class, and if one did feel "jealous" of an enslaved person, they should not act upon it in such a fashion.

Slavery and slaveholding were also critical ingredients of pride. Some slaveholders derived caste pride from enslaving people because it meant that their children or wives did not have to labor in the fields.[49] Others based their self-respect and notoriety on their abilities to heal, buy, or break enslaved bodies.[50] Reputation was paramount to White Southern elites, and they depended on being viewed favorably by their peers. Any damage to that reputation, a source of so much pride, produced a much less desirable emotion: anxiety. In his study of Southern social classes Daniel Hundley claimed that one's public estimation was of particular importance to those who aspired to the upper ranks of the planter class, saying that middle-class men who yearned to be large slaveholders experienced "torturing anxiety . . . to be well spoken of by the world."[51]

In the antebellum South enslaving people was not just an economic calculation: it was a means to accrue social capital. But that capital, and all attendant pride and reputation, could be lost if one was publicly perceived as an inept slaveowner. An author in *DeBow's Review* observed that "a shivering servant is a shame to any master," while a slaveholder in Louisiana swore to Olmsted that "nobody would have respect for a man that treated his niggers cruelly."[52] Their main concern was not being a "cruel" or negligent master; instead, they feared being put on trial in the court of public opinion, where town gossips were judge, jury, and executioner and the sentence was pride or shame. As Frederick Douglass observed, "Public opinion is, indeed, an unfailing restraint upon the cruelty and barbarity of masters, overseers, and slave drivers."[53] Some enslaved people did believe that fear of losing "the good opinion of the public" provided a check on slaveholders and saved them from further beatings.[54] On the other hand, Keckley saw firsthand what occurred when a slaveholder disregarded the opinion of their peers after she was severely punished by her owner. She remembered that these recurring beatings "created a great sensation at the time," as her owners' brutality became "the talk of the town and neighborhood." Keckley's only solace was the knowledge that her owners were disgraced because they "were not viewed in a light to reflect much credit upon them."[55] Since owning slaves could be a source of pride or of humiliation, affective and social norms were some of the only checks on slaveholders' behavior.

Slave mistresses were also painfully aware that to avoid gossip, and protect their reputation as a supposedly kind mistress, they had to maintain, or at least perform, certain relationships with enslaved people. Harriet Jacobs recalled that when her grandmother grew ill many of the local elite, White women stopped by to visit her and "to bring her some little comforts." When Jacobs's Aunt Nancy asked their mistress, Mrs. Flint, if she could go care for her mother, Mrs. Flint refused, claiming that there was not "any need" for Nancy to go and that she could not "spare" her. But Jacobs remarked that once Mrs. Flint learned that "other ladies in the neighborhood were so attentive" to the sick woman who had once been enslaved by Flint, and "not wishing to be outdone in Christian charity," she hurried to fawn over the woman on her sick bed.[56] Mrs. Flint must have suspected that public estimation of her character would suffer if her peers were visiting her former slave and she was not. By going to see Jacobs's grandmother, but not permitting Nancy to attend to her own sick mother, Flint also revealed that she was much more invested in the appearance of being an "attentive" and "Christian" woman than in actually being one.

Slave narratives indicate that, at times, enslaved people were able to use slaveholders' fears of being grist for the rumor mill to their own advantage. Slaveowners not only were concerned about what other members of the planter class might say about their affective relations with enslaved people, but also were anxious about what enslaved people might reveal. Harriet Jacobs claimed that her grandmother's respected position in the community offered her "some protection," because "Dr. Flint was afraid of her" and "dreaded her scorching rebukes." In particular, he was concerned that because she was well known locally as "Aunt Marthy" for her homemade "crackers and preserves" and also widely admired, if he abused her granddaughter she would make "his villainy . . . public," which could damage his own reputation irreparably. Jacobs conceded that this was another benefit of living in a town, rather than a more anonymous city or an isolated rural area, because everyone knew "each other's affairs." This demonstrated the power of gossip and the importance of location to avoiding punishment.[57]

Flint had reason to worry that the free woman's word would trump his own. He no doubt recalled that when he had tried to sell her, despite the fact that she had long been promised her freedom, there had been an intense public backlash. According to Jacobs, her grandmother's "long and faithful service in the family was also well known," as was "the intention of her mistress to leave her free," so Flint's actions were viewed with universal distaste. Because of this, when Jacobs's grandmother came up for auction "many voices" in the audience cried "Shame! Shame! Who is going to sell *you*, aunt Marthy? . . . This is no place for *you*" and "no one bid for her." Finally her former mistress's sister, who was well acquainted with Marthy, and her sister's promise, purchased the woman. The sister was only able to afford her because no one else placed a bid, and after buying Jacobs's grandmother, she freed her.[58] In small Southern towns in particular, public shame was a powerful deterrent for slaveholders. Their reputation as slaveholders was a critical asset, but reputation mattered for enslaved people as well, as it could function as a shield or as a weapon.

Making Fear

Nowhere was the emotional influence of enslaved people clearer than when slaveholders talked about what scared them. Reading through *DeBow's Review*, it is evident that slaveowners were plagued by a variety of fears. They feared crop failure and that the slave population would grow until the institution became "utterly unprofitable" and unaffordable.[59] They feared competition from other American cities and foreign powers.[60] They experienced "fear of exposure and shame," afraid they would lose face with their peers.[61] But they were truly concerned about enslaved people, which the people they enslaved knew all too well.[62] Charles Ball opined that Southern slaveholders were like "inhabitants of a national frontier" because they were surrounded at all times by "hostile" people who might resent them enough to resort to violence.[63] Terror about slavery was a critical ingredient of the institution from its inception. Fear that enslaved people and indentured servants would ally themselves along class lines to rebel against their masters led colonies like Virginia to establish more laws that restricted enslaved people and also differentiated between the legal statuses of enslaved people and White indentured servants. Such laws included harsher punishments levied against enslaved people and prohibitions on any mass meetings of enslaved people, including "feasts and burialls [*sic*]," because of the fear that a critical mass of enslaved people would spawn a collective uprising.[64]

Fears of enslaved people pervaded the letters and conversations of members of the planter class in the antebellum period. In an August 1835 letter to his father, Caleb Green, Jr., described the climate of terror haunting slaveholders in the region. Green claimed that residents in Opelousas, Louisiana, were "pretty excited by insurrectionary moments among the slaves." Green did not think these were imagined anxieties, declaring that "there is no doubt but a widely extended conspiracy has embraced the whole Southwestern country." He cited victims of this supposed slave "conspiracy," including a friend of his who "was shot down near his own house" only weeks before, and his wife's uncle, who detected the taste of poison in a glass of water. Green blamed both crimes on enslaved people, and he expressed relief that the attempted poisoner had been "sent into the chain gangs of New Orleans" as punishment.[65] Nor did these fears subside with time. In a letter written to his father five years later, Green wrote that "insurrections are continually taking place . . . a few weeks ago a most formidable one was 'nipped in the bud.' . . It aimed at nothing short of indiscriminate slaughter of the whites." Though this most recent "insurrection" had been prevented, they were not put at ease, for Green noted ominously that slaveholders were "sleeping upon a volcano."[66]

Slaveholders throughout the South slept fitfully, worrying about enslaved people's intentions and tormented by nightmares of race war. A woman in East Texas told Olmsted that abolition was unthinkable because former slaves would "murder [them] all in [their] beds." As evidence she mentioned a recent case of a local enslaved woman who had "killed her mistress with an axe, and her two little ones." The woman assured Olmsted that the perpetrator had been executed, which she could only hope would serve as "a good lesson to the rest."[67] One enslaved man could paralyze whole communities with fear. In the summer of 1860 an enslaved man in Alabama named

Battiste was brought up on a variety of charges, including hosting meetings for enslaved people and "harboring" fugitives. According to court documents "various citizens of Mobile had frequently complained to the police that they lived in terror" because of Battiste and "were afraid to leave their houses." He was ultimately convicted of being a "disorderly person," but fear of enslaved people remained the order of the day.[68]

While one enslaved man could inspire community-wide anxiety, the greater fear for White Southerners was the enslaved conspiracy theories that Caleb Green, Jr., dreaded. As British journalist James Stirling opined while visiting America in 1856, "such feelings are fermenting in many an African heart," a theory he based entirely on the "suspicions and fears of slaveowners." Stirling perceived that some slaveowners tried to "make light of" the potential danger of enslaved insurrection in order to cope with their fear, but even those boasts were revealing, as he suspected that "a vast amount of distrust and fear lurks under their bravado."[69] Whether slaveholders expressed fear or spoke glibly about the threat with visitors, the menacing shadow of the murderous, rebellious enslaved person occupied a great deal of space in slaveholders' thoughts and imaginations. In order to quell collective White terror, some Southern newspapers elected not to cover slave revolts, only mentioning a recent uprising if it had been successfully thwarted so that any fears of insurrection were assuaged by editors' assurances that hypothetical insurgents would be caught before their wills were realized.[70] But the idea of enslaved people's latent anger fomenting into organized mass rebellions remained terrifying to Southern slaveholders; whenever there was news of a successful armed slave revolt, the aftershocks were felt even in other states and counties. In an essay on Nat Turner, abolitionist Thomas Wentworth Higginson shed light on slaveholders' fears that insurrectionary sentiments were commonplace. Higginson observed that even after Turner and his co-conspirators were executed, slaveholders throughout the South were chilled to the bone, awakened to the dreadful "suspicion that a Nat Turner might be in every family."[71] This statement captured the nuance of the emotional politics of slavery: enslaved people could simultaneously fall under a slaveholder's definition of "family" and also be a source of terror and mistrust.

These fears gave proof to the proslavery lie of the mutual affective relations of master and slave. Despite using the paternalistic language of "family" to describe enslaved people, slaveholders clearly understood that the people who fed, bathed, and nursed them might also want to kill them. Little wonder then that White people throughout the South projected their fears about Nat Turner's rebellion onto local enslaved people, whipping and even lynching innocent slaves from North Carolina to New Orleans in the hopes that doing so would stave off future revolutions and exorcise their terror.[72]

Fear of enslaved people, and of armed slave insurrections in particular, was rampant among slaveholders in the antebellum South, but these anxieties rarely translated into concrete policy changes, even after large, successful rebellions. Terrified of the Haitian Revolution, then in its tenth year, South Carolina closed its ports to the international slave trade. Tellingly, the decision was reversed the following year, after the Louisiana Purchase. South Carolina slaveholders likely still harbored fears that they might import the next Toussaint L'Ouverture, but they could not ignore the siren song of the western expansion of slavery, which depended on more enslaved bodies.[73] Meanwhile, city officials in New Orleans were concerned enough about the possibility of armed insurrection that during the Haitian Revolution they drew up plans to build ramparts that would wall in the city.[74] Those walls were never built. Three decades later Nat Turner's rebellion shocked the South, enough that mere months after Turner was hanged Virginia's legislature debated abolishing slavery in the state. In the end, every slave state in the South decided to enact stricter slave codes in the wake of Turner's rebellion.[75] In the intervening decades since the Haitian Revolution haunted their shores, the price of cotton had only skyrocketed, giving slaveholders less incentive to abolish an institution, even if it could prove lethal.[76] Like those in South Carolina and New Orleans before them, Virginia slaveholders decided that the benefits of slavery outnumbered the risks, that self-interest outweighed fear.

Enslaved people were extremely familiar with what their owners feared, and both enslaved people and formerly enslaved people sought to deliberately invoke White terror as a means of antislavery resistance. A number of historians have written about how enslaved people used deceit or theft as a survival mechanism.[77] Inspiring dread in the people who enslaved them, whether through overt acts of violence or more subtle forms of inducing fear, was another mode of resistance. Some formerly enslaved people used their slave narratives to provoke slaveholders' fears of murder and rebellion, and to remind slaveholders of what the people they enslaved were capable of. In his first two narratives Frederick Douglass refused to disclose how he had escaped. In his second memoir he explained that he did this in order to "keep the merciless slaveholder profoundly ignorant of the means of flight" used by runaways, hoping that this would keep slaveowners in a heightened state of vulnerability and anxiety. Douglass asserted that the slaveholder "should be left to imagine himself surrounded by myriads of invisible tormentors" and "be made to feel, that, at every step he takes . . . he is running the frightful risk of having his hot brains dashed out by an invisible hand."[78] Douglass hoped to keep planters in perpetual terror, unsure of which enslaved people wanted to run away or who might be plotting "torment" or murder instead of escape.

Northup also threatened slaveholders with the specter of revolt, warning that "a day may come—it *will* come. . . . A terrible day of vengeance, when the master in his turn will cry in vain for mercy."[79] Northup emphasized the gravity of his prediction by correcting his initial assessment that insurrection "may come" to the more confident threat that it "*will* come." By describing such an event as "vengeance" and suggesting that it was the slaveholders' "turn" to experience merciless cruelty, Northup also pinned the blame for this supposedly imminent and unavoidable uprising on slaveholders themselves, suggesting they would reap what they had sown. Douglass and Northup were free of their chains when they wrote these passages, but they knew from their time in bondage how to incite slaveholders' fears. And they knew just how difficult it was to combat an invisible but ubiquitous enemy like dread.

* * *

Enslaved people and slavery fundamentally shaped how slaveholders felt about their families, spouses, children, and peers, playing an integral part in how slaveowners expressed love, hostility, jealousy, pride, and fear. Even slaveholders' practices for commemorating emotional turning points in their lives, like growing up, marriage, and death, involved enslaved people. Because that process began in childhood and was woven into the fabric of their daily emotions, it was all too easy for slaveholders to overlook the myriad ways that their feelings, relationships, and affective rituals depended on slavery and enslaved people. Former slaveholders would only begin to grasp that enslaved people had always been inextricably tangled in their affective life once slavery came to an end. Historian W. E. B. Du Bois surmised that it took Emancipation for former slaveowners to truly realize the profound emotional role enslaved people had played throughout their entire lives, from the enslaved women that "at his behest . . . laid herself low to his lust," to the countless enslaved people that "had bent in love over the cradles of his sons and daughters, and closed in death the sunken eyes of his wife."[80]

Whether or not slaveholders recognized the extent to which their very emotions and familial relations had been forged by enslaved people, enslaved people knew the vital emotional labor they performed, and how they could manipulate slaveowners' affective bonds and feelings in order to survive or even resist enslavement. Of course, enslaved people did not learn those emotional survival skills overnight, any more than children of the planter class were born knowing how to compel enslaved people's joy or fear. Slaveholding children and enslaved children both had to be taught the emotional politics of slavery, including its affective practices and norms. For enslaved children in particular, that learning process began in infancy, and the knowledge they gained of the emotional dynamics of their world would ultimately cut their childhoods short.

CHAPTER 2

"Born and Reared in Slavery"

In recounting their childhoods in bondage, many formerly enslaved people described the experience of a fleeting, liminal period of happiness before they became aware of their slave status.[1] For some, the moment of clarity came when they were separated from a parent by sale or death, leaving children like Harriet Jacobs and Lizzie Gibson suddenly exposed "for the first time" to their "condition . . . as a slave."[2] For many, the realization was precipitated by their relationships with slaveholding children. As a young boy Henry Bibb was hired out to work in order to earn tuition money for his owner's daughter, his own former "playmate." For Bibb this first experience of commodification marked his introduction to "sorrow and suffering," when he "first commenced seeing and feeling that [he] was a wretched slave, compelled to work."[3] By comparing his lot with that of his childhood friend, and realizing that his labor and "suffering" were for her benefit, he became cognizant of his enslavement and the new feelings that accompanied that status. Lunsford Lane experienced a similar epiphany as a child when he began to apprehend the ways that his life differed from those of his "master's white children," noting that they were taught to read while he was barred from doing so, and that he could be sold without warning. Grasping those fundamental inequalities had a profound emotional impact on Lane: "all things now made me *feel*, what I had before known only in words, that *I was a slave*."[4]

These revelations occurred before the authors reached adulthood, but each of them felt that their childhood had been truncated by the devastating realization of what it meant to be enslaved. As Bibb and Lane articulated, these rude awakenings about their place in the world also represented an emotional metamorphosis, a transformation from the happiness of childhood to the "sorrow and suffering" of bondage. These discoveries irreversibly altered enslaved children, ushering them into the specific affective norms expected of enslaved people. Those moments also threw into sharp relief just how much their experiences and emotional lives differed from those of children of the planter class.

Having endured his own childhood in bondage, Frederick Douglass observed in his second autobiography that "nature has done almost nothing to prepare men and women to be either slaves or slaveholders," and that to learn to be slave or master required lengthy and "rigid training."[5] Sources from the antebellum period demonstrate that the feelings of slaveholders and enslaved people were individually learned, collectively constructed, and socially embedded in the slave South, and that enslaved people and slavery played a critical role in that socialization process. In the antebellum South, enslaved children, slaveholding children, and even adults who did not grow up in slaveholding households had to be taught the emotions and affective norms of slavery. Slaveholding and enslaved children became versed in the affective rules and expectations that governed them from their parents, from observing the world around them, from other adults, from fellow children, and from the process of play. However, enslaved children and slaveholding children were taught widely diverging lessons about how to feel, what to emote, and what emotions to suppress.

Though they might grow up playing alongside slaveholding children, enslaved children experienced abbreviated childhoods and needed to learn different emotional rules. Enslaved children were inculcated with a set of affective survival skills for negotiating the emotional politics of slavery. This included the ability to cope with loss and hardship, to read emotions, and to identify emotional allies in order to create affectively supportive social networks. Meanwhile children of the planter class may have been encouraged to foster childhood friendships with enslaved children, but part of their maturation process was shedding those friendships and learning how those relationships were inextricably tied to power. Over time they were taught the building blocks of paternalism and how to bring domination and violence to the fore of those affective relations.

This chapter examines how enslaved people learned the affective norms of slavery as children, and how slaveholding children were indoctrinated with the feelings and emotional expressions that were expected of them as members of the planter class. Of course, children were not the only ones in the antebellum South who needed to be instructed how to feel and express emotions. Sources written by enslaved people and members of the planter class indicate a widespread belief that White people who were not raised in the South, or did not grow up in slaveholding households but became slaveholders as adults, had to be taught the affective norms of slavery. Thus the final section of the chapter elucidates how slaveholding adults were taught which emotions were appropriate and inappropriate.

Childhood in the Antebellum South

Historians of slavery have asserted that in order to understand the lives of enslaved people, it is crucial to examine their experiences as children and how their formative years shaped them.[6] Yet there are many challenges that confront anyone writing about the history of children in general and enslaved children in particular.[7]

First, there is the question of who is defined as a "child," as childhood itself is a modern concept that is socially, culturally, and temporally constructed as well as heavily contingent on race, class, and gender.[8] Childhood in the antebellum South not only looked different from childhood in the South today, but also varied wildly for the enslaved and free children living under slavery. Thus it is important to avoid presentism when trying to locate the historical experience of enslaved children.[9]

The second challenge when studying the history of children is the problem of available sources. The study of slavery and children involves limited source material, which is compounded when researching enslaved children.[10] Many of the existing sources about slaveholding or enslaved children are adults' later recollections, raising questions about the problems of memory.[11] As if to counter potential accusations that they did not remember their childhoods, authors of slave narratives often described events from their youth as "never to be forgotten" or leaving a "lasting impression."[12] Some historians argue that despite debates about the accuracy of memory, adults' narratives about their childhoods in slavery should not be dismissed as untrustworthy.[13] Rather, scholars should be aware of the challenges of studying children as historical subjects, and they must read across sources about slaveholding and enslaved children to identify commonalities in their experiences and affective development. Ultimately, examining the emotional development of children in the antebellum South sheds light on the lived experiences of enslaved children and children of the planter class, showing how children are socialized, and the role emotional politics play in learning how to maneuver through social interactions.

Learning Affective Norms

In order to become versed in the affective norms of slavery, children of the antebellum South needed to understand the social hierarchies that structured their world.[14] Identifying who possessed or lacked power was especially important for enslaved children. Enslaved people learned the emotional politics of slavery by reading the feelings of the people around them, a process of observation that began in childhood. Growing up enslaved in Maryland, Frederick Douglass quickly grasped hierarchies of slavery and the particulars of his master, Colonel Lloyd. He did this in part through discerning how the enslaved people around him felt about Lloyd, noting that the "name" of his master "seemed ever to be mentioned with fear and shuddering," never "with affection but always with fear." Even before he met Lloyd, he knew how much power was wielded by the man with "the ominous title of 'old master'" by the emotional reaction other enslaved people had to Lloyd. In this way, Douglass swiftly learned to fear the man and to avoid him.[15]

To weather the complex emotional politics that structured the slave South, children first had to learn how the hierarchy of their family intersected with the power structures of slavery. Harriet Jacobs described how her brother William was schooled in the scaffolds of power that surrounded him one day "when his father and his mistress both happened to call him at the same time." William paused before responding, unsure who "had the strongest claim upon his obedience," before deciding to answer the call of his mistress. Afterward, their father chastised him for this decision. When William confessed his confusion about who to respond to, their father replied, "You are *my* child . . . and when I call you, you should come immediately, if you have to pass through fire and water."[16] Clearly enslaved parents still sought to hold disciplinary sway over their children, but at a young age William already recognized that his father was not the only person he answered to, nor was his father the highest authority on the plantation.

For enslaved children who had been raised to respect their parents it was all the more sobering when they realized that those parents were also subject to the tyranny of members of the plantocracy. Jacob Stroyer never forgot the "first time" he was "whipped by anyone except father and mother," when he was beaten by a groom in the stable where he worked. He appealed to his parents for help, leading his mother to be beaten as well. Confronted with this injustice it occurred to Stroyer that his entire family and "the rest of [his] fellow Negroes" were "doomed to cruel treatment through life." Unable to enlist his parents' aid in challenging their shared oppressor, Stroyer decided "to appeal to the sympathy of the groom" but to no avail.[17] Once he became cognizant of the relative power that he and his parents possessed, Stroyer, ever the savvy jockey, saw that he had to learn new pathways through the affective norms of enslavement. The passage illustrates that in order to understand the emotional politics of slavery, children in the antebellum South not only needed to determine the *social* hierarchies of the institution, they needed to calculate the *affective* hierarchies around them, who would emotionally respond to them, and what feelings to express or suppress.

Learning from Parents

As Stroyer learned, parents were not the only people enslaved children answered to, but they served as the primary source for lessons on affective norms for enslaved children. Enslaved parents taught their children what emotions to repress, they modeled how to create and maintain family ties, and they prepared children for the inevitability of loss. Enslaved children were often urged to mask their sadness and tears outside of the home, particularly if they were in the presence of members of the plantocracy. They were also warned against giving free rein to anger.[18] But many enslaved parents also worked diligently to provide children with a nurturing home environment in which children experienced love and support and could freely express their feelings.[19] As a result of such efforts, family functioned for many enslaved children as an emotional bulwark from the totality of the grim reality of slavery.[20] Unlike so many children in bondage, Harriet Jacobs was born and raised in a two-parent household "in a comfortable home," which led her to feel "so fondly shielded" that she "never dreamed" that she was "a piece of merchandise."[21] Living with family also helped fortify Frederick Douglass against the objectification of slavery. Douglass claimed, after being raised by his doting grandparents, "it was a long time before I knew myself to be *a slave*." As a result, he knew of "no higher authority over [him] or the other children than the authority of grandmamma."[22] Jacobs's and Douglass's recollections demonstrate that it was possible, even if only temporarily, for enslaved families to create a home life that sheltered children from the full extent of their enslavement.

Slave narratives detailed the lengths some enslaved parents went to in order to create a relatively stable home environment amid the uncertainties of slavery. This was especially challenging for parents who were in "away marriages," enslaved on different, and often distant, plantations. As a child Charles Ball lived with his mother as his father was enslaved on another plantation. Ball saw his father on weekends only, but his memoirs are a testament to how cherished those abbreviated homecomings were. Ball recalled his father's "gay social temper" during those visits, suggesting that his father was happy to see his family but also cognizant of maintaining a cheerful disposition during their brief time together. Ball's father worked to make those nights special, as he "always brought [them] some little present," including "apples, melons, sweet potatoes," which, in Ball's burnished memory, "tasted better in [their] cabin, because he had brought it."[23] Given the grueling workdays for enslaved people, a visit with his family was already a gift, yet Ball's father made additional unknown sacrifices in order to provide a tangible present each week. Perhaps it was knowing what his father had given up to sustain these weekly acts of generosity that made those "little present[s] . . . taste better," leaving indelible recollections of happiness and affection.

While growing up enslaved outside of St. Louis, Mattie Jackson related that her parents regularly proved that the conditions of bondage, and the nature of their away marriage, would not determine the tenor of their relationship. Mattie Jackson wrote admiringly of her father, Westly Jackson, and his "deep affection for his family." His commitment to his family was repeatedly tested as he was sold to successive owners who lived farther and farther away from his partner, Ellen Turner, and their three children. Because Westly lived so far away, the then three-year-old Mattie was able to see her father only on the weekends. Father and children alike relished what little time they had together. Mattie noted that she could "well remember the little kindnesses" her father "used to bestow upon" them as well as "the deep affection and fondness he manifested."

Westly's visits with his family were perhaps so memorable because they were infrequent and because of the effort he put into making those moments possible. At the time his owner lived twenty miles away from Turner and her children, but the slaveholder allowed the abroad marriage to continue. This meant that to see his family Westly had to walk twenty miles each Saturday night, only to walk twenty miles back on Sunday night so that he could return to the fields on Monday. After a week of backbreaking labor he subjected his body to that journey, all for the sake of his wife and children.[24] On a weekly basis Westly Jackson measured out his devotion to his family in footsteps and, in doing so, modeled love and fidelity for his three children. Ball's and Jackson's homages to their fathers serve as an important reminder that enslaved children did not just experience the division of their families; they also bore witness to the commitment enslaved people had to keeping families and communities together. In a world of uncertainties, in which a parent might be repeatedly sold, Ball and the Jackson children nevertheless saw that it was possible to preserve family bonds, and that it took diligence and dedication to do so.

Enslaved parents' efforts to make time for their families, despite their excruciating work schedule, instilled in their children how love could transcend slavery.[25] Lunsford Lane hinted that what he remembered most about his mother was her absence, as his "infancy was spent upon the floor, in a rough cradle, or sometimes in [his] mother's arms."[26] As a result the attempts enslaved parents made to steal away from work to be with their family left lasting impressions on their children. William Wells Brown's mother frequently told him "how she had carried" him "upon her back to the field" when he was a baby and "how often she had been whipped for leaving her work to nurse" him but how happy he had appeared when she took him into her arms.[27] William was too young to remember the brief reunions between mother and son; what he was instead recalling was his mother affectionately describing her daily acts of loving rebellion. In recounting what she went through to care for him she conveyed her feelings for her son and reminded him that though he may not remember them, they had shared happy moments together.

Even brief visits with family provided children with the strength and support needed to endure the harsh realities of slavery. Lizzie Gibson, born in 1852, recalled that she was seven when she was first hired out to cover her owner's debts. Though this separated her from her mother and siblings it "was not so grievous at first" because they were still able to see one another occasionally. During these reunions the Gibson family fantasized about what life as free people might be like, imagining all the "good things" they would eat at their "new home."[28] For Gibson the most critical emotional succor her family could provide was hope. Though their homecomings were short, that time together was invaluable because her family was able to reunite and collectively envision a future in which food was "good" and plentiful, their home was their own, and they were free from bondage.

One of the most important lessons enslaved parents taught their children was how to anticipate the affective road that lay before them. Some parents did that through stories. The trickster tales that were told and retold in slave cabins helped teach enslaved children about the emotional power dynamics of slavery in parable form, as such fables typically depicted "the victories of the weak over the strong." Whether human or animal, the heroes of these stories usually succeeded by outwitting their more powerful foe or by knowing the value of concealing their feelings or motives.[29] Because of their allegorical nature such stories could be viewed as entertaining by young enslaved children, and innocuous to any slaveholder who chanced to overhear, while older children and adults could see the radical subtext and even get ideas about tactics for resistance. There were moral lessons embedded in trickster tales, often related to respecting family, obeying parents, and honoring the Sabbath.[30] But just as importantly such stories could also fortify enslaved children with hope, hope that the dispossessed could fight back and prevail.

Enslaved adults also had to figure out how and when to introduce enslaved children to the prospect of being sold. It was a harsh reality that children needed to be prepared to be sold away from their family, given that enslaved youths represented an increasing amount of interstate slave sales in the antebellum period. Because children cost less, were perceived to be a more liquid asset and a malleable *tabula rasa*, many enslaved children were destined for the auction block before they reached adulthood.[31] Enslaved parents found a number of ways to broach the subject of separation with their children. Some parents tried to console their children through faith in religion and with the promise of reunion in heaven. Born in 1816, Tabb Gross explained that when he was about to be sold with his brothers at the age of fourteen his mother gathered her sons to tell them that "they would perhaps never see her again in this world, but she trusted to meet them in heaven."[32] Henry Box Brown recalled that his mother prepared him for sale with a poignant parable about the inevitable change of the seasons. She took him to the woods and, gesturing to the surrounding trees left bare "by the winds of autumn," explained that "as yonder leaves are stripped from off the trees of the forest, so are the children of the slaves swept away from them by the hands of cruel tyrants." Her timing was apt and may have been prompted by rumors of an impending sale, as Brown noted that this conversation with his mother was one of the last "enjoyments of maternal feeling" that they shared before he was sold. Because they were parted soon after, Brown may have idealized the way that his mother depicted the issue of separation. No matter how the lesson was disseminated, Brown remembered his mother's efforts to help him anticipate imminent loss.[33]

Some relatives elected not to tell children about a forthcoming sale. Frederick Douglass lamented that when his separation from his grandmother was drawing nigh she "kept the sad fact hidden" from him. Slave narratives contain many descriptions of the terror children experienced when they discovered they were to be sold, so perhaps some relatives remained quiet in the hopes of reducing children's anxieties. When Douglass learned he was to be taken from his grandmother's home once he was old enough to work, he claimed that while he could not yet "comprehend the full import of the intelligence . . . a shade of disquiet rested upon" him, and he was "haunted" by the "dread" of being sold.[34] Though not yet able to understand the forces that were taking him from his grandmother, he was gripped with terror. Lunsford Lane experienced similar "fear" when he learned that he "might be sold away from those who were dear" to him. Like Douglass, he could not shake the sense of foreboding: "deep was this feeling, and it preyed upon [his] heart like a never-dying worm."[35] Even children who were thought to be too young to understand the possibility of sale were consumed by dread of it. The constant threat of separation flooded these children with wracking feelings of uncertainty and powerlessness, highlighting the importance of parental preparation and the armor of family bonds.

Other enslaved children learned what it meant to be sold through second-hand experience. When Lizzie Gibson was only seven years old she witnessed an event she swore she "never forgot": a family of enslaved people being dismembered by a slave sale in the middle of a city street. Gibson watched as an enslaved man was unexpectedly told that he had been sold away from his family. Before he could even say goodbye to his wife and children, his new owner took him away. Another man proceeded to buy the enslaved man's wife and infant child but was unable to afford the couple's older child, who was brusquely advised "tell your mammy good-bye." This scene left Gibson paralyzed by emotion, crying "briny tears" in the street. Gibson claimed that the event filled her with her "first dread of slavery," and from that day forward she lived in fear of being sold away from her own family. Witnessing this abrupt division no doubt convinced her that these separations could come at any time, leaving her in a state of perpetual anxiety long before she ever had to "stand on the block." Perversely, these feelings may have prepared her for the sale she feared was inevitable. Gibson wrote that when she finally was sold, though she was separated from her sisters and brothers forever, the event was not "so hard" as the sale she had seen in the street.[36]

This scene is exemplary of how enslaved children learned the emotional terrain of the antebellum South. First, it illustrates that enslaved children were as likely to absorb the affective norms that structured their world from their own observations as from a loved one. Gibson's writing also indicates that many enslaved children realized at a very young age that theirs was a world fraught with loss and emotional uncertainty in which they were forced to constantly adapt. Finally, Gibson alludes that the horrifying sale she witnessed helped her come to terms with the possibility of being sold, and in some small way it made her own sale seem not "so hard." This speaks volumes about the methods enslaved children deployed to cope with the emotional turmoil of slavery. This event may have softened the blow of her eventual sale, but there is little doubt that seeing another family being sold and experiencing the division of her own family played a pivotal role in Gibson's emotional development.

Navigating Emotional Politics Alone

Since they were often deprived of parents or other relatives through death or sale, enslaved children had an even more pressing need to understand how to navigate the emotional politics of slavery, and they had to do so largely on their own. The writings of former slaves demonstrate that enslaved children needed to learn three crucial skills in order to do so: how to read emotions, how to self-soothe, and how to identify potential allies. Like Gibson, many enslaved children discovered the affective norms and boundaries of slavery by studying the emotionally charged interactions and relationships around them. Separated from their families other enslaved children sought methods for self-soothing. Finally, many enslaved children identified new sources of support, including other adults and children who could serve as fictive kin or mentors.

The ability to decipher the emotions of others was vital to survival for enslaved children.[37] In the nineteenth century scientists like Charles Darwin were already examining how children interpreted and responded to affective expressions.[38] By studying other people's emotions children learned how to feel, what affective expressions were acceptable, and how to respond to the emotions of others, all of which helped them persevere in a world in which they faced vast power differentials. In describing his childhood in bondage Douglass shed light on how enslaved children read faces in order to make sense of complex affective relations and emotional events. For example, Douglass did not merely describe his grandmother as upset when they were separated, he wrote that his "Grandmamma looked sad" and that this expression was how he "knew she was unhappy." Enslaved children may have learned how to interpret feelings by watching their loved ones, but they also used those skills to read the emotions of members of the planter class. Douglass's narratives provide a wealth of information about how children began to pick up on the emotional cues of slaveholders and how they used this affective information strategically. As a child Douglass not only monitored what his owner *did*, but also observed how his owner *felt*, claiming that Colonel Lloyd "very early impressed me with the idea that he was an unhappy man. Even to my child's eye, he wore a troubled" expression that "awakened my compassion." Douglass emphasized just how "unhappy" he perceived Lloyd to be, remarking that he could feel "compassion" for the man who owned him and had subjected him to so much pain.[39]

By watching the slaveholder Douglass quickly gathered that Lloyd was prone to intense and dangerous emotions, having "seen him in a tempest of passion" comprising "all the bitter ingredients of pride, hatred, envy, jealousy, and the thirst for revenge," and Douglass used this affective information for self-preservation. Thus Douglass knew that whenever Lloyd's "gestures were violent," Douglass needed to be cautious, for during these spells one "had only to be near him to catch punishment, deserved or undeserved." Tracking the man's emotions helped Douglass predict Lloyd's future affective states and avoid their ramifications. Even when Lloyd displayed the occasional "affectionate disposition," Douglass remained wary, knowing that "the pleasant moods of a slaveholder are remarkably brittle . . . they neither come often, nor remain long." Douglass had only to mentally scan his store of emotional data, collected over time, to know that Lloyd's "pleasant moods" were transient and not to be trusted.

Douglass believed it was critical to anticipate his owner's feelings, but this system was hardly infallible: Douglass also recounted situations when he incorrectly inferred how slaveholders would react emotionally. Douglass recalled an incident when one of his enslaved cousins came to Captain Anthony to tell him about an abusive overseer. Douglass "expected to see [Anthony] boil over with rage" at the overseer, but instead he replied to the enslaved woman in "an angry tone" that she had likely "deserved every bit of" abuse. From observing interactions like this Douglass could course-correct perceptions of how his owner would respond and also better predict slaveholders' future emotions. His memory of this event is evidence that from a young age enslaved people were constantly trying to interpret their owners' moods and motives. Furthermore, this process had to begin anew each time an enslaved person encountered a new slaveholder, or even after returning to an owner after a lengthy separation. Douglass explained that when he was brought back to Thomas Auld's plantation, Douglass's lessons "concerning his temper and disposition, and the best methods of pleasing him, were yet to be learnt."[40] Despite their previous time together Douglass believed that affective dynamics could change dramatically over time, so to anticipate Auld's moods Douglass had to relearn the slaveholder's feelings. Douglass rebuilt his bank of affective information from scratch in the hopes that knowing his owner's emotions could provide him with a modicum of predictability and protection from Auld's "temper."

While Douglass touted his ability to discern slaveholders' feelings, he also contended that members of the plantocracy were blithely unaware that those they enslaved were watching and analyzing their emotions. Douglass claimed that Lloyd would never have "thought that the little black urchins around him, could see, through those vocal crevices, the very secrets of his heart."[41] Perhaps slaveholders like Lloyd could not believe the affective acuity of enslaved people, let alone enslaved children, or perhaps it was too sobering to contemplate being subject to that level of constant emotional scrutiny by the people they enslaved.

Enslaved children also gained crucial affective information from studying the complex relations among members of the planter class and also between enslaved people and slaveholders. Harriet Jacobs suggested that through these observations enslaved people perceived the nexus of hate, jealousy, and fear that had especially explosive ramifications for enslaved girls. Jacobs explained that any enslaved child that worked closely with members of the planter class "will learn, before she is twelve years old, why it is that her mistress hates" certain enslaved women. Jacobs claimed that by listening to the fights that took place between slaveholding couples an enslaved child might learn that her "own mother is among the hated ones." Nor were young enslaved girls ignorant of "the cause" of such "outbreaks of jealous passion." As a result Jacobs believed that the enslaved girl "will become prematurely knowing in evil things," and she will quickly "learn to tremble when she hears her master's footfall."[42] This elucidates the process of how enslaved girls in particular became aware of the intricate and gendered dynamics of the emotional politics of slavery. Perceiving that her mistress "hated" certain enslaved women educated Jacobs about the threat of sexual abuse within slavery while also shaping her own emotions. Guided by knowledge of the root cause of her mistress's hatred she learned to fear "her master's footfall," in the hopes that such wariness might help her avoid sexual assault herself.

As many enslaved children learned, it did not suffice to identify and understand the feelings and relationships of the people around them; enslaved children also needed to grapple with their own emotions, often alone. Separated from their parents by work, sale, or death, enslaved children were compelled to learn how to cope with loss and how to comfort themselves. Some children gained experience in managing their emotions when their parents had to leave them for work.[43] These daily estrangements often meant that children were left to deal with their intense feelings about separation alone. As a boy, William Wells Brown was a domestic servant, which he admitted was "preferable" to field labor because he received better clothes and rations, and he was able to get another thirty minutes of sleep. His mother was required to rise earlier, and "though the field was some distance from [the] house," young Brown "could hear every crack of the whip, and every groan and cry of [his] poor mother." Brown said that because of these sounds he "wept aloud" alone, yet "found no consolation" except in tears.[44] The routine theft of his mother was doubly felt as he bemoaned her treatment and had no one to provide him with solace.

In the end Brown "found . . . consolation," or at least catharsis, in the unchecked expression of his grief. In pondering how enslaved children dealt with sadness, Douglass asserted that the enslaved child "cries but little, for nobody cares for his crying," and he "learns to esteem his bruises but slight, because others so esteem them."[45] Douglass intended this as proof that enslaved children were comparatively content, but it insinuated that some enslaved children quickly absorbed how to temper their emotions, learning ways to quell tears and feelings that would otherwise go ignored. Unable to seek comfort from their parents, children like Brown and Douglass learned through necessity to control how they felt by self-soothing or by stifling their emotions.

Through their discussions of the many losses and separations that enslaved children endured, slave narratives illustrated that enslaved children often experienced intense feelings that exceeded their nascent coping strategies.[46] That affective unpredictability, combined with physical and emotional deprivation, led some enslaved children to experience bouts of depression. In his second narrative in particular Douglass detailed the profound desperation he felt as a child. Douglass's feelings of loss began at a young age, as he poetically observed that "early did clouds and shadows begin to fall upon [his] path." These stormy emotions intensified with age, and as he "grew older and more thoughtful" he spent more time dwelling upon them. According to Douglass, "The cruelty of Aunt Katy, the hunger and cold I suffered . . . together with what I almost daily witnessed, led me, when yet but eight or nine years old, to wish I had never been born. I used to contrast my condition with the black-birds, in whose wild and sweet songs I fancied them so happy! Their apparent joy only deepened the shades of sorrow."[47]

As he would throughout his second autobiography, Douglass lyrically invoked nature to convey the emotions slavery provoked. Scholars have argued that Douglass, like so many authors of slave narratives, was heavily influenced by sentimental literature, which placed emphasis on empathy and sorrow.[48] But in this passage Douglass was describing feelings not just of sadness, but also anger and bitterness. The "black-birds" he saw made him feel "deepened . . . sorrow," but only in contrast to their joy and "wild[ness]," which he envied acutely. The "wish" that he "had never been born" was a melancholy sentiment, but also a violent one.

Some children responded to overwhelming feelings of sorrow and anger by acting on such despondent and violent impulses. When they were both quite young, Moses Grandy's brother was sold to a man who was notorious for how he "very much ill treated many colored boys." His brother was subjected to severe punishments: when some cattle were lost his brother was flogged and was informed that he would be whipped each day until they were located. Perhaps unable to find them, and fearing being flogged again, or perhaps out of defiance of his master, Grandy's brother "piled up a heap of leaves, and laid himself down in them, and died there." Grandy reported that his brother "was found through a flock of turkey buzzards hovering over him; these birds had pulled his eyes out."[49] It is unclear how the story got back to Grandy or how anyone could have known that Grandy's brother intentionally "laid himself down" to die. Nevertheless, regardless of how Grandy learned about his brother's fate, or whether his brother's death was by suicide, it is telling that Grandy believed it was plausible that one so young could be distraught and determined enough to will themselves to die. Of course, if bondage could make young Douglass wish that he "had never been born," other enslaved children might also have felt that death was preferable to the emotional and physical brutality they endured.

Fictive Kin and Supportive Allies

Enslaved children found other ways to exert a small measure of control over their affective lives. This was done through a two-pronged campaign of seeking out allies and attempting to emotionally influence the people around them. Some enslaved children sought fictive kin for protection or as an alternative support network if they had been separated from family.[50] Fictive kin figures could provide a wealth of information about how to maneuver through the emotional landscape of slavery, particularly relations with slaveholders. Douglass's narratives provide a window into the affective process for children as they worked to identify allies and potential sources of emotional and physical sustenance. Having lost his mother and grandmother, Douglass knew how crucial loving relationships were to surviving slavery. He saw the ability to forge emotional bonds as divine, claiming that "the germs of affection with which the Almighty . . . arms the helpless infant" were to be used to combat "the ills and vicissitudes" of slavery. Cast into the unfamiliar world of the Lloyd plantation, Douglass "gradually" embraced new sources of assistance with "the little tendrils of affection, so rudely and treacherously broken" when he was taken from his grandmother's home. He also learned that kindness could come from unlikely sources, as he found that even Aunt Katy, who deprived him of food when he first arrived at the plantation, "was not destitute of maternal feeling" and eventually showed him affection. Other "sympathizing old slaves" supplied him with extra food when they could, as well as encouragement, offering "the comforting assurance" that he would "be a man some day," and to "never mind, honey—better day comin'." Douglass observed that such "gentle" gestures helped "to convince him that though *motherless*, he was not *friendless*."

Finding sympathetic mentors and creating fictive kinship networks helped enslaved children manage their emotional lives and cope with loss, but the process also taught enslaved children a critical survival technique: how to inspire affection in others, including slaveholders. It is clear from Douglass's narratives that enslaved children realized from a young age that endearing oneself to a member of the planter class could yield a variety of advantages, from emotional aid to more tangible support. Douglass noted that in addition to the comforting "words and looks" he sometimes received from Lucretia Auld she also occasionally slipped him "a piece of bread and butter."[51] Similarly, Douglass benefited from his relationship with his owner's son, Daniel Lloyd, because the young Lloyd shared food with Douglass and functioned as a "sort of protector," shielding Douglass from the harassment of "the older boys."[52] Slaveholder Edward Pollard also wrote about bestowing favors upon enslaved children. Pollard described an enslaved boy named Tom as his "best friend," recalling, "I had a great boyish fondness for him, gave him coppers, stole biscuits for him from the table, bought him a primer and taught him to read."[53] The gifts of extra food to a no-doubt-undernourished child and of reading lessons to a person systemically denied a right to literacy were invaluable. Douglass and Tom would have been keenly aware that they relied on a combination of the largesse of members of the planter class and of their own abilities to provoke and sustain "fondness."[54]

For a child starved for affection as well as food, it might have been difficult to differentiate between an affective caregiver and a food provider. It is evident in Douglass's and Pollard's accounts that members of the planter class also conflated gifts of food with affection. Regardless of what Pollard and the Lloyds felt toward the children they gave "biscuits," protection, and "coins" to, enslaved children like Douglass learned that they could convert slaveholders' sympathy into food and other advantages. It is also impossible to know how Tom felt about Pollard, or if Douglass genuinely saw Daniel Lloyd and Lucretia Auld as friends, but these passages underscore how complicated and vital friendships between free and enslaved children could be.[55]

Emotions, Friendship, and Play

Children of the antebellum South also learned about the emotional strictures of slavery through interactions with other children, testing their nascent knowledge of affective norms in the social laboratory of play.[56] Play helped children grasp and adapt to the emotional politics of slavery because it prepared them for their future roles and work, it helped them transgress social boundaries, and it could function as a source of comfort. Enslaved children were subtly educated in the affective boundaries of slavery through the myriad ways that play and work overlapped.[57] Some enslaved children pretended to set tables and bake, preparing them for the tasks that lay ahead.[58] Play and work became particularly intertwined, and emotionally loaded, for children like Linda Brent, Frederick Douglass, Elizabeth Keckley, and Sella Martin who served as caretakers for children of the planter class. Tasked with attending to another child, it could be difficult to tease apart the bonds of friendship from the obligations of work.[59] Enslaved children were also aware that their slaveholding playmates might someday be their legal owner. Moses Grandy was close to his owner's son from birth because they were born just two days apart. Moses recalled how they "used to play together," and that his companion's slaveholder father "always said he would give" Grandy to the son following his own death. The boys' friendship was encouraged, but it was overshadowed by constant reminders of the true, unequal basis of their relationship: ownership.[60]

Some authors of slave narratives insisted that early in their childhood interracial friendships flourished between slaveholding and enslaved children in the transitional period before slavery had intruded fully into their consciousness. Lunsford Lane claimed that he spent his "early boyhood in playing with the other boys and girls, colored and white," before any of them "had learned that they were of a superior" race and he "of a subject race." Douglass argued that race did not matter to children, as much as their need for friends. He stressed how simple the criteria for friendship were for children, asking "are you a child with wants, tastes and pursuits common to children... ? Then, were you black as ebony you would be welcome to the child of alabaster whiteness."[61] Ultimately these depictions of picturesque childhoods, whether real or idealized, contrasted with the moment when enslaved children became aware of their chains. Perhaps such descriptions of a singular epiphany about one's slave status were primarily a literary trope, intended to invoke the sympathy of mostly Northern readers who were steeped in a sentimentalist culture that adulated children and childhood. Romanticizing their childhoods as a period of color-blind play, a happy respite from slavery, would certainly heighten such readers' umbrage at the fact that these contented children had been robbed of their carefree youth. Or maybe these writers really remembered experiencing a transformative moment of realization about their enslavement. There was perhaps a grain of truth in these scenes, speaking to the authors' senses, as adults, that their childhoods had been abbreviated at best, and that they had never been like the childhoods of their slaveholding playmates.

Play could also provide a forum for children to challenge members of the planter class. In a 1934 interview Jeff Hamilton, a ninety-year-old man who was a former slave of General Sam Houston, recalled playing with Houston's daughter, "Miss Nancy." As a child Hamilton played a prank on her that nearly caused her "to drown." He explained that Houston owned a "very spirited horse" that would become "enraged if anyone spit in his face." One day, when he was "feeling mischievous," Hamilton convinced Nancy to do just that. She spat at the horse, which "reared up on its hind legs and advanced towards her, snorting in anger." Backing away in terror the girl tumbled "into a deep part" of a creek. Hamilton managed to drag her out, but not before the sound of her screams attracted her "family . . . to see what the trouble was." They did not see that Hamilton had saved her, only that he had endangered her life, and because of this "Gen. Houston gave [him] a thrashing."[62] Though Hamilton chalks his behavior up to "feeling mischievous" he deliberately tricked his master's daughter into doing something he knew would provoke a temperamental horse. At the very least, he knew the "very spirited horse" would scare Nancy, but he might have anticipated that the horse would react with physical violence. Whether he intended her harm or not, Hamilton pushed boundaries by placing a member of the planter class in danger. Within this loaded context his actions were not taken as "playful."

As Hamilton learned, because play could be used to test the limits of slavery and free status it could have serious consequences.[63] The very real impacts of play were clear in an event from James Pennington's childhood in bondage. Pennington recalled "an extremely cruel" overseer who was never without a "long hickory whip." One day Pennington chanced upon one of the whips on the ground, so he "picked it up, and boy-like" pretended to ride it like a pony until the overseer found him, absorbed in his game of make-believe. The overseer proceeded to beat young Pennington savagely. This did not appease the overseer, who commenced a campaign of terror against the boy who had dared to play with his whip. Pennington explained that after that he "lived in constant dread" of the overseer, who took every opportunity to "show how much he delighted in cruelty by chasing [Pennington] from [his] play with threats and imprecations."[64] When Pennington picked up the hickory stick and imagined it as his horse the boy may not have intended his actions to be subversive, but it certainly angered the overseer. Because Pennington had defied the man by playing with a tool of discipline, the overseer set out to abuse the boy physically and emotionally. Whether it was because the overseer felt mocked, or because he recognized the liberatory possibilities inherent to play, Pennington's game of make-believe was viewed as threatening enough to warrant punishment and policing, ensuring that Pennington's future play was undergirded by fear.[65]

Rather than using play to challenge members of the slavocracy, and their violent forms of discipline, some enslaved children longed to play at being a master themselves. Jacob Stroyer remembered an enslaved boy named Gilbert who was, in his words, "a cruel boy" who delighted in taking smaller enslaved boys into the woods to whip them "until their backs were all scarred." Several times a week Gilbert would play the role of slaveholder or overseer, beating the boys and then threatening them with further violence if they told anyone. This continued until the day that Gilbert decided to whip Stroyer. When begging for mercy did not work Stroyer ran to tell a relative about Gilbert's reign of terror. As a result, "Gilbert was brought to trial, severely whipped," and then made to apologize to all his victims.[66] Stroyer does not specify whether the punishment was ordered by his owner or overseer or whether justice was meted out by members of the enslaved community, though both would have disapproved of Gilbert's ad hoc brutality for different reasons. A slaveholder might be angered by Gilbert's impudence and by any damage done to the boys, who were valuable property. The enslaved parents of Gilbert's victims would also want to see the "cruel boy" punished, albeit for hurting their children. It is not clear if Gilbert was also disciplined for daring to act out a fantasy of being master, not mastered.

Play served as an emotional outlet from slavery for many enslaved children. Douglass described how "play and sports" often took him "from the corn and tobacco fields . . . where scenes of cruelty were enacted and witnessed."[67] By removing him from the site of so much "cruelty," play offered Douglass temporary emotional, and perhaps physical, respite. Play also helped him adjust to life at Colonel Lloyd's plantation. Brought there to be separated from his grandmother, Douglass was suddenly surrounded by an excited assembly of children who were eager to greet the "new comer," demanding that he "play with them." He declined at first, hesitant to spend his last moments with his grandmother playing with strangers, but she insisted that he join them, reminding him that some were even related to him. His separation anxieties were warranted, as his grandmother snuck away while he watched the other children play. Perhaps she knew that he would need to start acquainting himself with his estranged family in order to establish new support networks once she departed. It was his cousins and other children who tried to cheer him up, telling him "don't cry" and offering him fruit, though Douglass recalled that he was so distraught that he tossed aside their gifts and "refused all their kindly advances."[68] Even if they had never been abandoned in a similar fashion the other enslaved children were quite familiar with the instabilities that characterized their world. It is possible that the children knew all along that Douglass's grandmother was preparing to leave and purposefully tried to distract him. In a society where children had little power or certainty they sought to comfort Douglass with the few methods they had at their disposal: "kind" words, food, and the diversion of play.

Slaveholding Children and Affective Norms

Like enslaved children, slaveholding children were indoctrinated in the affective norms of the antebellum South, learning the emotional strictures of society from personal observation, from their parents, and from other adults and children. But while enslaved children were being taught affective survival skills, children of the planter class were schooled in emotional mastery and dominance. A passage from Fanny Kemble's diary of her time on her husband's three Georgia plantations shows how quickly children of the planter class comprehended the emotional politics of slavery. Kemble remarked that she did not know how or where her daughter "gathered her information" but she remarked that "children are made of eyes and ears, and nothing, however minute, escapes their microscopic observation." As a result, one day her daughter announced to an enslaved woman named Mary "some persons are free and some are not . . . I am a free person, Mary—do you know that?" The woman replied "yes, missis," but the child continued to press the issue, asking if Mary was aware that not all people were free.[69] Just like enslaved children, free children recognized the power dynamics that existed within and outside of their families. Kemble's daughter understood that she, at three years old, had rights that an enslaved woman did not. She had also already learned that power only functioned if others acknowledged it, as her repeated questions to Mary all served to highlight their unequal positions.

In the eighteenth and nineteenth centuries both abolitionists and proponents of slavery worried that early exposure to the hierarchies of slavery had a deleterious effect on children of the planter class, arguing that the power dynamics of slavery did irreparable damage to their character and emotional capacity. In *Notes on the State of Virginia*, Thomas Jefferson expressed concern that being raised amid the "tyranny" of slavery had a pernicious and lasting impact on slaveholding children.[70] Writing over seventy years later, an author in *Southern Planter* offered a similar caution, that after extended intimacy with enslaved people "an impression is made upon the mind and heart" of slaveholders that was "sown in their hearts . . . in the days of childhood."[71] Some authors were more explicit about how slavery irrevocably altered the disposition and temperaments of slaveholding children, contending that slavery did not merely influence their emotions, it deadened them. In his Southern travelogue Frederick Law Olmsted observed that people who were "accustomed from childhood to see men beaten . . . to see other men whip women without . . . any expression of indignation, must have a certain quality, which is an essential part of personal honour . . . greatly blunted, if not entirely destroyed."[72]

Olmsted suggested that because the system was characterized by such ignominious actions, a child raised by slaveholders could not help but become "accustomed" to cruelty. This in turn stunted them emotionally and "blunted" their ability to possess "honour" or to fully "express" certain feelings. Solomon Northup claimed to have witnessed this phenomenon in action, observing that his owner's son "possessed some noble qualities" but had become "pitiless" while growing up on a plantation. Nor did Northup think this was mere anecdotal evidence. He believed that if one was raised abusing enslaved people then as an adult "the sufferings and miseries of the slaves will be looked upon with indifference." In this way Northup believed that slavery "necessarily fosters an unfeeling and cruel spirit" in members of the planter class.[73] So slavery not only "blunted" one's sense of "honour," but also apparently robbed one of the ability to feel pity, and left one "indifferen[t]" and "unfeeling."

To counter arguments that slavery perverted young slaveholders, some proslavery authors asserted that the social conditions of slavery were instructive, helping children of the planter class to develop emotional mastery of themselves and of others. Thomas Roderick Dew challenged Jefferson's claim that the "tyranny" of slavery emotionally impaired children of the planter class, arguing instead that "there is nothing which so much humanizes and softens the heart, as . . . *authority*."[74] Similarly, Daniel Hundley reasoned that the very character and "dignity" of the Southern planter stemmed from "his habitual use of authority from his earliest years." According to Hundley, wielding that "authority" imbued young men of the planter class with a "sense of the responsibility and . . . obligations" that was necessary to teach them "first to control themselves" and then, inevitably, to exert control over others.[75]

Many proslavery authors argued that in order to achieve lasting, intergenerational bonds between master and slave the seeds of such relationships must be sowed in childhood friendships. In his defense of slave society James Henry Hammond asserted that childhood relationships with slaves helped master and slave alike "cultivate the tenderest and purest sentiments."[76] Daniel Hundley's proslavery essays were a paean to the trope of the loyal, enslaved childhood friend. He waxed romantic about the supposed lifelong bonds of enslaved people and "young gentlemen," how they played side by side, enslaved people "shadowing" their masters. As they grew older, the relationship began to evolve. The enslaved person now followed the slaveholder to school, and instead of playing they hunted together.[77] *Southern Planter* magazine was less sentimental when justifying friendships between slaveholding children and enslaved people. One author suggested that such relationships were beneficial to the growth and self-esteem of children of the planter class, who enjoyed the company of enslaved children or adults in part "because the deference shown them makes them feel perfectly at ease." The author even intimated that their childhood interactions with enslaved people were perfectly suited because even enslaved adults were, in his view, so childish that the "subjects of conversation are on a level with [the] capacity" of slaveholding children.[78]

Sources from slaveholders and formerly enslaved people suggest that many slaveholding parents agreed with authors like Dew, Hundley, and Hammond, as they encouraged friendships between their slaveholding children and enslaved children. Edward Pollard nostalgically recounted how he "was trained in an affectionate respect for the old slaves on the plantation." He "was permitted to visit their cabins, and to carry them kind words and presents."[79] Though Pollard's parents "trained" him to go "visit" enslaved people himself to maintain relations with them, other slaveholding parents were more directly involved in ensuring proper affective ties between slaveholding and enslaved children. The Auld parents made clear their investment in forging bonds between their son Thomas and young Frederick Douglass, who was charged with caring for Thomas. Douglass was presented as a gift to Thomas, who "was affectionately told by his mother, that '*there was his Freddy*,' and that 'Freddy would take care of him.'" Douglass in turn "was told to 'be kind to little Tommy.'"[80] Thomas may have become attached to Douglass out of love for his "present," or because he now had another child to play with, but Douglass's narrative emphasized that their introduction and their first feelings about one another were mediated by Lucretia Auld. She subtly guided the growth of their relationship by speaking of Douglass "affectionately" and by giving them both nicknames. Of course, the difference in their status was also delineated. Douglass was referred to as "*his* Freddy," underlining that he was more than a friend or caretaker: he was "Tommy['s]" possession. While Douglass was warned to be "kind" to his new master, Thomas was not issued a similar injunction. In doing so, Mrs. Auld was instructing them in what emotions were expected of people in their positions, emphasizing that the job of human chattel like Douglass was to provide affection, to "care" for Thomas in every sense of the word. The effort Mrs. Auld put into the first meeting between Douglass and her son indicates how invested some slaveholding parents were in orchestrating the emotional relations between slaveholding and enslaved children.

Interactions with enslaved children had a profound emotional impact on children of the planter class. Pollard wrote enthusiastically about playing with his "sable companions" as a child, but a description of his time spent in solitude revealed even more about what he felt about his enslaved associates. Pollard recalled that when engrossed in his "own boyish enjoyments," while "having a pleasant ride . . . or feasting on delicacies," his pleasure was sometimes interrupted when it occurred to him that his "poor little slave companions" were hard at work. He also thought about "what poor food they had, and with what raptures they would devour 'the cake'" with which he was "pampering" himself. Overcome by these thoughts, young Pollard reported feeling "gloomy, embittered, and strangely anxious to inflict pain and privation" on himself.[81] Perhaps when a young Pollard contrasted his comfortable existence with that of his "slave companions" he was overcome by guilt. It is also possible that as a child Pollard used these meditations on difference and the emotions they provoked in an attempt to simulate what he thought his "poor little slave companions" felt and thus empathize with their "pain and privation."[82] Or perhaps Pollard described how "gloomy" and "embittered" he had felt as a child because he was writing in the sentimental mode, which romanticized sorrowful feelings and sympathy in particular.[83]

Given the complex relations that could form between slaveholders and enslaved people, it is little wonder that some parents of the planter class were anxious about the intimacy that existed between slaveholding and enslaved children. Harriet Jacobs claimed that she "loved" her child mistress, who "returned [her] affection," but the Flint parents were wary of Jacobs's emotional influence over their daughter. One day Jacobs overheard Dr. Flint refer to his daughter's "attachment" to Jacobs, while Mrs. Flint countered that the "attachment . . . proceeded from fear." This upset Jacobs, as it made her wonder, "did the child feign what she did not feel? Or was her mother jealous of the mite of love she bestowed on me?" Jacobs eventually decided that Mrs. Flint's assessment was rooted in envy, assuring herself that children were incapable of emotional guile.[84] This passage showcases the conflicting feelings planter parents could have about their children's relationships with enslaved people. Though Dr. Flint thought his daughter was devoted to Jacobs his wife argued that this affection was false and coerced. Of course, the conversation also reflected the larger web of emotional politics in the Flint household. Since Dr. Flint was already sexually harassing Jacobs he had a vested interest in encouraging his daughter's attachment, thereby ensuring Jacobs's continued place in the household. The jealousy that Jacobs perceived in Mrs. Flint's comment might have had as much to do with her worries about her daughter's affections as they did with her growing concerns about Dr. Flint's own "attachment" to Jacobs.

Slaveholding children also established relationships with enslaved adults, sometimes because of tensions within their families. Pollard exposed the competing affective relations of his childhood when he described his "poor 'mammy'" who "would protect . . . and humor" him when he was "chided . . . by [his own] mother."[85] Though his mother may have held authority over Pollard (and the enslaved woman), during emotional conflicts Pollard knew the enslaved woman would give him the "protection" and solace he desired when his mother sought to discipline or scold him. Pollard does not address the power dynamics inherent to the situation, that the enslaved woman was charged with looking after Pollard and thus had reason to be reluctant to "chide" her possible future owner. Nor was Pollard the only member of the planter class who found enslaved allies. Josiah Henson explained that his master, "Mr. R," was the legal guardian of Francis, the master's wife's young brother. Unfortunately for the orphaned Francis, Mr. R was an abusive alcoholic who did not give him enough food. Henson recalled how Francis frequently sought him out, "tears in his eyes, to tell me he could not get enough to eat." Henson explained that he made the boy his "friend for life, by sympathizing in his emotions" and "sharing" his family's small ration of food with him.[86] When the boy needed it most, Henson provided him with emotional and physical sustenance, nurturing him in ways that his own family would not. Pollard and Francis may have found true comfort and care in the homes of enslaved people. Of course, they may also have suspected that enslaved people would be hard-pressed to turn down a request of food or sympathy from a member of their owner's family.

Slaveholding parents may have encouraged friendships between their children and enslaved people, but planter parents were also clear that they expected these childhood relationships to end with the onset of adulthood. When Douglass returned to Baltimore and was reunited with his former friend, "Little Tommy," it was clear that "the loving relations" they once shared had dissolved. Douglass attributed this change to the fact that Tommy now "felt himself a *man*" who now demanded "more suitable associates," so "the time had come when his *friend* must become his *slave* . . . we must now take different roads."[87] An enslaved child may have been a "suitable" youthful companion, but the process of becoming an adult member of the planter class entailed the evolution of relations with enslaved people, from friendship to domination. Other authors suggested that slaveholders did not organically outgrow their enslaved friends; rather, they were told what kinds of emotional relationships with enslaved people were appropriate. For example, Lunsford Lane described how his former playmates "began to order" him about, because they "were told to do so by [his] master and mistress."[88] Evidently some slaveholding parents were explicit in urging their children down the "road" to proper slaveholding and away from their childhood relationships with enslaved people.

Saying goodbye to one's childhood playmates was a harrowing experience for some young members of the planter class. Virginia slaveholder John M. Nelson detailed this difficult process "from painful childhood sympathy to manly callousness." He confessed that as a youth "he would try to stop the beating of slave children," and when they were whipped he would "mingle [his] cries with their, and feel almost willing to take a part of the punishment." After his father chastised him repeatedly for his excess of "compassion," Nelson "became so blunted" that he "could not only witness their stripes with composure" but also "inflict them . . . without remorse."[89] Nelson's father was unequivocal that one was not supposed to feel "compassion" for enslaved people, and he may have even ordered his son to "witness" or "inflict" punishments in order to correct those feelings. Over time Nelson learned to check his tears and feel no "remorse" at watching or administering beatings. It is telling that Nelson did not describe his feelings toward slaves as having been altered, but rather "blunted" by deliberate repression. This illustrates how slaveholding parents used enslaved people as vehicles for an emotional transition, teaching slaveholding children how to be the master of enslaved people and of their own emotions.

The primary way that parents taught slaveholding children about the emotional politics of slavery was by example. Many proslavery authors stressed the importance of modeling healthy affective relations between master and slave, for as Hundley cautioned his reader "children learn a great deal more from example than precept."[90] This was far from a newfangled idea; almost eighty years before, Thomas Jefferson advised that children learned how to emotionally relate to enslaved people from observing their parents interact with enslaved people. According to Jefferson, when slaveholders failed to check their emotions in the presence of enslaved people "children see this and learn to imitate it; for man is an imitative animal. . . . From his cradle to his grave he is learning to do what he sees others do." Because of this, Jefferson recommended that a parent should "restrain" their "passion towards his slave," at least whenever "his child is present." All too often, however, parents did not guard their tempers when their children were watching. Instead, "the parent storms, the child looks on" and "catches the lineaments of his wrath," only to later reenact this "wrath" on their own on "smaller slaves."[91] Here Jefferson warned that if parents did not control their feelings toward enslaved people then slaveholding children would swiftly absorb these emotional lessons and treat enslaved children with the same "passion" they had seen their parents display. In Jefferson's view this was a problem of plantation management and of child development, a sign of how slavery tainted future generations.

Enslaved people also testified to the profound impact parents' behavior had on slaveholding children's views of affective relations between master and slave. One of Solomon Northup's owners, a man named Epps, maintained a campaign of sexual violence, harassment, and physical abuse toward an enslaved woman named Patsey, a fact that was well known on the plantation. One day Epps demanded that Northup whip Patsey while the Epps children stood nearby with Mrs. Epps, who watched the beating "with an air of heartless satisfaction." As other enslaved people and the Epps family looked on, all cognizant that Patsey was being punished for Epps's infidelity and his wife's jealousy, Northup whipped her at his master's behest. The Epps children might not have known the full extent of their father's relationship with Patsey, but they may have noticed that their mother was "satisfy[ied]" by the spectacle of the beating.[92]

Northup emphasized that witnessing these daily scenes of violence left their mark on slaveholding children, noting that "the effect of these exhibitions of brutality on the household of the slave-holder is apparent." He had watched as the oldest Epps son, on the brink of puberty, delighted in "chastising" enslaved people, especially an older man named Abram. If Epps's son deemed the enslaved man guilty of some offense then the boy mimicked his father, "sentenc[ing] him to a certain number of lashes," which he administered himself. The tangled knot of family ties and violence was even clearer when the boy accompanied his father into the fields "with his whip, playing the overseer, greatly to his father's delight. Without discrimination . . . he applies the rawhide, urging the slaves forward with shouts, and occasional expressions of profanity, while the old man laughs, and commends him as a thorough-going boy."[93]

As a boy becoming a man and growing into his planter status, Epps's son was already exploiting the authority that he possessed over an elderly and esteemed man. He may have been imitating his father's method of punishment when he whipped Abram, but when he joined his father the dynamic grew more complex. If he had not already begun to associate pleasure with enslaved pain from watching his mother and father's interactions about Patsey he would no doubt do so once he was repeatedly praised by his father for whipping and verbally abusing enslaved people.

As the recollections of Nelson and Northup show, as young men of the planter class grew up, enslaved people's bodies often became a vector for father-son bonding. Enslaved people were acutely aware that they bore the brunt of the process of indoctrination as young people of the planter class who yearned to win their fathers' love and approval learned how to be slaveholders. As a young man William Wells Brown was hired out to a Major Freeland whose favorite method of disciplining enslaved people was to tie them "in the smokehouse," whip them, and then burn "tobacco stems" to "smoke" them. According to Brown, Freeland euphemistically referred to this ritual torture as "Virginia play" since it involved his home state's cash crop. Brown experienced this "play" firsthand after running away. When Brown was caught Freeland "flogged [Brown] to his satisfaction" before fetching "his son Robert, a young man eighteen or twenty years of age, to see that" Brown "was well smoked." As Robert explained to Brown, "this . . . was the way his father used to do his slaves in Virginia." Clearly Freeland had taught his son that this was the best way to discipline enslaved people, and Robert saw the perverse delight and "satisfaction" his father derived from whipping enslaved people before subjecting them to smoke inhalation. It is unclear why Major Freeland made his son perform "Virginia play" rather than doing so himself. It is also unclear how Robert felt as he forced Brown to breathe in the noxious fumes. Perhaps he was reluctant, or feared disappointing his father, or perhaps he too felt pleasure and even pride at being entrusted with his father's beloved exercise in nostalgia, domination, and violence. Regardless of how Robert felt, Brown found the son to be a quick study, proclaiming him "a 'chip off the old block.'"[94]

Through observing how adults physically and emotionally disciplined enslaved people, slaveholding children absorbed the affective norms of slavery and began exercising their ability to provoke enslaved people's feelings, particularly fear. Pollard recalled that as a child he and his brother tormented enslaved people with what he termed "practical jokes," ranging from pelting them with apples to ordering them to go on fake "errands" that took them away from their work.[95] Though he swore these "jokes" were not rooted in "cruelty" he confessed that they were at times motivated by vengeance. Pollard explained that enslaved adults were sometimes tasked with punishing Pollard and his brother; thus the siblings "perpetrated revenge for such 'rough kindness' on the old ill-natured blacks." Even as a child Pollard experienced a specific shame or anger at being disciplined by an enslaved person. Tellingly, his response was to reassert his status, sending enslaved people on "fools' errands" to underscore the authority he possessed over them.[96]

Throughout Pollard's narrative it appears that the "practical jokes" perpetrated against enslaved people were dress rehearsals for wielding authority and fear as slaveholding adults. Pollard wrote at length about a devout enslaved woman named Judy and how he and his brother "thoughtlessly" and "wrongly—delighted to tease and annoy her." His brother Dick in particular targeted Judy for her religious fervor, calling her the "'Preacher,' or sometimes 'Old Nat Turner,'" ominously reminding her about "the tragic fate of Nat Turner." Not content with mocking her faith, Dick also felt compelled to intimidate the woman with warnings that if she was too outspoken she would be hanged like the insurrectionary Turner. The references to Turner reflect how much slaveholding children learned from their parents about the emotional politics of fear. Dick's threats were meant to frighten Judy, but also betrayed slaveholders' anxieties that any charismatic religious leaders like Judy might lead the next slave rebellion.[97] Little wonder then that Pollard believed that their bullying of Judy "was sometimes replied to in great bitterness."[98]

Young slaveholding girls also learned how to terrorize and intimidate enslaved people.[99] While traveling, Olmsted met an adolescent girl of the planter class. As they spoke an old enslaved man walked by, and she stopped him to "demand to know where he was going, and by what authority" before commanding the man to "return to his plantation." When the enslaved man "hesitated," she responded with "turbulent anger . . . threatening that she would have him well whipped if he did not instantly obey. The man quailed like a spaniel, and she instantly resumed the manner of a lovely child with me, no more apprehending that she had acted unbecomingly, than that her character had been influenced by the slave's submission."[100] This passage speaks volumes about how children of the planter class understood the nexus of feelings and power that operated in the slave South. Olmsted watched as the girl initially experienced anger, which made the enslaved man feel fear, or at least led him to "quail . . . like a spaniel," in a manner so convincing that the young girl and Olmsted were fooled. She was quick to don the role of authority figure but also was swiftly appeased by the enslaved man's obvious terror. Though only twelve, the young girl knew how to adopt different demeanors when interacting with enslaved people. As she seamlessly returned to being "a lovely child" while chatting with Olmsted she made manifest that she had learned what emotions were appropriate and inappropriate when addressing Black people or White people.[101]

While Pollard's, Olmsted's, and William Wells Brown's writings demonstrated that slaveholding children recognized how to inspire fear in enslaved people, sources also indicate that some enslaved people sought to influence children of the planter class by frightening them. A *Southern Planter* article on the management of enslaved people cautioned that "the witch and ghost stories so common among negroes, excite the young imagination and enlist the feelings" so parents should be mindful of what fairy tales enslaved people told to slaveholding children.[102] In his memoir Pollard recalled that there were a number of enslaved people on the plantation who scared him as a child, including one woman whose fables would "fill [their] youthful minds with awe, superstition, and an especial dread of being alone in dark rooms." As he said, "We are told by her of every variety of ghosts, of witches that would enter through the key-hole . . . and worse than all, of awful and terrible visions that had been afforded her of the country of the dead."[103] It is notable that these stories made Pollard and his siblings feel "awe," which the woman may have intended. She clearly wanted them to believe that her powers were uniquely hers and not accessible by all, as she proclaimed that she was "afforded" "visions . . . of the dead." Her legends may also have been calculated to keep them suspended in a state of "dread." She spun yarns in which "ghosts" were ubiquitous and "witches" could access any room. She also told the Pollard children that a local bird that was known for its "plaintive" song was no ordinary creature; rather, it contained "the transmigrated soul of a little child that had been the victim of the cannibalism of its parents." The enslaved woman told the Pollard children that if they listened closely they could hear the birds describing their fate in their song:

My mammy kill me,
My daddy eat me,
All my brudders and sisters pick my bones,
And throw them under the marble stones.[104]

Many of the woman's tales had the same effect, instilling slaveholding children with apprehension about the mundane, including fear of the dark, of birds, and of their own parents, who might eat them. All these stories shared the ominous theme that the children's world was more frightening than they imagined and that the enslaved people around them might be more powerful than they knew. Similarly, another enslaved woman frequently told Pollard that she could speak to his dead sister, Rosalie, and that she often did.[105] Perhaps the enslaved woman was hoping to scare him or trying to establish some power over him as the sole channel for communicating with his sister. Such stories may also have been intended as a creative way to punish or reward a slaveholding child that they were not permitted to discipline.[106] In either case these enslaved women were portraying themselves as people to be feared and respected by the children who might someday be their legal owners.

Learning the Affective Norms of Slavery in Adulthood

Children were not the only ones who needed to learn the affective norms of the slave South. The writings of enslaved people and members of the planter class share the widespread notion that White people who did not grow up in slaveholding families but became slaveholders as adults had to be taught the emotional expectations of slavery, as well as how to interact properly with enslaved people. These authors contended that nonslaveholding White Southerners, Northerners, and foreigners who were transplanted to the South did not know either how to feel about enslaved people or how enslaved people were supposed to feel about them. Discussions of how newcomers to slavery were cruel or inadequate as slaveholders are indicative of the importance placed on learning the affective norms and practices of the antebellum South.

Planters found novice slaveholders to be a convenient scapegoat, while enslaved people also castigated them, with Douglass noting that "of all men, adopted slaveholders are the worst."[107] While enslaved by Thomas Auld, Douglass saw the effects of such inexperience firsthand. Douglass specified that "Auld was not a born slaveholder" because he had inherited slaves through marriage. Because of this, Douglass posited that Auld did not know how to emotionally manage enslaved people, instead he "was cruel, but cowardly . . . at times rigid, and at times lax." Douglass pointed out that Auld seemed aware of these norms and strived to adhere to them in order to be perceived as a feared and respected slaveholder. But Douglass found Auld's performance wanting, noting that though Auld's "airs, words, and actions, were the airs, words and actions of born slaveholders," Auld could not fully or naturally embody the correct demeanor, and as a result Douglass claimed Auld "was an object of contempt" among slaveholders and enslaved people. Furthermore, Douglass claimed that enslaved people's "want of reverence" had a profound impact on Auld, making him "fretful" and even more inconsistent. This implied that one could never truly obtain the appropriate behaviors and emotions of slavery if one was not born into a slaveholding family. Auld's inexperience served as a cautionary tale to would-be slaveowners: if they could not instill fear, then enslaved people would disrespect them, their peers would hold them in "contempt," and they would be "fretful" and unhappy.[108]

According to Douglass, people who became slaveholders later in life also needed to learn how to feel about the people they enslaved. Douglass's mistress, Sophia Auld, came from a more modest, nonslaveholding family. As a result, she did not know how to behave toward enslaved people, nor could she recognize what was and was not emotionally appropriate. Douglass outlined Sophia Auld's atypical affective relations with enslaved people to exemplify what was considered inappropriate. First, Douglass pointed out that unlike other slaveholders Auld did not demand emotional censorship from enslaved people, because she "did not deem it impudent or unmannerly for a slave to look her in the face." Nor did she suppress her own feelings; Auld listened to the travails of the people she enslaved, and "there was no sorrow or suffering from which she did not tear." Rather than keep enslaved people at an affective distance, Auld offered material and emotional care to those who needed it, providing "comfort for every mourner" so that "none left without feeling better for having seen her."[109] She was particularly unsure of how to feel about Douglass, her son Tommy's companion. Douglass argued that it was difficult for her "to feel" that the enslaved boy "who was loved by little Tommy, and who loved little Tommy . . . sustained to her only the relation of a chattel" because she could not reconcile Douglass's status as property with the way she felt about a child who was integral to her household and family.[110] In detailing Auld's unusual affective responses, Douglass shed light on the complex emotional relations that developed between slaveholding and enslaved children, and within slaveholding households, while implying that experienced slaveholders knew how to handle those affective tangles.

Douglass also witnessed how quickly new slaveholders embraced the affective norms of slavery and how that affectively altered them. Though he initially believed Sophia Auld to possess "the kindest heart and finest feelings" he bemoaned that she swiftly socialized, evolving into a cruel slaveholder. According to Douglass, this emotional metamorphosis manifested physically, as her "cheerful eye, under the influence of slavery, soon became red with rage" and her "tender heart became stone."[111]

Some slave narratives discussed the inculcation process of Northerners and foreigners who moved to the South, describing how people who had not been raised in slave states had even more to learn about the emotional expectations of slaveholders. Harriet Jacobs claimed it was "a miracle" that one slaveholder showed kindness to her family. Though he owned many enslaved people Jacobs swore that he "was not quite deaf to that mystic clock whose ticking is rarely heard in the slaveholder's breast," implying that unlike most slaveholders he listened to his heart in matters concerning enslaved people. In order to explain such exceptional sympathy on the part of a slaveholder Jacobs noted that "this gentleman was a Northerner by birth" who had married into a slaveholding Southern family, and that his anomalous affective reactions stemmed from this upbringing.[112] Similarly, in addressing why one of his owners exhibited excessive sentiment toward enslaved people, Sella Martin claimed that his mistress was a "simple-hearted lady, who had been brought up in the North" and only recently come to the South: "therefore, she had little knowledge of slavery, and still less the feelings of slaveholders." Martin was more critical of an Italian man who bought him, deriding him because he had not been "born and bred" as a slaveholder. Rather, "he had come from a land that held no slaves" and had deliberately chosen "to stain his hands with the iniquities of slavery for mere gain."[113] Here Martin hinted that foreign-born slaveholders were worse than those raised with the institution and its norms because they could not claim they had inherited slaves or been steeped in the institution since childhood. Martin suggested that such outsiders naturally possessed a more objective perspective on slavery, and they should therefore reject the brutal system. If they still elected to become slaveholders then they were, in his view, motivated solely by greed.

Though authors of slave narratives might attest that outsiders, whether Northern or foreign-born, did not possess "the feelings of slaveholders," they also discussed how rapidly newcomers adopted the emotional relations and practices of slavery. Jacobs remarked to her readers that "when northerners" traveled to the slave South "they soon imbibe the sentiments and disposition of their neighbors."[114] James W. C. Pennington declared that Northerners did not just learn to mimic Southern-born slaveholders: they quickly exceeded them in brutality, and Northern transplants "readily become the most cruel masters."[115] Defenders of slavery remarked on this supposed phenomenon as well. In a proslavery essay Thomas Roderick Dew declared that it was a "fact, known to every man in the south, that the most cruel masters are those who have been unaccustomed to slavery." Because of this, he claimed that it was universally believed that Northern men who married "southern heiresses, are much severer masters than southern gentlemen."[116] Likewise, Hammond opined that the "Scotch and English are the worst masters among us, and next to them our Northern fellow-citizens," arguing that because they were not "born and bred" around slavery, they were less "humane."[117] In this way formerly enslaved people and proslavery authors simultaneously blamed any excesses of slavery on outsiders, and they demonstrated the extent to which they believed that the affective norms of slavery were socially constructed.

* * *

Since emotions like happiness, trust, and fear were used to both challenge and maintain slavery, it is little wonder that so much emphasis was placed on children and novice slaveholders becoming adept in the affective norms of slavery. Of course, children of the planter class received very different emotional training. Like enslaved children, they learned the affective norms of the antebellum South from observing daily interactions on the plantation, from their parents, from older enslaved people, and from enslaved children. But though some enslaved and slaveholding children may have shared playtime in their youth, for children of the planter class such friendships served as a dress rehearsal for their future master-slave relations. Beginning in childhood, members of the planter class were taught how to master emotions, their own and those of others. Meanwhile, enslaved children developed an arsenal of affective tactics that they could use to ward off punishment, gain rewards, or seek comfort and affection. These techniques proved crucial for weathering the daily interactions, conflicts, and negotiations of slavery, and they also helped them survive and resist the institution as adults.

Throughout their childhoods enslaved children bore witness to the power of emotions and what sorrow, rage, love, and jealousy could do, but the majority of them also experienced a childhood that was cut short by the realization of their condition. Just as enslaved children experienced the epiphany of recognizing they were enslaved, they would also come to understand that their feelings were contingent on their bondage, that the people who enslaved them expected them to feel and express emotions differently.

From a young age enslaved people learned that the emotional politics of slavery dictated that they suppress emotions like anger or sorrow, which were deemed undesirable by slaveholders. In place of those emotions enslaved people were expected to embody a performance of happiness that was believable enough to make their owners forget it was being compelled.

CHAPTER 3

"The Pursuit of Happiness"

In 1841 thirty-two-year-old Abraham Lincoln saw a slave coffle firsthand in St. Louis, leading him to muse about "the effect of condition upon human happiness" in a letter to a proslavery family friend, Mary Speed. Lincoln observed how twelve enslaved men and women had been "separated from . . . their friends, their fathers and mothers . . . and many of them, from their wives and children," and were on their way down the river to be sold. He claimed that while "we would think" it "distressing" to be torn away from family and friends the enslaved people in the coffle "were the most cheerful and apparently happy creatures," as evidenced by their dancing, singing, fiddling, and card playing. From this, Lincoln deduced that divine powers must ensure that even "the worst of human conditions" remained "tolerable."[1] Though Lincoln conceded how harrowing it would be to be "separated from" loved ones, he insinuated that this loss had not profoundly impacted the enslaved people he encountered, as they seemed to him to be superlatively contented.

Lincoln's description of enslaved men and women on their way to be sold highlighted a number of prevalent assumptions about slavery and happiness. First, Lincoln hinted that enslaved people experienced feelings differently, employing terms like "we" and "they" to contend that an event that would be "distressing" to "us" was not heartbreaking for enslaved people. Second, he was wholly convinced that cavorting and making music were proof of unalloyed happiness, and that this "apparent" contentment was sincerely felt, rather than a conscious act.[2] Given the numerous incentives enslaved people had to maintain a façade of joy in the presence of members of the planter class, and the punishments that awaited them if they gave free rein to feelings like anger or sorrow, it is little wonder that so many enslaved people excelled at performing the role of happy slave. As Elizabeth Keckley observed in her narrative of her journey to freedom, "the sunny face of the slave is not always an indication of sunshine in the heart."[3] But it is telling that Lincoln, who acknowledged the cruelty of slavery, accepted signs of merriment as confirmation that life in bondage must be "tolerable." Throughout his legal and political career the man who would later be known as "the Great Emancipator" was ambivalent about Emancipation.[4] But in this 1841 letter he voiced a popular dual assumption about American slavery: that enslaved people were happy in bondage, and that this presumed contentment justified the entire institution. Just a few years before Lincoln reflected on enslaved people's happiness, a Southern slaveholder assured English author Harriet Martineau that American slaves were "the most contented, happy, industrious peasantry in the world."[5] These passages demonstrate that slaveholders and nonslaveholders alike posited that enslaved people were happy in order to defend slavery as a moral economic system.

In the antebellum South enslaved people's emotions could function as liabilities or commodities, and no emotion was more highly valued by slaveholders than happiness. Amid increasing sectional polarization, the North and South were united by a shared cultural obsession with contentment that played out in countless newspapers and journals. Enlightenment-era debates about happiness evolved amid the market revolution of the nineteenth century, leading many authors to pontificate about whether the path to genuine joy was work and wealth, and whether the secret to an efficient labor force was contentment. These claims were freighted with implications. The argument that happiness was not rooted in material wealth challenged the capitalist paradigm, and it could even be used to explain why the nation's burgeoning middle class might be financially secure but still unhappy. Ultimately, however, employers embraced such theories about the causes of happiness to rationalize paying low wages or no wages at all.

Discussions about the relationship between work, money, and happiness were applied in different ways in the slave South. In the hands of proslavery advocates and slaveholders these arguments were the root of a damning syllogistic fallacy: if people with money were not happy, then money did not lead to happiness; thus unpaid labor (i.e., slavery) was defensible. This proslavery axiom took on an insidious and enduring form: the myth of the happy slave. In letters, agricultural journals, and proslavery essays, advocates of slavery insisted that enslaved people were contented, happier than free laborers or even slaveholders.[6] For members of the planter class enslaved contentment was more than paternalistic rhetoric used to condone slavery to outsiders. In the antebellum South enslaved happiness was also an asset and a method of control. Meditations on what constituted happiness were not simply philosophical exercises; they were practical tools for plantation management and for marketing enslaved people.

Once proslavery authors established the debate, that enslaved people were contented in bondage, and thus slavery was justified, White abolitionists dismissed those claims by arguing that enslaved people were inherently and unconditionally unhappy. Enslaved people recognized that the myth of the happy slave misrepresented their experiences in bondage, and elided Black pain.[7] But the White abolitionist trope of the miserable enslaved person was also an oversimplification of enslaved people's emotions. Aware of these two opposing caricatures, and of the rhetorical and commercial value assigned to enslaved happiness, formerly enslaved people worked to portray the more nuanced emotions they felt while in bondage. Authors of slave narratives explicitly dismantled the myth of the happy slave and implicitly countered it by depicting events from their lives in which joy and sorrow were reversed or went hand in hand. Despite these efforts, the myth of enslaved contentment persisted as a defense of slavery long after Emancipation.

Life, Liberty, and the Pursuit of Happiness

The definition of happiness is a topic that has fascinated and frustrated philosophers, historians, and artists for millennia. Was happiness tantamount to godliness or to carnal pleasure, or was it exemplified by the absence of misery, fear, and pain? Was happiness equated with knowledge, or was ignorance indeed bliss?[8] Were "happiness" and "contentment" fungible, or was contentment merely complacency, a dulled simulacrum of joy?[9] Was freedom a prerequisite for happiness, or was it happiness, or at least its pursuit, that constituted liberty?[10] Debates about whether happiness was internal or external, spiritual or material, increased during the Age of Enlightenment, with philosophers of the period asserting that happiness was not a divine gift to be achieved only in heaven; it was conceivable that one could realize joy in this life.[11] That did not necessarily make happiness more attainable for the earthbound. As Jean-Jacques Rousseau pondered in *Emile*, "where is happiness? Who knows?"[12] Other Enlightenment-era authors were less concerned with the nature of happiness and more interested in the political and social implications of individual contentment. For John Locke, felicity and freedom were inextricably linked. Humans must be free to choose what made them happy, and they should pursue that goal to the extent that it did not impede the joy or liberty of others.[13]

Out of this cauldron of debate emerged modern ideals of emotions, including the radical notion that earthly happiness was not only possible but also a basic human right. Abbé Pestré asked in his article on happiness for Diderot's famed Age of Enlightenment encyclopedia "does not everyone have a right to happiness?"[14] What Pestré posed as a question in the mid-eighteenth century was widely accepted by 1776, when lawyer Thomas Jefferson stressed the importance of "the pursuit of happiness" in the opening salvo of the Declaration of Independence. Delegates to the Continental Congress offered a number of revisions to Jefferson, including a suggestion that he modify "inherent and inalienable rights" to "certain inalienable rights," but no changes were made to the rights themselves, "life, liberty and the pursuit of happiness."[15] Perhaps they had no quibbles with his wording because many other contemporary documents proclaimed happiness, or the quest for it, to be a natural right. Many of the state constitutions drawn up by the thirteen colonies also included references to the emotion, including Virginia's Declaration of Rights, also penned in the summer of 1776, which stated that "men . . . have certain inherent natural rights," including "the enjoyment of life and liberty, with the means of acquiring and possessing property, and pursuing and obtaining happiness and safety." Other revolutionary-era politicians reiterated the sanctity of these rights. James Madison proposed amending the Constitution to include mention of the natural rights of "life and liberty," "property," and "happiness and safety."

The inclusion of "property" in the Virginia Declaration of Rights and in Madison's revisions speaks volumes about how many colonial politicians and intellectuals viewed some rights as interchangeable. Other authors and policy makers simply substituted "property" for "happiness." In 1764 lawyer James Otis maintained that government existed "to provide . . . the happy enjoyment of life, liberty and property."[16] Ten years later the delegates to the first Continental Congress approved a document declaring that the colonists' basic rights were "life, liberty, and property." In 1776 Thomas Paine produced an even more pared-down list of rights in *Common Sense*, writing that a proper governing body "should be strictly limited" to "securing freedom and property to all men."[17] Over the course of the American Revolution and the founding of the United States the conversation about the basic rights of citizens evolved from property and liberty for all, to the widespread idea that happiness was a right. Within a matter of decades the debate morphed once more, into a question of whether people who were held as property were happier in the absence of liberty.

On both sides of the Atlantic a number of eighteenth-century intellectuals pondered the relationship of money, property, and happiness. In his two-volume treatise on the subject the Marquis de Chastellux worked to establish "indices du bonheur," or measurements of happiness. He believed that by examining factors such as an individual's financial health, workload, and leisure, one could quantify their contentment. Chastellux also saw "slavery and war as the greatest impediments to public happiness," because collective contentment could not exist unless all were free of coercion.[18] In colonial America Benjamin Franklin wrote at length about the origins of happiness, questioning the causal relationship between joy and wealth in his autobiography and in the pages of *Poor Richard's Almanack*. In a 1757 issue he opined that "happiness depends more on the inward Disposition of mind than on outward circumstances."[19]

The Age of Enlightenment preoccupation with happiness did not fall out of fashion after the Revolution; rather, nineteenth-century Americans were fervently committed to realizing their affective inalienable right. In his American travelogue Alexis de Tocqueville marveled at the infatuation with achieving happiness that characterized the incipient republic, writing that "no one could work harder to be happy" than Americans, who lived in perpetual "fear of missing the shortest cut leading to happiness."[20] Little changed in the ensuing decades, as a writer for *Harper's New Monthly Magazine* conjectured in 1857 that since Americans were "a race of pioneers . . . always moving and looking ahead . . . restless" that happiness was a perpetual but doomed quest, as "the satisfaction of a want to-day is but the basis of a new desire tomorrow."[21] Half a century after the Declaration of Independence was written, Americans seemingly took the dictum to pursue happiness seriously, performing the task with equal parts perseverance and anxiety.

Nineteenth-century authors continued to plumb the topic of happiness and wealth. In a series of articles on happiness that appeared in *Lady's Book* in 1839 the author, Mrs. Harrison Smith, pondered the relationship between penury or prosperity and joy. Smith swore that "there is no necessary or indissoluble connection between riches and happiness—misery and poverty," that contentment or unhappiness were "indiscriminately distributed," without regard to wealth or social status.[22] Despite her claim that the ability to achieve happiness was individual, random, and wholly democratic, Smith went on to argue in the following month's column that rich people were unhappier than the indigent. According to her the critical component was not assets, but work; she posited that "employment is an essential ingredient of happiness." Smith cited the number of monied individuals who had all the leisure time in the world but remained discontented, producing nothing but "ennui." She even hypothesized that the "pastimes of the rich" are "often more fatiguing than the labours of the poor," assuring her reader that "happier, far happier are those who are thus forced into activity, than those whom wealth abandons to the tyranny of idleness."[23] The economy was rapidly changing in the first half of the nineteenth century, and as more people began working outside of their home it is little wonder that writers would tackle the subject of labor and happiness. Smith's convictions about wealth, work, and contentment were a secularization of the Protestant work ethic, adapted to the modern era. No longer must people work to achieve divine salvation, they must work to attain happiness in life.

Other authors questioned the belief that working more correlated to increased contentment. The author of "Are We a Happy People?" noted that the average household income was on the rise in the mid-nineteenth century, but they saw no concomitant growth in the nation's store of happiness. The author readily admitted that Americans were hard workers, to the point of excess, observing that they "exhaust" their "energies in the hard drudgery of . . . daily labor." Yet despite all this work, and in spite of what Mrs. Harrison Smith espoused about labor being an "essential ingredient of happiness," the author of the *Harper's* article could not answer the titular query in the affirmative. Instead the writer lamented that Americans were "by no means a cheerful people." Work did not produce happiness; instead, for all too many people happiness was a distraction that impeded work, as "Americans have no appreciation of quiet enjoyment . . . they seem to despise it, as if it were a waste of time." According to the author, Americans' vacations were infrequent and brief, viewed as "interferences with the all-absorbing business of the year, " and "retirement" was "hardly known in America." Ultimately, they explained, an American's "only sense of enjoyment" was derived from profit, from "making more . . . he groans beneath a self-imposed burden that no slave can be made to lift under the whip of his owner."[24] Working ceaselessly without holidays, postponing retirement, continuing to labor even when there was no more material need for wealth: to the writer these were all signs that work did not empower people and enrich their quality of life. Instead, it only shackled them to more work.

As tensions between North and South were increasing over the course of the 1850s it is no surprise that the author used the metaphor of slavery to decry the national overworking plague. Written for periodicals with mostly Northern audiences, these pieces were critiquing the social and emotional impacts of the ongoing market revolution, but the authors may not have fully grasped how their arguments about work and happiness also directly related to proslavery propaganda. Smith contributed to the popular perception that material wealth did not create happiness, while the *Harper's* author even implied that excessive work was worse for free laborers, that they struggled under an even weightier "burden."

Arguments about contentment, wealth, and work served a distinct agenda in the slave South. In the antebellum South, where emotions were based on enslaved people, and where intensifying abolitionist attacks led the planter class to be defensive, debates about happiness could not occur without discussing slavery, and no debate about slavery was complete without a discussion of happiness. This was the quintessential syllogism for proslavery Southerners: that work was synonymous with happiness, and enslaved people worked, thus the enslaved must be happy. That supposed happiness, in turn, was used to externally justify the institution of slavery and was internally valued as a management tool and commodity.

Three years before he was elected the first president of the United States, slaveholder George Washington illustrated how revolutionary-era proponents of slavery viewed contentment and enslavement as intrinsically tied. In a 1786 letter he discussed slaveholders' concerns that enslaved people were traveling with their owners to Philadelphia and seeking assistance from the local Quakers in suing for their freedom. Washington declared that no one wished "more sincerely than [he did], to see a plan adopted for the abolition of" slavery. Washington averred that he did not want "to hold the unhappy people" who were seeking manumission in Philadelphia in bondage, but he qualified his support for their freedom, opining that "when slaves who are happy & content to remain with their present masters, are tampered with & seduced to leave them . . . it introduces more evils than it can cure."[25] He did not explain why some enslaved people might be "unhappy" if most were "happy & content" in bondage. Nor did he offer a litmus test for quantifying happiness. But he insinuated that the happiness produced by the institution exceeded the unhappiness, and thus this outweighed his professed desire to abolish slavery.

This line of affective argumentation, that slavery and happiness were congruent, became particularly popular among slavery's defenders in the antebellum period. It was also evident in the converse claim, that emancipation made enslaved people unhappy. One editorial from *DeBow's Review* shared the story of a lawyer who was executing the last will and testament of a New Orleans slaveholder who had asked that the thirty-eight people he enslaved be manumitted upon his death. The article explained that the thirty-eight individuals were freed and taken to New York City, but before long some of them wrote to the lawyer and "*begged*" him "to take them back . . . saying [he] might keep them as slaves, or sell them—that they were happy before and wretched now."[26] Published in a planter's journal, such anecdotes may have been intended to discourage slaveholders from manumitting those they enslaved. But the tale also served both as a ringing endorsement for the "happy" institution of slavery and as a condemnation of the misery produced by Northern freedom.

The Myth of the Happy Slave

Nearly every defense of slavery penned in the antebellum period included passages attesting to how "happy" and "cheerful" enslaved people were and how slavery was "promotive" of their "happiness."[27] Whether these authors were arguing the superiority of slavery on an economic, religious, pseudo-scientific, or White supremacist basis, all were implicitly refuting abolitionist critiques of slavery with effusive descriptions of enslaved people's ostensible contentment. In a speech at an 1851 medical convention in Louisiana, Doctor Samuel Cartwright concluded that "the negro is a slave by nature and can never be happy . . . in any other condition."[28] Similarly, in an 1853 treatise, "The Morals of Slavery," William Gilmore Simms stated that "there are few people so very well satisfied with their condition as the negroes,—so happy of mood, so jocund, and so generally healthy and cheerful."[29] Other defenders of slavery were even more emphatic: enslaved people were not merely happy, they were the "happiest," "happier" than any other people on earth.[30] Thomas Roderick Dew contended that Black people were "the happiest of the human race," avowing that "a merrier being does not exist on the face of the globe, than the negro slave."[31] James Henry Hammond concurred that "slaves are the happiest three millions of human beings on whom the sun shines."[32] After his travels through the South even Frederick Law Olmsted evinced that there were no "other people in the world with whom the Negro would be as contented" or "so happy, as with those who are now his masters."[33]

To demonstrate that happiness was not determined by free status or wealth, but rather in working conditions, defenders of slavery compared the contentment of enslaved people to other groups.[34] A frequent argument was that enslaved people were happier than other people of African descent, be they free Black people or "the wild African . . . in his native woods."[35] Advocates for slave labor often discussed the relative merit of slavery and free labor, and they found free labor less efficient, more expensive, and generally lacking.[36] By far the most common claim was that enslaved people were happier than free workers, in the North or abroad.[37] An 1859 article from

Southern Planter discussing the "difference" between free labor and slavery held "that negro slavery was so much the better for . . . the well-being and contentment of the slaves."[38] In an essay comparing the two labor systems, author Edmund Ruffin devoted a great deal of ink to the comparative happiness of free and enslaved workers, stressing that "in comparison" to the "suffering hireling laborer . . . the general condition of . . . negro slaves is one of comfort, ease and happiness."[39] Edward Pollard pointed to the allegedly mutual affectionate relations fostered under paternalism as the factor that separated the plight of the enslaved "so happily from that of the free laborer, who has nothing but a menial intercourse with his employer."[40] The idea that enslaved people were happier than wage laborers was also the crux of George Fitzhugh's notorious *Cannibals All!* In it Fitzhugh castigated anyone, particularly abolitionists, who would "shed crocodile tears over the happy negro and boast of British Liberty," while "miscalled freemen" endured "poverty . . . and downright starvation."[41]

In order to argue that enslaved people were happier than free laborers, some proslavery authors even questioned whether money was the root of happiness. Hammond wrote that anyone who believed free laborers were happier than enslaved people was also presuming that "gold and silver" were "the greatest test of happiness." According to Hammond, if one accepted the assumption that contentment stemmed from wealth, then naturally they would also believe that "the American slave must be wretched . . . because he is not compensated for his services in *cash*."[42] In doing so Hammond deftly combined proslavery critiques of free labor with claims of authors like Mrs. Harrison Smith that happiness was wholly independent from material conditions or "gold and silver."

Proslavery authors contrasted the contentment of enslaved people and free laborers so as to find free labor wanting as an affective and economic system, but many also compared the happiness of enslaved people and slaveholders. The only time that defenders of slavery embraced egalitarianism was in their argument that both were equally capable of happiness.[43] Proslavery authors typically painted a picture of mutually contented slaveholders and enslaved people, conflating the "happiness of both master and servant."[44] A senior editor of *Southern Planter* remarked that he had "seen no situation yet so enviable as that of" a Virginia planter, "surrounded by his . . . cheerful negroes, to whom he is not less a protector and benefactor than a master."[45] Fitzhugh observed that "the interests of master and slave are bound up together, and each in his appropriate sphere naturally endeavors to promote the happiness of the other."[46] Some defenders of slavery went farther, declaring that enslaved people actually experienced *more* satisfaction and contentment than slaveholders. Dew speculated that while one might believe "the slave . . . unsusceptible of happiness in his humble sphere . . . he may indeed be much happier than we are."[47] Likewise, Pollard declared that enslaved people were "as happy as, and perhaps happier than," himself, while politician William Smith swore in an 1861 speech that "in nine cases out of ten, in positive contentment, the Alabama slave is happier than his master."[48]

No one spent more time recording their thoughts on the comparative happiness of enslaved people and slaveholders than Pollard, who vacillated between positing that slaveholders and the enslaved were equally happy, that enslaved people were happier, and that happiness could be neither compared nor judged. Written in the style of a series of letters to a Northern friend, Pollard's book *Black Diamonds* relied on personal anecdotes, and emotional arguments to defend the institution of slavery. Pollard repeatedly returned to the democratic nature of happiness, sharing that he was "profoundly convinced that the negro-slave has naturally as much of happiness" as he did, as enslaved people possessed "the same sum of happiness as . . . their masters." In Pollard's view no one group was singled out for undue joy or misery; instead, "every human lot has its sorrow and its agony."[49]

The claim that happy masters made for happy slaves, and vice versa, was the apotheosis of proslavery arguments about happiness. Advocates of slavery were no doubt trying to allay abolitionist claims that slavery was physically and emotionally cruel, but that was not the only goal. Contending that the happiness of both enslaved people and slaveholders were inseparable supported the related idea that happiness was divorced from material conditions. The appearance of such hypotheses in agricultural journals like *DeBow's Review* and *Southern Planter* hints at more pragmatic uses for this rhetoric. For members of the planter class the myth of the happy slave was not just proslavery discourse: it was a critical tool of plantation management and enslaved productivity.

According to proslavery authors the converse was true as well: unhappy enslaved people would make for unhappy slaveholders, and if enslaved people were happy in bondage then Emancipation would usher in mass misery. Proslavery author William Harper wrote that enslaved people "are too well content with their condition"; thus Emancipation would inevitably result in "the most intolerable mischiefs and calamities to both master and slave."[50] Some portended even more widespread affective ramifications should slavery be abolished. In an 1832 diatribe about slavery, Dew warned that the abolition of slavery would "be utterly subversive of the interest, security and happiness of both the blacks and whites."[51] Similarly, politician A. H. H. Stuart exhorted his audience that abolition would emotionally impact the entire nation, predicting that "a deluge of free negro migration will pour its desolating flood over the whole North and West, sweeping before it the peace and happiness . . . of the people."[52]

In an effort to defend slavery by swearing that enslaved people were happier than slaveholders, and that joy did not correlate to wealth, defenders of slavery succeeded in revealing the depths of both their unhappiness and their debts. William Smith noted that compared to a slaveholder who might be plagued by worries about everything from finances to the weather, an enslaved person had all their physical wants taken care of, so their thoughts of the future were not of impending "bills" and responsibilities but of "holidays."[53] Pollard also alluded to his dire financial and emotional state when comparing his feelings to those of enslaved people. Pollard was clear that his planter status brought stress rather than satisfaction: "all that I suffer from struggles, from disappointments, from agonies in a superior career, [an enslaved person] is a happy stranger to."[54] Nor did he think he was alone in experiencing more anxiety than enjoyment, as Pollard confessed: "I have suffered more of unhappiness in a short worldly career than ever did my 'Uncle Jim' or any other well conditioned negro slave in a whole lifetime. How many of us, who are so blessed with so many external gifts of fortune, can lay our hands on aching, unsatisfied hearts, and say the same." Here Pollard intimated that he had experienced more sorrows in his young life than an older enslaved person did in their "whole lifetime," and that the root cause of this diverging happiness lay in their differing degrees of "external . . . fortune." All the money, status, and natural-born privilege had not made Pollard happy, while penniless enslaved people were, in his view, "happy stranger[s]" to such material concerns and insecurities. Furthermore, he assumed that other people of his class shared his dilemma of hefty bank accounts and "aching . . . hearts." Later Pollard posed the rhetorical question of how one could even imagine an enslaved person, who "has his . . . wants supplied," could ever be "more unhappy than his master, who may see nothing in his own career but a struggle with the great necessities of life, closing in a grave as readily forgotten as that of his slave?"[55] No doubt Pollard's intention in tackling the issue of wealth and comparative contentment was, like that of Mrs. Harrison and Hammond, to advance the idea that wealth did not buy happiness. But in his musings that enslaved people were much happier than he was, he divulged far more about his own feelings, including his profound anxieties about his own mortality and his legacy, or lack thereof.

Rather than solely resorting to alleging that enslaved people were happy or happier in bondage, some proslavery authors adopted a different line of reasoning: attacking the idea that happiness was a natural right. Simms questioned the rights themselves, asking whether "life, liberty, and the pursuit of happiness" truly "are inalienable . . .? Do we not alienate them every day?," citing executions and prison sentences as examples. Instead he asserted that these rights were "only *conditional* possessions or endowments."[56] His argument was clear: if these rights were merely "conditional," and not owed to all citizens, then those rights need not be extended to enslaved people. Harper devoted even more space to debating the natural rights outlined in the Declaration of Independence. Though Harper swore he had the utmost "respect for the important document" he disagreed wholeheartedly with the famous preamble that "*All men are born free and equal*," countering that it was more accurate "to say that no man was ever born free, and that no two men were ever born equal." As evidence that these rights were already regularly abrogated, and thus far from unimpeachable, Harper pointed out that "females are human . . . yet who complains" when "they are excluded" from full citizenship? Like Simms, Harper mentioned how rights were denied to prisoners and those judged to be criminally insane, noting that "every government does, and . . . must, deprive men of life and liberty for offences against society," which in turn restricted their right to freely pursue happiness.[57] Simms's and Harper's readings of the Declaration of Independence did not contradict the myth of enslaved contentment. Instead the two theories reinforced one another: enslaved people could still be presumed to be inherently happy, but if they were not contented then there was no legal obligation to protect their right to seek joy and fulfillment.

The myth of the happy slave took on such potent meaning and staying power because it was defined in opposition to its counterpoint, the angry, rebellious slave. Members of the slavocracy configured an emotional spectrum from the ostensibly loving and loyal mammy, a figment of White longing and nostalgia, to the terrifying waking nightmare embodied by Toussaint L'Ouverture and Nat Turner, figures of White fear. Whether perceived as contented, affectionate, childlike innocents, or vengeful, ungrateful, bloodthirsty killers, this White supremacist emotional continuum for enslaved people was predicated on a belief that the controlling paternalism and violent policing of slavery were more than justified: they were mandatory. Enslaved people would have been aware of this binary and of its ramifications: they should strive to imitate the paragon of the happy, and therefore nonthreatening, slave, not its frightful polar opposite, if they wanted to reap rewards rather than punishment. Since Black contentment was so highly prized by White people in the slave South almost any other Black emotions, especially feelings that were not intended for White consumption, were seen as dangerous, both to the hallowed figure of the happy slave and to White supremacy.

The Price of Happiness

Proslavery authors spent so much time defending the happiness of enslaved people not just to foreclose abolitionist claims, but also because enslaved happiness held real worth in the field and on the auction block for slaveholders. Slave narratives illustrate that enslaved people were keenly aware of how happiness was commodified in the slave market. William Wells Brown recalled that in the slave pens the human merchandise was encouraged to seem merry, "set to dancing . . . some to singing, and some to playing cards," in order to "appear cheerful and happy" and entice buyers.[58] Happiness, or at least the appearance of it, was a selling point for customers, while enslaved people who expressed sorrow were viewed as damaged goods and sold at significantly lower prices. To prevent lost sales or diminished profits enslaved people were verbally chastised and physically disciplined for crying in front of potential buyers. Solomon Northup described how one enslaved woman who could not stop weeping after being separated from her children rapidly lost value in the slave market and was ultimately sold "for a trifle."[59] Enslaved people who were deemed malcontents, or "disaffected," were also sold off at deeply discounted prices.[60] Little wonder then that Frederick Douglass remembered a slaveholder telling him that Douglass's "leaden, downcast, and discontented look, was very offensive to her."[61] Douglass observed that it was for this reason that enslaved people "almost invariably say they are contented, and that their masters are kind."[62] An enslaved person who dared to expose their misery or dissatisfaction was not just forcing their owner to confront the cruelty of slavery; they were also actively depreciating their own retail value.

Happy enslaved people were so highly prized in part because of the widespread belief that contented enslaved people were more productive workers. As a result, many defenders of slavery purported that enslaved happiness was commensurate with enslaved utility and value. According to Fitzhugh, slaveholders should provide sufficient clothing, food, and shelter in order to "make his slaves happy and profitable."[63] An 1859 article in *Southern Planter* explained that for a person of African descent "enslavement . . . is his most useful and happy condition."[64] Slaveholders frequently spoke of the enslaved being "happy" and "industrious" in the same breath; Cartwright avowed that "the most efficient, and, of course, the most profitable laborers are those who are the most active, healthy, happy, and contented."[65] Whether in prescriptive literature written for other slaveholders, or in writing intended to defend slavery to outsiders, members of the slavocracy maintained the party line that a happy slave was a productive slave, and a productive slave was a contented one. Some slaveholders framed the causal relationship between work and contentment in another way. Harper warned that if permitted to malinger enslaved people would become "unprofitable" and "discontented."[66] Similarly, Dew maintained that slavery was beneficial to the enslaved because it turned "his slothfulness . . . into industry," which in turn made "his labor more productive . . . and his happiness more secure and constant."[67] This was paternalism taken to its ostensibly logical conclusion. In their view, masters were not only providing for enslaved people's contentment in return for work, but keeping enslaved people working made them happy.

Because so many slaveholders saw enslaved productivity and contentment as ineluctably intertwined, happiness was considered essential for plantation management. This is confirmed by the advice given to slaveholders and overseers in agricultural journals like *Southern Planter.* An 1858 article entitled "All About Overseers" proposed that a good overseer should ensure that enslaved laborers were contented and that slaveholders were profiting. The author emphasized the important role of overseers in achieving this, noting that "upon their discretion . . . depends the happiness, to a great extent, of the millions of slaves." An overseer was so crucial to maintaining the emotional and financial stasis of a plantation that the article warned that if an overseer was not diligent then "the interests of his employer would be jeopardized, while the happiness of the negroes themselves would be in no wise enhanced."[68] An 1851 article on managing enslaved people was more explicit about the mechanics of how joy translated into output. The author counseled that contentment increased efficiency because "whistling or singing" a happy "lively tune" helped set a good pace for enslaved workers, while "*drawling* tunes" should be prohibited because they slowed the workers' pace.[69] Rather than give free expression to their feelings enslaved people were expected to sustain a constant façade of happiness to guarantee slaveholders' profit margins.

Since enslaved happiness, or the appearance of it, was highly valued as a commodity and as a labor practice, proponents of slavery wrote at length about what conditions they believed fostered enslaved happiness. Some slaveholders preached that religion was a source of enslaved contentment.[70] Others contended that, for enslaved people, ignorance was bliss.[71] Some slaveholders even believed that they were the wellspring of happiness for the people whom they enslaved. An 1851 article in *DeBow's Review* assured its planter audience of their role in enslaved felicity, explaining that "so long as the paternal authority was absolute, the slaves . . . were happy."[72] Pollard swore that he had seen firsthand that "a great and peculiar source of happiness to the Southern slave is the freedom of intercourse and attachment between himself and his master." Pollard cited the example of his younger sister in particular, who he claimed was "the light and the joy of them all," for she "cheered the dark lot of the poor slaves."[73] Given that Pollard represented slaveholders' and enslaved happiness as a symbiotic relationship it was fitting that he saw slaveowners as a "source of happiness" for enslaved people. One of Douglass's owners went even further, arguing that as Douglass's master he should be the singular fount of happiness for the enslaved man, that Douglass should "depend solely upon him for happiness."[74] Of course, there was truth to his owner's narcissistic claims: slaveholders could have a powerful impact on enslaved people's expressed and felt emotions.

Defenders of slavery could be incredibly vague about how slaveholders should cultivate enslaved contentment. In order to assure both the "happiness" and "the value of the slave" Professor Holcombe stated that a master should provide "for the comfort of the slave" and limit themselves to "steady, though mild discipline."[75] George Fitzhugh was equally broad when theorizing about the ingredients of enslaved happiness. Fitzhugh wrote that "good treatment and proper discipline . . . renders the slave happier . . . and contented."[76] Each were convinced that enslaved people should be overjoyed that their basic needs were minimally met and that their physical punishments were "mild" and "proper." Neither author acknowledged how imprecise these definitions of happiness were. They did not explain what would meet collectively accepted standards of sufficient "comfort" or "good treatment," nor did they articulate what would constitute a transgression of the limits of "proper discipline." With such general, subjective expectations of treatment any slaveholder could claim they provided adequate "comfort" and did not exceed "mild" punishment.

Holcombe and Fitzhugh were not alone in equating enslaved happiness with freedom from physical pain. In his "Letters on Slavery" Hammond declared that "if pleasure is correctly to be defined by the absence of pain" then "slaves are the happiest . . . of human beings."[77] Author Timothy Flint agreed, arguing that "to the Negro, remove only pain and hunger" and they would be in a "state of enjoyment."[78] In an article about plantation management a planter from Mississippi reported that reducing whippings guaranteed "the happiness of both master and servant."[79] Of course, despite such prescriptions about the fungible value of enslaved happiness, and the role of minimal pain and corporeal punishment in ensuring that happiness, records from slaveholders and enslaved people illuminate how frequently slaveholders resorted to brutal physical abuse to control those they enslaved. This suggests that the value of enslaved happiness may have been primarily rhetorical, and that the appearance of contentment was much more highly prized among slaveholders than enslaved people's authentically felt joy.

The Value of Holidays

Given slaveholders' ideas about how to use happiness to increase production and maintain control, it is little wonder that debates arose about how slaveholders should handle holidays. Some members of the planter class believed that sporadic, limited "holydays" were a source of happiness that could be used to occasionally reward enslaved workers.[80] Others worried that the risks of unchecked, enslaved joy were too great, and they did not justify the lost labor time. It had long been common throughout the slave South to provide some work holidays for the enslaved population, often timed to annual religious or seasonal celebrations. Missionary Timothy Flint recalled that in New Orleans and the surrounding areas "every year the negroes have two or three holidays," including Mardi Gras.[81] What holidays were permitted varied greatly, depending not only on regional culture but also on the predominant crop regime. *Southern Planter* reported that in "many parts of Virginia" it was "customary" to have corn-shucking parties for enslaved people to facilitate the harvest.[82]

Slaveholders throughout the South typically gave the people they enslaved time off for Christmas. Some owners justified it as a way for enslaved people to visit family on other plantations.[83] But sources from slaveholders and formerly enslaved people make clear that how many days of vacation enslaved people received depended entirely on the whims of their particular slaveholder. Northup noted that his owner provided a three-day holiday from work while other slaveholders in that area of Louisiana gave as many as six days of respite.[84] Douglass also reported receiving an annual holiday of six days.[85] Plantation account books document the holidays given and how much they could fluctuate from one year to another. The owner of Bayside Plantation recorded that "Hollidays commenced" Thursday, December 24, 1846, and continued through Saturday, December 26, when they noted that the

"Hollidays continued. Gave black people a dinner." With the 27th falling on a Sunday the people enslaved at Bayside managed to receive a four-day break that year.[86] Some slaveholders gave significantly fewer days off. In his Affleck "Cotton Plantation Record and Account Book," Pierre Prudhomme recorded that in 1857 and 1860 the people he enslaved worked a half-day on Christmas Eve, with respite from work all day Christmas, before returning to work on December 26.[87] Enslaved people could also never be certain that a holiday given one year could be expected the next.[88] For all their self-professed interest in enslaved happiness, slaveholders ultimately viewed enslaved contentment as a commodity. If an owner believed that the net value of happiness gained from providing a vacation did not outweigh the loss of output, then the holiday would be abbreviated or canceled altogether.

The discrepancies in number and length of holidays also reflect diverging opinions among slaveholders about whether they should provide holidays at all and, if so, when. Antebellum agricultural journals targeting slaveholders offer insight into debates about the wisdom of allowing enslaved people the time and space for holidays and celebrations. Based on these sources the two principal concerns about permitting holidays were that celebrations promoted vice or that they were poorly timed to the harvest calendar. In November 1858 an anonymous planter from Virginia wrote to *Southern Planter* to complain about a local harvest celebration. According to the author it was tradition to gather enslaved people from many plantations for corn shucking, encouraging them to attend and husk corn by promising copious quantities of food and liquor. The author explained that this model meant that "a large amount of corn is shucked, many songs are sung, a hearty supper eaten," but he claimed it also inevitably led to "quarrels and fights." After one of his own slaves died in a fight after a harvest party the slaveholder warned that such "assemblies were improper, because they tended to corrupt and debase the slaves."[89] This sheds light on how slaveholders weighed the costs and benefits of holidays and celebrations for enslaved people. Clearly the slaveholder decried the harvest party for facilitating drunken "quarrels" only once the value of the corn shucked was outweighed by his personal financial loss from the enslaved man's death.

As the planter from Virginia demonstrated, some slaveholders employed paternalistic language of concern for the moral and physical well-being of enslaved people in order to elide the commodification of enslaved bodies, labor, and joy. This was apparent in Prudhomme's account of Christmas 1860 on his plantation. Prudhomme noted in his records that there was "excitement as usual of Christmas. Most of gang enjoy themselves." Despite "danc[ing] all nite" the people he enslaved were back at work on the "cold and cloudy" morning of December 26, 1860, their annual day-and-a-half recess now a memory. Prudhomme was pleased to report that there had been "good behavior" at the Christmas ball, based on the fact that there was "not one ill not many drunk."[90] Slaveholders could act like they were worried about the moral well-being of enslaved people, but Prudhomme's focus on inebriation, paired with the early return to work, signals another concern: that time would be lost by enslaved people suffering from Christmas hangovers. For all their paternalistic bombast the primary goal for slaveholders was ultimately not to provide happiness for those they enslaved but to ensure they did not lose a valuable enslaved person or their productivity.

Other proslavery authors took issue with how holidays led to debauchery and how they often occurred at inconvenient times during the harvest. An 1843 article on "the Agricultural Year" from *Southern Planter* advised against giving "the usual indulgence of a holyday at Christmas" because they believed it was preferable for enslaved people to "be at work than encouraged in dissipation and vice, or even in the comparatively innocent pleasure of visiting." Instead of a holiday at Christmas the author suggested that "the health and comfort of . . . negroes would be promoted by giving the annual holyday in the last week of October," with the new agricultural year beginning on the first of November, rather than in January.[91] An 1851 article entitled "Management of Negroes" expressed similar reservations that "the strolling about of negroes for a week" each Christmas "is productive of much evil," profaning what ought to be "observed as a *sacred festival.*" The author conceded that enslaved people "need . . . rest and recreation," but he recommended "giving a week in July when the crop is laid by, to giving three days at Christmas."[92] The author's proposed alternative holiday elucidates that his underlying fear was not idleness. Rather, he was most worried about losing precious work time at the height of the harvest, as evidenced by his willingness to provide a longer holiday at a more convenient date on the agricultural calendar.

Slaveholders in Louisiana were especially vexed about the timing of celebrations or breaks, allowing the rigorous sugar-cane harvesting schedule, not the calendar, to dictate holidays. In 1860 the cane harvest commenced in October and ended in early December. To mark the occasion the enslaved people at Bayside were given a holiday that started on Thursday, December 6, before they returned to work on Monday, December 10, to start planting a new batch of cane. Despite that four-day holiday the enslaved laborers were given a second recess that December on Christmas Day and Boxing Day. However, the following year found the enslaved people at Bayside "hard at work making sugar" on Wednesday, December 25. It was still a holiday for the slaveholder, who hosted "a gathering of neighbors" that day. As part of the itinerary of Yuletide events the planter brought his guests on a tour of the sugar mill to watch as the enslaved workers processed freshly cut cane. The Bayside accounts show that the people enslaved there were finally given five days of holiday in mid-January 1862, once the cane processing was over.[93] As with previous planters who gave alternate holidays, the fact that breaks were typically moved rather than canceled altogether is telling. This indicates that slaveholders were loath to lose time at the height of the harvest, but they still recognized that holidays were too valuable to abolish them completely.

While members of the planter class debated the cost of days off versus the happiness they yielded, formerly enslaved people were also divided about the emotional payoff of holidays. According to Northup the enslaved people he knew had many reasons to "look forward" to the annual Christmas festivities, their sole "respite from constant labor." A break from work meant "deliverance from fear, and from the lash." During this time enslaved people were also typically given more latitude to travel between plantations to see loved ones. This vacation from work, the alleviation of anxiety, and the "temporary relaxation" with friends and family were "brief" but transformative; Northup claimed the holiday created "an entire metamorphosis" in the community. Because of this Northup called Christmas "the happiest day in the whole year for the slave," as it fostered "genuine happiness, rampant and unrestrained."[94] Douglass had a very different view about the role of holidays for enslaved people and about slaveholders' reasons for providing them. Douglass recalled that during the six days of the Christmas break some visited family, while others used the time to hunt or make items to sell or use. But, according to Douglass, most enslaved people passed the holidays less constructively, "fiddling, dancing, and drinking whisky." Douglass observed that these activities pleased slaveholders most, as they believed that any enslaved person who spent the holidays working, not making merry, was ungrateful.[95]

Considering slaveholders' motives for providing annual recesses, Douglass condemned holidays as "the most effective means . . . of the slaveholders in keeping down the spirit of insurrection." Rather than seeing the days as a benevolent gift, he argued that "holidays serve as . . . safety-valves, to carry off the rebellious spirit of enslaved humanity." Without the yearly distraction of temporary merriment Douglass believed that enslaved people would be forced to confront the "wildest desperation" of their situation, which he implied would lead to collective revolt. He contended that "the slave's happiness is not the end sought, but rather the master's safety." To achieve this goal slaveholders promised an annual oasis of joy to stave off rebellion.[96]

Douglass questioned slaveholders' rationale for providing vacations, and he wondered if holidays even generated genuine happiness for enslaved people. He believed that to safeguard against enslaved mutiny, slaveholders discouraged pragmatic, healthy, or "rational enjoyment" of the season. Instead slaveowners hoped "drunkenness" and "degradation" over the holidays would "disgust the slaves with their temporary freedom" until they were "glad to return to their work." According to Douglass this cycle of gleeful debauchery and regret was solely for the benefit of slaveholders.[97] He saw the holidays as a tool of plantation management and control, arguing that any breaks were not meant to make the enslaved feel happy. Quite the contrary: the slaveholders' goal was for enslaved people to feel ashamed for celebrating and enjoying their brief taste of liberty.

Challenging the Myth of the Happy Slave

As sectional tensions over slavery intensified in the decades before the Civil War, proslavery authors claimed that only abolitionists viewed enslaved people as unhappy. Pollard chided an antislavery associate, noting that "Northern politicians would represent the slaves of the South as sullen, gloomy . . . [but] nothing could be further from the truth."[98] Other authors leveled more serious charges at abolitionists, asserting that antislavery ideas made enslaved people unhappy. Dew surmised that "since the slave is happy" it was not right "to disturb his contentment" with daydreams of freedom that would "inevitably dry up the very sources of his happiness."[99] Similarly, Harper asked of abolitionists "is it not cruelty to make men restless and dissatisfied in their condition?" Harper claimed that doing so did "the greatest injury . . . to their happiness."[100]

By repeating claims that enslaved people were happier than free workers, African people, or even slaveholders, and that it was abolitionists who made enslaved people unhappy, members of the planter class set the terms of the debate about the emotional politics of slavery. According to them, the institution of slavery was defensible because enslaved people were supposedly so happy, and enslaved people were happy because slavery was such a successful labor and social system. Rather than inquiring how one could prove if another person was happy, or if happiness was a proper metric for judging if a society was just, White abolitionists responded that enslaved people were unhappy and thus slavery was cruel. Many antislavery authors from Britain tackled the topic of slavery and happiness in their writings about America, all concluding that enslaved people were deeply unhappy. Fanny Kemble wrote in 1838 that rather than being innately happy, enslaved people were distinguished by a "predominant . . . mixture of sadness and fear."[101] A decade later Harriet Martineau remarked on the "look of the depressed slave" she encountered everywhere in her travels, while British abolitionist James Stirling noted in his 1856 travelogue that enslaved people in America were "not happy," instead they "struck [him] as depressed" and "gloomy."[102] Kemble's, Martineau's, and Stirling's beliefs about the innate and constant sorrow of enslaved people reflected the prominence of the "suffering slave" that became a popular emblem in antislavery texts in the 1830s. For White abolitionists a totalizing sadness defined slavery and enslaved people. It would be Black abolitionists in particular who sought to complicate these affective narratives of slavery, challenging one-dimensional representations of the blissfully happy or utterly miserable slave.[103]

Formerly enslaved people who wrote narratives before Emancipation were authoring consciously abolitionist texts, so they knew that detailing the misery of slavery had commercial and political value for the antislavery cause. But rather than simply depicting enslaved people as entirely characterized by sadness, formerly enslaved people deliberately countered the myth of happy slaves, emphasizing instead the nuances of enslaved joy and sorrow. As people who had experienced enslavement firsthand, they may have been motivated both by an urge to dispel proslavery stereotypes and by the desire to repudiate authors who purported to know how enslaved people truly felt. Through depictions of the layered and at times contradictory ways that enslaved people experienced joy and sorrow, slave narratives explicitly and implicitly debunked the cliché of the happy slave and refuted White abolitionists' oversimplified image of the depressed slave. In particular formerly enslaved authors portrayed the complex nature of enslaved emotions by discussing how unadulterated happiness was confined to childhood, by describing the limits to enslaved people's contentment and by highlighting how often joy and sorrow were juxtaposed or reversed for people in bondage.

Some authors consciously used slave narratives to dismantle the fictions spun by members of the plantocracy about the happiness of enslaved people. James Bradley intimated that the figure of the happy slave was little more than slaveholder propaganda, remarking in his 1835 memoir "how strange it is that anybody should believe any human being *could* be a slave and yet be contented!"[104] Writing a few decades later, Douglass disputed the concept that the happiness of slaveholders and enslaved people was equal and mutually assured, arguing, "I was about as hard to please by a master, as a master is by a slave."[105] Henry Bibb addressed the related idea that enslaved people were more contented than slaveholders because they were not burdened by the preoccupations of free people. Bibb observed that enslaved people experienced the "calamities of sickness, death" that befall all humans while also being "denied the consolation of struggling against external difficulties, such as destroy the life, liberty, and happiness of himself and family." Rather than being a boon that enslaved people did not have to "struggle against misfortune," for Bibb this was another sign of the rights and power that were withheld from them, leaving them "helpless."[106] This was the crux of the vaunted pursuit of happiness: one was not guaranteed happiness itself, but people were promised the right to struggle for its attainment, including, Bibb suggested, the right to fail in that endeavor.

Authors of slave narratives were particularly dismissive of the proslavery chimera that enslaved people were happy because their material needs were met by their owners. Douglass rejected this as a complete fabrication, noting that his own "experience contradicts" slaveholders' tall tales that "slaves enjoy more of the physical comforts of life than the peasantry of any country in the world."[107] Northup responded to multiple happy-slave myths. Looking back on the deprivations he endured while enslaved, Northup observed that he never came "to the conclusion, even once, that the southern slave, fed, clothed, whipped and protected by his master, is happier than the free colored citizens of the North."[108] In doing so Northup linked the notion that enslaved people were well provided for to the belief that enslaved people were happier than their free Northern counterparts, calling both arguments into question. According to Douglass, perhaps the biggest lie about enslaved happiness was that slaveholders genuinely cared about it at all. As human property Douglass opined that he was "but the sport of a power which makes no account, either of [his] welfare or of [his] happiness."[109]

The amount of space Black abolitionists devoted to attacking the proslavery shibboleth of happy slaves speaks volumes about how insidious formerly enslaved people thought the convention was. Douglass repeatedly attacked proslavery misconceptions about enslaved happiness in his pre-Emancipation narratives, especially the widespread perception, popular even in the North, that "singing, among slaves," was "evidence of their contentment and happiness." Rather than being a symptom of enslaved contentment Douglass wrote that "slaves sing most when they are most unhappy," as the melodies "represent the sorrows of [their] heart[s]." To Douglass these tunes functioned as catharsis, and he compared this musical solace to how "an aching heart is relieved by its tears."[110] In parsing this scene Douglass was asking what "evidence" could be considered proof of contentment. Douglass returned to this subject again in his second narrative, mentioning how often he heard that "slaves are the most contented and happy laborers in the world" because "they dance, and sing," but Douglass cautioned his reader that "slaves sing more to *make* themselves happy, than to express their happiness."[111] His remark about how often people equated singing with happiness, and the fact that he repeated lengthy passages from his first narrative verbatim, hints at his contempt for this belief and conveys how little the popularity of this myth had waned in the intervening decade.

Authors of slave narratives also implicitly contested idealized depictions of contented slaves by describing the sorrows they had endured while enslaved.[112] This was acutely clear in discussions of enslaved people who died by suicide. Keckley recalled the defiant desperation of an uncle who hanged himself "rather than be punished the way Colonel Burwell punished his servants."[113] A similar unwillingness to face another lashing led Moses Grandy's brother to "[lay] himself down" in the woods "and die . . . there."[114] Suicide need not always have been a deliberate act of rebellion in order to resist the institution of slavery and rebut representations of contented slaves.[115] Depressed over being sold back into slavery after years of freedom, Mattie Jackson's grandfather sank into "deep despair." "Overwhelmed with grief" he decided to run away in the winter, intending to "put an end to his sorrows by perishing with cold and hunger." His plans were thwarted when his owner learned the enslaved man was missing and tracked him down the following day. Her grandfather survived his night in the woods, but he suffered severe frostbite in "his fingers and toes, and was thenceforth of little use to his new master."[116] According to Jackson her grandfather had made the choice to die of starvation or exposure rather than suffer life in slavery once more. The frost damage to his extremities would serve as a constant reminder of this choice. Though he had not died by suicide, making his sorrow manifest might have disabused his owners of any happy slave stereotypes they harbored, and it certainly depreciated his potential market value.

Rather than allow proslavery authors to represent how enslaved people felt, formerly enslaved authors used their narratives to discuss the realities of happiness and sorrow for enslaved people. Many authors of slave narratives reiterated the unhappiness of slavery by depicting their childhood in bondage as a sheltered period of joy that was abruptly cut short. Portraying that innocent, undefiled contentment and how it was violently interrupted served to heighten the contrast with the sorrow they endured as enslaved adults.[117] Many authors referred to having had a "happy childhood" and talked about the "happy" or "happiest days" they experienced as enslaved children.[118] Slave narratives also underscored how "carefree" this happiness was, depicting an idyllic time in which "troubles" fell away "like water on a duck's back," and sorrows were briefer than a spring rainstorm.[119] Some authors accentuated the role of racial parity in their abbreviated childhood happiness, describing childhood as a liminal period in which they knew "the same joyful freedom as the little white children" and possessed "a heart as free from care as that of any free-born white child."[120] Douglass described this ostensibly color-blind, democratic bliss of childhood as a period where there was "little difference in the measure of contentment felt by the slave-child neglected and the slaveholder's child cared for and petted. . . . [I]f cold and hunger do not pierce the tender frame, the first seven or eight years of the slave-boy's life are about as full of sweet content as those of the most favored and petted *white* children of the slaveholder." Douglass continued that enslaved children were capable of almost as much happiness as children of the planter class in part because the enslaved child was rarely subjected to "lectures on propriety of behavior, or on anything else."[121] Of course, "cold and hunger" were all too familiar for many children, many of whom also experienced sale or loss of their family before they were the age of seven. Douglass's claim that enslaved children were "content" because they did not have to sit through "lectures" was also glib given Douglass's own unslakable thirst for knowledge as a child. That he portrayed childhood for the enslaved as happy, pastoral, and egalitarian after his own experience of early sorrows reveals the cultural currency of the image of the happy enslaved child in abolitionist texts, even for those who vehemently refuted propaganda about happy enslaved adults.

Equally critical to the trope of the blissfully happy enslaved childhood was the depiction of the unexpected moment when that state of contentment was shattered, and the author was forced to confront their slave status. Whether it was when a parent died, or when an enslaved child was first sold or put to work, slave narratives recounted the "sorrowful change," the moment when innocent happiness ended and "sorrows and sufferings commenced."[122] As Harriet Jacobs explained, the "happy days" of her childhood were blotted out by "that blight, which too surely waits on every human being born to be a chattel" when her "kind mistress died."[123] Though authors of slave narratives acknowledged that this affective epiphany was different for each enslaved child, Jacobs's remark implied that the experience of emotional rupture was universal and inevitable for "every human . . . born" into slavery.

Joy amid Sorrow and Sorrow amid Joy

Because of the cultural endurance of the "suffering slave" in antislavery texts, formerly enslaved authors may have been reluctant to write about feeling unmitigated joy in bondage both because it perpetuated the myth of the happy slave and it defied the rules of the slave narrative genre and thus their abolitionist audience's expectations. This authorial quandary surfaces in many slave narratives, as most references to happiness during slavery were accompanied by qualifying statements. When chronicling how her grandfather fell in love with an enslaved woman amid the "sorrow and hopeless toil" of bondage, Mattie Jackson did not describe their relationship as one of unadulterated joy; rather, she noted that "they lived as happily as circumstances would permit."[124] This careful wording insinuated that there were limits to the amount of happiness that was possible during the "hopeless . . . circumstances" of enslavement. The notion of circumscribed happiness was often invoked when formerly enslaved people described being sold. To refute both the fantasy of the kind slaveholder and that of the happy slave, authors of slave narratives were explicit that even if their owner changed, any happiness they felt was relative because they remained enslaved. For example, when Northup was sold to a cruel man named Tibeats, Northup stated he was "doomed . . . to lead no more the comparatively happy life" he had while enslaved by a Mr. Ford, while Sella Martin recalled that when his family was bought by Dr. C. that "for three years [they] were as happy as it falls to the lot of slaves to be."[125] Neither Northup nor Martin unequivocally stated that they had been content in bondage; instead they maintained that any joy they experienced was "comparative," conditioned upon their enslavement. They could only be "as happy" as enslaved people could be, their potential happiness constrained by "the lot of slaves."

Douglass disavowed feelings of joy while in bondage even more forcefully, stressing how dangerous he thought it was to depict unreserved enslaved happiness. Douglass specified that "much of the happiness—or absence of misery" that he felt while enslaved by a Mr. Freeland was due to the "ardent friendship of [his] brother slaves" and the love they bore for one another. Despite these strong, supportive bonds he "hated slavery" so intensely that in the last few years that he was in bondage he was "not only ashamed to be contented in slavery, but ashamed to *seem* to be contented."[126] Rather than unconditionally aver that he had felt some joy while enslaved, Douglass tempered his admission of "happiness" by claiming that he had only experienced "the absence of misery" and that the two were not synonymous. Over time

Douglass came to see that purported "absence of misery" as false and shameful. With the benefit of hindsight he denied having ever felt happiness while in chains, and he even decried feigning contentment. Published in the mid-1850s, as conflicts between abolitionists and proslavery advocates grew more aggressive, Douglass's narrative stated that desire to repudiate any happiness he had felt in bondage, and his implicit criticism of enslaved people who endeavored to "*seem* . . . contented," elucidates how threatening the figure of the happy slave was to antislavery rhetoric. He could not admit to feeling unchecked joy, nor did he want enslaved people to perform happiness, or even appear content, lest it give members of the slavocracy more ammunition to defend the institution.[127]

In addition to challenging the conceit of the happy slave, illuminating enslaved sorrow, and qualifying their definitions of happiness, many formerly enslaved authors also described the often-contradictory nature of happiness and sadness for enslaved people. Slave narratives are saturated with scenes portraying moments of joy amid feelings of sorrow and of moments of sorrow amid times of joy. Depicting the complex ways that enslaved people experienced those feelings was another rebuke to the legend of the happy slave and to all the simplistic feelings that fictitious invention represented. In his discussion of the cathartic role of singing, Douglass observed how song was able to capture how antipodal emotions could intertwine for enslaved people. He recalled that enslaved people "would sometimes sing the most pathetic sentiment in the most rapturous tone, and the most rapturous sentiment in the most pathetic tone," thus "revealing at once the highest joy and the deepest sadness."[128]

Other authors asserted that rather than existing simultaneously, "the highest joy and the deepest sadness" were often inverted for enslaved people. This meant that events that were celebrations for free people could be mournful for enslaved people, while situations that free people met with sadness might be cause for joy for people in bondage. For example, holidays enjoyed by free people often triggered entirely different sentiments for enslaved individuals. Harriet Jacobs explained how enslaved families could be divided on January 1, as slaveholders rented out enslaved people for year-long contracts. Jacobs spoke directly to her readership, declaring, "O, you happy free women, contrast *your* New Year's day with that of the poor bond-woman!" While for free people "the day is blessed," full of "friendly wishes . . . and gifts," Jacobs noted that for enslaved mothers "New Year's day comes laden with peculiar sorrows."[129] In the sentimental era, flipping the affective script in this fashion to reverse the traditional valence of feelings and emotional occasions would have been powerful for readers. The frequency with which formerly enslaved authors illustrated how "the highest joy and the deepest sadness" were compounded or switched for people in bondage also confirms that many authors saw this as a defining trait of enslaved emotions.

Nowhere were the conflicting emotions of enslaved people thrown into sharper relief than in slave narratives' discussions of rites of passage like courtship, marriage, and childbirth. Rather than portraying them as happy occasions, authors delineated the different associations these life events held for enslaved people. Bibb recalled his hesitance to marry, or even court, an enslaved woman, fearing that their union would only serve to "obstruct [his] way to the land of liberty."[130] Douglass concurred that love could limit rather than liberate, arguing that "thousands would escape from slavery, who now remain, but for the strong cords of affection that bind them."[131] Jacobs experienced firsthand that falling in love in bondage produced more anguish than joy, asking her reader "why allow the tendrils of the heart to twine around objects which may at any moment be wrenched away?"[132] A number of authors of slave narratives conceded that love had brought them a glimmer of joy, but this was typically immediately accompanied by their recollections of the inevitable heartbreak for enslaved lovers. Once again formerly enslaved people warned their sentimental readers that they should not expect a happy romantic story; instead, their experiences of love were laden with ambivalence.[133]

Slave narratives also depicted the mixed emotions enslaved people had about becoming parents. Keckley expressed hesitation about motherhood because she "could not bear the thought of bringing children into slavery—of adding one single recruit to the millions bound to hopeless servitude."[134] Jacobs was also loath to have children because she "shuddered to think of being the mother of children that should be owned by [her] old tyrant." This reluctance did not subside when her first child was born; she described her feelings for her infant son as "a mixture of love and pain." Amid her love for the newborn she "could never forget that he was a slave," which cast "a dark cloud over [her] enjoyment."[135] Enslaved fathers experienced similar complicated sentiments. After his daughter was born Bibb did not feel the joy that might be expected of a free man who had become a new father because he could not "look upon the dear child without being filled with sorrow and fearful apprehension, of being separated." Even once he became free Bibb confessed that he had "to lament" that he was "the father of slaves."[136] Over the course of the nineteenth century more importance was placed on children and childhood, which would have made these authors' anxieties about parenthood all the more harrowing for their audience.[137]

Formerly enslaved authors argued that even reunions between siblings, spouses, or parents and children were not purely joyful if they occurred in the confines of slavery. After successfully running away Bibb dared return to the

South to see his wife and child. But his homecoming was marred by warring emotions, as he recalled that "the sensation of joy at that moment flashed like lightning over [his] afflicted mind, mingled with a thousand dreadful apprehensions" known only by the "heart-wounded slave father and husband."[138] Leonard Black experienced these clashing feelings when he got to see four of his brothers for the first time in many years. Black noted that he "was glad to see [his] brothers, but yet [he] was a slave," so even this momentous event left him depressed, "crushed by the cruel spirit of slavery."[139] In depicting how supposedly joyous occasions were freighted with sorrowful or competing emotions former slaves stressed that in bondage there could be no purely happy moments.

Formerly enslaved people also outlined how occasions that might be tragic for free people might be celebrated by the enslaved. This was exemplified in scenes that discussed how it felt when an enslaved loved one ran away, was sold, or died. Jackson bore witness to both her sister and her father running away to seek freedom, but rather than depicting this as a tragic loss, Jackson emphasized how happy her remaining family was to know that their loved ones would be free. To avoid being punished Jackson's mother even "pretended to be vexed and angry" in their owner's presence when she was told that her eldest daughter had run off. But Jackson saw how her mother truly felt, describing "how wildly mother showed her joy at Nancy's escape when [they] were alone together." Her sister ran away when Jackson was young, but it left a distinct impression on her. Beyond teaching her to conceal certain emotions from slaveholders, Jackson's mother modeled the complexities of love for her daughter, showing Mattie that one could rejoice at the loss of a family member if it meant that they had escaped enslavement. This early lesson was repeated a few years later when Jackson's father ran away rather than be sold away from his family. Jackson would "never forget the bitter anguish of [her] parents' hearts . . . or the profusion of tears" they cried when her father came to say goodbye. "The parting was painful," but Jackson explained that her mother even helped her husband implement his plan for escape because she wanted him to be free.[140] As a child Jackson repeatedly saw the lengths one might go to in order to see a loved one become free, even if that meant relinquishing them forever, and that such an occasion could be met with acceptance and joy.

Nowhere was the reversal of traditional sentimental emotions clearer than in slave narratives' discussions of how death might be welcomed rather than grieved. Jacobs observed that she "had often prayed for death" and even found herself wishing that her newborn child might die too, claiming that "death is better than slavery."[141] Northup expressed similar fatalistic sentiments throughout his narrative. After watching Patsey recover from a savage whipping by their owner, Northup opined that "a blessed thing it would have been . . . had she never lifted up her head in life again." Northup pined for death himself, noting that there were multiple times in bondage "when the contemplation of death as the end of earthly sorrow . . . has been pleasant to dwell upon." Just as Jackson's family rejoiced when family members escaped to freedom, authors of slave narratives painted the death of an enslaved person as a "pleasant" or "blessed" event, not a tragedy. Taken together these depictions of the inversion of sorrow and joy felt by so many enslaved people recapitulated the horrors of slavery while also repudiating any claims that enslaved people led lives of simple, blissful contentment.[142]

Though Northup detailed the suffering endured by enslaved people, he was clear that he was not merely falling into the reactionary trap of claiming that enslaved people were miserable in order to counter the myth of the happy slave. Rather than accept proslavery fictions of contented slaves, Northup rejected the debate itself. In his narrative Northup opined that "there may be slaves well-clothed, well-fed, and happy, as there surely are those half-clad, half-starved and miserable; nevertheless the institution . . . is a cruel, unjust, and barbarous one."[143] Instead of responding to slaveholders' fantasies of merry slaves with tales of unrelenting woe, Northup contended that even if some enslaved people were happy, which he doubted, a few "happy" slaves did not represent all enslaved people. Stirling made a similar point in 1857, writing that "even if" proslavery authors were right "and the slaves were really as 'happy' as they would have us believe," he was undeterred in his staunch opposition to slavery. He would not be bogged down in a false dichotomy debating "happiness or unhappiness"; he was more interested in slavery "as a matter of right or wrong."[144] Like Northup, Stirling counseled that happiness was a misleading metric for the health of a society, or of slavery, and should not be used to measure their justness.

Emancipation and the Myth of the Happy Slave

Even after Emancipation, the myth of the happy slave did not lose its talismanic power for slavery's defenders. White romanticization of master-slave relations only intensified in the wake of war as Confederate apologists and former slaveholders sought to safeguard slavery's legacy by characterizing enslaved people as contented.[145] Exalting representations of benevolent masters and contented slaves was part of the "Lost Cause" agenda. As former general P. G. T. Beauregard opined, members of the planter class needed to take the helm in crafting the narrative of slavery and the war in order to "see that it is correctly written." For them, a "correct" depiction of the South was one in which enslaved people were as faithful as they were happy.[146]

The obdurate myth of the happy slave is evident in Lost Cause novels, films, and historical texts and also in continued efforts by African Americans to dispel that stereotype in the decades after slavery's end.[147] Charlie Moses of Mississippi reflected on his time in slavery over half a century later in an interview for the Federal Writers' Project, observing, "the young folks now-a-days are happy an' don't know 'bout war an' slavery times, but I does. . . . [T]hey are happy. We was miserable."[148] Tellingly Moses did not say that he had been alone in his misery in bondage; rather, he stated that "*we* was miserable." In doing so he underlined that enslaved people's unhappiness was universally felt, not individual or singular. He also hinted that as time passed it was even more critical that survivors of slavery speak about their affective experience in order to inform young people about the realities of the institution and disabuse them of such myths.

The writings of Black Southerners also reveal how tightly many White Southerners clung to the belief not only that enslaved people had been happy, but also that Black people remained contented with their status as second-class citizens in the Jim Crow South. For White Southerners to preserve that deluded assumption, the emotional politics of Jim Crow dictated that Black Southerners must cultivate and maintain a happy façade during all interactions with White people. Richard Wright wrote at length about White Southerners' expectations that Black Southerners appear content at all times in his memoir about his formative years in 1920s Mississippi. Wright recalled that as a teenager a White employer asked him, "Why don't you laugh and talk like the other niggers?" Wright admitted, "Well, sir, there's nothing much to . . . smile about," deliberately "smiling" as he replied.[149] Wright's White boss had evidently become so accustomed to the forced happiness displayed by Black Southerners that he may have believed Wright was anomalous for not expressing that familiar contentment. Or he may have been warning Wright that he found Wright's affective performance wanting, putting Wright's job (and life) at risk. Regardless of the man's intentions, Wright's response indicates that by seventeen he knew the emotional politics of Jim Crow, though he chafed against their constraints, and he recognized that smiling carried more weight than any words he might say.

Wright's memoir also sheds light on how difficult it was to sustain a cheerful countenance. At a subsequent job at a drugstore Wright described how he was struggling to maintain an adequate performance of happiness. This culminated in an interaction with a White customer when Wright found that he "had to figure out how to perform each act and how to say each word." He "could not grin." Growing up in Mississippi, Wright was schooled in the affective expectations White Southerners had of Black Southerners, but that perpetual burlesque of contentment was no less exhausting because it was familiar. As a result, Wright was relieved when he was hired as a night janitor, as he would not encounter White customers. His colleagues were also young Black men, so Wright "was happy": "at least I could talk, joke, sing, say what I pleased."[150] White Southerners like Wright's bosses and customers could disregard their complicity in compelling his feigned contentment, even as they demanded that Black people "laugh" and "smile" in their presence and threatened punishment when Black people failed to do so. Ignoring their role in establishing the affective norms of Jim Crow enabled White Southerners to pretend that happiness was genuine rather than coerced. In the eyes of Wright's White bosses, when interactions with Black people did not go as anticipated the problem was not the oppressive, racialized expectations of the emotional politics of Jim Crow, but the Black people who "could not grin" or "figure out how to perform."

As a child in Alabama and Florida, Zora Neale Hurston was also well acquainted with the expectation that Black people should always appear cheerful and nonthreatening. In the introduction to a 1935 anthology of African American folk tales, Hurston wrote that "the Negro, in spite of his open-faced laughter, his seeming acquiescence, is particularly evasive" and that it was common practice for Black people to "smile and tell him or her something that satisfies the White person because, knowing so little" about Black people, they did not "know what [they were] missing." According to Hurston the "seeming" deference and smiles were a Trojan horse, "evasive" maneuvers that helped Black people carve out sites of opposition and emotional sanctuary in an otherwise violent, segregated society. She called it "feather-bed resistance," observing that try as White people might to squeeze information or sincere feelings from Black people their efforts were thwarted by "laughter and pleasantries."[151] Hurston insinuated that concealing genuine emotions was not always oppressive for Black people. Instead it could function to protect the Black community and to shelter Black individuals' authentic inner selves.[152]

The debate over the myth of the happy slave that had divided abolitionists and proslavery authors in the nineteenth century also played out in the historiography of slavery. In the early twentieth century many historians accepted Lost Cause propaganda texts at face value, leading to histories that affirmed slaveholder rhetoric of contented slaves. U. B. Phillips's 1918 monograph,

American Negro Slavery, is one of the more notorious examples of idealized master-slave relations. Phillips invoked the White supremacist rhetoric of authors like Thomas Jefferson, James Henry Hammond, and Samuel Cartwright when he wrote that the "typical negro" was "sociable and amorous . . . and contented."[153] Phillips's theory was still the accepted narrative in 1941 when Wilbur Cash declared in *The Mind of the South* that "the negro . . . is a creature of . . . facile emotion and, above everything else under heaven, of enjoyment."[154] But in this era the myth of the happy slave was deployed not just to rationalize slavery but to justify the steady creep of Jim Crow–era segregation nationwide.[155]

* * *

The myth of the happy slave did not die with the coming of Emancipation. Rather, it was perpetuated with new fervor in order to defend slavery's legacy and its ideological successor, Jim Crow. The debate once fought between proslavery and abolitionist authors over whether enslaved people were singularly contented or wholly miserable continued to be waged in the historiography of slavery and the popular memory of the institution, in service to many different political agendas. But authors of slave narratives were not just trying to dismantle the trope of enslaved happiness; they were challenging any accounts that reduced the experience of bondage to simplistic emotions and relationships. Rather than replace the happy-slave conceit with one of misery, such authors rejected all one-dimensional affective depictions of enslaved people in favor of portraying the complex gradations and inversions of feelings that people in bondage endured.

Meanwhile the goal for formerly enslaved authors was exactly what proponents of the myth of the happy slave found most unnerving, the idea that behind their façade of coerced happiness Black people concealed deep veins of thoughts and nuanced emotions. Because of that, members of the planter class required happiness from enslaved people at all times and were also paradoxically obsessed with determining whether enslaved people's emotions were authentic. For slaveholders the question of whether or not enslaved people's feelings or motives were sincere was of great consequence, because slaveholders' very lives and livelihoods depended on their ability to trust the people that they kept enslaved.

CHAPTER 4

"Breach of Confidence"

In the pages of her diary actress Fanny Kemble frequently pondered the subject of enslaved people and honesty, debating whether the people enslaved on her husband's plantations could be trusted or not. During her stay in Georgia, Kemble also spent a great deal of time with an enslaved man named Jack. Kemble recalled that one day she asked him how he would feel about freedom, to which he "hesitated" before protesting, "Free, missis! What for me wish to be free? . . . me no wish to be free, if massa only let me keep pig!" She interpreted this to mean that he was afraid to "offend" her if he confessed a desire to be free or expressed "the slightest discontent." Instead she believed he hoped to win her "favor," even if that required "strangling the intense natural longing" for freedom that "glowed in his every feature."[1] Kemble clearly thought Jack was lying, denying an "intense . . . longing" for liberty that his face could not conceal. But Kemble was not displeased by this lie; rather, she was touched that he would suppress the truth to appease her and curry "favor." Jack may have "hesitated" to say how he felt about freedom, but he did not pause when insinuating that he could be sated without manumission for the price of a pig. It is impossible to know how Jack felt about liberty or if he was deliberately trying to flatter his mistress with a performance of contented fidelity, but it is evident that Jack understood this conversation to be a negotiation of loyalty and trust.

Regardless of whether Jack was genuine in his sentiments he deftly turned a potentially contentious discussion into a bargaining opportunity. The request for a pig was seemingly unrelated, but Jack was implicitly suggesting a trade: his continued loyalty, in return for permission to keep livestock. Jack's quick response shows that enslaved people became adept at performing the role of trustworthy slave, relying on established scripts to successfully navigate loaded interactions with slaveholders. However, enslaved people like Jack also knew that feigning loyalty was a gamble. Faithfulness could help an enslaved person avoid future punishments, earn them a pig, or other material benefits, perhaps even freedom. Or they could gain nothing. Worse, they might be perceived as liars and lose the currency of trust.

The way that Jack and Kemble responded to one another illustrates a great deal about the affective bargaining that occurred between slaveholders and enslaved people around questions of trust and sincerity. Though Kemble did not intend to test Jack's loyalty with her inquiry, it had that effect. She questioned his honesty, but she saw his deceit as an attempt to please her, which flattered her enough that he still succeeded at being seen as faithful, if not honest. However, other slaveholders were less favorably inclined toward enslaved people they viewed as deceitful or untrustworthy. This passage highlights the paradox inherent to relationships built on coercion: distrust between slaveholders and enslaved people was rampant, yet for all involved there were numerous incentives to establishing trust. The writings of former slaveholders and enslaved people detail a litany of mutual mistrust and broken promises. Though trust was essential to the daily interactions of slavery, it was a nebulous process to fabricate it.[2] When trust was established it was usually temporary, threatened by betrayal, and highly contingent on the space in which it was created. As a result of this instability mistrust between slaveholders and enslaved people persisted and had far-reaching impacts on the social, legal, and political landscape of the South.

Though enslaved people and slaveholders had profound distrust for one another, trust was nonetheless crucial, facilitating the many daily exchanges that took place between them. For slaveholders building trust, even if only briefly, helped them manage the daily operations on their plantations; it protected their investments, it enriched their coffers, and it could save their lives. For enslaved people knowing when to lie, when to tell the truth, and when to be (or act) loyal could also be a life-or-death issue, helping them survive bondage, obtain benefits, avoid punishments, and even escape enslavement. Mistrust was forged in the crucible of broken promises and emotional politics of slavery, so making trust required time and familiarity. Sociologist Trudy Govier defines trust as a set of "expectations" that includes the assumption that a person who is trusted is not a threat, while acknowledging that trusting another person inherently involves "risk and vulnerability." This theory of trust helps explain why slaveholders and enslaved people were both so concerned with creating or feigning trust: to reduce both danger and fear, even temporarily.[3] Slaveholders valued trust, so they sought ways to ascertain and reward loyalty and punish deceit. Meanwhile many enslaved people sought the benefits of being trusted, even as they continued to mistrust members of the slaveocracy.

This chapter examines how trust and loyalty were hindered and fostered in the antebellum South, and how they functioned in the daily interactions between slaveholders and enslaved people. The chapter also delves into the value and fungibility of loyalty in the slave South, and it reveals the rewards and risks involved in trusting, lying, and breaking promises. Master-slave relationships were riven by deep distrust, but trust and honesty were concerns among enslaved people as well. Enslaved communities built trust and disciplined the untrustworthy through their own established customs and practices that were taught to children at a young age and kept concealed from slaveholders. Finally, the chapter focuses on the trust issues that fugitive slaves and newly freed people faced, as runaway attempts in particular show how trust could help enslaved people escape bondage, but mistrust issues also followed them to freedom.

The antebellum period was an era that was greatly concerned with sincerity. In an article about charlatan doctors in *DeBow's Review* the author, "Dr. D. McCauley," declared, "If anything marks the present age, it is the prevalence of imposture, and the very great readiness with which men and women . . . allow themselves to be beguiled." The doctor believed that deception and fraud had become so commonplace that they defined the era. But his criticism was not aimed at mountebanks who traded in "imposture"; rather, he chastised the public for not being more skeptical and discerning. He also lamented that the formerly "honorable" medical profession had "been infested by quackery and humbug."[4] The overarching argument of his essay was clear: widespread trust issues plagued nineteenth-century society. Many of these anxieties about trust and sincerity stemmed from increasing feelings of alienation and anonymity triggered by major social forces like urbanization, immigration, and market revolution. As a result, residents of northeastern cities in particular developed a number of rituals and signifiers to navigate what was increasingly becoming a "world of strangers."[5] But as Dr. McCauley's essay demonstrates, concerns about trust and sincerity were not an exclusively urban or Northern phenomenon, restricted to social dealings with unknown individuals. Preoccupations with the trust and loyalty of enslaved people indicate that the era's anxieties about authenticity and truth were widespread and, especially in the South, laden with racial connotations. The environment of mutual mistrust brewed by slavery ensured that despite daily contact and the ineluctable intimacy bred by proximity, enslaved people and slaveholders were, in many ways, also operating in a "world of strangers."

A Natural Tendency to Untruth

Concerns about the sincerity of enslaved people gave rise to debates among slaveholders about whether or not enslaved people were inherently deceitful. An 1857 article on plantation management for overseers in *Southern Planter* warned that "the only way to keep a negro honest is not to trust him."[6] In her diary, Kemble devoted a great deal of attention to whether enslaved people were capable of honesty. Given her frequent discussion of enslaved people's trustworthiness it was a subject of much interest to Kemble, and a popular topic for members of the planter class. One local slaveholder opined that enslaved people were very similar to the Irish, citing the shared propensity to "lying and pilfering . . . of both peoples." During a visit to another neighbor, Kemble recalled that they debated "the credibility" of enslaved people with some positing that "no negro was to be believed on any occasion or any subject." Kemble's own husband averred that "it was impossible to believe any word" enslaved people uttered.[7]

The fact that Kemble's husband believed enslaved people to be liars had a profound impact on plantation policy, and it became a source of tension between Kemble, her husband, and the plantation's overseer. Kemble found that the prevalent stereotype that enslaved people were deceitful promoted a climate of suspicion on plantations and put enslaved people's lives at stake. In an article in *DeBow's Review* Dr. McTyeire addressed whether to call a doctor when an enslaved person was ill, advising readers to "guard . . . against feigned sickness," as though this were a common phenomenon.[8] Because of the ubiquity of the idea that enslaved people's physical self-assessments were not credible, Henry Bibb claimed that enslaved people were given minimal care when they were sick. Bibb attributed this to slaveholders' conviction that any enslaved person who said they were ill was "a liar and a hypocrite" who "only wanted to keep from work."[9] Kemble repeatedly encountered this perception when, on behalf of some women on her husband's plantation, she tried to reduce the workload required of enslaved women when they were pregnant or postpartum. Kemble brought the issue to the overseer who told her that enslaved women on the plantation were faking pregnancy, "constantly . . . *shamming* themselves in the family-way" to shirk their duties.[10]

The stereotype that enslaved people lied about their health to avoid work was so enduring that enslaved people were even thought to feign death, a practice referred to as "playing possum" or "possuming."[11] Sella Martin recalled the story of an enslaved man named Flanders whose owner ordered that Flanders be hung up and given over "four hundred . . . lashes." The slaveholder whipped Flanders long after he appeared to be unconscious, even after another slave pointed out that Flanders was not responding and might be dead. The owner continued the beating unabated, claiming that Flanders was merely "playing possum." Eventually the slaveholder realized that Flanders had stopped moving, at which point he stabbed the enslaved man in the foot several times to be sure. When Flanders still did not respond, the slaveholder finally pronounced him dead.[12] This scene is a testament to the brutality of slavery and is proof of how little slaveholders trusted enslaved people. The slaveholder not only disregarded the enslaved person who pointed out that Flanders was "dying," but also ignored all signs that he was flogging a dead man, so convinced was he that enslaved people could not be believed on any subject.

The perception that enslaved people were born liars was codified by the legal system of the antebellum South, which denied enslaved people and free Black people the right to testify in court unless it was against another person of color.[13] For enslaved people like Moses Grandy, this meant that "the evidence of a black man, or . . . many black men, stands for nothing against that of one white." Grandy bemoaned that a White person could do anything they wanted to a Black person as long as they made sure there were no White witnesses.[14] Jacob Stroyer pointed out the folly of such laws when recounting the tale of an infamously cruel "slave hunter" who was suspected of killing some fugitives, but the only people who had seen proof of his brutality were enslaved people. As a result, the man was not brought to justice until a White individual who suspected him of murder befriended him and wheedled a confession out of him.[15] With this example Stroyer elucidated that any number of criminals might go free because enslaved people were not considered trustworthy in a court of law.

Slaveholders also worried about whether enslaved people's dishonesty extended to theft. While some members of the planter class argued that enslaved people were as prone to stealing as they were to lying, other slaveholders contended that enslaved people primarily stole food, a crime that could be avoided if a master provided "sufficient wholesome food."[16] One Maryland slaveholder even swore that he "would trust a nigger with [his] money a great deal sooner than [he] would with cows and hogs."[17] Indeed, for all the assertions that enslaved people were thieves, a number of slave narratives and slaveholder memoirs described incidents of enslaved people being “entrust[ed]” with money or valuable property, including a slave mistress’s diamonds.[18] Although these anecdotes supported slaveholders being able to trust enslaved people with their lives, food, and valuables, other stories about how enslaved people stole food or robbed from only stingy masters functioned as cautionary tales for slaveholders. Rather than be shadowed by anxieties of enslaved thieves, slaveholders could increase food allowances or reassure themselves that they provided ample food and thus had nothing to worry about.

Kemble frequently remarked that enslaved people were “habitual liars” not because of a “natural tendency to untruth,” but because they were unable to differentiate “between truth and falsehood.” Despite believing that they had a habit of lying, Kemble was struck by how bad enslaved people were at deception. She recalled that an enslaved cook was accused of stealing meat, and Kemble was convinced of his guilt because the “lies he told . . . were so curiously shallow, child-like, and transparent, that . . . they confirmed the fact of his theft quite as much, if not more, than an absolute confession.” Her contention that she easily saw through his lies hints that Kemble thought she excelled at reading the sincerity of enslaved people, and that she assumed that enslaved people could not intentionally lie. This was underscored when she wrote that she believed enslaved people’s accounts of life under the previous overseers, claiming “let the propensity to lying of the poor wretched slaves be what it will, they could not invent, with a common consent, the things that they . . . all tell” her about the cruelty of the former overseers.[19] Kemble concluded that their similar stories corroborated one another, but she also implied that since enslaved people could not deliberately lie on their own they certainly could not create and sustain a collective lie.

Despite the popular notion that enslaved people were incapable of telling the truth, whether by birth or through social conditioning, a number of proslavery texts contained impassioned defenses of enslaved people’s honesty and trustworthiness. Many slaveholders provided convoluted or condescending reasons why enslaved people could not or did not lie, perhaps to assuage their concerns about the veracity and sincerity of those they enslaved. Slavery advocate Thomas Roderick Dew declared that many slaveholders “would sooner rely upon their slaves’ fidelity and attachment” during a crisis “than on any other . . . individuals.”[20] William Harper weighed in on the subject in his own proslavery essay, noting that he had “never heard or observed, that slaves have any peculiar proclivity to falsehood,” or had ever known an enslaved person to lie “for a malicious purpose.” Instead he suggested that they usually lied to protect another enslaved person, which he applauded, as such deception was at least rooted in "some semblance of fidelity." Similarly, Harper gave enslaved people the benefit of the doubt that if they lied it might be because the "truth could not be told without breach of confidence." Harper was so intent on defending enslaved people's trustworthiness, and the institution as a whole, that he assured his reader that enslaved people's lies were infrequent or were due to "fidelity" and a desire to protect their owners' discretion. He decried the perception that enslaved people were untrustworthy, observing that "even if" a slave harbored "no feelings or designs" of deceit "they will be attributed to him." In his view enslaved people were viewed with unwarranted and excessive suspicion because of slaveholders' paranoid imaginations. Harper conjectured that if these irrational misgivings could be checked, then "confidence and good will" would flourish between trusting slaveholder and trusted enslaved person.[21]

Harper praised the loyal nature of enslaved people at length, claiming that their "fidelity to their masters is not to be shaken," especially when they had "confidence" in their owner.[22] Harper saw trust as shared and mutually reinforcing; an enslaved person who had "confidence" in their owners could then be trusted to be unerringly faithful. (Harper did not entertain the notion that enslaved people might not trust those who owned them.) Many proslavery authors discussed enslaved people's capacity for loyalty, effusively praising enslaved men and women who had provided a lifetime of faithful service. James Henry Hammond penned a lengthy homage to enslaved people who were loyal from "cradle" to grave, their owner's or their own, whichever came first.[23] George Sawyer commended an enslaved man named Jack who "had lived to see three generations" of children born to his owner's family, and how they held him in high esteem because he was "faithful" and "devoted." Of course, Sawyer was quick to point out that this "fidelity . . . to their masters" was not rooted in "intellect" or a "refined sentiment of gratitude" but was an "instinctive impulse" akin to the faithfulness exhibited by dogs.[24] It is typical of White supremacist proslavery arguments that in lauding enslaved people for loyalty Sawyer also dismissed the trait as animal "instinct" rather than an acquired virtue or skill.

Those who clung tightly to the idea that enslaved people were sincerely loyal even found a way to explain enslaved people's untrustworthy acts: attributing them to Northern abolitionists. Southern court cases and proslavery texts provide a window into the widespread conviction that abolitionists' primary objective was convincing enslaved people to run away.[25] Harriet Jacobs recalled that when her brother William accompanied his owner to the North the slaveholder initially wrote a letter complimenting William for being "most faithful," even though "abolitionists had tried to decoy him away." However, news arrived shortly after announcing that the abolitionists had "succeeded." The slaveholder expressed shock that William had escaped, declaring that he had "trusted him" as if he were his own brother, so he did not believe that the "abolitionists . . . could tempt him."[26] Eventually the slaveholder placed the blame on abolitionists, since that was easier for him to believe than accepting that William would leave of his own volition. Other proslavery writers feared that Northern abolitionists had infiltrated the South, aided by poor, nonslaveholding White Southerners. Daniel Hundley fretted that the "Yankee" was in league with poor White Southerners to identify "discontented" enslaved people and encourage rebellion.[27] Edward Pollard cautioned against trusting Northern transplants in the slave South who pretended to be "the greatest admirers of the *peculiar institution*, and, to honey-fuggle" Southerners, even vociferously critique the North, all while covertly "tampering with the slaves" and insulting the South at every "secret opportunit[y]."[28] Hundley and Pollard were drawing distinct battle lines of who could and could not be trusted. Not only did they consider all Northerners to be covert abolitionists, but they implied that anyone who did not own slaves should be viewed with suspicion.

These elaborate conspiracies that framed enslaved people as victims of abolitionist chicanery rather than willing agents in their own liberation reveal slaveholders' intense desire to trust the people they enslaved. Such slaveholders swore that enslaved people never told "malicious" lies, that they stole only food, and that any enslaved people that rebelled had been duped by abolitionists. Slaveholders were so invested in the idea that enslaved people were loyal because at stake were slaveholders' very lives and their way of life. Members of the planter class could not admit the extent of their skepticism about the people who fed, nursed, and dressed them. Instead advocates of slavery had to blame any breakdowns in trust on enslaved people's innate shortcomings or on external factors like abolitionists. It was too dangerous to concede that slavery as a system was the problem.

Distrusting Masters

While proslavery advocates and slaveholders pondered whether enslaved people were inherently deceitful or incapable of lying, consensus among formerly enslaved people was that slaveholders, and most White people in general, were liars and hypocrites. Jacobs observed that "slaveholders pride themselves upon being honorable . . . but if you were to hear the enormous lies they tell their slaves, you would have small respect for their veracity."[29] This critique called into question the planter class's vaunted sense of "honor," while also implicitly repudiating notions that enslaved people were the deceitful ones. This learned mistrust of White people was so pervasive that even ostensibly sympathetic White people were viewed with suspicion. While hired out to a shipyard Douglass encountered two Irishmen who advised him to run away. Douglass was skeptical, aware that "white men have been known to encourage slaves to escape" in order to catch them for a bounty, and Douglass feared that the Irish workers, though "seemingly good men," planned to do the same.[30] Whether or not the men intended to trick Douglass, other White people had clearly realized they could profit from convincing enslaved people to run away. However, based on such tales, enslaved people like Douglass learned to be cautious around White people who spoke of freedom.[31] Such mistrust, indoctrinated over generations and reinforced daily through interactions with members of the slavocracy, was hard for formerly enslaved people to shake. Jacobs remembered that a White ship captain who helped her escape from slavery was upset that she "had so little confidence in him" after all he had done for her. "Ah, if he had ever been a slave he would have known how difficult it was to trust a white man," Jacobs sighed.[32]

Sources show that trust between slaveholders and enslaved people was so hard to cultivate because of how frequently planters made promises to enslaved people that were never realized. No promise was more often made and then broken than the guarantee that enslaved families would be kept together, that an enslaved person and their children or spouses would not be sold. Henry Box Brown's owner "promised faithfully" not to sell Brown's wife, and he "pretended to entertain an extreme horror of separating families." Because of his "apparent sincerity" Brown and his family believed him, but after barely a year of marriage "his conscientious scruples vanished" and he sold Brown's wife.[33] Similarly, when Grandy was a child, his intemperate owner sold off many enslaved people to cover his debts, but he swore he would never sell Grandy's mother and her eight surviving children. He did not keep the vow long; Moses was not sold, but most of his siblings were.

One of the bitterest betrayals for enslaved people was when the promise of freedom was denied. Some slaveholders gave assurances that an enslaved person would be manumitted or permitted to buy their own freedom, often with little intention of following through. Grandy discovered this after he bought his freedom for $600 from his owner, Mr. Grice, only to be sold by Grice to a Mr. Trewitt. Grandy would pay for his liberty twice more before he was finally freed, ultimately spending a total of $1,850 to purchase himself.[34] Brown shared that situations like this were not uncommon, that he had "known many slaves" who worked and saved diligently in an effort to purchase their freedom, only to find that "after they paid for themselves over and over again" they were still denied their liberty by "unprincipled" owners.[35] Time and time again slaveholders proved that for all their talk of loyalty and mutual affection profit took precedent over sustaining trust with enslaved people.

Because of this familiar pattern of broken pacts, enslaved people knew there were a number of reasons why a slaveholder's guarantees might not pan out. Jacobs explained that "the promises made to slaves, though with kind intentions, and sincere at the time, depend upon many contingencies for their fulfillment." Interestingly, she was not saying that all slaveholders' "promises" were tantamount to lies; instead, their pledges could be entirely "sincere" yet still never be realized. Jacobs's brother William hinted at how little he trusted his owner's word when he ran away, despite the slaveholder repeatedly swearing that he would free William in five years. Even if the slaveholder was not making false promises to secure William's labor and loyalty, a variety of other factors could intervene and determine his fate. William knew that the slaveholder might decide to "postpone the promise," he might fall into debt, so "his property might be seized by creditors; or he might die, without making arrangements" for William to be freed. William ruefully noted that he "had too often known such accidents to happen to slaves who had kind masters."[36] The Jacobs siblings knew that even "sincere" or "kind" slaveholders answered to higher economic and legal powers. The lesson here was that slaveholders' promises and professions of affective ties were of little worth in a society in which people were commodified, and market forces dominated.

A passage from Sella Martin's narrative of his time in bondage sheds light on how slaveholders' promises were extracted and on how the process of trust could break down. After being abruptly separated from his family years before, Martin learned that his mother was alive, though not well, and living only sixty miles away. When Martin begged permission to visit her, his master "seemed glad" that Martin had learned his mother's whereabouts and "promised in the genuineness of his joy to take [Martin] himself . . . shortly." However, as time passed, the slaveholder grew "cool on the subject," realizing "how sentimental, and therefore how silly, to slaveholders, it would appear" to travel that distance simply to reunite an enslaved family. He tried to discourage Martin from making the trip, finally telling Martin that he could not take him and "would not trust [him] to go alone."

Despite the man's change of heart Martin was adamant that his owner had planned on taking him to see his mother initially. In his view the slaveholder decided against it when it occurred to him that the act would be perceived as an inappropriate emotional response to an enslaved person, even one viewed as loyal, because it would be seen by other slaveholders as "sentimental" or "silly." The fact that the slaveowner succumbed to imagined peer pressure is evidence of the power of the affective norms of slavery and of how those norms were internally policed. Nonetheless Martin framed the event charitably, alleging that the slaveholder did not renege on the deal from "want of feeling," as the planter had vowed to consider purchasing Martin's mother even though he was not in the market for another slave.[37] Maybe Martin was giving the slaveholder the benefit of the doubt, or he tried to appear forgiving in his narrative. Or perhaps Martin sincerely believed that the slaveholder had entertained the idea of buying Martin's mother. It is possible that he had contemplated reuniting the two in some way, but it is also incredibly likely that the slaveholder's "maybe" was always intended as a "no."

During her time in bondage Jacobs learned that some of the least credible promises were those made by slaveholders who hoped to trade a pledge of benefits for sex. Jacobs saw this when Dr. Flint sold an enslaved woman who was believed to be the mother of one of his children. As the woman was taken away she cried out to Flint, "You *promised* to treat me well." Dr. Flint's actions confirmed for Jacobs that he was not to be trusted. More importantly, the sale of the enslaved woman demonstrated that even if an enslaved person had sexual relations with a slaveholder it was no insurance that they would receive any of the favors or security they had implicitly or explicitly bargained for. Later Jacobs made the calculated decision to engage in a sexual relationship with a Mr. Sands, who was not her owner, rather than succumb to the harassment of Dr. Flint, partially due to her hope that intimacy with Sands could protect her from Flint. However, she was once again reminded that the exchange of sex was no guarantee that freedom would be given or that assurances could be kept. Jacobs and Sands had two children, Benjamin and Ellen, whom Sands purchased and vowed to free. But after becoming a congressman and having children with his White wife, Sands made Ellen a maid for her White half-sister, and Jacobs feared their pact would be forgotten.[38] Her narrative illuminates that even enslaved people who knew that slaveholders would likely break their promises either had few other options or still held out hope that sexual relations could be traded for long-term or short-term gains. Her memory of how Sands had once offered so many assurances, and the anger the enslaved woman felt at Flint breaking his promise to "treat" her "well," suggest that slaveholders knowingly exploited the belief that a transaction of favors had been negotiated in order to coerce sexual relations.

Authors of slave narratives often shared stories of enslaved people being betrayed by White people. Stories about once-trusted White people who had stolen free papers or betrayed information about fugitives were passed down from one generation to the next, preserving family history and teaching young enslaved people how to navigate the emotional politics of slavery and avoid being fooled.[39] Other anecdotes circulated within enslaved communities in order to warn against specific slaveholders. Douglass had heard many times of an infamous interaction between his owner, Colonel Lloyd, and an enslaved man. According to Douglass, Lloyd owned so many human beings that he did not recognize them all, and the people enslaved on his satellite farms did not know Lloyd by sight. As a result, Lloyd encountered a Black man on the road one day and asked who his master was, and the man replied, "Colonel Lloyd." Lloyd did not reveal his identity, but asked "does the colonel treat you well?," to which the enslaved man answered, "No, sir." Lloyd pressed him further and the enslaved man candidly responded that he was worked "too hard" but was fed "enough, such as it is." Lloyd never admitted that *he* was in fact the man's owner, and the enslaved man continued on, unaware of whom he had spoken to. Several weeks passed until Lloyd's overseer told the enslaved man that for critiquing his owner he was to be sold.[40]

The moral of the story, as Douglass warily observed, was that there was a "penalty" for "telling the truth," but the woeful tale provided two related lessons to enslaved people: treat all White people as though they were one's own (untrustworthy) owner, and lie when asked about life in bondage. Douglass mentioned that as a result of incidents such as this, when asked about their treatment, enslaved people "almost universally say they are contented, and that their masters are kind." Enslaved people had been led to believe that slaveholders would circulate "spies . . . to ascertain their views and feelings" about their owners. Whether this was true of many slaveholders or not, the rumor was powerful enough to encourage enslaved people to self-censor, and, more grievously, it fomented distrust instead of solidarity among enslaved people. Douglass vouched that these lessons were effectively ingrained in him, as while enslaved he had often been "asked . . . if [Douglass] had a kind master," and he never responded with "a negative answer."[41] This passage exemplifies that some of the scripts enslaved people used to enact loyalty were learned from other enslaved people, sometimes through their trial and error. Each time an enslaved person passed down a story of a breach of confidence, it served as a cautionary tale about trusting that individual master, while also helping to perpetuate the belief that slaveholders and White people categorically could not be trusted.

Aware that enslaved people did not trust them, and the obstacles this might present, some members of the planter class made concerted efforts to at least seem trustworthy. Brown detailed how a man who was trying to buy Brown's wife came to him because the slaveholder did not have enough money, and he hoped Brown would lend him fifty dollars. In return, the slaveholder swore that Brown and his wife would not be separated. Brown was "a little suspicious about being fooled out of [his] money," so he asked the man "what security" he had that his wife would not be sold anyway. The man responded defensively, asking Brown, "Do you think . . . that I could have the heart to sell your wife to any person other than yourself, and particularly knowing that your wife is my sister and you are my brother in the Lord?" Brown was skeptical of the man's religious professions, but he ultimately decided to lend him the money, not because the man "feigned piety" or because he had any "faith" in the man's assurances, but because he believed that the man would feel an "obligation" to him based on the loan.[42]

This exchange is particularly interesting because while trust was established long enough for the money to be lent, neither man trusted the other for the expected reason. The would-be buyer clearly believed that a show of religion, couched in the language of family, could function as emotional collateral and make Brown trust him. Brown did not place any credence in that, but he believed that lending the man money would encourage him to keep his word. Sadly, the man should not have been trusted; he sold Brown's wife for a profit, which was likely his plan all along.[43] This betrayal highlights that some members of the planter class tried to make themselves appear trustworthy in the hopes of obtaining a short-term goal (a fifty-dollar loan) or a long-term gain (the profit he made from the sale.) When slaveholders recognized that they could not create trust even temporarily, they might enlist the help of enslaved people to serve as a more trusting proxy. After Jacobs ran away her owner sought the assistance of her family in locating her. He asked her Uncle Phillip to go to New York to look for her, arguing, "You are her relative, and she would trust *you*," while "She might object to coming with *me*."[44] Her owner, like Brown's, saw the difficulties of establishing trust, and the benefits of doing so, even if betraying that trust was their ultimate objective.

Some slaveholders deliberately fostered an environment of apprehension and suspicion, often in the hopes of increasing productivity. One tactic described by Bibb was for overseers to motivate enslaved people to pick cotton by trying to "deceive them" into working harder for a prize or other "inducement." With the lure of a reward enslaved people would pick tirelessly, but once the overseer saw how much each enslaved person was capable of picking they were whipped if they picked less in the future.[45] Douglass recalled that the enslaved people hired out by a local man named Covey labored diligently "in his absence almost as well as his presence" because the slaveholder kept them on guard by frequently "surprising" them. One of his methods was to sneak up on them and startle them while they were working in the field. Because of this the enslaved laborers knew that "it was never safe to stop" working, even for a moment, because Covey's every waking hour was "devoted to planning and perpetrating the grossest deceptions."[46] It is possible that Covey wanted to keep the enslaved people in a state of anxiety, rather than trying to secure their trust, because unlike a slave*owner* who could create an environment of mutual trust through promises, Covey had only *hired* them. Since Covey leased the enslaved people for a year, he could not guarantee them care in their old age or manumission in return for their loyalty. The only affective promises he could afford was that they would live in fear until the lease was done.

Establishing Trust

In the slave South trust did not just facilitate negotiations of power: trust *was* power, with very real economic, political, and social value.[47] Slaveholders and enslaved people had to weigh the costs of trusting and distrusting in order to navigate their daily interactions, so they employed a variety of strategies to establish trust and ward off dishonesty. According to Douglass, slaveholders often resorted to force to compel enslaved people to be sincere, observing that "suspicion and torture are the approved methods of getting at truth here."[48] Other members of the planter class decided that the best method of obtaining sincerity was to reward enslaved people who were faithful or honest with compliments, minor benefits, or even the promise of freedom.

Some slaveholders concurred with Harper's claim that enslaved people were "excitable by praise" and thus could be encouraged to be loyal or truthful by complimenting such behavior. Perhaps this is what William Jacobs's owner intended when he penned a letter to the Jacobs family, marveling that William "had proved a most faithful servant, and . . . that no mother had ever trained a better boy."[49] This insinuated that enslaved parents were responsible for inculcating their children with a sense of loyalty, but "faithful" service was still notable enough to be lauded. The Crafts' narrative shows that this commendation could come from strangers. Having observed William Craft interact with his supposed owner (Craft's wife, Ellen, in disguise), a gentleman on a train in Virginia exclaimed, "I reckon your master's father hasn't any more such faithful and smart boys as you," to which William replied, "'O, yes, sir, he has . . . lots . . .' Which was literally true."[50] William simultaneously deflected the comment and exhibited his dry humor. He was not being modest; he was making light of the fact that of course "lots" of the people his owner enslaved were more "faithful," as he was in the process of running away. Though the joke was at the expense of the man who had misread the nature of the loyalty William held for "his master," the observer was correct in perceiving that William was loyal to Ellen, who was pretending to be his owner. Regardless of the stranger's ability to accurately read people, his words indicate that it was acceptable to praise other slaveholders' enslaved people for their fidelity.

One strategy many slaveholders believed would secure long-term trust was to give their word that enslaved people would eventually be freed or taken care of in their old age. Through both implicit and explicit promises of liberty or comfortable retirement, slaveholders hoped to establish that past and present loyalty would be rewarded in the future. Slaveholder D. B. DeBow counseled that enslaved people cherished the idea of care for the elderly, so a vow to do so was a gift in and of itself, noting, "For such a green and cheerful old age, should every faithful servant be permitted to hope."[51] Thus the stories planters like Hammond and Sawyer told about loyal, lifelong enslaved companions did more than romanticize the relations of slavery; they helped perpetuate the idea of what enslaved people could "hope" to expect in their "old age" in return for prolonged "faithful" service. Whether or not enslaved people saw being cared for in their "cheerful old age" as an adequate exchange for a lifetime of unpaid labor, many slaveholders believed this was a useful bounty to motivate enslaved people. This speaks volumes about how slaveholders wanted enslaved people to perceive them and about what they thought enslaved people wanted in return for their work and trust. It is impossible to determine how many slaveholders intended to fulfill vows to manumit enslaved people, and how many only gave assurances of freedom and retirement to instill short-term loyalty, with no plan that they would ever come to fruition. Court records disclose that slaveholders did, on occasion, manumit enslaved people, ostensibly as a reward for their loyal service, but the infrequency of such cases proves that it did not happen as often as enslaved people hoped.[52] Nevertheless, the fact that these vows were sometimes realized shows that either some slaveholders perceived exemplary fidelity to be worthy of reward, or they saw value in keeping their promises.

One case in particular illustrates that at best the exchange of loyalty for freedom was still a lengthy and unfulfilling process. *Scranton v. Rose Demere and John Demere*, brought before a Georgia court in 1849, concerned the wishes of the late Raymond Demere that an enslaved couple, Joy and Rose, and their children, John and Jim, be manumitted for their "fidelity" and "faithful conduct." In Demere's will he shared how Joy and Rose "not only saved and protected" his plantation during the British invasion of St. Simons Island, "but actually buried . . . a large sum of money," which he recognized that they could easily have stolen and used to "obtain . . . their freedom." For the slaveholder this was the truest test of loyalty, made all the more meaningful because most of the enslaved people on the island took advantage of British occupation to run away. His description of what the couple could have done with the money hints that other enslaved people did just that, or that in moments of reverie in the intervening years Raymond Demere had stopped and imagined what his life might be like if Rose and Joy had chosen differently. Court records do not explain why the couple stayed and protected their owner's home and valuables, but they capture the protracted legal battle as the executors of Demere's estate refused to honor his wishes. Eventually the court decided in his favor, and Rose and her surviving son, John, received their freedom, as well as over four thousand dollars.[53] Decades after the British invasion, loyalty paid dividends for Rose and John, but for Joy and Jim, who had passed away, it was too late. Even when enslaved people did reap some benefit for loyal behavior it was never on their terms.[54]

Enslaved people may rarely have been freed by their owners, but many still dreamed of being manumitted when a slaveholder died. The strength of this conviction is evident in the ways that enslaved people reacted when they were *not* freed after their owner's death. When Brown's owner was on his deathbed, he called for Brown and his mother. Brown wrote that they rushed hopefully to his side, as they "both expected that [they] should be set free when master died." Brown invites the reader to "imagine [their] deep disappointment" when the dying man instead gave them only advice, telling Brown to "be an honest boy and never tell an untruth." He also informed them that his son William would be their new owner. Brown felt that his owner "deceived [them] by his former kind treatment and raised expectations" that they would be free. Brown did not say if the man had ever explicitly promised they would be manumitted when he died, but they had received enough assurances that they were astonished by his last words, "left to mourn, not so much [their] master's death" as the fact that their most likely path to freedom had been foreclosed.

While many slaveholders believed that enslaved people longed for nothing more than to be cared for in their old age, what enslaved people truly desired in exchange for loyalty was freedom. Brown affirmed that little could "buoy up the spirit" of an enslaved person like "the hope of future freedom." Furthermore, Brown contended that slaveholders were well aware of this desire and used it to their advantage, sustaining the fantasy that enslaved people might receive or be able to buy their liberty in order to extract more labor from them "without . . . entertaining the slightest idea of ever fulfilling their promise."[55] Clearly this was a topic that enslaved people had discussed; they had perhaps warned each other about dreams of freedom being raised and dashed at their owners' deathbeds, and they commiserated over vows that were never realized.

Though they were often empty, slaveholders' promises of freedom produced hope, which could have an immense impact on an enslaved person's outlook. After Douglass tried and failed to run away, his owner, Thomas Auld, guaranteed the defiant would-be fugitive that if he "behaved . . . properly" Auld would free him when he turned twenty-five. Douglass expressed gratitude "for this one beam of hope," though he feared it was "too good to be true."[56] Douglass admitted that even if Auld's assurances were unlikely to come to fruition they still provided him with a sliver of optimism to cling to. Perhaps that is exactly why slaveholders like Auld made lavish declarations that they may or may not keep: even the slimmest "beam of hope" could compel an enslaved person who was prone to rebellion or running away to "behave" if it might lead to freedom one day.

Enslaved people understood that some owners were willing to exchange large and small favors in return for trustworthiness. From a young age Jacobs sensed that there was a value to fidelity, and that loyal behavior could be traded for a variety of advantages. As a child Jacobs was frequently permitted to "share some indulgences" with her owner's children. At the time Jacobs thought being included was "no more than right," but she was still "grateful" enough for this treatment that she endeavored "to merit the kindness by the faithful discharge of [her] duties."[57] This implies that while enslaved children like Jacobs might believe that the modicum of "indulgences" they were given was a "right" rather than a privilege, she was also aware that such acts of "kindness" would disappear if she did not respond with "faithful" service. Even enslaved children grasped that enacting loyalty was a strategic choice that could be mutually beneficial.

Aware of the importance placed on fidelity by members of the planter class, enslaved people sometimes expressly communicated that their loyalty and honesty had a price. These bargains could be transacted in letters, in private, or on the auction block. In 1834 James Hope wrote to his owner to voice his "desir[e]" to return to the plantation where he had been born. Hope swore that if the slaveowner allowed him to do so, then he would give his "reverence" and "ever . . . obey his master." Hope reiterated his promise of fidelity by signing the letter "from you obt [obedient] servant."[58] His owner may already have assumed that, as an enslaved man, Hope should be "obedient," so Hope's offer of future "reverence" emphasized that he believed that deference was not a given: it had to be earned. The letter also contained the tacit threat that if Hope was not permitted to return to his family that he would not be "ever" obedient.

Enslaved people understood that loyalty could be bartered. Therefore, many also believed that obedience and trustworthiness could not be expected if negotiations fell through. Josiah Henson prided himself on his honesty, so he was committed to buying his freedom rather than running away. However, after his owner betrayed him by inflating Henson's price, Henson began to plot his escape, declaring that if his owner had "been honest enough to adhere to his own bargain," Henson also would have stayed loyal. By breaking his promise to Henson, the slaveholder ensured that he would receive neither loyalty nor honesty. In Henson's view, a trade had been brokered, and if his owner would not abide by the terms, then neither would he. Of course, sometimes slaveholders realized that they needed to fulfill certain promises in return for continued loyalty or sincerity from enslaved people. When Henson's owner was reluctant to sell him, Henson sought the aid of the man's brother-in-law, who warned the slaveholder "that if he did not take care, and accept a fair offer" from the enslaved man then Henson might run away. This convinced the slaveholder, and Henson negotiated the price of his freedom for $450.[59] Although Henson's owner was motivated more by fear of property loss than by gratitude, this incident underscores that some planters understood that if they did not reward fidelity they would reap deceit.

The Price of Loyalty

Henson's struggle to purchase his freedom demonstrates the price of loyalty for slaveholders and also the cost of that fidelity for enslaved people. Though Henson's owner eventually let Henson purchase himself for $450, the terms of the agreement changed after the slaveholder fell deathly ill. Henson nursed the slaveowner back to health, which only accentuated his loyalty and value.

Based on that quality of care Henson's owner reneged on their initial deal, abruptly raising Henson's price to $1,000. Instead of rewarding Henson for his reliability, the slaveholder proved his own inconstancy and illuminated the cost-benefit analysis of faithfulness. Henson felt cheated so he disparaged the slaveholder for his lack of "obligation" to himself, frustrated that saving the man's life did not make him feel indebted to Henson; rather, Henson's fidelity served "only to enhance [his] money value."[60] This experience taught Henson that loyalty was a form of currency in the slave South, but enslaved people rarely profited from it.

Some enslaved people were able to use their record of loyalty to their advantage when negotiating their own price. When Elizabeth Keckley tried to buy freedom for herself and her son, her owner initially would not agree to the arrangement. Instead he gave her a few dollars and said that if she wanted to go she could use it to take a ferry across the river to freedom. Since he disdainfully refused her offer to purchase her liberty, Keckley was understandably wary of her owner's motives in giving her fare money and telling her to run away. A cagey Keckley responded by stressing her loyalty, endearing herself to him by proclaiming that she did not want to run away, though she had ample opportunity to do so. She reminded him that though it would be easy to take the local ferry to free territory that she would never do so because it was illegal. According to Keckley her master had hoped for such a response, so she knew she had "pleased" him with both her profession of loyalty and her commitment to the law. Keckley believed that this test of her fidelity succeeded, as not long after her owner announced that he had changed his mind because she "had served his family faithfully," and he offered freedom for Keckley and her son for $1,200.[61] Keckley knew how to fully embody the role of the "faithful" enslaved person, and that such a performance would "please" her owner. In mentioning the proximity of the ferry Keckley was highlighting how easily she could have run away, and that she could still escape in the future.

Bibb witnessed how the commodification of fidelity operated in the marketplace when his owner fell into debt and was forced to sell many of the people he enslaved. As the planter tried to auction off an elderly enslaved man named Richard, a buyer inquired if the aged man was still able to work. The slaveholder responded that though the man could do little "manual labor" due to his age that he would prefer Richard over younger enslaved people "who are able to perform twice as much labor—because [the slaveholder knew] him to be faithful and trustworthy, a Christian." It is impossible to say if the slaveholder meant that "trustworthy" and "faithful" Richard was worth more than a younger, stronger man. However, the fact that he made this declaration at an auction, when he needed desperately to cover his debts, suggests he believed that the assembled prospective buyers recognized a market value for these qualities. The sales pitch succeeded, as Bibb observed that someone was willing to spend almost "two hundred dollars" on Richard because of his reputed "good Christian character."[62]

Bibb also saw how dishonesty could depreciate an enslaved person's value when another owner tried to sell the defiant Bibb for running away so often.[63] Whenever potential buyers asked Bibb if he had escaped in the past, his owner would invariably "answer this question for [him] in the negative," denying that Bibb had ever run away and expounding upon his "Christian character" in order to make Bibb seem "pious and honest." Bibb noted that he had "never had religion enough to keep . . . from running away," thus pointing out the double deception taking place on the auction block, as his master lied about Bibb's nonexistent faith and his constancy.[64]

But the monetary value attached to Christianity was not the sole reason to encourage religiosity among enslaved people; many slaveholders believed religious training made enslaved people more docile and loyal. Henry Box Brown explained that from a young age, enslaved children were indoctrinated with the Christian precepts of honesty and obedience.[65] Of course, if members of the planter class hoped that enslaved Christians were more truthful and trustworthy, that religious inculcation also made the hypocrisy of supposedly faithful slaveholders all the more blatant. Bibb saw this when a man who interrogated him about his trustworthiness before buying him was "one of the basest hypocrites that [he] ever saw," who spoke "like the best of slave holding Christians, and acted at home like the devil."[66] Brown explained that enslaved people could not "believe or trust in such a religion" as that of slaveholders because its sole aim was deluding enslaved people into adhering to the biblical dictum: "servants be obedient to your masters." Brown believed that White people could "lie, and rob the slaves, and do anything else" as long as they "read the bible and joined the church."[67] As a result of enslaved people's suspicions about the sincerity of slaveowners' faith, Douglass opined that slaveholders could give some credence to the religiosity of enslaved people, but enslaved people could not have the same "confidence in the piety of their masters."[68] Unbeknownst to slaveholders their tactic for making enslaved people trustworthy and trusting had the unintended effect of convincing enslaved people that their owners were liars and hypocrites who could not be trusted.

Cognizant of the rewards for honesty, and the punishments for disloyalty, enslaved people were often faced with difficult decisions about how and when to lie. Some formerly enslaved people went into great detail about their calculations; Henson in particular dramatized his conflicted feelings about deceit. Throughout his narrative Henson frequently defended his honesty, cataloging treacherous deeds he could have committed but did not, including killing slave traders and inciting a group of enslaved people to run away.[69] When Henson's owner asked him to lead a slave coffle to his brother's Kentucky plantation, it dawned on Henson how close they were to Ohio and freedom. Henson remarked that though he greatly desired liberty he had never considered running away because of his "sentiment of honor" which he "would not have violated even for freedom." While he admitted that he had often stolen food from his owner in order to dole out extra rations to other enslaved people, Henson clarified that his sense of "honor" would not permit him to steal for himself. Still, Henson was faced with an unexpected chance for him and his fellow enslaved travelers to escape their owner "whom . . . none of [them] [had] any reason to love, who has been guilty of cruelty . . . and who had never shown the smallest sympathy" for them. Even Henson's internal debate over whether to run or not was framed in emotional terms. Henson defended running away because he and his fellow enslaved people did not "love" their owner, and he charged the slaveholder with lacking even "the smallest sympathy with" those he enslaved. Henson's insights show how heavily emotions and affective relations weighed into the valuation of being trusted.

Though Henson stated that running away from his dissolute owner would have been entirely justified, he still did not take advantage of their proximity to a free state, nor did he even tell the others how close freedom was, because he "had promised" his owner that he would deliver them to his brother. Henson recognized that he passed up the chance to escape "the sentiment of high honor" he knew and did "prize," but that he would not trade his honor even for freedom.[70] Henson had any number of reasons for outlining the opportunities he had to be deceitful and why he did not take them. As an author and the protagonist of his own memoir Henson had incentives to portray himself as principled and credible. Henson may also have been trying to create a more exciting tale for his reader, embellishing what was otherwise a straightforward vignette with a hypothetical escape, or building suspense for when he did become free. Or perhaps Henson was depicting the thought process for enslaved people when the possibility arose to deceive or cheat a slaveholder. In any case, this illustrates how much slaveholders could benefit from rewarding enslaved loyalty and honesty. Even when he was out of reach of his owner Henson protected the slaveholders' property, valuing his supposed "honor" over freedom.

Deciding to lie required savvy on the part of enslaved people, especially since they were already perceived as dishonest.[71] Knowing all too well that enslaved people were encouraged to lie to facilitate sales, one potential buyer tried to compel honesty from Bibb. The buyer swore that if Bibb told "the truth like a good boy, perhaps I may buy you with your family." He also asked Bibb if he knew how to read and write, and if he had ever run away before, repeating to him "don't tell me no stories now." Bibb concluded that since he had no obligation to give this man "the whole truth," he gave only part of it, answering that he had only "run away once." This appeased the man enough to purchase Bibb and his family.[72]

Bibb's decision to admit that he had "run away once" confirms that some enslaved people believed that if slaveholders expected them to lie then admitting a minor transgression would be seen as the most plausible response. Sella Martin did just that when his owner confronted him about rumors that Martin could read, and had been reading to other slaves, as Martin felt that it was "safest" to confess that he was literate. His owner issued him "a threatening warning" not to tell "a falsehood" and perhaps because of this "threat," or because Martin feared that his reading sessions had been betrayed by another enslaved person, Martin swiftly elected to bend the truth. He knew that in a society laced with informants and bounded by mistrust he could not deny the charges outright. Instead he swore that he had read only the Bible, hoping that the slaveholder would view this pastime as harmless or even virtuous. Ultimately his lie may have helped; the slaveholder made him promise that he would stop reading, but Martin was not punished.[73]

Depending on the seriousness of a master's accusations, admitting a partial truth was not always an option, forcing enslaved people to weigh the risks of lying. When Solomon Northup's owner demanded to know if he had asked a local White man to mail a letter for him, Northup mounted a three-part defense of his innocence. First Northup vehemently denied the charge, swearing that "there is no truth" to the accusation. Then he discredited Armsby, the local man who had betrayed him to his owner, saying that "Armsby is a lying, drunken fellow . . . and nobody believes him anyway." Finally Northup cited his own history of honesty, reminding his owner "you know I always tell the truth." Northup had, in fact, asked the man to write the letter. Armsby was a poor White man who lived nearby with an enslaved woman and their mixed-race children, all of which marked him as a transgressive figure on the fringes of Southern society. It was because of that liminal status that Northup had believed that he could trust Armsby with the letter, but once Northup was caught he knew that Armsby's marginal status also meant members of planter class thought he was disreputable. Because Armsby's character could be cast in suspect light, while Northup could boast of his own consistently trustworthy track record, Northup succeeded in convincing his master that he had been falsely accused, with Epps declaring "I'm d____d . . . if I don't believe you tell the truth."[74] Northup could take a gamble and lie because he had shored up trust and goodwill over time and because he knew who in the community was perceived as even less trustworthy.

Trust in Enslaved Communities

Trust issues plagued master-slave relationships, but they were also a problem among enslaved people. Some of the distrust stemmed from social divisions among the enslaved. As Bibb detailed to his readers, "domestic slaves are often found to be traitors to their own people, for the purpose of gaining favor with their masters."[75] Whether or not "domestic slaves" were more likely to inform on other enslaved people, and did so to win their owners' approval, this was evidently a common conception among enslaved people. The material deprivation of slavery also led enslaved people to worry about theft within their community.[76] The subject of enslaved people's treachery toward one another was clearly of great interest to readers of slave narratives; Stroyer mentioned that he was often asked if enslaved people would "betray their fellow negroes . . . to the white man?," hinting that the stereotype that enslaved people could not be trusted by slaveholders or by their fellow slaves was widespread and a matter of a great deal of curiosity.[77] Slave narratives provide many accounts of incidents in which an enslaved person betrayed another, but the authors also showed how enslaved people responded by establishing elaborate methods of identifying and punishing theft and deceit, and forging trust.

The process of fostering trust and honesty within the enslaved community began at a very young age. Enslaved children received a variety of lessons about who to trust, and how trust worked inside and outside the family, but they were also inculcated with the importance of distrust.[78] Many authors of slave narratives reported that as children they were told "not to steal" or develop "habits of untruth." Some owners and overseers taught enslaved children that if they lied, stole, or "disobey[ed] their master . . . they would be sure to go to hell."[79] Stroyer recalled how enslaved parents were instrumental in educating children about deception and honesty. According to Stroyer enslaved children were trained to believe that before a person died "he had to tell the truth and had to own everything he had ever done."[80] Enslaved children would have been well aware that death was a frequent and often sudden visitor, which made the warning against deceit all the more urgent and persuasive.

As enslaved children aged though, they began to be taught that there were subtle gradations to truth and trust. Enslaved parents instructed children not to lie to them, and not to steal from fellow enslaved people, but that there was a different standard of honesty when dealing with slaveholders. Part of children's inculcation in the nuances of truth came from trickster tales, which valorized the importance of guile when fighting an opponent with significantly more power. Beyond providing specific examples of cunning, and how the weak could triumph over the mighty with strategic deceit, many animal trickster stories centered on acquiring food.[81] These tales encouraged children to use cleverness themselves in order to obtain food, even if that meant stealing for themselves or their family from plantation kitchens in order to survive.[82]

First, however, enslaved parents had to ascertain if their children could be trusted with sensitive information.[83] Afraid that a child might accidentally divulge the truth about stolen food or goods, or about plans to run away or resist, enslaved parents raised children to understand that some of the things they saw in their insular community were to remain "in their sleeves" and were not to be mentioned in front of members of the slavocracy.[84] But it was one thing to teach secrecy to children; it was another to put those lessons to the test. When Jacobs's daughter was about to be sent North, Jacobs decided to leave her hiding place to say goodbye to her. Jacobs's grandmother worried about Jacobs revealing herself, but Jacobs assured her that she trusted her daughter and was "sure she would not betray" Jacobs. Because of this confidence in her daughter Jacobs's grandmother relented, and mother and daughter were able to spend several hours together. Before leaving Harriet made her daughter swear that her "secret would be safe," and the girl promised that she would "never" expose her mother's location.[85]

Jacobs's narrative attested to how quickly enslaved children absorbed the importance of keeping secrets. After Harriet's son Benjamin, or Benny, unwittingly saw another runaway slave, he told his great-grandmother, who ordered the boy "never to speak of it, explaining to him the frightful consequences." Benny demonstrated how well he had learned discretion after he realized that his fugitive mother was concealed in the attic of his great-grandmother's house. When Harriet was about to go North and spoke with her son for the first time in seven years, she realized how long he had known she was there and how hard he had worked to keep her secret. Benny shared that he had "heard somebody cough" in the attic, leading him to speculate that his mother was hiding there. After that he encouraged his friends not to play next to the house, for fear that they would also hear suspicious noises emanating from her hiding place. Once he became aware of the dangerous position they were all in, Benjamin kept watch for Dr. Flint, growing nervous if he saw the slaveholder. Jacobs remembered that he had often appeared "uneas[y] . . . when people were on that side of the house," and now she knew his cautiousness stemmed from his desire to protect her. Lest her reader think that her children were unique, Jacobs averred that his cagey behavior was common; since enslaved people faced so much betrayal, they had to "early learn to be suspicious and watchful . . . prematurely cautious and cunning."[86]

Jacobs's narrative exhibited how learning "to be suspicious" could be a vital skill for enslaved children like her daughter Ellen. When Ellen moved North to live with her White father's family, the Hobbses, her freedom was far from secured. She was occasionally able to see her mother, who had since escaped North, but the rest of her time was spent working as a maid for the Hobbs family. When Ellen became convinced that a member of the family was in contact with Dr. Flint about the whereabouts of her mother, Ellen began to closely monitor the man. While she and the Hobbs children were outside one day, she watched as the man ripped up a letter and threw the pieces on the ground. Because Ellen was "full of suspicions of him" she collected the fragments. Piecing it together the letter did indeed inform Flint that Jacobs was in the area and advised him how to capture her. Ellen was able to use her distrustful intuition to protect her mother, passing the letter's contents along to her.[87]

Enslaved people had to learn how to keep family secrets and to be wary of members of the slavocracy, but they also needed to learn to navigate trust relations with other enslaved people. In his narrative Stroyer spent a great deal of time discussing how enslaved communities built trust and disciplined the deceitful. He explained that it was common on his plantation for multiple families to share a cabin and how those close quarters could breed mistrust. Stroyer noted that if one family stole food from their owner they had to conceal it, or eat the contraband meal at a friend's home, "for fear of being betrayed by the other family." Stroyer knew one enslaved man who stole and butchered a hog, only to be caught by an enslaved person he lived with. That enslaved man told the overseer, and the thief was flogged. As revenge, the man slaughtered a second hog several months later and concealed the carcass amid the traitorous family's belongings. He proceeded to tell the overseer, who now whipped the other man for supposedly being a thief. This revenge served to physically punish the enslaved man for having informed on him, but it also potentially helped damage the trust the overseer had in the man who initially "betrayed" his neighbor.

According to Stroyer revenge was not the only way to address trust issues that arose among members of the enslaved community; they also had multiple strategies for "detecting thieves" or dishonesty. If someone in the community was believed to have stolen something from another enslaved person, a Bible (or a sieve, if there was no Bible available) was suspended from string and carried by four men who came to each cabin to accuse the head of household of the theft. If the object "was to turn around on the string," that was accepted as conclusive "proof" that the enslaved person in question was guilty. Because this process was repeated three times at each cabin for accuracy, it could take weeks to identify the perpetrator on a large plantation. Stroyer recalled that if the Bible or sieve turned and the accused person did not confess, the defendant was required to admit to anything he had stolen "previously . . . or that he had thought of stealing at the time when the chicken or the dress was stolen" and to provide restoration. In this way the ritual sought to redress a particular theft, it attempted to resolve other cases, and it was used to identify, and perhaps even prevent, deceitful "thought[s]."

The last technique for "detecting thieves" was learned from enslaved parents. Stroyer explained that since enslaved people believed that a person had to confess any dishonesty before dying to avoid damnation, "graveyard dust" was seen as the "truest" substance to use in rituals for identifying robbers. He described how "dust would be taken from the grave of a person who had died" recently and mixed with water. The accused thief was told that if they were innocent they could drink the water without harm, but if they were guilty and they drank from the bottle they would "burn . . . in fire and brimstone." If the accused was indeed the culprit they would admit "it rather than take the water" and then be required to pay damages to their victim, providing four chickens for every bird taken, for example. If they could not repay the debt they had to swear never to steal in the future.[88] This illustrates how hard enslaved communities worked to root out deceit, even if it took an entire month to determine guilt. The lengths some enslaved people were willing to go to is evidence of how seriously they took these transgressions and how committed they were to uncovering the truth, preventing future theft, and mitigating distrust within their community.

Douglass wrote at length about how important trusting other enslaved people was to surviving slavery. Though Douglass spoke of how enslaved people sometimes betrayed their fellow bondsmen, he was also intent on proving that trust flourished in enslaved communities. In his second autobiography Douglass reminisced about the enslaved people he befriended while they were hired out together. He refuted the notion that distrust was rife in enslaved communities, observing that though people often "charge slaves with great treachery toward each other, and . . . believe them incapable of confiding in each other," this was not his experience, for his enslaved friends "were as true as steel." As a result of the trust and affection in this close-knit group, none of them took "advantage . . . of each other; as is sometimes the case where slaves are situated as [they] were" and there was "no tattling" to their owner. Douglass does not say what came first, friendship or trust, so it is not clear exactly how these men were able to join in amity and common cause rather than be divided by informing. But it is clear that these bonds of confidence provided the men with emotional support, enabling them to contemplate escape together.[89] Once again the stakes of trust were thrown into sharp relief: no less than love and revolution were possible when enslaved people could unite without mistrust.

Still, the constant tribulations of slavery meant that even the most trusting relationships between enslaved people could be built on shaky foundations. Douglass wrote wistfully about an enslaved man named Sandy who took Douglass into his home after an escape attempt, even though Sandy would have been brutally whipped or "worse" if his complicity had been discovered. Douglass admired Sandy's bravery and selflessness in helping a "brother bondman." Throughout the passage Douglass displayed his gratitude to Sandy, underlining how trustworthy Sandy was and how much some enslaved people were willing to gamble on their comrades. Perhaps because Sandy had proven himself as a confidant, when Douglass and other enslaved men contemplated running away together, they invited Sandy to join them. As the plan developed, however, he decided not to go, and before long their plot was uncovered. Because Douglass and his other conspirators trusted each other so much it was all the more shocking when it became clear that someone had given away their plans. They vowed to find out "who had betrayed" them, but while they might obviously have suspected one another of informing, Douglass swore that their "confidence in each other was unshaken." Douglass ruefully noted that all evidence pointed to Sandy as the "betrayer." In spite of this, Douglass claimed that he and his fellow conspirators "loved" Sandy too much to give credence to this theory and still believed that another spy must be responsible.[90] This demonstrated the strength of their confidence in one another; they continued to believe Sandy rather than the accusations against him. Douglass's hesitance to condemn someone who had been loyal in the past is a testament to the fact that slavery could kindle mistrust, but it also cemented lasting bonds of confidence that could be difficult to break once they had been established.

Trust and Freedom

Slaveholders and enslaved people knew that trust could be a life-and-death issue, but enslaved people were also keenly aware that trust and loyalty were critical factors in successfully escaping from slavery. Many enslaved people contemplated fleeing slavery on their own because of concerns about being betrayed by allies like Sandy. But even enslaved people who ran away alone were faced with questions of whether or not to trust other enslaved people, White people, or free people of color in order to escape. This was the quandary for Northup when he decided to try to write to former associates in the North to tell them that he had been enslaved. To do so Northup had to find a person who could safely send the letter, leading him to initially ask his neighbor Armsby. Because Northup feared that Armsby could betray him, Northup bribed the man and did not disclose the letter's contents. Northup's fears were justified, as Armsby told Northup's owner that one of the men he enslaved had asked him to mail a letter. This left Northup despondent, both because his letter attempt had failed and because he knew building trust was vital to his plan but he did not know if he could be trustful in the future. This sheds light on the decision process for enslaved people when determining if they could trust a White person or not, especially when freedom hung in the balance. The incident also shows that while Northup thought money would buy Armsby's trust, it may only have kindled the man's suspicions. Money could accompany trust but not necessarily forge it or replace it.

Though Northup felt hopeless after Armsby's betrayal, he was able to use the breach of confidence as a learning experience for future escape attempts. Later that summer a White man named Bass, who was openly opposed to slavery, came to stay at the Epps plantation. With time Northup "became convinced he was a man in whom [Northup] could confide," but his misadventure with Armsby led him to be much more "cautious" about approaching Bass. After watching Bass for days, waiting for an opportune time when the two men were alone, Northup finally confessed to Bass that he was a free man from New York and that he hoped to get a letter to his Northern friends. Northup begged Bass not to divulge his story, and Bass promised Northup "he would keep every word" that Northup spoke "a profound secret," providing

Northup with many "assurances . . . that [he] should not be betrayed." Eventually Bass sent the letter, setting into motion Northup's eventual emancipation.[91] While Bass's antislavery statements were a clue that he might be trusted to help an enslaved person what mattered most to Northup in this equation was the time he spent observing Bass, learning if he was sincere.[92]

Even enslaved people who tried to escape alone sometimes had to improvise and place their trust in other enslaved people who became apprised of their plan. During one runaway attempt Sella Martin fled to the plantation where his mother lived, but another enslaved man saw him creeping through the slave quarters that night. Having been caught in a dangerous position Martin hazarded his luck by confiding in the stranger that he was a runaway and that he was there only to see his mother. Martin noticed that the man appeared aloof, but he agreed to bring Martin's mother to him. Waiting in the dark for him to come back, Martin wrote that "it was an age of anxiety," as he wondered if the enslaved man had "gone to betray" him. As time passed Martin feared that the man "must be informing his master." To quell his apprehension during his seemingly interminable wait, Martin reminded himself of the man's straightforward, "honest way" which made him believe that the enslaved man "was not a traitor." Indeed, the man returned with Martin's mother, and the two were reunited for several hours.[93] Having been betrayed by another enslaved person before, and with so much to risk, it is little wonder that Martin worried that the man was "informing" on him. Faced with the option of trusting the man or running without seeing his mother Martin assured himself that he had correctly read the man's character: therefore he could be trusted. Nevertheless, his concerns while waiting underscore both the dangers of trusting other enslaved people and also what was possible if trust could be built, even briefly.

It is little surprise that enslaved people who betrayed runaways were reviled by authors of slave narratives. Stroyer observed that while enslaved people often aided runaways in their flight, if a fugitive encountered enslaved people who were known informants then the runaway "would mob or kill" any double-crossers.[94] Bibb revealed his aversion to such traitors, and how they were recruited, after he was captured escaping. Because he was a notorious runaway, local slaveholders interrogated Bibb about the "whereabouts" of other fugitives. Through this process he learned that he had been exposed by two Black men he met in Cincinnati who were paid to befriend him before relaying information about him for a reward. His inquisitors offered him the same deal, promising him enough money to buy his family's freedom if he would help identify and catch other runaways. Bibb refused, proclaiming that though he cherished his family and longed for them to be free he was "unwilling" to achieve that "by betraying and destroying the liberty and happiness of others who have never offended" him.[95] Though Stroyer and Bibb both conceded that there were those who were all too willing to serve as spies for slaveholders, they also insisted that many enslaved people would not agree to serve as turncoats.

These passages highlight the extent to which trust was contingent on space and how much enslaved people's mobility hinged on being trustworthy. Enslaved people understood that how much their owner trusted them could be measured by how far they were allowed to travel from their owner's home and how often.[96] As Martin learned, though his owner generally had confidence in him he refused Martin's request to visit his mother sixty miles away.[97] That slaveholder quantified how much he trusted Martin, and that trust had geographic limits. Jacobs's brother William deduced that seeming trustworthy could lead to increased mobility and thereby could facilitate escape. Mr. Sands repeatedly praised him for being "faithful" for not running away as they traveled through the North. William relied on that shored-up trust when he left their hotel on the last morning of their tour carrying his trunk. When Sands inquired about his plans, William replied that he was going to trade his old trunk for new luggage. Sands did not question this errand and even offered William money to purchase a new suitcase. According to the slaveholder William "thanked" him but declined and left. Little did Sands know that the "shabby" trunk was filled with all of William's belongings, and that he was escaping in plain sight.[98] William was able to run away because he was trusted to come and go freely, but his plan would have been impossible for an enslaved person who was not considered honest or loyal.

Enslaved people who were perceived as untrustworthy recognized the greater mobility permitted to faithful enslaved people, and some saw this as reason enough to at least perform a semblance of loyalty. Douglass acknowledged that "a slave who is considered trust-worthy" could persuade their owner to hire them out, permitting them to leave their owner's home to work. In return for giving up most or all of their weekly wages, the enslaved worker could usually "dispose of his time as he likes." Enslaved people who were trusted were able to use that time to earn more money, raise crops, or visit loved ones. Unfortunately for him, Douglass "was far from being a trustworthy slave." Being viewed as honest and loyal could win an enslaved person a modicum of control over the terms of their labor, and diligent work could also provide the means for enslaved people to seem more trustworthy. When Douglass realized that his "insolent answers" and "sulky deportment" were raising his owner's "suspicion that [he] might be cherishing disloyal purposes," Douglass made a show of tirelessly laboring in the hopes that this would allay the slaveholder's "suspicion." Douglass's efforts paid off, as he was able to mask his "disloyal purposes" with cheery industriousness, convincing the slaveholder that Douglass had never been happier when in reality he "was planning . . . escape."[99]

Mobility was linked to trustworthiness and loyalty in part because of broader concerns about building trust with strangers.[100] Slaveholders and enslaved people developed a variety of methods for discerning or concealing deceit in their daily interactions, but beyond the plantation, different tactics were necessary to establish trust and truth. While a slaveholder might learn through time and observation which enslaved people they could trust, in the public spaces of the antebellum South all Black people were assumed to be enslaved and suspected of being runaways. This is most evident in descriptions of how White people, including children, would interrogate any Black person they saw alone on a street or road.[101] But at times members of the planter class were in a predicament: how to win the trust of a Black person they did not know. This was also a question for enslaved people, especially runaways, as they debated whether to try to create trust with or lie to strangers they encountered. Even before James W. C. Pennington was caught trying to run away, he agonized over what to tell anyone who might stop him on his way. He knew that if he admitted he was a fugitive he would be swiftly returned to his owner and punished. Hoping to avoid that fate, he realized his remaining options were to remain silent or "tell an untruth." Pennington decided upon the latter, so when he was apprehended by several White men he "resolved . . . to insist that [he] was free." They did not believe him, however, so they bound him and set out to find a magistrate to hear his case.[102]

As they traveled the men tried to wheedle the truth out of Pennington, alternating between inducements and threats in an effort to gain his confidence and determine whether he was honest. When they saw that Pennington was having difficulty walking with his hands tied, they unbound him, hoping this small act would make him trust them. He explained that after he was "untied . . . they began to parley," as one of the men told Pennington that if he had escaped it would behoove him to confess, for he would receive "better" treatment. Pennington, undaunted, swore that he was free.[103] Clearly the men thought they were negotiating, and that promising a lighter punishment in return for confessing was an enticing proposition. However, Pennington no doubt saw the offer for what it was, a thinly veiled threat of what would happen if he did not admit he was a runaway. Pennington's account illuminates just how much the scripts enslaved people relied on to perform trustworthiness depended on mutual familiarity.

With so much mistrust hanging over interactions between Black people and White people in the liminal spaces outside of plantations, a runaway was faced with the dilemma of how to quickly secure the trust that was supposed to take a lifetime of ostensibly faithful labor to accrue. As Martin tried to escape North, he discovered that unsolicited trustworthy actions could function as currency, even in a land of strangers. Martin described how he encountered a "Californian" on a steamboat headed North whose friends "were being cheated out of their money by cardsharpers" early in the trip. Martin told the Californian about the con men before his friends lost more money, and as a result of this altruistic act the stranger felt obliged to Martin. Luckily for Martin, he ran into this man in an Illinois railway station after he was told that a Black person could not buy a rail ticket unless someone could "vouch for their freedom." The Californian took Martin aside and demanded to know if he was indeed a free man. Martin vowed that he was and showed him some free papers he had falsely obtained, and the Californian proceeded to buy Martin his train ticket to true freedom.[104] Because Martin had gone out of his way to be honest before, the man believed him now, enough to put his own reputation on the line by vouching for him.

Nothing illustrates the challenges runaways faced to establish trust with strangers better than the critical moments in many slave narratives when fugitives were forced to confide in or rely on free people, including White people, in order to escape slavery. The stakes were high, and secrecy was imperative, so confiding in a stranger while in flight from slavery might lead to freedom or to capture and reenslavement.

Because of what they were risking, and because of the caution with which many authors approached escape, these scenes shed light on the process of how enslaved people ascertained if someone was trustworthy. After a night spent in the cold William Wells Brown had to overcome feelings of mistrust to seek someone who would shelter a fugitive. He initially hoped to be harbored by "some colored person, or, if not, someone who was not a slaveholder: for I had an idea that I should know a slaveholder as far as I could see him." Brown hid when a man approached who "looked too genteel," and he eventually flagged down another White man who passed by only after discerning from his less "genteel" appearance that he was likely not a wealthy planter.[105] His gamble paid off, as the man was a Quaker who concealed Brown in his house. Away from their owner's home, and all that was familiar, runaways like Brown might have to trust White people but were still hesitant to trust anyone they suspected was a member of the planter class. If forced to confide in a White person, the goal was to find someone poor, an identity that Brown believed could be gleaned from visual signifiers, which he hoped would make them more sympathetic and more likely to help him.

Slave narratives indicate that mistrust, especially of White people, lingered for many fugitives long after they reached free soil. While recounting the rush of mixed emotions that he experienced upon reaching New York, Douglass shared that his mantra remained "trust no man!" It may have been a self-fulfilling prophecy, as he "saw in every white man an enemy, and in almost every colored man cause for distrust." Douglass still feared that any White person and many Black people might give away his plans and condemn him to enslavement once more.[106] Ellen Craft felt similar suspicions when the Crafts reached Philadelphia and were taken in by a Quaker. Ellen was initially at ease with the Quaker because he "was not of the fairest complexion," so Ellen concluded that he was also a person of color. When she realized that he was White William tried to dispel her concerns, but she responded that she had no "confidence whatever in white people" because she feared they intended to deceive the Crafts, capture them, and return them to their slaveholder for a reward. Eventually she was reassured by William and the Quaker, and the experience helped convince her "that there are good and bad persons of every shade of complexion."[107] For enslaved people who had been inculcated into the emotional hierarchies of slavery, it was difficult to shed the idea that White people could not be trusted. That Douglass and the Crafts were so apprehensive around people they met in free states delineates how deeply enslaved people were ingrained with mistrust and how that suspicion could hinder efforts to construct new affective relations.

Even after they were free, formerly enslaved people sought to repudiate the stereotype that enslaved people were inherently deceitful. This became a subtext of slave narratives, in which formerly enslaved authors repeatedly insisted that they had been "faithful" or "loyal," and they gave impassioned defenses of any lies that they had told while in bondage.[108] Former Georgia slave Harry McMillan stated in 1863 that dishonesty was strategic, as enslaved people "learned to talk false to keep the lash off their backs."[109] Bibb and Jacobs wrote nearly identical rationalizations, saying that "deception" or "cunning" was "the only weapon" available to enslaved people.[110] In spite of the way that they framed lying as a justifiable tool for the dispossessed, Jacobs clarified that she hated being dishonest; forced to lie once she reached New York as a fugitive, she did so regretfully, "reluctant to resort to subterfuges."[111] Beyond refuting the convention that enslaved people were dishonest, formerly enslaved writers may also have felt it necessary to explain any deceptions from their past to prove that they were reliable narrators.[112]

The number of slave narratives that began or concluded with authenticating documents, often by White editors, also suggests that publishers and audiences believed that formerly enslaved people's stories needed to be substantiated. Northup defended his own authorial integrity, introducing his text by explaining that his objective was "to give a candid and truthful statement of facts," to tell his "story . . . without exaggeration."[113] But most slave narratives included excerpted letters from White acquaintances or other documents to "corroborate" their accounts.[114] George Thompson opened Grandy's narrative by describing Grandy's "unsurpassed faithfulness" and asserting that he had "entire confidence" in what he called Grandy's "artless tale." Such letters provided credibility by association, insinuating that the reader could trust the author of the slave narrative because the White editor or acquaintance did. Thompson provided two different arguments for why Grandy could be trusted. First, he assured the reader of Grandy's integrity, then he claimed that Grandy was incapable of guile, as evidenced by his supposedly "artless tale." This enabled the reader to proceed "with entire confidence" that Grandy's story, though incredible, was true.[115] A review in the abolitionist paper the *Anti-Slavery Advocate* praised Harriet Jacobs's *Incidents in the Life of a Slave Girl* for its "truthfulness and integrity," hinting that the emphasis on reliability was not just for the peace of mind of readers, but that slave narratives were of little use as abolitionist texts if they were not considered credible.[116]

The belief that enslaved people could not be trusted even had far-reaching impacts on formerly enslaved people. Because North Carolina law required recently manumitted people to leave the state, Lunsford Lane had to seek special permission to stay in North Carolina after he was freed so he could purchase his family. This required him to obtain letters from White people attesting to his character. One man, known to him through his former owner, wrote an 1840 letter describing Lane as "prompt, obedient and faithful." The man also wrote a petition to the North Carolina legislature in which he praised Lane for his fidelity.[117] In order to thrive as a free Black person in the South, one still had to prove they were trustworthy and loyal to members of the planter class.

* * *

In the antebellum South mistrust simmered beneath the surface of almost every interaction between slaveholders and enslaved people. But with so much to risk for both groups, there were also incentives to find strategies for building trust or at least feigning it. The forced proximity of slavery may not have forged emotional intimacy, but the dynamic meant that slaveholders had to trust enslaved people with property (including the enslaved themselves) and with their own lives. Meanwhile, the emotional politics of slavery dictated that enslaved people had many reasons to be mistrustful of slaveholders, and there were few methods for compelling owners to be honest. Even after they shed their shackles newly freed people discovered that liberty did not free them from being suspicious of White people or dispel the stereotype that people of African descent were prone to untruths. An untrusting intuition helped many enslaved people survive bondage, and escape to freedom, but that deeply ingrained mistrust could prove to be an obstacle when trying to navigate life outside of the emotional politics of the South.

The letters written on Lunsford Lane's behalf, more than anything, highlight both the value that White people in the antebellum South placed on trust, and the anxieties they harbored about enslaved people that could not be made faithful. The ramifications of these fears and that mistrust would be felt for generations to come. Slaveholders recognized that loyalty and honesty were more easily feigned than compelled. When trust between slaveholders and enslaved people broke down, then scripts failed, promises held no sway, and loyalty was not sufficient currency. If enslaved people could not be induced to be faithful and trusted through rewards, then slaveholders would resort to punishment.

CHAPTER 5

"Fear No Lash, nor Worse"

After a plan to run away failed, Frederick Douglass found himself alone in a jail cell, accused of orchestrating the plot, while his coconspirators were freed. Douglass was despondent during this lonesome incarceration, writing, "thirty-nine lashes on my naked and bleeding back, would have been joyfully borne, in preference to this separation from . . . the friends of my youth."[1] Douglass's moving passage attests that the sting of the whip was not the only way to punish an enslaved person; there were also a variety of ways that slaveholders could discipline enslaved people emotionally. Furthermore, Douglass posited that the experience of being whipped was preferable to affective modes of control, including being isolated from loved ones. Douglass's contention that a whipping would be "joyfully borne" compared to being torn from his closest companions was intended in part as a direct response to proslavery rhetoric that said that enslaved people felt emotions less acutely.[2] But he also hinted that emotional modes of discipline were deliberately employed by masters and were the cruelest weapons in a slaveholder's arsenal.

Historians writing about antebellum American slavery have generally concentrated on the physical violence of the institution.[3] In his work on the history of punishment in America, Lawrence Meir Friedman argued that "punishment on the plantation was essentially physical punishment," with the whip serving as the chosen "correctional instrument of all purpose."[4] When discussing types of punishment used by members of the slavocracy, many historians list physical methods like branding, flogging, paddling, or the stocks, neglecting the myriad ways that slaveholders deployed and targeted emotions when punishing enslaved people.[5] Other authors deny that emotional modes of correction existed at all.[6] Focusing solely on corporeal punishments of enslaved people ignores the crucial role that individual feelings and collective affective norms played in disciplining enslaved people and maintaining slavery in the antebellum South.

Affective discipline may be overlooked because it lacks the bloody spectacle of the physical violence slaveholders used to subjugate and terrify enslaved people. But examining how slavery was enforced through emotional discipline and affective manipulation sheds light on the lived experience of slavery and on the critical place of emotional mastery in discipline. Studying how slaveholders often used corporeal forms of discipline to compel specific feelings in enslaved people and to punish them for expressing certain emotions challenges traditional notions of how discipline operated on plantations, and it exposes contradictions in the proslavery rhetoric that enslaved people felt emotions and family ties less keenly. A variety of forms of correction functioned as affective discipline, including punishments that aimed to elicit a specific emotion in an individual enslaved person or in the enslaved community and also punishment for someone because they expressed a specific emotion. This is not to deny the physical violence of slavery or the many types of corporeal punishment that members of the planter class wielded. In fact, affective discipline and physical punishment often went hand in ruthless hand. Exploring forms of affective discipline broadens definitions of what constituted discipline, how it was used to shore up slavery, how such punishments were gendered, and how enslaved people responded to their emotions being punitively provoked or suppressed.

Corporeal Punishment Versus Affective Discipline

In the daily interactions that took place between slaveholders and enslaved people emotions were often central to discipline, frequently serving as both the means and ends of punishment. Slaveholders disciplined enslaved people by inciting certain emotions, but enslaved people also faced punishment, physical or emotional, if they were perceived to be feeling or expressing the wrong sentiments. Slave narratives are full of accounts of enslaved people who either were whipped for seeming proud, "insolent," or untrustworthy or were sold for grieving too long over the death or sale of a spouse or child.

Slaveholders punished enslaved people for expressing certain emotions, and at times they used discipline to prevent specific feelings from intensifying, which could lead to running away, or the dreaded affliction known as "disaffection." In an 1851 article entitled "Diseases and Peculiarities of the Negro Race," Dr. Samuel Cartwright opined that "before the negroes run away, unless they are frightened or panic-struck, they become sulky and dissatisfied."[7] He intended this as evidence that slaveholders could keep enslaved people from running away if they worked to ensure enslaved people's contentment. But his assertion that "sulky" moods and discontentment presaged flight could also convince slaveholders that rather than trying to make enslaved people happy, and watching for signs of their dissatisfaction, they should ward off escape attempts by punishing enslaved people who expressed the discontentment that supposedly preceded running away.[8]

The writings of slaveholders and formerly enslaved people detail the emotional abuse of slavery, illuminating disputes about which was crueler and more effective, physical or affective discipline. In his autobiography, Henry Box Brown explained that punishments that targeted emotions were far worse than those that aimed to injure the flesh, venturing in his introduction that "the whip, the cowskin, the gallows, the stocks, the paddle, the prison . . . although bloody and barbarous . . . have no comparison with those internal pangs which are felt by the soul when the hand of the merciless tyrant plucks from one's bosom the object of one's ripened affections." Brown catalogued the arsenal of tools of physical torture enlisted by members of the slavocracy, methods that would have been quite familiar to abolitionist audiences accustomed to slave narratives that told woeful tales of corporeal cruelty, only to say that there were crueler methods. Later in the text he clarified that he based this comparison on personal experience. When recalling the anguish of being sold away from his mother, he swore that the heartrending event was "a thousand fold more cruel and barbarous than the use of the lash" because the wounds inflicted by a whip would "heal" eventually, "but the pangs which lacerate the soul" as a result of the separation of loved ones "only grow deeper and more piercing."[9] His repeated use of the term "pangs" to describe the anguish of losing a loved one was a testament to how sorrow left no legible scars to heal yet could still cause a grieving person physical pain. Lunsford Lane invoked a similar idea in his narrative when he said that enslaved people were "spirit-bruised," which he claimed was "worse than lash-mangled."[10]

While enslaved people wrote about the excruciating emotional and physical brutality of slavery, members of the plantocracy were filling letters, agricultural journals, plantation books, and legislative halls with musings about the most effective ways to police and discipline the enslaved population.[11] Enslaved people were familiar with this obsession, as Jacob Stroyer dryly noted that "how to control negroes . . . was the principal topic of the poor white man South, in the days of slavery."[12] Slaveholders used a number of methods for emotionally exploiting and correcting enslaved people. But the writings of slaveholders and court records suggest that not all members of the planter class agreed about what types of punishment to employ. However, no matter what sort of punishment an overseer, slaveholder, or slave trader favored, emotions were integral to debates about discipline.

Corporeal punishment had many advocates among the planter class, and they trotted out endless justifications to defend their disciplinary practices to both abolitionists and opponents of physical punishment. Some declared that corporeal punishments were the only kind that worked on enslaved people, while others claimed that whipping was not excessive or brutal.[13] One author writing in the agricultural journal *DeBow's Review* went so far as to surmise that after enslaved people were whipped they would "laugh . . . at '*Massa*,' who thinks, 'dat kind o' lashin ebber hut nigga.'"[14] In adopting dialect to say that enslaved people laughed at the notion that whipping could "hurt" them, the author made light of corporeal punishment, and distanced the responsibility for beatings. The author also alluded that enslaved people were inured to physical pain and hinted that the joke was on any slaveholder who believed that an enslaved person could be physically hurt. Other members of the planter class countered accusations that whipping was cruel by pointing out that the same punishment was used to correct children, and sailors in the U.S. Navy.[15] William Harper invoked this argument, concluding that beating an enslaved person could not be "degrading to a slave" any more than a whipping was "degrading to a child."[16] Like the author in the pages of *DeBow's Review* Harper dismissed the impact of physical discipline, comparing it to the widely accepted practice of spanking a disobedient child. By equating the treatment of enslaved people to children he downplayed the possible severity of such beatings and framed correction as a necessary duty for paternalistic patriarchs in order to dominate all members of the family and plantation.

Some advocates of slavery even touted physical discipline as a superior, kinder alternative to affective punishment. One author in *DeBow's Review* observed that an enslaved person who received a whipping had a better fate than that of an English criminal, who would be jailed and thus "banished from hearth and home, wife and children."[17] Like so many defenders of slavery, the author implied that enslaved people were better treated than free workers in Britain (measured by the supposed relative happiness of slaves and "misery" of British workers). But the author also insinuated that enslaved people and free workers alike preferred physical correction, like a whipping, to the emotional punishment of being separated from one's family in prison, separated "from hearth and home." A similar argument was made in a poem called "Negroes in the Field" from an 1850 *DeBow's Review*, which portrayed enslaved people happy at work and their frequent "jocund laughs" as they labored. In verse the author proclaimed that enslaved people "fear no lash, nor worse! The dungeon's gloom, / Nor nurse the sorrows of a hopeless doom."[18] The poem perpetuated the myth that enslaved people were naturally happy, "gay" and laughing as they worked, while also alleging that enslaved people were not afraid of punishment, whether it was corporeal or "worse." Ultimately the poem provides insight into how planters viewed the hierarchy of punishment, which they hinted mirrored enslaved people's preferences. The "gloom" of incarceration was deemed "worse" than whipping, intimating that some members of the planter class believed that affective discipline was harsher than corporeal correction.

Still other slaveholders insisted that physical discipline was risky or ineffective. Some worried about the impact whippings and beatings had on an enslaved person's price. According to slaveholder William Harper, the goal in punishing enslaved people was to "produce obedience or reformation, with the least permanent injury."[19] Enslaved people with severe or prominent scars were worth less on the slave market, so concerns about the value of their investments inspired slaveholders to find modes of correction that left less visible marks.[20] The children of a Mississippi slaveholder even sued their father in court in 1846, concerned that he was "always cruel to his slaves" and therefore he was devaluing the enslaved human property that they hoped to one day inherit.[21]

Some members of the planter class questioned the efficacy of corporeal punishment as a tool of plantation management, believing that whipping had a negative impact on master-slave relationships, which in turn lowered worker productivity. This line of argumentation frequently appeared in agricultural journals, the very sources planters turned to for advice on best practices for farming and slaveholding. An 1851 essay in *Southern Planter*, "The Management of Negroes," counseled that slaveholders should avoid using the whip to excess, because "if a master be a tyrant his negroes may be so much embarrassed by his presence as to be incapable of doing their work properly when he is near."[22] The author underscored that relying on the whip harmed the affective relations between slaveholder and enslaved people, and it made the enslaved feel "embarrassed," but the crux of the issue was that this emotional damage rendered the enslaved "incapable of doing their work," reducing worker efficiency and planter profits.

Other authors warned that physical discipline created unhappy enslaved people, which led to reduced output and higher rates of running away. That same year Cartwright cautioned *DeBow's Review* readers against displaying cruelty toward their slaves or "frighten[ing] them by a blustering manner," contending that a contented slave would not run away.[23] In this same vein, a planter from Mississippi described his plantation management techniques in *DeBow's Review*, advising that slaveholders should employ the whip less frequently. Doing so would assure "the happiness of both master and servant" and, in the long run, if slaveholders and enslaved people were contented then even fewer whippings were needed.[24] A slaveholder perusing *Southern Planter* throughout the 1850s would have repeatedly read that they should use physical punishment minimally, that instead overseers and owners should compel work through "good temper, conciliation," and "encouragement."[25] Whether prescriptive literature posited that physical discipline stirred up negative emotions or shaped the affective bonds between slaveholders and enslaved people, all their advice was based on the premise that emotions and discipline were inextricably tied.

Emotional Mastery and Affective Discipline

In the antebellum South, a world that placed great stock in patriarchal control, self-mastery and the ability to master others were inextricably tied, and legal, emotional, and physical domination went hand in hand.[26] Sources from and about members of the planter class indicate that consummate domination required the control of one's own emotions and those of others. Even in a society in which affective self-control was prized, few were more absorbed with achieving total emotional mastery than South Carolina planter and politician James Henry Hammond. Hammond's letters, journals, and plantation records expose his lifelong battle to "control" himself "in every particular."[27] According to a biographer, Hammond was hardly unique; rather, he was a product of a society whose norms dictated that "that he always dominate those around him." Hammond himself opined that members of the planter class were "accustomed . . . to control and scorn to be controlled."[28]

In particular, slaveholders were advised in planter journals and etiquette books, and even by their peers, that managing one's emotions was a critical component of plantation management. This was most evident in numerous essays in journals like *DeBow's Review*, *Southern Planter*, and *American Cotton Planter*, which urged slaveholders to quell their feelings, especially anger, when disciplining enslaved people.[29] In one article in *DeBow's Review*, entitled "Plantation Life—Duties and Responsibilities," H. N. McTyeire argued that emotions should play no part in debates over discipline, or in the actual punishment itself. First he dismissed critiques of "corporal punishment" as mere "mawkish sentimentalism." But he admitted that a master should resort to physical punishments only to achieve the "legitimate" goal of "correction and prevention," and that moderation was key, because "anger is fierce and wrath cruel."[30] McTyeire declared that emotions should be divorced from both discussions and practices of discipline, lest the debate devolve into "sentimentalism" or a slaveholder resort to "anger," leading them to be overly "cruel." "Management of Negroes" from *Southern Planter* in 1851 hinted that it was the manifestation of anger that most needed to be checked, cautioning that "the negro should . . . see from your cool, yet determined manner that [the punishment] is not in consequence of your excited temper, but of his fault."[31]

While the idea of exhibiting emotional restraint while disciplining enslaved people was especially widespread in the emotionally focused sentimental period, this was not new advice. Thomas Jefferson shared similar cautions about emotional mastery, recommending that slaveholders "restrain" their "passion towards his slave," especially in front of children of the planter class. He believed that all too often parents ignored this, giving free rein to their "storms" of "wrath."[32] Jefferson's concern was that displays of unchecked emotion were more than unseemly: they were contagious and could infect a future generation of slaveholders. McTyeire was more apprehensive about external critics than internal impacts of such punishments, arguing that emotionless modes of discipline could stave off "mawkish" debates with "sentimental" critics of physical coercion, namely abolitionists. In either case the message was clear: to control enslaved people, a slaveholder needed to control their own emotions, particularly anger.

But the master who exhibited emotional control when punishing enslaved people was an ideal conjured up by proslavery authors and planters in order to defend the institution of slavery; this restraint was not reflected in the daily practices of slaveholders and their proxies. Prescriptive literature may have advised members of the plantocracy to exercise emotional restraint, particularly when disciplining enslaved people, but the recollections of formerly enslaved people highlight how commonly and brutally those precepts were ignored. Charles Ball would never forget the day his slave mistress arrived on her husband's newly built plantation and promptly whipped an enslaved woman when the mistress's baby "cried, and could not be kept silent" by the enslaved nursemaid. Though the beating was intended to punish the enslaved woman for being unable to subdue the baby, Ball believed that the whipping instead revealed that the "mistress possessed no control over her passions."[33] Airing their passions could have a price. Stroyer gave an example, noting that some slaveowners asked slave hunters to return fugitives "unbruised," but others, "in a mad fit of passion," told would-be slave catchers "'bring my runaway nigger home, dead or alive.'"[34] In Stroyer's view, savvy planters did not allow their emotions to reign at the cost of injury to their bonded property, but, crazed by "passion," other slaveholders demanded corporeal punishment to sate their anger, leading them to potentially devalue or even lose their enslaved human investment. In an age in which emotional control was so highly valued Stroyer may have been trying to highlight how unreasonable slaveholders were, particularly if they allowed their impractical "passions" to outweigh their economic self-interests, while denigrating their ability to master their own feelings.

Those who had experienced the whip knew all too well that slaveholders did not merely punish enslaved people *while* they were upset, they did so *because* they felt that way. Solomon Northup observed that the people enslaved by his master, Epps, were as likely to be punished for how Epps felt as for an actual offense. Northup claimed that Epps was frequently felled by "periods of ill-humor," and during these moods a "trivial . . . cause was sufficient with him for resorting to the whip."[35] Knowing that slaveholders were inclined to exorcise their feelings through the lash, enslaved people learned to be watchful for slaveholders' fits of anger or "ill-humor." James W. C. Pennington warned about the direct impact of slaveholders' vacillating moods on enslaved people's lives, observing in his slave narrative that "to-day you may be pampered by his meekness, but to-morrow you will suffer in the storm of his passions."[36] Stroyer witnessed such a "storm of . . . passions" when a local slaveholder became "fretful and peevish" after he was cheated out of a great deal of money by a business partner. The other enslaved people on the plantation were uneasy about the financial loss, both because they realized that they served as the "security" backing the investment and because they knew "slaveholders would revenge themselves on the slaves whenever they became angry."[37]

In the pages of trade journals slaveholders publicly exhorted other members of the slavocracy to keep their feelings in check, particularly when disciplining enslaved people, but Douglass surmised that some slaveholders deliberately promoted the idea that they would lash out in anger as a different sort of managerial strategy. According to Douglass, some slaveholders worked to "convince" enslaved people that while an overseer might not mete out punishment in anger, that their owners' "wrath is far more terrible and boundless, and vastly more to be dreaded, than that of the underling overseer." Douglass knew firsthand that this was more than an idle threat, noting that if a slaveholder let their "temper be stirred" and their "passions get loose" then that slaveholder would inevitably "go *far beyond* the overseer in cruelty."[38] Douglass implied that slaveholders sometimes deployed intermediaries, whether it was overseers, jailors, or law enforcement agents, in order to whip enslaved people for minor crimes, but also to maintain the perception that masters only personally wielded the lash when overcome by emotions, thus ensuring that their floggings went "*far beyond*" the supposedly comparatively dispassionate punishment of an overseer. Ultimately slaveholders believed this helped them maintain control of the enslaved population by fostering a climate of fear, and it encouraged enslaved people to avoid angering their owners at all costs.

But there could be downsides for slaveholders who propagated the perception that they were cruel and quick to anger. When a slaveholder debated using corporeal punishment, often they were thinking not of venting their rage, jealousy, or desire, but of protecting their pride and honor, as being known as physically brutal could damage their reputation with fellow slaveholders and enslaved people.[39] As an 1852 article on hiring out enslaved people observed, "harsh discipline . . . is repugnant to the feelings of every refined nature."[40] Even if the stated disapproval of "harsh discipline" was feigned in order to refute abolitionists' criticisms of slavery, the suggestion that anyone who wanted to claim they possessed "refined" "feelings" disavowed such punishments highlights once more the defining part emotions played in disciplining enslaved people. Slaveholders were not just punishing enslaved people for how those in bondage felt: slaveowners were crafting a public image of their own emotional life. Douglass theorized that some slaveholders even tempered whippings or avoided them altogether because they did not want to be known locally as "a cruel master." Douglass averred that only a truly "desperate slaveholder" would risk the "shame" and "odium" of their peers by beating their slaves so violently that their neighbors could hear.[41] Indeed, one Virginia court ruled in 1827 that additional laws prohibiting the abuse of enslaved people were not necessary because "the tribunal of public opinion . . . will not fail to award to the offender its deep and solemn reprobation."[42] Like the 1852 *Southern Planter* article mentioned above, this judgment assumed a collective understanding of a standard of treatment of enslaved people as well as a widespread belief that the court of public opinion policed norms for slaveholders.

Physical punishments were particularly visible and audible and were thus harder to conceal from the scrutiny of one's peers, a phenomenon Harriet Jacobs knew all too well. Her owner, Dr. Flint, "had never punished" her directly and would not allow anybody else to punish" her, even though Jacobs knew that his wife frequently urged him to. According to Jacobs, this amnesty from physical punishments was not due to mercy or kindness, but rather because he was afraid of what Jacobs might say, fearing that resorting to "the lash might have led to remarks that would have exposed him in the eyes of his children and grandchildren."[43] Because Flint was concerned about his relationship with Jacobs being made public, and because he hoped to avoid being shamed before his loved ones, Jacobs escaped whippings but was still subjected to affective discipline.

Though slaveholders first and foremost considered their own emotional state when weighing which forms of punishment to deploy, there were ultimately few consequences if one was a "cruel master." As this chapter shows, enslaved people could be punished for failing to suppress their own emotions, or punished for how a slaveholder felt, but despite injunctions against disciplining in anger, slaveholders faced no legal consequences for affective intemperance, even if it resulted in homicide. A law passed in South Carolina in 1821 stated that it was a felony to plan to murder an enslaved person but that "killing" an enslaved person "in sudden heat and passion is the same as manslaughter," a lesser charge.[44] Journals and other proslavery essays might outline emotional norms for slaveholders, but laws like those in South Carolina effectively decriminalized killing an enslaved person if one claimed it was affectively motivated. The same anger and "passion" that slaveholders were cautioned against enacting on enslaved bodies were also their ticket to acquittal should their emotions prove deadly.

Provoking Enslaved Emotions

While members of the plantocracy debated whether affective discipline was more efficient and instructive than corporeal punishment, and the role of their own emotions in punishment, sources show that slaveholders often used physical discipline toward affective ends, with the goal of curbing or provoking individual or collective emotions in enslaved people. Henry Bibb remarked that the whip was used in the slave yard in order "to make the slaves anxious to be sold."[45] Physical violence was occasionally used as a deterrent and to give weight to another tool in slaveholders' affective armory: threats. Focusing on affective discipline, and its relation to physical punishment, demonstrates the extent to which members of the planter class relied on intimidation and cultivating fear in order to maintain slavery. Slave patrols, for example, often used corporeal violence, but they were also known to threaten to beat an enslaved person, only to let them go, terrified but physically unharmed. This was done not out of mercy or clemency, but with the intention of heightening enslaved people's fears of the patrols and of what would happen if they were caught committing a second offense.[46] Some slaveholders believed that physical and emotional discipline were both tools for governing enslaved people. Douglass commented that Thomas Auld, his master, was "incapable of managing his slaves either by force, fear or fraud."[47] In Douglass's view fear was one of several ways to "manag[e]" or affectively discipline slaves, but it was often used alongside bodily "force" and bullying.

Individual slaveholders also relied on the threat of physical cruelty or labor to instill certain emotions in enslaved people. Jacobs remembered that when she was resisting Dr. Flint's sexual advances he threatened to send Jacobs and her children to a plantation where they would all be forced to do grueling manual labor. Flint stated that the strenuous work would correct her "feelings" which "were entirely above [her] situation."[48] This functioned as affective discipline on two levels. First, the possibility of hard labor was supposed to intimidate her into compliance by inducing fear and anxiety for her children. Moreover, he implied that the drudgery was meant as an affective punishment, rather than a physical one, as the work was meant to rectify her emotions, which were inappropriate for an enslaved woman. In this way he hoped to simultaneously discipline her feelings and to punish her *through* emotions.

Some members of the planter class were more explicit when justifying why physical and emotional punishment worked best concomitantly. Enslaved people recognized that slaveholders deployed this two-pronged affective attack, which only served to make them mistrustful of any emotional overtures by a master. Jacobs explained that Dr. Flint wielded a variety of methods to make his slaves do as he pleased, several of which relied on emotions for implementation and impact. According to Jacobs, "Sometimes he had stormy, terrific ways, that made his victims tremble; sometimes he assumed a gentleness that he thought must surely subdue." For Flint, fear and affection were two sides of the same coin and should be used in concert to exert control over the people he enslaved. Interestingly, Jacobs vowed that between the two affective expressions, "I preferred his stormy moods, although they left me trembling."[49]

Corporeal punishment could be used or foreshadowed in order to incite certain emotions in enslaved people, but it was also introduced at other times to discipline enslaved people who expressed feelings that were deemed unacceptable. In the slave South the myth of the happy slave was more than an idealized figure valorized by slaveholders: it was a cudgel for enslaved people who dared to feel or express anything less than contentment on a slaveowner-prescribed emotional continuum from happy to furious. Enslaved people were well aware that if they wanted to avoid punishment they needed to censor any emotions on that spectrum that slaveholders viewed as objectionable, undesirable, or even threatening. Moses Grandy wrote that "slaves are under fear in every word they speak," anxious to avoid any "expression of discontent" lest they be whipped.[50] Similarly, Madison Jefferson recalled that when his sister was sold his family was disconsolate, "but . . . they were obliged to conceal their grief from their oppressors" because if their owner "caught them crying" the grieving family would be punished further.[51]

No matter how much "discontent" or "grief" they felt, enslaved people could not publicly articulate that sadness if they wanted to avoid a physical punishment. Nor was sorrow the only problematic feeling that needed to be suppressed; expressing "insolence," anger, hatred, or sorrow could get an enslaved person whipped for being an emotional outlier.[52] Beating an unhappy enslaved person would not make them any more contented, or reduce their hatred or anger toward their owner, but such punishments had far-reaching impacts. Flogging an enslaved person who dared to display an emotion that slaveholders considered inappropriate served as an immediate punishment for the individual who transgressed the affective norms of slavery, and it might prevent them from openly displaying an array of offensive feelings in the future.

Whipping enslaved people who expressed inappropriate emotions was also intended to have a chilling effect on the broader enslaved community, enforcing the internal boundaries of the emotional politics of slavery by reminding enslaved people that they were under ubiquitous affective surveillance, so they needed to maintain constant self-censorship. The physical punishment of an individual enslaved person could have a communal impact by invoking fear in the enslaved populace in general. Douglass observed that slaveholders often targeted one enslaved person for "especial abuse" and frequent beatings, not because they believed it would "improve" that person but because of the whipping's "effect upon others."[53] This was sometimes done in a highly public forum, to maximize the number of enslaved witnesses who were impacted.[54] This is exemplified by a story Frederick Law Olmsted shared about an enslaved man who was publicly executed for allegedly bludgeoning his owner to death. The enslaved man was "roasted" over "a slow fire," purportedly at the site of the murder, in front of an audience of "many thousand slaves" brought in "from all the adjoining counties" by their owners for the express purpose of making them watch the man be tortured to death. Afterward the enslaved man's ashes were "scattered to the winds and trampled underfoot," and the enslaved people in attendance were forced to listen to preachers share cautionary speeches meant to deter them from killing their own masters. Only one enslaved man had been executed, but it is impossible to quantify the emotional toll of that gruesome spectacle, or how effective fear was in policing the future behavior and feelings of the enslaved observers who were present that day.[55]

An enslaved person did not have to kill their owner in order to be considered a mortal threat to the collective affective order of the South, thus earning a public execution. Douglass watched one day as an enslaved man named Demby was shot dead in front of many enslaved people because he was deemed to be "unmanageable" and disobedient. According to the overseer, killing Demby was necessary because "he had set a dangerous example," asserting that "if one slave refused to be corrected" and did not face consequences, the rest would follow suit, which would invariably lead to "the freedom of the slaves, and the enslavement of the whites."[56] This speaks volumes about how punishments, especially exaggerated and public punishments, reflected the fears of slaveholders. Demby was ostensibly murdered to teach the other enslaved people on the Auld plantation a lesson, but it was also meant to stave off White anxieties about slave rebellions, race war, and an end to the White supremacy that they maintained with an iron fist.

The fact that physical punishments were often accompanied by affective discipline indicates that some members of the planter class felt that bodily pain was insufficient. Grandy noted that "many mistresses will insist on the slave who has been flogged begging pardon for her fault on her knees and thanking her for the correction."[57] Clearly it was not enough for an enslaved person to be physically punished for a perceived infraction: they must also ingratiate themselves to their owner in a ritual of shame, forgiveness, and submission. Douglass experienced this firsthand under the tenure of his former overseer, Mr. Gore, who he said "was just proud enough to demand the most debasing homage" from enslaved people.[58] Douglass believed that Gore was driven to discipline because of his own feelings of pride, which "demand[ed]" that enslaved people show him respect. This illustrates that members of the planter class used a combination of physical and affective punishments both to kindle certain feelings in enslaved people and to curate their own emotions, in order to feel "proud," revered, or feared.[59]

According to Douglass, Gore wanted to be seen as a capable overseer, and he wanted to command respect in the enslaved laborers he oversaw. Evidently Gore, like many members of the plantocracy, believed that the best way to dominate and correct enslaved people was by eliciting certain emotions, including fear (of physical harm or loss of loved ones), awe, anxiety, pride, and shame.[60] Gore was embodying the recommendation laid out in a *Southern Planter* article titled "All About Overseers," that a good overseer must be able to "secure the respect as well as the fear of the negro."[61] The Douglass, Jacobs, and Olmsted sources shed light on how many slaveholders and overseers followed the latter advice, using threats or violence to evoke fear in an individual enslaved person or in the general enslaved population. Another *Southern Planter* author advised stimulating different feelings in order to discipline enslaved people. The contributor to the widely read journal warned overseers against relying too heavily on fear tactics, declaring that one should "never threaten a negro" because it might backfire, as "a violent and passionate threat will often scare the best disposed negro" to run away. Instead of inspiring terror, and possibly losing a valuable enslaved person or their productivity, the author surmised that the best way to discipline enslaved people was to humiliate them by placing them in "the stocks."[62] A Florida slaveholder agreed, bragging in a treatise on slavery that in his decades as a slaveholder he "hardly ever had to apply other correction than shaming" the men and women he enslaved.[63]

Slaveholders sought to elicit a number of emotions in order to affectively discipline the enslaved, but one of the most common methods for instilling fear in an enslaved person, or punishing them with sorrow, was to disrupt or destabilize their family. Douglass argued that when a slaveholder mentioned selling an enslaved person it was usually as a "threat," meant as "punishment of a crime."[64] The specter of the auction block was all the more terrifying for enslaved people who might be sold away from family members.[65] Other slaveowners took advantage of family bonds to enact discipline by beating, starving, or selling the family of an enslaved person, rather than the enslaved person themselves. This method was often used to punish runaways, but affective discipline via the family was also frequently utilized to punish enslaved women, usually to intimidate them into sexual relations.

Of course, manipulating the family relations of enslaved people as a form of affective discipline ran counter to proslavery arguments that enslaved people were fundamentally emotionally limited. Proslavery author George Sawyer swore that "the negro race" lacked the "emotions of parental and kindred attachment," while formerly enslaved man Lewis Hayden recalled a Presbyterian minister who preached to an audience of slaveholders that "there was no more harm in separating a family of slaves than a litter of pigs."[66] In spite of claims made in essays and from pulpits that enslaved people felt emotions less intensely, and could not forge strong family ties, enslaved people's relationships became a primary site of affective discipline. Once again proslavery rhetoric and White supremacist ideology were contradicted by the daily actions of slaveholders who sought to exert power over enslaved people and their emotions.

How enslaved people's familial feelings could be used as a mode of punishment was thrown into stark relief in situations where physical control was not or could not be used. When Bibb and his family were being sold down river to New Orleans there were times when his hands were not bound, even when the ship was docked at port. According to Bibb this was not because his captors trusted him to stay, as he was a notorious escape artist, but because his master "was not . . . afraid of [Bibb] running away" because the slaveholder still had Bibb's family. The slaveholder knew that Bibb's "attachment was too strong to run off," even if the opportunity arose. This was, in fact, one of the reasons the slaveholder kept the Bibb family together, rather than immediately selling Bibb's wife and daughter to punish Bibb. The slaveowner did not even hesitate to allow Bibb to explore New Orleans unfettered because the slaveholder kept Bibb's wife locked up while the enslaved man walked the city streets searching for someone to buy him and his family.[67] In this way the slaveowner demonstrated that he believed that Bibb's love for his wife and child chained him more effectively than literal bonds could. Or perhaps the slaveholder feared that if he sold Bibb's family he would have no more sway over the recalcitrant enslaved man and thus no other means of subduing him.

Bibb's owner held his family captive to keep Bibb from escaping, but other slaveholders threatened more aggressive punishments for the families of fugitives in order to discourage runaways. As Pennington struggled with whether to flee, thoughts of his parents and siblings gave him pause. It was "heartaching" to think of leaving them, not only because he feared he would never see them again, but because he worried that if he escaped they would be punished by being "sold off as a disaffected family," a practice he knew was common when a family member ran away. This was affective discipline in all its ruthless efficiency, as selling a runaway's loved ones simultaneously punished fugitives and their families and no doubt deterred other enslaved people from escaping. Unable to discipline Pennington physically if he ran away, his owner could still punish him emotionally by vicariously selling Pennington's family. Tainted by Pennington's disobedience, his parents and siblings would be deemed emotionally contaminated, labeled as "disaffected," and sold as devalued and dangerous property. Filled with fear that his loved ones would bear the brunt of his choice to escape, Pennington initially dismissed the idea, but in the end he fled North and his family was sold to a planter in Virginia.[68] Though Pennington decided to run away it is likely that not all enslaved people who weighed the risks to themselves and those they loved made the same decision. That he debated escaping, and the impact it would have on his family, for so long exhibits the chilling effect punishing fugitives' families had on the enslaved population as a whole. While he ultimately decided to run away, knowing full well the consequences for his family, it cannot be estimated how many enslaved people balanced their longing for freedom against concerns for their loved ones and then elected not to escape.

Gendering Affective Discipline

Affective discipline was employed to keep enslaved people in line and to prevent them from running away, but it was also a gendered punishment, frequently engaged to threaten or punish enslaved women in order to compel sexual relations. Many slaveholders and overseers comprehended that a woman who was isolated from her parents, spouse, or children might be more vulnerable to their sexual predations.[69] Not long after coming to one of her husband's Georgia plantations, Fanny Kemble wrote about an enslaved woman she met named Judy, who recounted tales of abuse at the hands of the plantation overseer, Mr. King. After rebuffing his sexual advances King "flogged her severely" for refusing to yield, before he "sent her off, as a further punishment, to Five Pound," a separate, remote plantation where she claimed slaves were "sometimes banished." Judy conceded that as "bad as the flogging was, she would sooner have taken that again than the dreadful lonely days and nights she spent on the penal swamp of Five Pound."[70] Like Brown and Douglass, Judy had experienced both physical and affective discipline, and she concluded that punishments that targeted her emotions were worse to endure. Judy's account also stresses the gendered aspects of affective discipline. As the most frequent targets of sexual harassment and assault, enslaved women were faced with two terrifying options: succumb to their owner or overseer, or face temporary or permanent exile from their loved ones.

An 1860 letter from a Maryland planter named T. D. Jones to an enslaved woman named Eliza is a harrowing example of a slaveholder selling an enslaved person as punishment rather than for profit, and it shows how this was used to affectively discipline enslaved women who resisted an owner's desires. In the biting letter Jones wrote that he had sold Eliza away from her daughter Jennie because he believed Eliza to be "ungrateful" and untrustworthy. However, over the course of the letter he insinuated that he had actually separated Eliza from her young daughter to punish Eliza for an unspecified emotional slight that he believed she had committed. Eliza had previously written to inquire about her daughter, "expressing the hope" that her master would permit Jennie to come live with her. Eliza longed for her daughter enough to write to her former owner, but his letter was calculated to make Eliza feel the pangs of separation all the more deeply. Jones blithely announced that he had read the letter to Jennie, adding that Jennie "seemed glad to hear from . . . Aunt Liza . . . (as she calls you)." Nevertheless, he replied that Jennie herself "doesn't want to go away from her master." In his response the tension of their affective tug-of-war was palpable, as was his desire to inflict heartache. The slaveholder first emphasized how little Eliza meant to her daughter, noting that Eliza was no longer referred to as "mother," but as the more cordial "Aunt Liza," before telling Eliza that her own daughter allegedly preferred to stay with her owner rather than be reunited with her mother. It is uncertain if these were Jennie's words or desires, if she felt impelled to say that she would rather stay with Jones, or if the entire conversation was fabricated to hurt Eliza. What was crystal clear to both author and reader was that the decision of whether to allow Jennie to go was in Jones's hands, and that he was magnifying his power over her family in order to inflict maximum emotional pain.[71]

Throughout the letter Jones reveled in his influence over Jennie's fate, drawing out Eliza's suspense by bemoaning that he could "hardly make up [his] mind," and that he "would be reluctant to part with her," as he would "miss her very much" if she left. His equivocating was calibrated to affectively provoke Eliza, contrasting Jones's control over the situation and her own powerlessness. While putting distance between Eliza and her daughter, he mentioned that he knew "how to estimate the claims of a mother" and could "appreciate the affection of a mother for her child." However, his unwillingness to part with Jennie shows that he had put a price on these "claims" and found the cost to be too high. His professed attempt at empathy served only to accentuate how he had undermined Jennie and Eliza's relationship.[72]

The slaveholder's punitive motives for keeping Eliza in a state of apprehension about her daughter became even clearer as he repeatedly referred to how Eliza had injured his own feelings. First, Jones disclosed that in an earlier letter Eliza had "made no inquiry after [his own] welfare" and wondered if this omission was deliberate, prompted by "indignation or malice" because he had sold her. He contrasted her churlishness with his own past behavior, insisting that she should "acknowledge that [he] was a kind and forbearing master" while she was "an ungrateful servant" who had been disloyal. Jones twisted his affective knife even deeper, opining that if Eliza *had* acted "faithfully" then he would not have sold her, as "no offer would have tempted" him to "part with" her. In doing so he placed the responsibility for her heartbreak solely on her own shoulders. Jones did not say how Eliza had acted disloyally, but he confessed that selling her away from her daughter was a punishment for her great betrayal, as Eliza's "tender affections" and care to his sick wife "created in [him] an attachment for [Eliza] that nothing but [her] ingratitude and faithlessness could have broken." He closed the letter by reiterating how he felt about her, perhaps because of the "attachment" he still had for her, or perhaps in order to make Eliza feel guilty. Jones's many attempts to hurt Eliza's feelings throughout the letter hinted at his own cruelty and pain and at his motives for selling Eliza. By continuing to keep her away from her daughter he proved that he did not just want to sell Eliza: he wanted to sever her ties to her daughter, and then contrast her estrangement with her daughter with his own close bond with Jennie. That Jones wrote this lengthy missive at all exemplifies how much his mission was affective discipline. It did not suffice to separate Eliza from her daughter; Jones wanted to exacerbate Eliza's grief by lashing out at her in writing, making her experience the pain that he believed he had felt.[73]

By alluding to his strong ties to Jennie, Jones also forced Eliza (and any other reader of the letter) to question the nature of his relationship with her daughter and the extent of his past relations with Eliza. According to Jones, one of the reasons why he was "reluctant" to let Jennie leave was, he told Eliza, "She is petted as you used to be. She is a watchful little spy as you used to be."[74] Maybe Eliza merely served as a nurse to Jones's invalid wife, or maybe Jones's anger over Eliza's supposed disloyalty signals that they had had a sexual relationship, or that he had felt a romantic "attachment" to the enslaved woman. Whatever the tenor of their relationship, it was close enough for Jones to feel slighted by Eliza. In this light, his remarks about Jennie being "petted" just as Eliza had been might have been intended to show that Jennie had privileged status in the Jones household, including a pampered lifestyle that Eliza could never provide. Or perhaps Jones referred to physical petting, thus implying to Eliza that he was planning to sexually assault her daughter. What is clear is the gendered nature of this mode of affective discipline, as Jones exploited Eliza's maternal feelings, invoked past memories of his treatment of her, and threatened her daughter with similar abuse.

Enslaved women who were targets of slaveholders' sexual assault and harassment also faced affective discipline if they dared to show affection for any man that was not their owner. Jacobs devoted much of her narrative of her time in slavery to describing the constant sexual harassment she suffered at the hands of her owner, Dr. Flint, and the methods he used to try to coerce sexual relations. He vacillated between bullying her and cajoling her, but the campaign of affective discipline intensified after he heard that she was in love with a free Black man. After learning this, Flint hit her, which Jacobs noted "was the first time he had ever struck" her, but most of his disciplinary methods relied on inducing fear. First, he tried scaring her, vowing that he would kill her or jail her. He also warned that he would force her to do backbreaking field labor, but according to Jacobs Flint was reluctant to follow through with this promise because of his "jealousy of the overseer." Finally, Flint resorted to trying to distance Jacobs from her lover and her family, stating that he planned to move to Louisiana and that he would bring her with him. In the end Flint succeeded in driving Jacobs and her lover apart, as she told the man to leave her and go North so that he could be truly free of the grasp of slavery. The effect of his departure was devastating for Jacobs, who remembered that once he left her "lamp of hope had gone out . . . [and she] felt lonely and desolate."[75] This illustrated that affective discipline could be used to compel emotions, but not always in a precise fashion. The jealous Flint had hoped to scare Jacobs into submission; instead he was the cause of her bitter heartache.

Douglass recounted the tragic treatment of an enslaved woman named Esther who was also punished when she "was courted" by an enslaved man named Edward. Their owner, Colonel Lloyd, set out to destroy "the growing intimacy" developing between Esther and Edward because of his own desire for Esther, demanding that she not see the enslaved man any more. Like Jacobs, Esther initially refused, and they carried on their courtship in secret. When Lloyd learned that their liaison continued, he felt "abhorred" by Esther and could no longer conceal "his rage." One morning Lloyd stripped her to the waist, bound her wrists, and whipped her ferociously. Douglass saw the beating through slots in the wall, watching as Lloyd took his time lashing her, appearing "delighted" by the task. Esther begged for mercy, but Douglass worried that her cries "seemed only to increase his fury."[76]

Though his primary mode of disciplining Esther was the whip, once again a slaveholder's goal was to punish an enslaved person both for the emotions they had expressed and for how the enslaved person had made their owner feel. Her crime was not only that she had loved Edward, or "abhorred" Lloyd, but rather that she had made Lloyd feel acute jealousy, rage, and rejection. Perhaps beating her brought Lloyd perverse "delight," or satisfied his thirst for revenge, or perhaps it only distracted him so that he did not have to acknowledge how he felt or the profound influence Esther had over his emotions. With every lash Lloyd was reasserting power over someone who had shaped his emotions, with a punishment meant to fit the perceived affective crime.

Resisting Affective Discipline

Affective modes of discipline were popular with the plantocracy, but enslaved people developed a number of responses to this method of discipline and domination. One way that enslaved people did this was by forging strong bonds with family and community in the face of a system that worked relentlessly to destroy or manipulate those kinship ties. That support network helped enslaved people endure and even challenge the vicissitudes of slavery.[77] But slave narratives highlight other ways that enslaved people actively resisted affective modes of discipline. This included refusing to stop expressing emotions, even when punished for doing so; defying slaveholders' attempts to incite a specific emotion; and taking advantage of how affective discipline was applied.

Since enslaved people were often affectively disciplined for expressing emotions that slaveholders deemed transgressive or otherwise undesirable, one way that enslaved people challenged this system of emotional correction and censorship was by refusing to suppress their rebellious feelings. While in the slave market awaiting transport, Northup encountered a woman named Eliza who, much to the chagrin of the slave traders, was heartbroken after having been sold away from her children. Eliza was repeatedly chastised by the traders for being "a blubbering, bawling wench" and was whipped for sobbing in front of customers. The limits of affective discipline became evident, as the slave merchants could think of no other way to punish a mother who had already been separated from her children. When beatings failed to staunch her tears, one slave trader could do little more than demand that she stop weeping or "he would soon give her something to cry about." Having seen that the lash could not dispel her anguish the slave traders had no other recourse but threats, which had no effect on Eliza's grief.[78]

Though Eliza managed to be sold, she continued to resist all efforts to censor her sorrow or command her fear. Northup recalled that when their new owner saw how inconsolable Eliza was, the slaveholder could not conceal his "regret at having bought her" to be a house slave. In his appraising eyes Eliza was depreciating in value by giving free rein to her emotions, sorrow in particular. The slaveowner's reaction reveals that enslaved people's feelings directly impacted their worth and productivity. And indeed, as Eliza grew increasingly despondent, her work began to suffer. According to Northup, Eliza also displeased their mistress by being "more occupied in brooding over her sorrows than in attending to her business" and as a result she was sent to do field work. The change did nothing to mitigate Eliza's expressions of heartbreak, and eventually she was sold "for a trifle" to another man. She continued to decline emotionally and physically, as Northup lamented that "grief had gnawed remorselessly at her heart, until her strength was gone." Because of the effect her agony had on her work, her new master beat her severely, but Northup observed that nothing could "whip back the departed vigor" and health she possessed before her children were taken from her.[79] The traders in the market, and each subsequent owner, were explicit that the punishments would stop if she checked her despair, but still Eliza refused. Once Eliza had been deprived of her children she had nothing left to lose, which meant slave traders and slaveholders had lost their most reliable method for disciplining an enslaved person: emotional leverage.

Since members of the planter class often applied affective discipline in order to arouse fear, heartbreak, sorrow, or shame in enslaved people, when enslaved people openly flouted attempts to provoke their emotions it was a form of resistance and an assertion of their personhood.[80] After Jacobs's Uncle Benjamin was caught running away, his owner declared that he would make an "example" of Benjamin by detaining him "in jail until he was subdued, or . . . sold." Benjamin had been imprisoned for months when passersby heard him singing and laughing in his jail cell. Jacobs explained that his "indecorum" was reported to Benjamin's owner, who requested that the enslaved man be chained up in his cell. For the act of exhibiting unrepentant joy while incarcerated, he was shackled, proof of how threatening that laughter was to the planter status quo and how little power the slaveholder had over Benjamin's feelings. Still not contrite, Benjamin diligently "worked at his chains" until he was able to slip out of them, before dropping the manacles out the window and asking that they be sent to his owner. By emphasizing that he could not be physically restrained, Benjamin was underscoring that he could not be emotionally chained either. The more Benjamin resisted the dual affective discipline of prison and of slavery the more his owner sought to "subdue" him, trying to chain the body of a man who was already in a jail cell since he could not shackle Benjamin's laughter.[81]

Jacobs also blatantly refused to be emotionally coerced by her owner's punishments or threats. Attempting to scare Jacobs into compliance, Flint asked her if she realized that he had the "right" to kill her at any time. Instead of inspiring fear, as Flint had hoped, Jacobs brazenly responded that she "wish[ed]" he would kill her, then challenged his assertion that he could, in fact, "do as you like." He replied with another threat, asking her how she would feel about being imprisoned for her "insolence." This also backfired, as she retorted that at least in jail "there would be more peace . . . than there is here."[82] Only then did Flint back down, realizing that he could not provoke the emotions in her that he desired. Like Benjamin, Jacobs could not be made to feel fear or contrition, and she would not quell her "insolen[t]" feelings.

Some enslaved people may even have taken advantage of their knowledge of affective discipline, exploiting the fact that "disaffected" and disrespectful slaves were typically swiftly sold to escape their owner, or slavery more generally. Sella Martin had a number of owners during his time in bondage, including a couple that resided outside of New Orleans. Longing to live in the city, where he believed he could more easily escape to freedom, Martin decided to sow discord with his owner's wife in the hopes that he would be sold as a "disaffected" slave. Martin set about "constantly quarrelling with her" in order to "provoke" his master "either to sell" him or release him from a "vigilance" that was "standing in the way" of his "plans for escape." Martin bickered with the woman until he "succeeded" and was then sold to a man in New Orleans.[83] This was a victory for Martin, paving the way for his eventual escape up the Mississippi River, but he was also clearly proud of having manipulated relations with his owners so expertly.

* * *

Physically brutal forms of punishment have long been the focus of historians of slavery, but that overlooks how discipline in the antebellum South was fundamentally shaped by emotions. Only through examining the less visible but no less damaging forms of affective discipline, and how physical and emotional discipline were used in concert, can scholars hope to more fully understand the lived experiences of enslaved people and the variety of ways that power operates through emotions. Enslaved people were punished for how they felt, punished for how slaveholders felt about them, and punished for daring to express emotions deemed rebellious. Proslavery authors may have claimed that enslaved people felt emotions less acutely, or lacked strong family bonds, but they were quick to punitively induce emotions by harming or selling an enslaved person's loved ones. Attention to the critical function emotions played in discipline provides insight into the daily interactions and abuses of slavery, and the specific ways that punishment was gendered, as well as how enslaved people endured and resisted emotional modes of correction.

Slaveholders' historic reliance on specifically affective modes of discipline was made abundantly clear after the Civil War. The post-Emancipation South was uncharted emotional waters for former slaveowners, who found themselves flummoxed by Black people whose feelings were now ostensibly out of their control. No longer able to whip a proud or angry enslaved person, or to quell or compel certain feelings with the emotional bludgeon of the auction block, members of the planter class were forced to find new methods to maintain the emotional politics of slavery. Meanwhile formerly enslaved people who had endured emotional methods of correction were more than ready to cast off those affective constraints to exercise their newfound emotional freedom.

CHAPTER 6

"Enjoying Freedom"

As a free resident of New York who was kidnapped into slavery, Solomon Northup knew what it meant to be free and what it felt like to be robbed of that liberty. Northup later recounted the experience of being taken captive in Washington, DC, the home of a government that was ostensibly founded on "man's inalienable right to life, LIBERTY and the pursuit of happiness!," dryly noting, "Hail, Columbia, happy land indeed."[1] Though he highlighted the irony of being enslaved in a town meant to represent "liberty," he also emphasized the hypocrisy of the supposedly universal right to the "pursuit of happiness," by sarcastically referring to Washington as "happy . . . indeed."[2] Nor was Northup alone in seeing the link between liberty and emotional freedom. Throughout his narrative Northup was emphatic that even people who had been born and raised in slavery understood the meaning of "life, liberty, and the pursuit of happiness," and that "ninety-nine out of every hundred" people in bondage yearned for those rights.[3] Furthermore, he contended that enslaved people fully comprehended the rights and responsibilities that came with freedom, and that liberty would "secure to them the enjoyment of domestic happiness."[4] According to Northup, enslaved people were well aware that freedom and their ability to "enjoy . . . happiness" were inextricably tied.

The writings of historians and formerly enslaved people alike reveal that the "enjoyment of freedom" was the overarching goal for many enslaved people.[5] Authors of slave narratives portrayed their dreams of "enjoying freedom" and of liberty as something to be "enjoyed."[6] Henry Bibb shared how much he "should like to enjoy freedom and happiness" with his wife and child, while Jacob Stroyer lamented the fate of enslaved people who died right before Emancipation, those who had come so close to "freedom but not living to enjoy it."[7] Notably they did not say that freedom was something to be possessed, or exercised; it was a right that was woven into the very fabric of happiness: to be free was to be able to pursue happiness, and great joy was derived from freedom. This language appeared in legal documents as well. Enslaved people who were manumitted in Louisiana were promised their "liberty, to have and to enjoy the same from this day henceforth."[8] The phrase was frequently found in court cases involving enslaved people and free Black people. A woman who claimed she was a free person who had been kidnapped and enslaved was described as having "been in the enjoyment of her freedom" for many years, but false enslavement had denied her this right.[9]

All these sources demonstrate that in the minds of enslaved people and formerly enslaved people, and in a court of law, freedom was fundamentally linked to joy, and the right to seek and expect happiness was a crucial component of freedom. In his groundbreaking work on the history of emotions, William Reddy defines "emotional liberty" both as the ability of a person to experiment with different emotional goals and expressions, and as a measure of the freedom of a given society. In his view, a society that allows for "emotional liberty" will permit and even encourage individuals to engage in affective "self-exploration," while repressive societies, like the antebellum South, allow only a limited range of emotions and will punish affective transgressors.[10] Thus Emancipation was not just a civic transformation, from slave to citizen, but an emotional metamorphosis as well.

Since the feelings and affective norms of antebellum society were predicated on slavery, widespread Emancipation was a seismic shift in the emotional terrain of the South. As a result, conflicts arose between free Black people and White Southerners over what the postslavery affective norms of the South would be, and if they would be radically different from the emotional dynamics that existed under slavery. Debates about whether being emancipated changed how newly freed people felt, and how freedom shaped relations between former slaveholders and enslaved people, began long before the Emancipation Proclamation came to fruition. Members of the planter class saw Black political freedom and emotional liberation as a menace to the affective norms of slavery, so White Southern elites fought to limit manumission, and after Emancipation they worked to maintain the affective relations of bondage. Because of the pressure on enslaved people to enact certain emotions while suppressing others, and because of the constant threats to enslaved families posed by the institution, enslaved people and formerly enslaved people asserted that the freedom of emotional expression denied to them while in bondage was an intrinsic component of liberty and citizenship.

Studying the emotional politics of the Reconstruction South lays bare that emotions continued to be the currency of power between free Black people and White people long after Emancipation. In the wake of war formerly enslaved people found a variety of ways to exercise what Reddy terms "emotional liberty" and to dismantle the emotional restrictions of slavery. Those methods included informing former owners of how their relationships had changed, trying to reunite families divided by slavery, engaging in public emotional performances, and establishing new holidays. But White Southerners, especially former slaveholders, did not respond well to this affective revolution. Threatened by free Black people's emotional liberation, many White Southerners employed legal and extralegal tactics, including laws and contracts demanding deference, and the use of violence to inspire fear and affectively discipline free Black people, all in an effort to preserve as many of the emotional hierarchies of slavery as possible. This chapter details the power struggles over establishing new affective norms, as well as the long-term impacts of racialized emotional restrictions and expectations in the post-Reconstruction South.

Emotions and Manumission

While many enslaved people and free Black people believed that emancipation meant freedom of emotional expression, many White Southerners thought differently. In the antebellum South, in which affective norms and expectations were based on one's status as free or enslaved, members of the planter class viewed free Black people as a threat to the social and emotional order of slavery. This was clear in the concerns some elite White Southerners had about relations between White people and free Black people. In his essay "On Slavery," Thomas Roderick Dew argued that manumission was detrimental to the contentment of masters and enslaved people, as emancipation was "utterly subversive of the interests, security and happiness of both the blacks and whites."[11] Prior to Emancipation slaveholders were particularly apprehensive about how free people of color might influence people who were still enslaved. In a speech published in *Southern Planter* in 1859 the author cautioned that the free Black population was "injurious" to the "contentment and happiness of the remaining slaves."[12] These convictions, that abolition would endanger the affective strictures of slavery, were frequently invoked to oppose individual and universal emancipation.

People who had escaped slavery were well aware of how elite White Southerners felt about free Black people. William Craft remarked that the "majority of slaveholders hate" Black people, and that members of the planter class had "no mercy upon, nor sympathy for, any negro whom they cannot enslave."[13] Paternalism might have been rooted in the belief that slaveholders could show "sympathy" to enslaved people, but Craft countered that only antipathy was reserved for Black people who existed outside the confines of slavery. In averring that slaveholders were unable to feel "mercy" for those they could "not enslave," Craft insinuated that slaveholders despised Black people if they could not dictate the terms of their affective relations. Formerly enslaved people also knew how concerned slaveholders were that free people of color would emotionally indoctrinate enslaved people, and how members of the slaveocracy tried to swiftly staunch any signs of free feelings in enslaved people. Harriet Jacobs recalled how her owner, Dr. Flint, threatened to make her perform manual labor because her "feelings were entirely above [her] situation" as a slave.[14] Clearly Flint wanted to remind her of her status and to instill in her how enslaved people were, in his view, supposed to feel. For Flint the appropriate feelings for a person in her "situation" were fear and awe of their owner.

Slaveholders' fears about the emotional influence of freedom and loss of affective control over the enslaved were concretized in manumission law, and how those laws were implemented. This is evident in a Georgia court case that arose after a slaveowner requested that four enslaved people be freed after his death. The slaveholder's will was contested in a trial in which the judge cited an 1818 law that the state needed to limit manumissions in order "to prevent a horde of free persons of color, from ravaging the morals, and corrupting the feelings of [the] slaves."[15] As a result, the four enslaved people were not granted the freedom they had been promised. By attesting that "free persons of color" would invariably "corrupt . . . the feelings" of "slaves," the law delineated that members of the planter class thought that free Black people possessed emotions that were not only dangerous but contagious.

To isolate the emotional contaminant of free Black people, some slave states permitted manumission only if a White person testified to the good character of the enslaved person seeking freedom. In 1847 Phillip Moore began the process to free an enslaved woman named Henrietta, as that was his mother's "dying wish." He affirmed that Henrietta had steady income as a laundress, and that she had always shown "good conduct" while enslaved; therefore she deserved freedom and would "not abuse its exercise." But Moore's word alone was not enough to free Henrietta. An acquaintance of the Moore family who knew Henrietta also testified to her character, saying that he had always "found her honest, well-behaved and industrious." Four additional people signed statements to this effect.[16] It did not suffice for an enslaved person to be seen as trustworthy and faithful to avoid punishment while in bondage; enslaved people were also expected to uphold the affective dynamics of slavery if they ever hoped to be manumitted. Policy makers and slaveholders clung to the notion that the emotional behavior of an enslaved person could predict affective relations after slavery. They could reassure themselves that anyone who had been faithful and "honest" while enslaved was not dangerous and would not try to corrupt enslaved people once free. Moore's promise that Henrietta would not "abuse" her freedom also hinted that some members of the planter class believed that other newly freed people had done just that after being manumitted.

This was not the only way in which slaveholders endeavored to safeguard the emotional politics of slavery even after Emancipation. When Louisiana slaveholder Sambo Bellastre freed fifty-year-old Suzanne, the manumission documents stated his wish that she should have "her liberty, to have and to enjoy . . . in as full, absolute, and complete a manner . . . as though she had been born free." In spite of his statement about her supposed "absolute" freedom, and the implication that this legal process was a symbolic renaissance in which Suzanne was declared to be a person "born free," the ties of master and slave were retained in a "promise" by Bellastre later in the document that in keeping with Louisiana law he would "oblige" himself and his heirs "to nourish and maintain the said Suzanne . . . whenever she shall be in want owing to sickness, old age, insanity, or any other proved infirmity."[17] By placing the onus of care on former owners, the state of Louisiana hoped to reduce the financial burden of providing for the indigent, but in doing so they effectively maintained the social obligations and paternalism of slavery.

Other states tried to isolate the contagion of freedom by expelling free Black people entirely. After Lunsford Lane purchased himself he was legally required to leave the state of North Carolina, a painful proposition since his family was still enslaved there. Lane observed that this law, which attempted to sever the bonds between manumitted people and their enslaved loved ones, reflected White resentment of free Black people. Lane protested being "banished," noting that from the moment he decided to buy his freedom he had intentionally tried "to conduct" himself so that he would not "become obnoxious to the white inhabitants, knowing . . . their hostility to the colored people."[18] This underlined that Lane believed that White "hostility" was codified as policy, but also that he hoped that the actions of individual free Black people could repudiate this stereotype and the attendant collective enmity it produced.

Lane was not alone; abolitionists had long warned enslaved people that in order to be treated as citizens formerly enslaved people would need to learn to adopt the feelings and affective behavior of free people. This is exemplified in a 1796 document printed by a Philadelphia-based antislavery society, a message to formerly enslaved people announcing that abolitionists wanted them to "act worthily of the rank [they] have acquired as freemen." According to the authors, formerly enslaved people could prove they had earned free status through proper social and affective behavior, including being "faithful in all the relations you bear in society, whether as husbands, wives, fathers, children or hired servants . . . be simple in your dress," "avoid frolicking, and amusements" that might incite "deserved reproach among your white neighbors," and always act "in a civil and respectful manner." If free people followed these injunctions the authors were confident that they could "refute the objections which have been made against you as rational and moral creatures."[19] Even once free, formerly enslaved people were expected to mute themselves and to maintain a defensive posture, anticipating criticism and precluding conflict.

The pamphlet's advice to newly freed people sheds light on how some White abolitionists viewed free Black people and their emotions. Cautioning free people to be "faithful" and demure in dress and demeanor suggested that they were seen, even in the North, as prone to disloyalty and excess. The abolitionists intimated that these measures were necessary because people of color were perceived as irrational and immoral, and the only way to disprove that was to learn the appropriate affective norms and practices of freedom. If formerly enslaved people did not practice restraint in their behavior, relationships, and affective displays, then they would, in the author's view, "deserve . . . reproach." All this assumed that White people already held "objections" to free Black people, and that it was the responsibility of the latter, rather than the former, to "refute" these ideas and resentments. Only then would free Black people be deemed "worthy" of their liberty and the rights associated with that freedom. Ultimately all these efforts to curtail the emotional expressions of free Black people, and to control their relationships with White people and enslaved people alike, stressed slaveholders' deep-seated need to emotionally control those whom they could not legally master.

The Transformative Power of Freedom

Though members of the planter class were determined to maintain the affective norms and practices of slavery for enslaved people and free Black people, this became increasingly difficult after the outbreak of the Civil War in 1861. Some slaveholders perceived affective shifts in enslaved people immediately. Mary Chesnut in particular became obsessed with reading enslaved people's faces for signs of emotional sea change, and she wondered if any fluctuations in demeanor were proof that enslaved people longed for freedom and Southern defeat. Just weeks after war began she wrote in her diary about "the demoralization produced by hopes of freedom" after an enslaved butler was noticeably distant. His work had not suffered, but he was quieter and "aloof," not engaging in his "usual . . . friendly chat." She compared this marked difference to the butler's wife, who, Chesnut claimed, "showed no signs of disaffection."[20]

The upheaval of war, and the number of enslaved people who took advantage of that disorder to run away, forced many slaveholders to acknowledge that enslaved people might actively resent them. Other members of the planter class found ways to convince themselves that enslaved people remained loyal and loving. Chesnut's husband, James, assuaged his concerns that enslaved people were "dissatisfied" and planning to escape by going to visit with them. Something in their behavior or manner must have reassured him, as Chesnut reported that her husband returned "charmed" with the enslaved people's "affection for him" and confident in their lasting fidelity. Chesnut herself sought solace in the idea that the last time the British occupied South Carolina the local "slaves certainly were faithful" rather than fleeing, a romanticization of the past given that many of her husband's grandfather's slaves had run away to join the British.[21] Clearly slaveholders like Chesnut were emotionally invested in the fantasy that slavery depended on enslaved people's love for slaveholders, and they were willing to ignore all evidence to the contrary.

While many Southern slaveholders were pondering what enslaved people were feeling, and if they would be devoted through the conflict, an article published in the *New York Tribune* in December 1861 gleefully surmised that slaveholders were deluding themselves. The author dismissed "attempts of Southern papers to pretend that the blacks are still loyal" as "absurd." Instead the writer wagered that any enslaved people who had "not yet escaped of course pretend to be faithful," even telling their owners that the South would win, while fervently hoping otherwise. During his recent travels in the South, the reporter had "observed a feeling of bitterness displayed by the blacks" and even "indignation" at slaveholders and their efforts to prevent enslaved people from running away.[22] By concluding that enslaved people were feigning being "faithful" while becoming increasingly and overtly "bitter," the author portended that enslaved people were still performing the familiar role of the "loyal" slave, but that they were less inclined to do so and were more unwilling to censor their feelings. Just a few years later, a Union officer charged with recruiting African American soldiers in Maryland shared that slaveholders' paternalistic fantasies of benevolence had not been shaken by years of war; rather, "nine owners out of ten will insist . . . that their slaves are much attached to them." Like the *Tribune* reporter before him, the officer dismissed this idea as "a delusion."[23]

Many slaveholders feared that war would lead not just to enslaved people's disaffection and escape, but to more violent manifestations of discontent. Members of the planter class had long been apprehensive that Emancipation would lead to vengeance-fueled violence. Dew speculated that universal Emancipation would be repaid in "horrors" and insurrection, while William Harper opined that if freed, formerly enslaved people would "be tempted to avenge themselves by oppression and proscription of the white race," and that such "retaliation" would lead to "open war" between the races.[24] These dire forecasts of post-Emancipation racial discord served to justify slavery, and it united slaveholders and nonslaveholding White people in common cause. Predictions of formerly enslaved people seeking collective, violent revenge became all the more apocalyptic as the Civil War began, though most enslaved people were more interested in using the situation to escape bondage than they were in retaliation.[25] Chesnut experienced one rare act of vengeance when her cousin was smothered to death during the war, allegedly by an enslaved person. The night that they learned of the murder Chesnut's friend Kate confessed that she was worried about how her enslaved maid felt, asking Chesnut, "Does she mean to take care of me—or to murder me?" Chesnut was also overcome by a combination of grief over her friend and misgivings about enslaved people, admitting "I feel that the ground is cut away from under my feet."[26]

Judging from Chesnut's diary, enslaved people's feelings were more than a personal preoccupation for Chesnut; it was a frequent topic of conversation among members of the planter class. At one party a friend conjectured "we have no reason to suppose a negro knows there is a war" and that she certainly did not discuss the conflict with the people she enslaved. Still, she feared that they knew more than they let on, because when the topic of war or the "Damn Yankee" came up, she repeatedly saw "the sudden deadening of their faces." Meanwhile, two friends told Chesnut worriedly "that the joy of their negroes" after the Union invasion was "loud and open."[27] These scenes demonstrate that not all enslaved people reacted the same to news of the war in the presence of their owners, but whether they exhibited "joy" or swiftly muted their affective responses, slaveholders were scrutinizing enslaved people's faces more intently than ever, hoping to discern the feelings that lay within and what those emotions foreshadowed about their own futures. Enslaved people knew they had to keep their feelings about the war in check, at least in the presence of Confederate supporters like Chesnut. Alonzo

Jackson testified after the war that while he "always rejoiced over Union victories," he shared those sentiments with only a trusted few while he was still enslaved in South Carolina, as he feared for his life "if it was known how [he] really felt about the war."[28]

As the war progressed, Chesnut was perturbed by the emotional revolution she was witnessing and how it was impacting relations between slaveholders and enslaved people. In 1863, Chesnut fretted that the enslaved people around her were "unreadable," certain that there was great significance in the "black masks" they donned. She worried that these "masks" conveyed more than outright rejoicing, since she contended that "on all other subjects except the war they are the most excitable of races." Because she thought enslaved people were generally emotionally transparent and easily "excitable," their lack of affective reactions about the war made her fear that enslaved people were cloaking their true feelings. By the summer of 1864 Chesnut was in a froth about the enslaved "sphinxes" divulging no feelings as Sherman approached, and she attributed even more meaning to the emotions they were not expressing. Chesnut noted that the people she enslaved were acting "more obedient and more considerate than ever" when they "*are in the house*," which she found most disconcerting. It had finally dawned on her that enslaved people performed emotions for the benefit of slaveholders, while concealing other sentiments only in her presence. Slaveholders like Chesnut had always tried to augur what enslaved people felt, but now that she expected a change in their emotions, and now that Confederate defeat and Emancipation were imminent, this task became all the more urgent and more maddening when she felt thwarted. Just three months before the end of the war Chesnut bemoaned that enslaved people still appeared "utterly apathetic," but she questioned if that would be the case "if they saw" the North was "triumphant."[29] For Chesnut, enslaved people's perceived apathy no longer signaled a lack of interest in the war: it was irrefutable proof of Union sympathies.

Slaveowners were convinced that merely anticipating freedom could alter how enslaved people acted and felt, and many formerly enslaved people concurred. Slave narratives brimmed with descriptions of how their feelings changed in relation to the promise of freedom, culminating in an emotional metamorphosis. Enslaved people who sought liberty, through purchase or by running away, typically characterized this affective process as a total and instantaneous transformation. For some the overwhelming exultation began as soon as they approached a free state, even before they were on free soil. William Wells Brown remembered that as he and his family drew closer to "a land of liberty" his heart "would . . . leap for joy."[30] Bibb used identical language to recount how, upon nearing the Ohio River, his "heart leaped up for joy at the glorious prospect that [he] should . . . be free."[31] In portraying the flood of completely new feelings Brown and Bibb emphasized that freedom from slavery was an emotional liberation.

For formerly enslaved people who bought their liberty, the affective epiphany could occur at different points in the purchasing process. Elizabeth Keckley wrote that as soon as she was told she could buy herself and her son the news felt like a "ray of sunshine," as she realized that "the bitter heart-struggle was over." According to Keckley she was forever altered; as soon as her owner said she could buy her freedom she saw the world in an entirely new light: now "the earth wore a brighter look, and the very stars seemed to sing with joy."[32] Lane reported that his feelings radically shifted when the transaction was over, that once "the money was paid to [his] mistress" he felt free finally: "And a queer and a joyous feeling it is to one who has been a slave."[33] Lane explained that the moment money was exchanged he felt different, and for the first time he felt "free." These passages illuminate that Lane not only felt "joyous" at being freed, but that liberty made him feel new and "queer" emotions that he had never experienced while enslaved.[34] For Moses Grandy, who had thrice paid for his freedom and been twice denied it, the emotional transformation did not come until he physically held legal documentation that freedom was truly his. Grandy recalled that once he had finally received his "free papers" his "feelings were greatly excited."[35]

Authors of slave narratives may have underscored their affective epiphany because they genuinely experienced a moment of emotional rebirth upon becoming free. The trope may also have been invoked to express the profound impact of freedom, in contrast to the affective oppression of slavery.[36] But formerly enslaved people also wrote about the moment of transformation because it was of great interest to their audiences. Steeped in sentimental culture, contemporary readers were preoccupied with feelings, articulating their own and reading about those of others, so they were captivated by the emotional experience of attaining freedom. Some authors addressed how popular the topic was and how difficult it was to answer questions about how it felt to become free. Frederick Douglass confessed in his first autobiography that he was "frequently asked how [he] felt" after he had entered "a free State," adding that he had "never been able to answer the question with any satisfaction" to himself.[37] Brown shared that in the years since escaping he had often "been asked how [he] felt" about being "regarded as a man" by White people after all his time in bondage. Like Douglass, Brown averred that he could "not say" that he had "ever answered the question yet."[38] Still, both authors tried to elucidate the moment when they first felt free, as did innumerable others.

While many authors depicted a spontaneous metamorphosis, writers like Douglass and Brown clarified that shedding the emotional expectations they absorbed while enslaved was a more complicated journey. For some the initial emotional epiphany of freedom was followed by a period of affective ambivalence. When Douglass attempted to capture the deluge of feelings he had about freedom, he called it "the highest excitement [he] ever experienced," but he conceded that this sentiment "very soon subsided; and [he] was again seized with a feeling of great insecurity," because he realized that he could be returned to slavery. That defenselessness tempered his elation, as did his feelings of isolation, as, after the incipient joy, "loneliness overcame" him. Far from the people he loved he also worried that he could not trust strangers, afraid that one would betray him to the "slave hunters."[39] Like Douglass, Jacobs was also thrilled to be free yet terribly lonely as she learned "what a desolate feeling it was to be alone among strangers."[40] Jacobs was plagued by a "constant feeling of insecurity," and though she yearned to "confide in" someone her options were limited, as she "had been so deceived by white people" that she "had lost some confidence in them." Whenever she did find people she could trust, her relief was palpable. In Philadelphia Jacobs was introduced to a free Black minister who housed her until she could travel safely to New York. This kindness helped mitigate Jacobs's fears and "insecurity," so that evening she "sought [her] pillow with feelings [she] had never carried to it before. [She] verily believed [herself] to be a free woman."[41] Far from being an immediate transformation, for many formerly enslaved people finding new support systems and allies was a slow emotional evolution that was nonetheless critical to their physical and affective survival.

Even before the passage of the Fugitive Slave Act, many runaway slaves felt vulnerable after reaching a free state, as numerous authors of slave narratives indicated that they did not feel an emotional liberation until they were in a country that had abolished slavery entirely. Peter Smith, who had been enslaved in Tennessee, did not feel secure until he arrived in Canada, which gave him the "feeling that there is more protection for him under the lion's paw than the eagle's wings."[42] David Barrett escaped enslavement in Kentucky first by fleeing to Ohio, but he disclosed in an 1837 interview that it was not until he reached Canada that he felt free, and affectively transformed, that once he "planted [his] feet upon British ground . . . [his] fears left [him] and [his] shackles fell!"[43] Levi Douglass posited that it was only once he was on

Canadian soil that he was freed from fear, confident that he could finally feel like a free man because no one could "make him afraid."[44] For many fugitive slaves their emotional liberation hinged on feeling safe from the grasp of slavery, and therefore, as Barrett and Douglass alluded, free from fear. Similarly, when Jacobs fled from New York to Boston to avoid being caught by Dr. Flint she reminisced that "the day after [her] arrival was one of the happiest of [her] life," because she was reunited with her children, and she "felt as if [she were] beyond the reach of the bloodhounds." But she knew that even this security was temporary, as long as Flint was after her. Jacobs eventually traveled to England with the Bruce family, to serve as their nanny and evade capture. Once more, Jacobs had an emotional renaissance. She detailed how once in London she felt immense relief as she slept, "for the first time, with the delightful consciousness of pure, unadulterated freedom."[45] By contrasting her anxieties in New York with the increased safety she felt in Boston, and the full security she finally experienced in England, Jacobs stressed how much fugitive slaves' feelings were tied to liberty and how their fear stifled affective freedom. Charting her emotional evolution from bondage to freedom reveals how the trope of an immediate affective metamorphosis belied the lengthy process many fugitive slaves underwent to leave behind the emotional politics of slavery.

Any sense of safety and affective freedom that runaway slaves felt evaporated with the Fugitive Slave Act. The Boston abolitionist paper *Liberty Bell* described the emotional climate in a meeting at Faneuil Hall shortly after the law passed. According to the author the hall was packed with fugitives who were "frightened, trembling . . . living in a state of mind bordering on distraction."[46] Jacobs also experienced the bill's chilling effect on runaways in New York. She was already nervous about her status as a fugitive, and that was "now greatly increased by the passage of the Fugitive Slave Law." She claimed that because of the law fugitives were once again "condemned to live in such incessant fear" of being recaptured. After returning from England Jacobs "lived in a state of anxiety" and "dreaded" the coming summer, when she worried Flint would return to the city to look for her. That inescapable apprehension rendered her a prisoner once more, as she woefully observed that she could not go outside "without trepidation at [her] heart."[47] By denying runaways affective liberty and plunging them back into a state of terror, the Fugitive Slave Act effectively extended the spatial parameters of the emotional politics of the slave South. For many fugitives, their sense of security and emotional liberation would not be fully restored until the Emancipation Proclamation.

Accounts of outpourings of joy at contraband camps after the Emancipation Proclamation was issued show that the affective transformation of liberation could be a communal experience. Several people wrote to abolitionist S. S. Jocelyn about the collective jubilation they witnessed at various camps. One recorded the scene at a Washington, DC, contraband camp, where "the first day of January was indeed a happy day to thousands. . . . In this camp there was much joy manifested by . . . freedmen."[48] James McCrea also wrote to Jocelyn in January of 1863 to chronicle his experience when the Proclamation was read out loud in a camp in South Carolina, and how the formerly enslaved people there "sent forth their glad shouts of joy . . . and the joyful sounds 'We are free, We are free' echoed far and wide."[49] As with formerly enslaved people who experienced an individual emotional change once they held their free papers, or reached a nation where slavery was already abolished, these letters demonstrate the shared affective impact of Abraham Lincoln's order. Of course, for many enslaved people throughout the slave South, January 1, 1863, did not bring freedom, so their emotional transition occurred not when the Proclamation was first issued, but when it was realized at the war's end. Lizzie Gibson asserted that as a slave in Virginia "the war came and went without [her] feeling it in the least. Then came Emancipation," which filled free people with joy that they could finally express "without being afraid" or having to censor their feelings.[50] Like authors who portrayed the emotional transformation of freedom as instantaneous, Stroyer represented the entire "spring of 1865" as though it were one joyful day, writing "the mocking birds and jays sing this morning more sweetly than ever before."[51]

An Affective Revolution

Emancipation was an affective revolution for former slaveholders as well. With the end of slavery an emotional lacuna opened up for them, as enslaved people would no longer function as dowries and living memento mori or serve as a source of honor and family affection. As they took stock of the social upheavals around them, White Southerners' responses to the postwar racial landscape were often couched in affective terms. They saw Emancipation, and the end of the war, not just as a military, political, and economic loss, but also as a personal blow to White Southern feelings and the emotional structure of slavery. Without these strictures former slaveholders were both unsure of how to emotionally react to formerly enslaved people and uncertain about the tenor of future interracial relations. Many White Southerners of all classes expressed loathing and resentment toward free Black people.[52] Union soldiers stationed in the South bore witness to this animosity. In the spring of 1865 Colonel Elias Wright voiced "concern over the sentiments" of White North Carolinians, who he claimed "regret" the ending of slavery and "deplore the presence of free negroes."

Many former slaveholders were also concerned about how free Black people felt about *them*, fearing the vengeful post-Emancipation backlash that proslavery authors had long predicted. Wright reported that just weeks after Lee's surrender White people in North Carolina "very much fear 'servile insurrection.'"[53] Former Confederate general Nathan Bedford Forrest justified the creation of the Ku Klux Klan in the months after war by arguing that the White supremacist terrorist group was necessary for defense since "the great fear" of White Southerners was of "a revolution something like San Domingo." Despite the fact that no postwar Toussaint L'Ouverture materialized, Forrest insisted "there was a general fear throughout the country that there would be an uprising" of formerly enslaved people, leading to "a war of races."[54] Race relations were still so charged in the years after war that multiple former slaveholders from Mississippi to South Carolina privately compared it to sitting atop "a volcano."[55] Rather than subsiding once Emancipation came and went peacefully, elite White Southerners' paranoid fantasies of former slaves seeking revenge only intensified.[56]

They may have felt fear, but what many former slaveholders conveyed was betrayal and grief over the affective relations they believed had been lost. Ryland Randolph, a former master and Alabama newspaper editor, alleged in 1869 that "Negroes, as bondsmen, were happier . . . than they are now," in contrast to the "grim countenances" born by free Black people and their newfound tendency to "grumble." Former slaveholder Charles Manigault also romanticized master-slave relationships and mourned their loss, complaining that once enslaved people were free "their heads and hearts are turned against . . . their former protectors and friends."[57] Like Randolph and Manigault, politician William Samford of Alabama placed the blame for any change in the affective climate on formerly enslaved people, opining in 1866 that "in spite of the most earnest efforts of their old masters to conciliate and satisfy them, the estrangement between the races increases in its extent and bitterness."[58]

These sources suggest that former slaveholders were quick to identify how free Black people's emotions had morphed, and how that abrupt shift had personally shaped them, but former slaveholders were less willing to admit their own role in the collective affective transformation. In her biography of slaveholder and politician James Henry Hammond, Drew Gilpin

Faust illustrates the emotional crisis Hammond underwent when enslaved people fled his plantation in droves at the war's end, "forc[ing]" Hammond "to recognize that what he had regarded as devotion from his slaves had been largely a form of manipulation." The mass exodus made Hammond confront how enslaved people had felt about him and how he had felt about them.[59] This array of reactions from members of the planter class demonstrates that there were a number of reasons why slaveholders depicted their feelings about the end of slavery in terms of loss and treachery rather than anger. Doing so placed the blame for any change in relations squarely on former slaves. Acting hurt over this emotional shift also enabled former slaveowners to protect their carefully curated image of themselves as benevolent slaveholders.

Some former slaveholders grappled with seeing the change in affective relations from the perspective of free people. After a formerly enslaved woman talked back to her, Susan Bradford felt "hurt and dazed," and she vowed that "never before had [she] a word of impudence from any of [her] black folks." The transformation in free people's demeanor may have "hurt" her, but it also made her realize the affective breadth of the revolution that had taken place. By responding to her with such "impudence," the free woman forced Bradford to confront how Emancipation had permanently altered the emotional politics of slavery, compelling her to understand that her servants were now "free to do as they pleased."[60] One member of the planter class even advocated for emotional reconciliation, writing in an 1867 letter that White Southerners had to cease giving "hard words and frowning looks" to free Black people in order to move forward socially and economically.[61]

Many of the objections members of the planter class had about interracial affective relations boiled down to their reluctance to adopt free labor after slavery's demise.[62] In particular, many White Southerners saw Black joy and pride as threats, believing them to be in direct conflict with White profits. In his 1865 diary, lawyer David Schenck griped that while newly free people were "going through this preliminary enjoyment" of liberty "the crops are suffering."[63] William Elliott wrote to his mother in the spring of 1866 to critique the comportment of free Black people as he tried to hire workers for his South Carolina plantation. He described a man named Jacob as "eaten up with self-esteem and selfishness." From Jacob's point of view, he may have been feeling proud and confident as a free man working for wages, but Elliott blamed Jacob's feelings for making him "indifferent" to work.[64]

The perception that formerly enslaved people were "selfish" or "indifferent" workers could have dramatic consequences, and it led to charged interactions between former slaveholders and free people. One White man from

Mississippi recalled an 1868 incident between Judge Henry Calhoon and a hired freedman. The man explained that the judge had "reprimand[ed]" a free Black man, supposedly for being idle, when the worker replied that "he was a free man now" and he would never again take orders from "any white man." According to the witness, "the judge was indignant at the negro's insolence" and threatened to whip the worker. The free man did not back down and instead raised his hoe. Before either dealt a blow the judge's son announced that in spite of the free man's work contract that he would shoot the formerly enslaved man if he did not leave the Calhoon estate at once.[65] This scene speaks volumes about how former slaveholders and formerly enslaved people were navigating the radically altered affective terrain of the postwar South. It is notable that the judge perceived the free man to be "insolen[t]," which in turn incited his own "indigna[tion]." Calhoon was confounded by the free man's unchecked display of emotions and wanted to physically discipline him for expressing feelings that would have been a death sentence for an enslaved person. Meanwhile, the worker openly scorned the emotional politics imposed by slavery, refusing to feign deference or suppress anger as a free man.

Because one of their primary tasks was arbitrating such contract disputes between landowners and newly freed people, members of the Freedmen's Bureau were deeply invested in the postwar affective relations of Black and White Southerners. However, members of the bureau had very different perceptions of the state of Southern interracial relations and thus widely diverging notions of how to ameliorate them. Appointed to head a Virginia branch of the bureau, Charles H. Burd attested that locally "the feeling between the white citizens and the freedmen is very good, and they seem mutually to understand and appreciate each other's distress."[66] Other Union officers and Freedmen's Bureau officials were less optimistic. As military governor of Kentucky, General John Palmer witnessed so much reluctance to accept Emancipation, and the new labor and affective dynamics that went with it, that he wrote a letter to local slaveholders that appeared in Louisville papers. Palmer warned that "to cling to the shadow of slavery . . . is to hug . . . discontent and disappointment to your bosoms," and instead slaveholders must endeavor to "gain or regain . . . the confidence of the colored people" in order to move forward. To Palmer the transition to Emancipation was an emotional challenge for both former slaveholders and formerly enslaved people. Notably though he argued that the problem could only be solved by sustained emotional labor from former slaveowners, that they were obliged to shore up trust with people of color after "generations" of "enjoying [their] unpaid and extorted labor."[67]

Freedmen's Bureau officer Rufus Saxton also worried that trust issues lay at the heart of the strained relations between former masters and newly free people, and he hinted that both groups bore responsibility for that. When Saxton was brought before the 1866 Joint Committee on Reconstruction to discuss Southern race relations in South Carolina and Georgia, he testified that planters did not truly "know" the people they had once enslaved, because "the system of slavery has been one of concealment on the part of the negro of all his feelings and his impulses." Saxton posited that the instinct to lie was "ingrained" in enslaved people, and that this "mutual distrust" hindered labor negotiations, because neither group had "any faith" in the other. Saxton concluded that it would take a great deal of time to dismantle this "distrust," as it was woven into the fabric of interracial affective relations and was reinforced through daily interactions.[68]

Amid tensions about the emotional politics of Reconstruction, many officials of the Freedmen's Bureau harbored their own prejudiced views about the affective capabilities of free people. Self-avowed abolitionist Samuel Gridley Howe surmised that "the white man seems to pass out of that phase of young life abounding in mirth and jollity" upon reaching adulthood, "while the Negro remains longer in it, if indeed he ever gets out at all." This implied that White people emotionally developed as they grew up, shedding the "mirth" and frivolous joy of youth, but that Black people never experienced an affective maturation. Even Freedmen's Bureau reports on the feelings and general well-being of free people that purported to praise them were infantilizing, perpetuating the idea that Black people were not in control of their emotions. An 1864 statement about the future for free Black people in the South noted that generally "the Africans were loyal men," that as laborers they were "willing" and "docile . . . not given to quarreling . . . cheerful and uncomplaining."[69] Another Freedmen's Bureau officer, Robert Dale Owen, anticipated that despite so many White Southerners' concerns, postwar-era race relations "would be mutually beneficial." According to Owen, Black people were "a knowing rather than a thinking race," who were "dominated by affections"; therefore, "the African would temper the cool and rational Anglo-Saxon."[70] Owen's hope that race relations could be "beneficial" to all involved was undermined by his speculation that Black people were emotional rather than "rational" or "thinking" and thus in need of White supervision and control. Tasked with assisting formerly enslaved people on their path to freedom, and impartially mediating conflicts between White employers and Black employees, instead many members of the Freedmen's Bureau embraced White supremacist planter propaganda that Black people lacked emotional self-governance and were happiest as laborers. This line of thinking could easily be used to justify legal and economic systems that encouraged "docile" Black people to cheerfully submit to the dominance of "cool and rational Anglo-Saxon[s]," just as they were expected to under slavery.

Challenging the Emotional Politics of Slavery

After the war, newly free people and former slaveholders were at odds over what post-Emancipation affective norms and interracial relations would be. The narratives of formerly enslaved people indicate that the newly freed thought that an affective coup was under way. As free people they firmly believed that they were entitled to the liberty of emotional expression that had been denied to them in slavery, and they worked to cast off the affective shackles of bondage. They did so by informing former slaveholders of how freedom had changed their affective relations, by uniting and protecting families that had been torn apart by slavery, and through a variety of deliberate and public acts of Black celebration.

One of the first ways that many formerly enslaved people defied the affective relations of slavery was by notifying former owners that they were happily free, like James Madison who wrote from Canada to let his former owner know that he was "now living in the enjoyment of liberty."[71] After Granville, John, and Lewis Bibb ran away together, the brothers delighted in the idea that the slaveholding family that had profited off of their "unrequited toil" was now "left . . . without a single slave." In an interview with their fellow fugitive and abolitionist brother Henry, they speculated gleefully that their former owner's "heart has been filled with grief over the loss of slaves."[72] It did not suffice to experience an emotional liberation upon becoming free; these formerly enslaved people wanted slaveholders to know about their affective change. Upon reaching freedom Brown longed to let his friends and family who remained in bondage know that he "was free!" But he also yearned to tell his former owners, joking that he was "anxious" to tell his former mistress "that she must get another coachman."[73] Brown was being glib in framing his message of liberation as a resignation notice, but he clearly wanted to let his master know he was not a slave and would no longer feign the deference expected of enslaved people. It was not just former enslaved people who fled North who seized the opportunity to tell planters that their emotional power dynamics had been irrevocably altered. An acquaintance of Chesnut mentioned that after the war he visited the formerly enslaved people on his Beaufort plantation. He vouched that they "were delighted to see [him]," expressing "overflowing affection," but they also "firmly and respectfully" told him that they "own this land now."[74] The newly freed people's "affection" paired with "firm . . . and respectful" claims of ownership delineated that their affective display had not changed, but their social relations had.

Other free people employed affective language with their former owners in order to reiterate that their relationship was forever changed. After planter Colonel Anderson wrote to his former slave, Jourdan Anderson, asking him to come back to his Tennessee plantation to work, Anderson responded with a letter thick with the language of endearment to negotiate. Anderson sent his "love" to the colonel's family and said he had been "proud . . . to call him master." But immediately following this compliment Anderson got down to business, requesting back pay for the decades that Anderson and his wife, Mandy, had worked for the colonel. Anderson calculated that those unpaid wages amounted to almost twelve thousand dollars, minus the colonel's minimal expenses for food, clothing, and health care. Still, Anderson framed the payment as an affective issue rather than a financial matter, adding that they had "concluded to test [the colonel's] sincerity" by asking him to send on their wages, assuring him that such an act would help them "forgive old scores." However, if the colonel "fail[ed] to pay," they stated that they could "have little faith" in his "promises in the future."[75] In discussing the terms of labor Anderson signaled that the master was now an employer, and the man who had once been "proud" to be his slave was now a free laborer and in a position to bargain. By requesting money as proof of the colonel's sincerity, Anderson also confirmed that trust was a valuable currency. The letter accentuated how much their affective dynamic had changed since Emancipation: no more was the onus on Anderson alone to be loyal; in the postslavery labor market, employer and employee had to be mutually faithful.

As the letter progressed it became evident that this was more than a written request for payment couched in affectionate language; Anderson, like the Bibbs and Brown, wanted his former owner to know how much he was enjoying his liberty. Anderson detailed what his life was like as a free man in Ohio, listing his good wages, better housing, and his children's access to education. But he also outlined the affective benefits of freedom, that his family was "kindly treated," including his wife, noting that "folks call her Mrs. Anderson," a more dignified appellation than "Mandy." In the North the Andersons received kindness and respect, and they could avoid the fear that their daughters would be "brought to shame by the violence and wickedness of their young masters" as they likely would be in the South. The more Anderson illustrated about their lives in the North, coupled with his request for almost twelve thousand dollars in back pay, the more obvious it became that the Andersons were never planning on returning to Tennessee.[76] Not content to merely seek out employers who would negotiate fair wages and terms of labor, newly free people desired emotional fulfillment as well as financial security. Some of that fulfillment, or at least satisfaction, may have been derived from the power to mock the people who once owned them and their families. Throughout the letter, Anderson subverted his relationship with his former owner with mounting sarcasm. Other free people may have exhibited even more open scorn toward slaveholders. One Kentucky planter wrote to President Andrew Johnson in July 1865 to complain that some formerly enslaved people who fled during the war were coming back "not . . . with the view of living in harmony with their old Master, but to taunt him with their free papers and threaten him with military power."[77] If the former slaveholder realized that free Black people's threats to appeal to authorities had driven him to write his own appeal to an authority, he did not mention it in his chronicle of grievances.

Another important way that free people repudiated the affective practices of slavery was in their efforts to locate loved ones that had been scattered by the auction block, self-liberation, or war. Formerly enslaved people employed a variety of tactics to do so, including both writing to Black churches throughout America and Canada with names and descriptions of their relatives and also traveling great distances to search for family.[78] Other free people enlisted the help of the Freedmen's Bureau and other military officials to find loved ones they had lost before or during the war. Having witnessed so many reunions of Black families during his time at the South Carolina Freedmen's Bureau, John William DeForest acknowledged how crucial it was for formerly enslaved people to locate their relatives, proclaiming that "the work of emancipation was incomplete until the families that had been dispersed by slavery were reunited."[79] One formerly enslaved man from Maryland named John Q. A. Dennis even wrote to the Secretary of War Edward Stanton in the summer of 1864, asking for help in finding and freeing three of his children.[80] Other newly freed parents sought the aid of local generals and military governors.[81] Such cases show that even before the Fourteenth Amendment was ratified free people firmly believed that the government was obliged to help its formerly enslaved citizens, including helping them defend their loved ones. If slavery had been defined by enslaved families being divided, freedom meant being able to protect one's family.[82]

In the months after war, many formerly enslaved people also took out ads in Black newspapers to seek information about lost loved ones. Such ads appeared in great numbers in the months after the war ended but would continue to be published for decades. In the brief announcements the author would generally provide their name and location, and any identifying information they could remember about the loved ones they were looking for, including names and places of former owners, or dates when they had been sold or separated.[83] One national Black newspaper offered this service for free in a weekly column for decades after the war. Their notification section opened with a message advising that "All Who Mourn a Missing Father, Mother, Brother, Son, Sister, Wife, Husband or Daughter, Should Read This," because "there are many persons throughout this great land who mourn some missing relative or friend," while "many home circles are rendered unhappy by the fact that there is a vacant chair."[84] By doing so the column was able to convey that the loss of an individual loved one was a personal tragedy and a widespread, shared experience, and that reuniting families was enough of a public good for the paper to offer the ads for free.

The ads themselves functioned as short, self-published slave narratives, as a few sentences could speak volumes about the heartbreak enslaved families endured and the lifelong efforts many enslaved people went through to try to find loved ones. Eliza Montgomery hoped to track down her brother Dick Bush, "the slave of Edward Bush, a negro trader," who was their father. In a matter of lines she recounted the harrowing tale of how this father had first sold their mother and left them as "very small children alone," before selling his own daughter away from her brother not long after. In 1892 when Eliza published the announcement she clearly still hoped to find the brother who had been her compatriot in anguish even though they'd been separated when they were "very small."[85] Jane Bell's brief 1871 notice was another tragic saga. She asked for information on "the whereabouts" of several children as she had "made every effort in [her] power to hear from them and having failed . . . [was] very unhappy." Bell mentioned that she had been separated from those children in 1858 before adding that she had "had *twenty-seven children*, and now [she did not] know the whereabouts of *but three*." More than an ad, this was a memoir of a mother's love and loss, and a testament to her untold efforts, having already found at least some information on twenty-four of those children.[86] Bell drew solace from at least having knowledge of her children. Nor was she alone. Many of the notices offered rewards simply for information, indicating that physically reuniting families was not the only objective of such ads. One announcement published just months after the war sought "information . . . of the whereabouts of Wesley Brooks," disclosing that his brother and sister were alive and searching for him, but "his father and mother, brother Sampson and sister Mary, are dead." Wesley's brother and sister might have included all those details in the hopes that it would help Wesley identify them and lead him back to them. But even if Wesley never read the ad, or saw his siblings again, they were still able to share their grief publicly. In this way, these notices could be both missing ads and obituaries, giving formerly enslaved people a space to speak their pain plainly to the world and to name those who had been lost, including, potentially, Wesley.[87] Though these searches were rarely successful the dedication to attempting to find loved ones underscores the precedent placed on restoring families that had been dismantled by slavery and slaveholders.[88]

Many formerly enslaved children had vivid recollections of the trials their parents endured to reassemble their families after the war. Nettie Henry's parents had different owners in Mississippi, so when her father's master moved to Texas after secession the Henry family was torn apart. She was only ten when the war ended, yet Henry remembered with pride that once free her father had "come back," having "walked almost all the way from Texas."[89] Anna Baker recalled that her mother's first action as a free woman was to confront Baker's owner and demand that he free her children. He initially refused, only acquiescing after Baker's mother enlisted the help of a Union Provost Marshal. Baker did not recognize her mother at first because she had been so young when her mother ran away, but her fear quickly subsided as her mother embraced her and carried her seven miles to their new home and their new life together.[90] By portraying the barriers parents and spouses faced in rebuilding their families, including time, distance, and reluctant slaveholders, these scenes prove how important it was to formerly enslaved people to find loved ones and how much they risked to do so. These passages also shed light on how free people were taking advantage of their newfound mobility and legal rights to challenge those obstacles. Years of forced separations and heartbreak could not be undone, but by prioritizing tracking down family free people showed that they hoped to right some of the affective wrongs of slavery. Finally, these texts demonstrate the lasting impression these brave acts of unconditional love made upon formerly enslaved children, as their parents introduced them to the affective possibilities of freedom.

Free people also signaled their commitment to reclaiming their families through their efforts to legally marry. The slave states did not allow lawful marriage for enslaved people, which left enslaved couples vulnerable to separation. Recognizing that many free Black people longed to legitimize their relationships post-Emancipation, Union General Lorenzo Thomas issued Special Order 15 declaring that any ordained minister could "solemnize the rites of marriage among the Freemen." A chaplain assigned to a Black regiment wrote to Thomas in 1865 to update him on the order's impact, stating that at his Arkansas camp "weddings . . . are very popular, and abundant." In the last month alone he had performed twenty-five ceremonies, "mostly [for] those who have families; & have been living together for years," suggesting that even couples in long-term relationships yearned for the legal validation of marriage. According to the chaplain free Black people were enthusiastically embracing marriage, particularly because they wanted to "have their Marriage Certificates, *Recorded*; in a *book furnished by the Government*." He surmised that they wanted that official proof in part because it created multiple records of their union, as the chaplain informed Thomas that a group of self-liberated people had been captured in January by Confederates and "had their Marriage Certificates . . . destroyed; and [been] roundly cursed, for having such papers."[91] The chaplain's letter shows how important free people felt it was to legitimize their relationships, and that many believed that legal marriage, and especially marriage certificates, provided newfound protection for their families. The fact that Confederate soldiers deliberately destroyed marriage certificates issued to Black people also emphasizes how threatening those legal unions were to some supporters of slavery.

Public Displays of Emotional Liberty

For many formerly enslaved people, true liberty did not just mean self-mastery, or freedom from violence; it meant being able to let one's feelings fly and to pursue pleasure, particularly publicly.[92] Following the war free people flouted the emotional politics of slavery by deriving pleasure from public spaces and performances that had been denied to them while in bondage. Free Black people's performative uses of public spaces, clothing, and holidays were in open defiance of the affective strictures and general oppression of slavery. But what formerly enslaved people viewed as opposition to generations of emotional censorship and coerced affective performances, White Southerners saw as a threat and an omen of social issues to come. White observers of all classes took particular umbrage over free Black people's public displays of joy or pride, increasingly referring to free people of color as "very insolent," "more and more insolent," and "impudent."[93] An Irish woman visiting Charleston immediately after the war grumbled that "the colored persons are awful sassy."[94] A Virginia newspaper reported in 1866 that the town of Petersburg was beset by Black soldiers, who were "strut[ting]" around "with an air of evident satisfaction." The author attributed this to them "feel[ing] the importance" of their contribution to the war, and that pride was allegedly clear "in every tone and action." The same paper later accused Black people of showing an "air of satisfaction" over the end of the war and slavery.[95] The author insinuated that any "satisfaction" or pride in the "importance" of free Black people was inherently disloyal, tantamount to delighting in the misery of Confederate defeat. They were not alone in asserting that Black joy came at the expense of White people. In recording the heightened racial tensions she experienced as she traveled in Reconstruction-era South Carolina, Elizabeth Botume made note of "the exultant faces of the Negroes, and the scowling faces of the rebels." To an observer like Botume, the two went hand in hand, because the joy of formerly enslaved people aroused anger and resentment for many White Southerners.[96] Taken in this light, every act of joy, pride, or confidence by a free Black person underlined for former slaveholders in particular how much had changed and how uncertain their future was.

In this tense climate, clothing became one of the sites where the emotional rights of the postwar South were hotly contested. The writings of White Southerners and formerly enslaved people indicate that free Black people found satisfaction in openly dressing as they pleased.[97] However, many White Southerners viewed the sartorial choices of free people as loaded affective signifiers. One Northern journalist examining race relations in the Reconstruction South spoke with several White women in North Carolina who lamented the number of free Black women wearing veils. An officer of the Freedmen's Bureau corroborated their complaint, informing the reporter that local White women saw Black women wearing black veils as such a "great offense" that many White women no longer wore black veils themselves. The reporter explained to his readers that a woman of color donning a black veil was interpreted as a grave insult to the "bitter, spiteful women whose passionate hearts nursed the Rebellion."[98] Southern women of all races were no stranger to death after four years of war, but the sight of Black women in mourning clothes elicited "spite" in White women rather than empathy or recognition of a shared experience of loss.[99] Perhaps the White women who were angered by these expressions of mourning inferred that a woman of color in a black veil was grieving over someone who died fighting for the Union. Or perhaps since arguments about racialized emotional difference had long been used to bolster slavery and White supremacy, many White Southern women simply could not acknowledge that sorrow and grief crossed the color line.

Black veils were not the only articles of clothing that were larded with emotions, representing freedom of affective self-expression for Black people while inspiring rage in White Southerners. Many Black veterans felt great pride about their service, represented by their Union uniforms, but some White Southerners saw their choice of garment as a celebration of Confederate loss. As a result, Black men in blue uniforms were excoriated in newspaper editorials and physically assaulted throughout the South.[100] Black people who wore stylish clothing were also viewed as dangerous to the Southern racial order. In the aftermath of war a White woman remarked that free Black women's fancy dress and proud "swaggering air" were enough to "inspire the most casual observer with a feeling of contempt" for them.[101] A formerly enslaved person mentioned that in Georgia "white men cut the clothes from the backs of ex-slaves" if they were deemed too "well-dressed."[102] For many White Southerners, Union uniforms and fine clothing were concrete reminders of defeat and of the dramatic revolution in race and labor relations. For Black people, clothes were a site for modeling new affective norms.

Free Black people also resisted the affective restrictions imposed by slavery in a collective, public manner, through parades, rallies, and holidays. A parade held in Charleston on March 21, 1865, showcased the mix of emotions free people were feeling about the end of slavery. The *New York Times* documented that the free people's parade, "in honor of their liberation from slavery," was "large and enthusiastic," drawing roughly four thousand people. The reporter was particularly taken with the symbolism involved, describing a slave auction scene staged on the back of a cart, where two Black women pantomimed being sold by a man playing auctioneer who shouted "how much am I offered?" as the cart rolled along. As though to punctuate the tragic scene that was so familiar to its audience, the next cart was a "mock hearse" bearing a coffin labeled "Slavery is dead," with solemn women in mourning garb processing behind. The reporter did not understand why the women appeared so somber, since he would assume "that the colored people would not be greatly afflicted with grief after having been assured of their freedom."[103] What the reporter missed was that the parade epitomized the complicated emotions produced by the dawn of freedom. Though enslaved people were generally overjoyed at the advent of Emancipation, a funeral for slavery did not necessarily indicate nostalgia for the institution, but rather a desire to acknowledge the sorrows of bondage, including the loss of loved ones by death or sale at the auction block.

The funeral was also satirical in purpose, allowing formerly enslaved people to commemorate the end of slavery while mocking any White Southerners who grieved the loss of the institution.[104] In doing so, the parade organizers highlighted the extent to which former slaveholders' feelings were based on slavery. Pretending to mourn the demise of slavery also reiterated the performative nature of emotions, perhaps giving further weight to former slaveowners' anxieties that enslaved people's supposed contentment and affection had been feigned all along. The *Times* journalist may have misunderstood the layered meanings of the pageant, including the potential irreverent message of the funeral, but he could not help but notice the White spectators' reactions, noting that "the expression on the countenances of many" in the crowd showed that the parade was "not altogether agreeable" to them, though "they wisely swallowed objections."[105] The crowd in Charleston may have quashed their opinions about the procession, but other White Southerners were less muted in their responses to celebrations of Black freedom. An 1868 article in the *Macon Telegraph* expressed "outrage" over a recent rally of Black people for several Republican candidates, saying, "A more humiliating scene was never witnessed."[106] This provided telling insights into why White Southerners were so upset by events thrown by the Black community. According to the author these celebrations did not just anger White Southerners, they provoked shame by reminding them of their military and social defeat.

In the Reconstruction period many White Southerners were particularly threatened by manifestations of Black joy. In an 1868 article in *Harper's New Monthly Magazine* novelist Harriet Spofford chronicled a recent "celebration of emancipation" held in Washington, DC. Though Spofford lauded the participants at first for processing in a "serious and stately" fashion, her other descriptions of the event undermined this praise. Spofford depicted the celebration as "an endless black cloud" or "mob," and she complained that "the throngs that compose it frolic . . . in exuberance and effervescence that know no bounds." While she could admit that the celebrants were "serious and stately," her comments suggested that there was something sinister about Black people celebrating, that their collective "effervescence" turned the participants into an unindividuated "black cloud" or "mob." Her wording also hinted that Black people could not restrain their emotions, for their feelings "know no bounds."[107] The article illuminates how White people from the North and South were processing the demise of the emotional politics of slavery. After decades of claiming that enslaved people were happy in bondage, many White people were now confronted with, and disturbed by, Black people's authentic joy over liberation. Of course, Black joy could only be seen as a menace by those who believed that Black rejoicing was fundamentally synonymous with White sorrow. To cope with anxieties about Black "exuberance," and about changes in race relations more generally, people like Spofford resorted to the White supremacist, proslavery rhetoric that Black people felt and expressed emotions differently and thus needed to be controlled.

Parades were not the only venue for displaying Black freedom and jubilation. Black Southerners also created and reappropriated holidays in order to deconstruct the emotional rituals of slavery. This was especially clear in postwar celebrations of January first, the anniversary of the Emancipation Proclamation being issued. For enslaved people the first of the year held tragic associations as the day that contracts for hiring out enslaved people for the upcoming year began. As a result, enslaved people feared the dawn of what some called "heartbreak day," as it often heralded separation from loved ones who were to be leased out.[108] Though only a fraction of the millions of people enslaved were actually freed on January 1, 1863, within weeks of the Proclamation's passage Frederick Douglass was among those calling for the day to be commemorated, vowing that it would be an "incomparably greater" holiday than July Fourth.[109] Though most enslaved people were not freed until the end of the war, by honoring the Emancipation Proclamation on a date that had long had devastating effects on enslaved families, Black people began the process of dismantling the significance of that fated day. By January 1, 1866, preacher Henry McNeal Turner announced in a sermon marking the anniversary that "the most bitter day of the year . . . shall henceforth and forever be filled with acclamations of the wildest joy and ecstasy."[110] By redefining January first as a day of exuberant "joy," rather than sorrow and loss, formerly enslaved people were consciously reclaiming the day and altering its emotional connotations. Its past as a day when families were divided was not forgotten, but formerly enslaved people were now free to determine the meaning and memory of that day for themselves.

Because most enslaved people were not freed until after Southern surrender many wanted to celebrate their Emancipation at the anniversary of the war's end. In Texas news of Confederate surrender and Emancipation was announced on June 19, 1865, leading to an annual celebration of "Juneteenth" regionally and later nationally to mark when all enslaved people were finally freed. Black and White Southerners recognized that freedom celebrations were construed as a direct challenge to the postwar emotional status quo. When free people in Richmond decided to organize an event in April of 1866 to mark the day Union troops liberated the city they knew that doing so might upset local White people, so event planners distributed broadsides to "respectfully inform the public that THEY DO NOT INTEND to celebrate the failure of the Confederacy." In spite of these conciliatory efforts numerous newspapers condemned the occasion, with editorials calling it "a jollification on the saddest of days" and warning that they would "wade through blood before the nigger shall celebrate the day." Incited by such rhetoric White residents of Richmond violently contested what was perceived as affective mutiny, burning down a Black church and threatening more violence if the event took place.[111] From editorial pages to the cinders of Black institutions, the holiday became a battleground for the emotional politics of the Reconstruction South. Black organizers anticipated the possible effect on the White populace, and the prospect of bloodshed, and they saw the need to differentiate between a commemoration of freedom and a celebration of White suffering. Nonetheless, White residents of Richmond interpreted any enactment of Black joy as an affront and hoped to quell it by spreading fear in the Black community. Remarkably the organizers would not be intimidated, and the celebration went on as planned.

Resisting Black Emotional Freedom

Faced with free Black people who could no longer be emotionally mastered, or affectively disciplined as they had been under slavery, White people turned to both legal and extralegal means to reinstate the social order of the emotional politics of slavery. As an article from the *Nation* from August of 1865 asserted, "White southerners sought to 'retain the slaveholding spirit without keeping the slaves.'"[112] In the years after the war many White Southerners resorted to illegal methods to emotionally master free people, employing real or implied violence against individual free people in order to foster a collective state of fear among Black Southerners. White terrorist organizations like the Ku Klux Klan perpetuated forms of affective discipline used during slavery, wielding dread to establish political and social control in the South. Accounts of formerly enslaved people reveal widespread fear of such White terrorist organizations, particularly in more isolated, rural areas.[113] A primary goal was to systematically frighten Black people into voting Democrat or to otherwise stifle the Republican vote. As one formerly enslaved man from Mississippi explained, "The Yankees tried to get men to vote, but not many did 'cause they was scared of the Ku Kluxers."[114]

The scope of these terrorist tactics, and their far-reaching political implications, came to light during congressional inquiries into the Klan's activities. A Black woman from South Carolina named Harriet Simril testified about how masked Klansmen visited her home three times, calling her husband a "radical" and vowing that "if he joined the democratic ticket they would have no more to do with him." When her husband persisted in his allegiance to the Republicans, the Klansmen visited the Simrils a final time, hauling Harriet into the street and repeatedly raping her. The Simrils spent the next four nights hiding in the woods, terrified the men would return. Abram Colby recounted how, after Emancipation, he was elected to the Georgia state legislature as a Republican and promptly offered a bribe by local Democrats to vacate his seat. Days after Colby refused, dozens of Klansmen arrived at his home, and when he denied their request again they beat him for hours. Colby testified that the "worst thing about the whole matter" was that his family saw him be dragged into the woods and whipped. When his daughter followed and pleaded with the men not to take her father they aimed a gun at her. Colby swore to the congressional panel that this "actually frightened her to death," as "she never got over it until she died" less than a year later.[115]

The Colby case elucidates how Black community leaders and politicians were specifically targeted in the hopes that threatening or assaulting an influential person would terrify the broader community into compliance. James Alston, for example, was a Republican member of the Alabama state legislature. White Montgomery citizens offered Alston thousands of dollars to convince local Black men to vote for Democrats. When Alston turned them down, masked gunmen fired hundreds of rounds into his home, wounding Alston's wife and child. After receiving mounting death threats, the Alstons were forced to flee. The Klan also targeted ministers for their prominent role in the Black community. A Baptist deacon from Alabama spoke before the congressional committee about how his church was burned down because the Klan believed the congregants "were too strong republicans" and they hoped to "break up this arrangement of the republicans." Even more symbolically the Klan set fire to the church, which the congregation had built themselves, on January 1, the anniversary of Emancipation.[116] In spite of the Enforcement Acts passed in 1870 and 1871 to curtail White supremacist terrorist groups, an 1875 report to Congress on White terrorism in Mississippi noted that free Black people throughout the state were "thoroughly intimidated, and will not vote . . . for fear of their lives." According to the report, these scare tactics were highly successful, as no Republicans had won in the last election.[117]

The Klan deployed fear to limit the Republican vote and scare Black communities in general, but they also wielded violence in order to discourage emotions and affective expressions that they deemed inappropriate for free Black people. A Black woman named Caroline Smith was woken up one night in 1871 when Klansmen arrived at her Georgia home. Ten men took turns whipping her, supposedly for her defiance to a White woman, as one of the assailants warned Smith "we don't want to hear any big talk; and don't sass any white ladies." Nor was this an isolated incident. Two days after Smith spoke before Congress, another Black woman from Georgia, Sarah Ann Sturtevant, testified that she was stripped to the waist, beaten, kicked, and pistol-whipped, all as a preemptive measure, "for fear [she] would sauce [sass] white women."[118] It is unclear what, if anything, Smith and Sturtevant had done to make those White men believe that they had or would show disrespect to White women. Perhaps the only infraction they had committed was being Black women who dared to be confident, which was coded by White Southerners as "sass" and treated as a punishable offense.

White supremacist terrorist groups and lynch mobs also tried to curtail expressions of Black joy through violence. Sam McAllum recalled that during Reconstruction some African Americans in Meridian, Mississippi, "were havin' a party one Sat'day night" at the home of a formerly enslaved man named Miler Hampton when some White men in disguise arrived on horseback, accusing Hampton of having "done somethin' bad," without elaborating further. The masked men captured Hampton without any struggle from the partygoers since, as McAllum confessed, they "were all scared" they would be killed, too, if they fought back. Hampton was murdered that night. Interestingly, while the vigilantes insinuated that Hampton had committed some infraction other than throwing a party, some of Hampton's guests saw a clear link between the festivities and the appearance of the lynch mob. This is evident in the reaction of those who witnessed Hampton's abduction. McAllum and the other men who had been in attendance at Hampton's home went to town the following day to "buy all the ammunition" they could get" because they were "having another party the next week," remarking dryly that the masked murderers "didn't come to that party."[119] This event exemplifies the ways that some White Southerners deployed violence to incite fear and suppress emotions like joy in the Black community. But it also offers insights into how some Black people were responding, willing to fight for their inalienable right to pursue happiness, including by throwing a party on a Saturday night.

After Emancipation elite White Southerners were desperate to find alternatives to the affective strictures of slavery in the hopes of keeping free Black people meek and manageable. Former slaveholders seemed particularly furious that free Black people were no longer forced to maintain an attitude of servile compliance in the presence of White people, nor compelled to smother their emotions as they had while enslaved. A Freedmen's Bureau agent shared that White Southerners were "quite indignant if they are not treated with the same deference that they were accustomed to" from enslaved people.[120] The answer to former slaveholders' anxieties about losing the hierarchies of slavery lay in writing new laws like the Black Codes, which codified affective norms and behavior for free Black people. Such laws circumscribed interracial affective relations and, in doing so, restored some of the emotional power dynamics of bondage. Mississippi's Black Code prohibited "insulting gestures, languages or acts" toward White people.[121] Florida's version defined the punishments for affective infractions, stating that anyone convicted of "willful disobedience . . . impudence . . . [or] disrespect to his employer" could be "hired out . . . imprisoned or whipped." Every Black Code included a statute that simultaneously legalized marriage between free Black people and also barred interracial marriage or sexual relations.[122] Through these statutes affective norms that had been custom under slavery became law, and the expectation returned that Black people must perform subservience and mask their feelings.

Some White employers also tried to legally preserve the emotional politics of slavery through labor contracts. In an 1886 contract between a Black sharecropper named Fenner Powell and a White landlord named A. T. Mial, Powell agreed to work land on Mial's North Carolina plantation for one year. In addition to detailing what tools and food Mial would provide for the year the document stated that "Powell agrees to work faithfully and diligently . . . and to be respectful in manners and deportment to . . . Mial."[123] Not content to have contracted labor, White employers like Powell hoped to formalize interracial affective relations, legally obligating laborers to maintain the emotional hierarchies so familiar under slavery, including the expectation of deference and loyalty.

When they could not control the emotions of living, breathing, free Black people, some White Southern authors took to memoirs, history, and literature to create the scenes of racialized affective dominance that they were nostalgic for. This was evident in the opening of Charles Colcock Jones's 1888 book entitled *Negro Myths from the Georgia Coast*, which he dedicated "in memory of Monte Video Plantation and . . . the family servants whose fidelity and affection contributed so materially to its comfort and happiness."[124] Abstractly referring to the "happiness" of the "plantation" as a whole suggested that the supposed contentment of slavery had been universally shared, even as enslaved people "materially" created those feelings. The emotional labor performed by enslaved people was downplayed in this dedication, just as the euphemistic language of "servants" elided the violence of slavery. Those "family servants" were now free women and men, but the expectation remained that they would be loyal and loving. The fantasy that the emotional support system of slavery remained steadfastly in place even after Emancipation was particularly insidious revisionism, allowing former slaveholders to believe that the emotional labors of enslaved people had been genuine rather than coerced. Nor was the myth of faithful, loving enslaved people solely attractive to former slaveholding Southern audiences. Quite the contrary, the nationwide popularity of "plantation nostalgia" literature and minstrel shows, and products like Aunt Jemima pancake mix illuminated that White longing for the emotional politics of slavery defied class and region. These rosy portraits of mutual and affectionate master-slave relations, consumed by audiences throughout the United States, were a critical component of the postwar, "Lost Cause" ideology, leading to the demise of Reconstruction and later serving as a defense of Jim Crow segregation.[125]

* * *

In the wake of Emancipation free Black people sought to establish new feelings and emotional practices, while former members of the slaveocracy tried desperately to maintain the affective relations and norms of slavery. In spite of their efforts to reinstate the emotional caste system of slavery post-Emancipation, many White Southerners continued to take offense to emotional expressions by Black people that they perceived as inappropriate. Almost a decade after Reconstruction ended, South Carolina poet Paul Hamilton Hayne decried the "insubordination and impudence" of Black people.[126] In the absence of federal occupation, even with increasingly restrictive laws that eroded rights for African Americans and prescribed Black feelings, many White Southerners continued to label any perceived misstep by Black people as "impudence," a catch-all for condemning and criminalizing Black behavior. In response to this perceived affective destabilization, White Southerners of all classes deployed legal and extralegal modes of violence and social control to reestablish the racialized emotional hierarchies of slavery. Many Black people, in turn, lost hope in the promise of Reconstruction, instead experiencing, as W. E. B. Du Bois noted, "bitter disappointment." Frustrated over efforts to perpetuate the dynamics of slavery, Du Bois observed that former slaveowners were "determined to perpetuate slavery under another name." That name, it soon became evident, was Jim Crow.[127]

Nevertheless, the repressive affective strictures of the Jim Crow South reinforced for many African Americans the urgent need to resist those emotional fetters. Seeking to exercise their freedom of affective expression, Black people in the postwar period used a variety of sites, including their bodies and public spaces, to deconstruct the emotional politics of slavery and to forge new affective norms, even amid disappointment over the death of Reconstruction-era progress. Just as free Black people in Richmond refused to sacrifice their celebration of freedom in the face of White supremacist intimidation, some formerly enslaved people combated the resurrection of the affective restrictions and censorship of slavery. They had been promised the inalienable right to the pursuit of happiness, so the denial of Black emotional liberty through legal and illegal means was not just an emotional disenfranchisement, but a political one. As a result, it would have far-reaching ramifications on Southern society and race relations, leaving a legacy of the emotional politics of slavery that reverberated for generations to come.

EPILOGUE

"The Sentiment Left by Slavery Is Still with Us"

Thirty years after the cessation of the Civil War, the prolific Frederick Douglass continued to denounce the racial injustice that plagued the nation, chronicling the rising number of lynchings of Black people by White vigilantes. Douglass lamented that the emotional politics of slavery still cast a shadow over the South. He observed that Black people were viewed with a "suspicion and increasing hate" that was rooted in slavery, and that this antipathy led White legal authorities to turn a blind eye when Black people were lynched by vengeful White mobs. Douglass contended that it was no coincidence that White people could "justify murderous assault upon a long enslaved and hence a hated people." White contempt for Black people was stoked over centuries of bondage and was considered justification enough for killing Black people for real or imagined crimes post-Emancipation. Douglass hinted that while it was supposedly White fears of Black rapists that motivated lynchings, it was Black Southerners who were left in a state of trepidation lest they or their loved ones become victims of a White riot. Watching as White resentment fomented a climate of terror meant to control the Southern Black population, the parallels to the emotional dynamics of slavery were unmistakable, leading Douglass to ruefully note that "the sentiment left by slavery is still with us."[1]

For Douglass both the dilemma and the answer were affective: Douglass argued that racial inequality should matter to all Americans, as "the solution" to racial violence and injustice "involves the honour or dishonour, the glory or shame, the happiness or misery, of the whole American people."[2] Less than a decade later, author W. E. B. Du Bois expressed similar concerns about the role of emotions, particularly fear, in post-Reconstruction race relations. Du Bois warned that "on the tainted air broods fear. Three centuries' thought has been the raising and unveiling of that bowed human heart," culminating at the turn of the century, leading Du Bois to famously predict that "the problem of the Twentieth Century is the problem of the color-line."[3] Like Douglass, Du Bois implied that the "problem" at the heart of race relations hinged on emotions, from the affective norms that had "bowed the human heart[s]" of the nation for generations, to the "fear" used to preserve the emotional dynamics of bondage.

Enslaved people had long been expected to perform certain emotions and camouflage others, to maintain the façade of the happy slave in front of slaveholders who believed that Black people felt less acutely, if at all. Faced with these affective restrictions, enslaved people and free Black people implicitly and explicitly challenged the idea that they were unfeeling or lacked strong familial ties and insisted that Emancipation meant not just legal and political freedom, but emotional liberation. As free people they could cast off the racialized affective norms forced upon them in slavery. No longer compelled to suppress sorrow and anger, or feign contentment and deference, no longer subjected to affective discipline and the division of their families, formerly enslaved people actively pursued happiness and the right to lead unimpeded, full emotional lives. But, devastated by the dual losses of military defeat and Emancipation, many White Southerners fought tooth and nail to maintain antebellum racial hierarchies, including the affective norms and expectations that had reinforced slavery for centuries. As a result, the legacy of the emotional politics of slavery continued long after Emancipation. Postwar affective norms were not identical to those that existed in the slave South, but they incorporated as many of the emotional customs of the institution as possible. Just as it had been under slavery, fear remained the quintessential ingredient of the emotional politics of postwar race relations.

Fear and Jim Crow

Scholars who study the history of emotions have shown that fear is both a physiological response and a social construct. Throughout the nineteenth century prescriptive literature dictated that being afraid was at odds with rational thought, and therefore it needed to be surmounted.[4] But during Reconstruction it became evident that when White Southerners inspired fear in free Black people it was not illogical, it was a systemic strategy for maintaining economic, political, and social White supremacy. Black Southerners recognized that White intimidation tactics were a deliberate backlash against the rights that African Americans had won in the years after war. In his memoir of his childhood in Mississippi, Richard Wright wrote extensively about emotions and race relations in the Jim Crow South, opining that when Black people "try to assert a claim to their birthright, whites retaliate with terror."[5] This White terror campaign was experienced by Black Southerners in ways both dramatic and mundane, knit into the cultural memory, linking the lived Black experience of past and present.[6] Slavery was gone, but White supremacist violence was still the modus operandi for scaring Black Southerners into submission and for exorcising manifold White anxieties.

Throughout the Jim Crow era White elites wrote laws to limit the freedoms of Southern Black people, including disenfranchising them.[7] These policies coincided with growing White nostalgia for antebellum affective relationships, all set against a backdrop of increasing national tensions around class, race, and the first wave of the Great Migration.[8] In his 1908 work on American racial relations, journalist Ray Stannard Baker shared that "many Southerners look back wistfully to the faithful . . . cheerful, old plantation Negro, and deplore his disappearance," making them "want the New South, but the old Negro."[9] One North Carolina lawmaker invoked that line of reasoning while defending Jim Crow and lynching, vowing that no Northerner could, in his words, "comprehend that ineffable, indescribable, unspeakable love that every southern man feels for the old black nurse who took care of him in childhood." Just as in proslavery ideology the myth of the happy slave existed as a foil to nightmarish figures like Nat Turner, in the twentieth century the legal and illegal violence of Jim Crow was packaged with gauzy nostalgia, justified by delineating the spectrum from loving, memorialized mammy to savage Black rapist. In this way the supposed love, always framed as mutual, of Black women was used to condone violence against Black people who were perceived to transgress the color line, including its racialized emotional parameters.[10] The increasing de jure segregation of public and private facilities went hand in hand with de facto social prescriptions that dictated the rules of interracial engagement, working in tandem to resurrect the affective hierarchies of slavery. Even decades after Emancipation Black Southerners were expected to embody deference and reverence toward White people at all times.[11] Authentic emotions, particularly negative feelings, were to be muted. Theories of racialized emotional differences, long championed by advocates for slavery, also persisted into the Jim Crow period. Civil Rights activist Jo Ann Robinson recalled in her memoir that in the Georgia of her childhood Black people were "still being treated as . . . things without feelings, not human beings."[12]

No text demonstrates how the emotional politics of slavery were resuscitated better than Richard Wright's memoir *Black Boy*, in which he wrote at length about growing up in the suffocating affective environment of Jim Crow. Paralleling the internal journey described in so many slave narratives, Wright discussed both how he learned the affective norms of Jim Crow as a child and how he attempted to perform and censor feelings, before going North in search of emotional freedom. For some Black children, learning to navigate Southern race relations was synonymous with learning to fear White people. Wright detailed this process, recalling that before he was even ten the mere mention of "white people" triggered a flood of "anxiety," until "a dread of white people now came to live permanently in my feelings and imagination."[13]

Wright's state of perpetual "dread" was exacerbated by knowing the consequences that awaited any Black people who upset the racialized emotional power dynamics of Jim Crow. Just as enslaved people knew they needed to appear happy and ingratiating to escape punishment, the racial etiquette of the South required that Black people suppress anger and sorrow, instead appearing meek and contented. Civil Rights activist Benjamin Mays saw those racialized affective performances constantly as a child in South Carolina at the turn of the twentieth century, explaining in his autobiography that in his town "most Negroes grinned, cringed, and kowtowed in the presence of white people."[14] Wright witnessed that daily emotional burlesque as well, but he voiced disdain for Black Southerners who enacted feelings for White audiences, including a Black coworker who "in the presence of whites . . . would play the role of a clown."[15]

Still, Wright recognized that Black Southerners were caught in a trap, loath to adopt certain emotions but afraid to not meet White people's affective expectations. Wright knew that many of his Black coworkers "hated and feared the whites," but if a White person appeared they "assumed silent, obedient smiles" and "false heartiness." Here was another way that the emotional politics of Jim Crow were internalized and built on the back of fear. Wright could profess contempt for the antics of his "clown[ish]" coworker, singing for White approval and money, but Wright, too, felt complicit in maintaining the affective hierarchies that White Southerners demanded. He knew that performing or hiding emotions was a matter of survival for Black Southerners, and also how much was at stake when choosing to counterfeit or cloak specific feelings. As Wright confessed, "The safety of my life in the South depended upon how well I concealed from all whites what I felt," for if he were to "lose control" of his emotions it would be a "sentence of death."[16]

In the Jim Crow South, Black people learned what feelings to feign and which to cover up based on direct and indirect feedback from White sources. At times the White press explicitly told Black Southerners which feelings to curb, and when. After a jury of White men dropped charges against a White man accused of raping a Black Montgomery woman in 1949, the local paper declared that "those colored people who have felt humiliated or angered over the Perkins case can now abate those emotions."[17] Black Southerners were also indoctrinated in the affective expectations of Jim Crow through more informal channels, primarily through their routine interactions with White people. Wright gleaned from conversations with White Southerners that they "did not like to discuss" a variety of topics including "Jack Johnson . . . the Civil War . . . the 13th, 14th, and 15th Amendments to the Constitution; or any topic calling for positive knowledge or manly self-assertion on the part of the Negro." Any remark that might be construed as praise for Black people, or that touched upon the subject of Black pride or courage, was to be avoided, leading Wright to deduce that White Southerners believed Black people should repress those feelings in particular.[18] Like Wright, Rosa Parks was reminded of how threatening Black dignity was to White people after seeing the reception of Black World War II veterans who returned to the South proud of their accomplishments and hoping for equal treatment. According to Parks, "Whites didn't like Blacks having that kind of attitude."[19] This suggests that what White Southerners wanted from Black people was less a performance of deference than a total absence of self-confidence.

From interactions with White employers, Black Southerners absorbed what emotions they should tamp down on the job. As an adolescent Wright needed to help support his struggling family, so he applied to do housework for a White family. In the interview Wright's would-be employer told him firmly "we don't want a sassy nigger." Wright responded that he was "not sassy," and he was told to return the following day at dawn to commence work.[20] This highlights what affective performances White employers found desirable or objectionable and what gradations of emotion were permissible for Black people. A Black employee should appear happy, but never verge on "sassy," which carried connotations of too much confidence and too little reverence.

Because of the ubiquitous messaging about what emotions were appropriate, and because failure to affectively masquerade could be a death sentence, it speaks volumes that some Black Southerners still could not bring themselves to simulate contentment in the face of segregation and injustice. Mays knew many Black Southerners enacted the expected emotions, but he also saw others that would not, and that "those who could not take such subservience" escaped to nearby cities or fled North.[21] This was Wright's eventual trajectory, as he found that as time went on he could no longer adopt the compulsory racialized emotions of Jim Crow. After a White Southerner observed that Wright did not "laugh and talk like other niggers" Wright was well aware of the dangers of failing to comply, but he could not maintain his false cheer; he "would remember to dissemble for short periods then . . . forget" and "act human again." It became even more difficult for Wright to fake happiness and cloak his contempt once he decided to leave the South. Worried that his intentions would be read on his face and perceived as traitorous, he tried to quash his true sentiments, and in their place he "smiled each day, fighting desperately . . . to keep [his] disposition seemingly sunny." He suspected that this carefully crafted mask was slipping, and he worried that he was not fooling his White boss, even when Wright "laughed in the way" he was "expected . . . to laugh." By depicting his boss's "preoccupation with curbing [his] impulses . . . [and] expressions," and how every night he was overwrought by his daily cache of "banked emotions," Wright was harrowing proof that constantly affectively performing and self-monitoring was emotionally and physically exhausting.[22]

Wright found some relief from the incessant barrage of dread when he moved from his rural Mississippi town to Memphis at the age of seventeen. He could still "detect disdain and hatred" in the way White people treated him, but it was less than what Wright was subjected to in rural Jackson. Yet even in Memphis Wright experienced life as a "continuously contained dream of terror, tension, and anxiety," making him contemplate fleeing the South entirely to "escape the pressure of fear." As nervous as he was to leave the South for the first time, Wright was also concerned about the extent to which he had internalized White supremacist affective expectations during his formative years. As he explained, growing up in the Jim Crow South, "I had learned to live with hate. But to feel that there were feelings denied me . . . that more than anything else hurt."[23] In the end what drove Wright North was the same impulse that compelled so many enslaved people to seek freedom: a desire for an emotional liberation that he believed was unattainable if he remained in the South.

But just as Harriet Jacobs and Douglass found that it took them time to unlearn the emotional dynamics of slavery, Wright was also surprised by how deeply ingrained the racialized affective norms of Jim Crow were when he arrived in Chicago in 1927. Having been "schooled to present an unalteringly smiling face" to White people, Wright found that he continued to perform emotions while his "true feelings raced along underground, hidden."

Like Jacobs and Douglass, Wright was also astonished to see that some of the affective hierarchies he associated with the South persisted in the North. Though he initially believed that in Chicago "there was no racial fear," he quickly saw that "color hate" existed in the North as well, simmering just below the surface, like his own true feelings.[24] As Douglass and Du Bois predicted decades before, the racialized emotional caste system of Jim Crow was not exclusive to the South and would need sustained systemic attention if it was to be fully extinguished.

Fear and the Civil Rights Movement

Whether it was fueled by the confidence of Black veterans returning from wars abroad, or an emboldening effect from the *Brown v. Board of Education* ruling, there was an emotional shift under way in the South in the wake of World War II.[25] The omnipresent racialized terror that Wright worked to escape continued to stifle Black Southerners, but there was growing momentum among African Americans throughout the South to more openly resist segregation and disenfranchisement.[26] White Southerners were reluctant to lose their grip on power, so as a Civil Rights movement coalesced the South saw an upsurge of White supremacist terrorist violence. This included a rise in lynchings, cross burnings, and membership in organizations like the Ku Klux Klan, in an effort to maintain the emotional politics of Jim Crow and intimidate Black Southerners who tried to vote or otherwise challenge the status quo.[27] Many White Southerners clearly worried that more rights for Black people meant a loss of rights for themselves. Once those White Southerners believed they were operating in a zero-sum political arena, their fears and anxieties were a volatile concoction, explosively triggered by even the inference of an interracial emotional transgression.[28]

Few cases were more indicative of White anxiety over losing the affective norms of Jim Crow, and of the ways White fear was used to justify violence, than the murder of Emmett Till. Fifteen months after the *Brown* ruling heralded the beginning of the long journey to end de jure segregation, a fourteen-year-old Black boy named Emmett Till traveled from Chicago to visit family in Money, Mississippi. The fact that he was from Chicago is often highlighted as a key component of the narrative, intended to convey that Till was not accustomed to the affective norms of Jim Crow, which dictated that Black men must be genial to, but never familiar with, White people, especially White women. It is unclear if Till winked, whistled, or made a cheeky comment to the White wife of a local grocery store owner; perhaps he did little more than exude cheer and confidence. Amid growing polarization over integration, even the slightest perceived infraction of the emotional politics of Jim Crow was, as Wright wrote a decade before, a "sentence of death."[29] It may never be known what took place on that fateful day in the store, but it threatened the White Southern affective status quo enough that the grocery store owner and another White man kidnapped, tortured, and killed Till.

In a piece published almost a year after Till's battered young body was pulled from the Tallahatchie River, and over eight months after Till's self-confessed killers were acquitted, novelist William Faulkner wrote about the case and the role of White fear in resistance to integration. Though Faulkner initially theorized that White anxieties stemmed from the economic competition posed by Black people, Faulkner quickly acknowledged that the real threat was how much Black people had accomplished since Reconstruction, despite being disenfranchised. In Faulkner's words, "That's what the white man in the South is afraid of: that the Negro, who has done so much more with no chance, might do so much more with an equal one." He believed that their underlying dread was that power structures that were rooted in racial inequality might dissolve. As more Black people migrated North to seek job opportunities and the vote, as the sharecropping system declined, and as more Black Southerners demanded rights and integration, White Southerners were afraid and manifested that fear on Black bodies like Till's. Faulkner did not discuss the graphic details of Till's lynching, but he parsed the emotional motives behind the murder, contending that the crime boiled down to the following "facts": "two adults, armed, in the dark, kidnap a fourteen-year-old boy and take him away to frighten him. Instead of which, the fourteen-year-old boy not only refuses to be frightened, but, unarmed, alone, in the dark, so frightens the two armed men that they must destroy him."[30]

Political philosophers and historians alike have explored how despots wield fear as a method of social control.[31] But in his summation of the case Faulkner identified a despotic dilemma: what happens when oppressors experience fear, when people in power feel threatened by those they have dispossessed? Faulkner hypothesized that though the murderers' initial goal might have been simply to terrify Till, ultimately his White supremacist killers experienced terror themselves and then enacted those fears on Till. Faulkner went on to ask the reader "what are we Mississippians afraid of?"[32] In 1950s Mississippi the answer to Faulkner's question depended very much on race.

Till's murder epitomized the fears of Wright and of so many other Black Southerners that failure to censure their emotions would end in death at the hands of White men.[33] But even if both Till and his killers felt afraid on that August night their fears were not seen as equivalent by society at large, nor were the stakes of their feelings the same. While being savagely beaten Till feared for his life, while his murderers merely feared for their way of life.[34] Moreover, his killers did not need to worry that there would be repercussions for their actions. Centuries of experience showed that they could act on their feelings with impunity, because killing a Black person based on White jealousy, anger, or terror had long been decriminalized in the South.[35] Because of those asymmetrical power dynamics, Till's and his killers' fears were treated differently, as were their respective abilities to invoke terror. In an essay about race, fear, and masculinity Robin D. G. Kelley acknowledged that it might seem empowering to be feared, even briefly, but he argued that "the power to scare is not real power."[36] Till's unwillingness to defer to White people may have frightened his attackers, but "real power" lay not in the ability to scare someone, but in being able to kill an unarmed adolescent and still claim one's own fear, rage, or jealousy as a legal defense.

The Emotional Politics of Race in the Twenty-First Century

It has been over a century and a half since Emancipation, yet the residue of the emotional politics of slavery remains in evidence throughout the United States. The language of emotions still comes to the fore when people discuss race relations in America. Resorting to affective and relational language frames racial inequality and discrimination as a problem of personal enmity and individual prejudice rather than a systemic issue of racial inequality that has accumulated over centuries.[37] Phrenology may have fallen out of fashion but the belief that Black people experience and express emotions differently from White people persists as well. The notion that Black people feel lust rather than love, or cannot express certain emotions at all, is evident in stereotypes of Black people as "lascivious" and hypersexual and in critiques of the welfare system that depict Black women as inadequate mothers.[38] The phantasm of the happy slave is still resurrected by some White people to defend slavery and other past racial injustices, dredged up to serve as a false point of comparison for contemporary race relations.[39] Reflecting on race in America through the prism of his childhood in Louisiana, Phil Robertson, a reality-television star from the show *Duck Dynasty*, told a journalist he recalled that "the blacks worked for the farmers. . . . They're singing and happy. . . . Pre-entitlement, pre-welfare . . . they were happy; no one was singing the blues."[40] In a matter of sentences Robertson conjured up the myth of the happy slave, and he conflated that with nostalgic claims that Black sharecroppers "were happy" in the Jim Crow South. He then explicitly contrasted that idyllic, ahistorical era of Black contentment with the present by labeling the period "pre-entitlement, pre-welfare," insinuating that African Americans were happier under Jim Crow. Robertson's comments were widely criticized but offered a peek into the enduring fable that Black people were happier in some imagined, purely anecdotal past despite, or perhaps because of, the racial hierarchies of slavery and Jim Crow.

With the proliferation of social media, when the figure of the happy slave resurfaces the response from many journalists, bloggers, and internet commenters is swift, critiquing these iterations and explaining what is at stake when White supremacist myths are perpetuated. In 2014 a food blog reported outrage on Twitter and Facebook after cooking-show star Paula Deen's Southern-style Georgia restaurant created an ad with an image of a smiling Black woman inviting people to eat by ringing a triangle. Critics claimed the advertisement invoked both the "mammy figure" and the myth that enslaved people were "contented, even happy."[41] In 2016 a children's book published by Scholastic entitled *A Birthday Cake for George Washington* was roundly condemned for its "depiction of 'happy' slaves." Scholastic pulled the book from shelves, conceding that without providing historical context about the harsh realities of slavery "the book may give a false impression . . . of the lives of slaves."[42] The author of the controversial book, Ramin Ganeshram, defended her work on the Scholastic website, asking, "How could they smile? How could they be anything but unrelentingly miserable? How could they be proud to bake a cake for George Washington? The answers to those questions are complex because human nature is complex," and because not all enslaved people experienced bondage in the same way.[43] Ganeshram was correct that enslaved people felt ambivalent and even paradoxical emotions, but without portraying that "complex" spectrum of feelings her book's affective portrayal of bondage parroted the myth of the "happy & content" slave that Washington himself touted over two centuries before.[44]

Even in the twenty-first century Black people are still expected to censor certain emotions, particularly anger, or face harsh criticism, especially if they are in the public eye. Audiences may clamor for the popular reality-television trope of the angry Black woman, but First Lady Michelle Obama was denounced throughout her husband's eight years in office for embodying the "angry black woman myth." The implication was both that she was not in control of her emotions and that any passion she showed was excessive and irrational, never a righteous, earned indignation.[45] The same critiques dogged President Barack Obama, as he was variously accused of being angry, not condemning the anger of other Black people, or not being angry enough.[46] The notion that President Obama repressed his emotions, especially fury, was so widespread that it spawned a recurring sketch on the comedy show *Key and Peele*, in which Obama had a person on staff named Luther who functioned as his "anger interpreter" to help him vent frustrations he could not voice himself.[47] At its core the injunction against Black anger is itself based on fear, fear that after centuries of being compelled to suppress emotions African Americans might grow weary of masking rage at their continued unequal treatment and thereby express unreserved and well-warranted anger.

Half a century after the murder of Emmett Till, race-based fear continues to be a flashpoint for violence and a defense invoked in courtrooms and the law.[48] The shooting of a Black seventeen-year-old named Trayvon Martin by George Zimmerman brought attention to Florida's 2005 "Stand Your Ground" law, which allows the "use of force" in self-defense if one has "a reasonable fear of imminent peril of death or great bodily harm."[49] In the wake of Martin's murder and Zimmerman's subsequent acquittal, many have observed that such laws codify implicit racial bias and violate the civil rights of victims like Martin. In an editorial in the *New York Times* law professor Kenneth Nunn explained how these laws disproportionately impact Black men because they have historically "been constructed in popular culture as violence-prone and dangerous," so "fear of black males, and consequently the use of deadly force against them, is 'reasonable.'"[50] Just as slave states decriminalized the murder of an enslaved person by a slaveholder in a fit of passion, such laws offered more protection for White fears than for Black lives.

Public outrage over the Zimmerman verdict led many people of color to write about how young Black men in particular were still expected to perform certain emotions in interactions with White authority figures, while also bearing the blame for any fear they inspired in White people. Cord Jefferson explored this in an article he published less than an hour after the Zimmerman verdict was announced. He shared his own tale of being racially profiled in a Virginia hotel parking lot before asserting that the acquittal was further proof that "people of color . . . must always be deferential to white people, or face the very real chance of getting killed." Jefferson lamented that to be "young, black and male in America" was to be simultaneously "aware that many people are afraid of you" and "apologetic for their fear." He related this barrage of daily microaggressions to the Trayvon Martin case, saying that given this set of racialized emotional expectations the onus was on Martin "to apologize" for being scary, rather than the burden being on White people to question why they were ruled by fear.[51]

Zimmerman's acquittal gave rise to the social movement hashtag #BlackLivesMatter, which in turn spawned a movement that has often asked why White fears rooted in racism have traditionally been privileged over Black fears of White supremacist violence. Though termed the Black Lives Matter movement, its founders, Patrisse Cullors, Alicia Garza, and Opal Tometi, have been clear that their focus was not only on threats to Black *lives,* but also on the material ways that historical racial inequality endangers Black emotional lives.

Cullors, Garza, and Tometi portrayed emotions as a constant refrain in Black social movements in an open letter posted to *Ebony.com* just weeks after the murder of Freddie Grey, a twenty-five-year-old Black man, by Baltimore police, writing, "Today, our hearts swell with the same current of love that coursed through the veins of those who faced the billy clubs and tear gas in Selma, Alabama. . . . There are those who do not acknowledge that our rage is a symptom of our grief . . . this is what Black Lives Matter is truly about. We support all of our emotions, from our bliss to our anger to our grief. All of it is welcome, as this is what it means to be human."

As they alluded in this short piece, it was not just the systems of oppression they were fighting that had historical roots; the emotions that accompanied those struggles against White supremacist violence had longer origins, too. Just as Solomon Northup had argued over a century and a half before, to be fully free was to have freedom to experience and express a litany of human emotions, including "anger," "bliss," and "grief," and to acknowledge how this constellation of emotions could operate in concert to challenge racial inequality. As they explained, battles over civil rights and human dignity had not been won with fear, or through love alone, but also with a "rage" based in "grief." One of the issues at hand was acknowledging the spectrum of emotions fueling the Black Lives Matter movement and the origins of those feelings. But according to Cullors, Garza, and Tometi, emotions were more than the reason to fight: emotions were also the means of resisting racial injustice. As they concluded, "We acknowledge that our uprisings are being fueled by the love we have for ourselves and for one another. A love that challenges silence, repression and death."[52]

* * *

Slavery in the United States was formally abolished with the Thirteenth Amendment, but it has proven difficult to dispel the affective norms and expectations that have their origins in the emotional politics of slavery and thus have accrued in hearts, minds, and relationships for centuries. Studying the emotional politics of slavery and racial injustice more generally makes transparent the formerly opaque process of how authority figures use emotions and affective norms to shore up power and how historically marginalized people can also deploy feelings to negotiate with or challenge those elites. Emotions can unite people, forming the filament of our most intimate bonds, but affective norms can also be used to preserve inequalities and divide people, by dehumanizing groups of people and delineating their supposed emotional differences. As Douglass observed over a century ago, racial inequality was a problem that impacted the entire country on an affective level. Douglass warned that "the glory or shame, the happiness or misery" of the nation was at stake, until all Americans could truly and equally exercise their rights to life, liberty, and the pursuit of happiness. Until the inalienable affective rights of all citizens are taken seriously, the question remains, what are we so afraid of?

NOTES

Introduction

1. Charles Ball, *Fifty Years in Chains; or, The Life of an American Slave* (New York: H. Dayton Publishers, 1859), 70, 235, 265, 304.

2. Catherine Clinton, *The Plantation Mistress: Woman's World in the Old South* (New York: Pantheon, 1984), 66.

3. *The Young Man's Own Book: A Manual of Politeness, Intellectual Improvement, and Moral Deportment* (Philadelphia: John Locken, 1842), 163. Similarly, an issue of *Southern Planter* advised that "by forgetting injuries we show ourselves superior to them; he who broods over them is their slave" (*Southern Planter* 20, no. 28 [August 1860]: 480). For more discussion about how emotional mastery and self-control were key components of slaveholding, see Michael E. Woods, *Emotional and Sectional Conflict in the Antebellum United States* (New York: Cambridge University Press, 2014), chap. 2, "Managed Hearts and Unmanageable Slaves," 72–95.

4. According to Ira Berlin, the difference between a "Society with Slaves" and a "Slave Society" was not only the centrality of enslaved labor, but also that in a "Slave Society . . . the master-slave relationship provided the model for all social relations," including family relations and dynamics between slaveholders and nonslaveholders. Ira Berlin, *Many Thousands Gone: The First Two Centuries of Slavery in America* (Cambridge, MA: Harvard University Press, 1998), 8. For more on how patriarchal master-slave relationships shaped Southern social and familial relations, see Stephanie McCurry, *Masters of Small Worlds: Yeoman Households, Gender Relations, and the Political Culture of the Antebellum South Carolina Low Country* (New York: Oxford University Press, 1995); and Jan Lewis, *The Pursuit of Happiness: Family and Values in Jefferson's Virginia* (New York: Cambridge University Press, 1983).

5. For example, one article, "Management of Negroes," cautioned that enslaved people should "see from your cool, yet determined manner that [the punishment] is not in consequence of your excited temper, but of his fault." "Management of Negroes," *Southern Planter* 11, no. 2 (February 1851): 39–43. For more examples of injunctions against disciplining in anger, see "Overseers," *Southern Planter* 16, no. 5 (May 1856): 147–148; "The Duties of an Overseer," *Southern Planter* 17, no. 7 (July 1857): 415; "From Affleck's Cotton Plantation Record and Account Book—the Duties of an Overseer," *American Cotton Planter* 2, no. 12 (December 1854): 333–355; and Thomas Jefferson, *Notes on the State of Virginia, with an Appendix* (Boston: H. Sprague, 1802), 223.

6. Some scholars have written extensively about the emotional rituals of White Southern elites, with particular attention to honor, but they do not consider the myriad affective interactions that took place between slaveholders and enslaved people, and the profound impact enslaved people had on the emotional lives of slaveholding Southerners (and vice versa). See

Steven M. Stowe, *Intimacy and Power in the Old South: Ritual in the Lives of the Planters* (Baltimore: Johns Hopkins University Press, 1987); Bertram Wyatt-Brown, *Southern Honor: Ethics and Behavior in the Old South* (New York: Oxford University Press, 1982); Bertram Wyatt-Brown, *Honor and Violence in the Old South* (New York: Oxford University Press, 1986); Bertram Wyatt-Brown, *The Shaping of Southern Culture: Honor, Grace, and War, 1760s–1880s* (Chapel Hill: University of North Carolina Press, 2001); and Kenneth S. Greenberg, "The Nose, the Lie, and the Duel in the Antebellum South," *American Historical Review* 95, no. 1 (February 1990): 57–74. For works on affective relations in enslaved communities, see John Blassingame, *The Slave Community: Plantation Life in the Antebellum South* (New York: Oxford University Press, 1972); Herbert Gutman, *The Black Family in Slavery and Freedom, 1750–1925* (New York: Vintage, 1977); Jacqueline Jones, *Labor of Love, Labor of Sorrow: Black Women, Work, and the Family from Slavery to the Present* (New York: Vintage, 1985); Brenda Stevenson, *Life in Black and White: Family and Community in the Slave South* (New York: Oxford University Press, 1997); Marie Jenkins Schwartz, "Family Life in the Slave Quarters: Survival Strategies," *OAH Magazine of History* 15, no. 4, Family History (Summer 2001): 36–41; Emily West, *Chains of Love: Slave Couples in Antebellum South Carolina* (Urbana: University of Illinois Press, 2004); and Rebecca J. Fraser, *Courtship and Love Among the Enslaved in North Carolina* (Jackson: University Press of Mississippi, 2007).

7. See Kenneth M. Stampp, *The Peculiar Institution: Slavery in the Ante-Bellum South* (1956; New York: Vintage, 1989); Eugene D. Genovese, *Roll, Jordan, Roll: The World the Slaves Made* (New York: Vintage, 1976); Bertram Wyatt-Brown, "The Mask of Obedience: Male Slave Psychology in the Old South," *American Historical Review* 93 (1988): 1228–1252; and Eugene D. Genovese and Elizabeth Fox-Genovese, *Fatal Self-Deception: Slaveholding Paternalism in the Old South* (New York: Cambridge University Press, 2011). More recent scholars of the history of slavery interrogate the performative and power-laden nature of paternalism, and in doing so they provide a more nuanced depiction of relationships between slaveholders and enslaved people. See Annette Gordon-Reed, *Thomas Jefferson and Sally Hemings: An American Controversy* (Charlottesville: University of Virginia Press, 1998); Saidiya Hartman, *Scenes of Subjection: Terror, Slavery, and Self-Making in Nineteenth-Century America* (New York: Oxford University Press, 1997); Walter Johnson, *Soul by Soul: Life Inside the Antebellum Slave Market* (Cambridge, MA: Harvard University Press, 2001); and Thavolia Glymph, *Out of the House of Bondage: The Transformation of the Plantation Household* (New York: Cambridge University Press, 2008).

8. For example, in his work on emotions and the French Revolution, William Reddy articulates how societies permit or repress certain emotions, but in a very top-down model. While his theory of how "emotional regimes" police and restrict affective expression is useful for understanding how the planter class saw themselves as emotional masters, of enslaved people and of themselves, the affective norms and practices of the antebellum South were not determined solely or even primarily by planters and policy makers. Barbara Rosenwein and the Stearnses provide a somewhat more democratic understanding of how affective norms develop in a given society, but they downplay the role of power in the formation of emotional standards and practices and, like Reddy, ignore the subject of race entirely. See William M. Reddy, *The Navigation of Feeling: A Framework for the History of Emotions* (New York: Cambridge University Press, 2001); Barbara Rosenwein, "Worrying About Emotions in History," *American Historical Review* 107, no. 3 (June 2002): 821–845; and Peter N. Stearns with Carol Z. Stearns, "Emotionology: Clarifying the History of Emotions and Emotional Standards," *American Historical Review* 90, no. 4 (October 1985): 813–836, at 828. Rebecca J. Fraser's very specific work on romantic

relationships for enslaved people, *Courtship and Love Among the Enslaved in North Carolina*, discusses how such bonds helped enslaved people endure and defy slaveholders who saw them as less human. However, Fraser does not discuss contestations over other emotions or how those debates resonated post-Emancipation. More recent scholarship by Michael E. Woods, *Emotional and Sectional Conflict in the Antebellum United States*, on the critical role of emotions in provoking the Civil War, also takes a broader view of feelings in the political arena. Since the work's focus is on regional divides over emotions in the leadup to war, Woods explores the real and idealized feelings of Southern slaveholders and of Northern elites, while enslaved people are more subjects testing slaveholders' romanticized emotional selves.

9. Jefferson, *Notes on the State of Virginia*, 190–195.

10. There is extensive scholarship on interracial sexual relations and sexual assault of enslaved people in the antebellum South. See Deborah Gray White, *Ar'n't I a Woman? Female Slaves in the Plantation South* (New York: W. W. Norton, 1999); Clinton, *Plantation Mistress*; Martha Hodes, *White Women, Black Men: Illicit Sex in the Nineteenth-Century South* (New Haven, CT: Yale University Press, 1997); Gordon-Reed, *Thomas Jefferson and Sally Hemings*; Joshua D. Rothman, *Notorious in the Neighborhood: Sex and Families Across the Color Line in Virginia, 1787–1861* (Chapel Hill: University of North Carolina Press, 2003); and Edward Baptist, "'Cuffy,' 'Fancy Maids,' and 'One-Eyed Men': Rape, Commodification, and the Domestic Slave Trade in the United States," *American Historical Review* 106. no. 5 (December 2001): 1619–1650.

11. Henry Box Brown, *Narrative of the Life of Henry Box Brown, Written by Himself*, ed. Richard Newman (New York: Oxford University Press, 2002), 51, 29. For more proslavery rhetoric about racialized emotional differences, see Edward A. Pollard, *Black Diamonds Gathered in the Darkey Homes of the South* (New York: Negro Universities Press, 1968), 38–39; George S. Sawyer, *Southern Institutes* (Philadelphia: J. B. Lippincott & Co., 1858), 200; Sterling Neblett, "For Southern Planter from the Nottoway Club, Brickland, Va.," *Southern Planter* 20, no. 6 (June 1860): 359–360; and William Harper, "Harper's Memoir on Slavery," in *The Pro-Slavery Argument: As Maintained by the Most Distinguished Writers of the Southern States, Containing the Several Essays, on the Subject, of Chancellor Harper, Governor Hammond, Dr. Simms, and Professor Dew* (Charleston, SC: Walker, Richards and Co., 1852), 17, 56–59. For more discussion about how ideas about racialized emotional differences were used to justify separating enslaved couples, see Fraser, *Courtship and Love Among the Enslaved in North Carolina*, chap. 1, "'Love Seems with Them More to Be an Eager Desire': Racialized Stereotypes in the Slaveholding South."

12. Quoted in *Slave Testimony: Two Centuries of Letters, Speeches, Interviews, and Autobiographies*, ed. John W. Blassingame (Baton Rouge: Louisiana State University Press, 1998), 697. Similarly, after Harriet Jacobs ran away she learned that her owner's wife had said that Jacobs "hasn't so much feeling for her children as a cow has for its calf." Of course, in spite of the prevalence of the opinion among women of the planter class that enslaved people lacked maternal feeling, records, including slave sales and the writings of former slaves and slaveholders, reveal that enslaved women were nevertheless charged with caring for Black and White children on many plantations. Clearly, the subject of enslaved women's emotional and maternal shortcomings was wielded in prescriptive literature and among slaveholders, but it was ignored when it was inconvenient. Harriet Jacobs, *Incidents in the Life of a Slave Girl* (Mineola, NY: Dover Publications, 2001), 86–87.

13. Ball, *Fifty Years in Chains*, 298–299.

14. Josiah Henson, *The Life of Josiah Henson: Formerly a Slave, Now an Inhabitant of Canada* (Boston: Arthur D. Phelps, 1849), 27.

15. Henry Bibb, "Narrative of the Life and Adventures of Henry Bibb, an American Slave, Written by Himself," in *Puttin' on Ole Massa: The Slave Narratives of Henry Bibb, William Wells Brown, and Solomon Northup*, ed. Gilbert Osofsky, 51–172 (New York: Harper & Row, 1969), 66; Jacobs, *Incidents in the Life of a Slave Girl*, 160. For more examples of the trope of enslaved people's unknowable but intense feelings, see Henson, *Life of Josiah Henson*, 3; Frederick Douglass, *My Bondage and My Freedom* (New York: Penguin, 1993), 207, 220; Ambrose Headen's words in Blassingame, *Slave Testimony*, 743–744; and William Wells Brown, "Narrative of William W. Brown, a Fugitive Slave, Written by Himself," in Osofsky, *Puttin' on Ole Massa*, 173–224, at 216. For examples of the unimaginability of enslaved parents' emotions, see Jacobs, *Incidents in the Life of a Slave Girl*, 116, 133; and Sella Martin's words in Blassingame, *Slave Testimony*, 715.

16. Notably the slave trade was closed in part due to slaveholders' fears about a revolt of enslaved people of the magnitude of the Haitian Revolution happening in America. Jed Handelsman Shugerman, "The Louisiana Purchase and South Carolina's Reopening of the Slave Trade in 1803," *Journal of the Early Republic* 22 (Summer 2002): 263–290; Howard A. Ohline, "Georgetown, South Carolina Racial Anxieties and Militant Behavior, 1802," *South Carolina History Magazine* 73, no. 3 (July 1972): 130–140.

17. For a discussion of how proslavery and abolitionist debates about "slave breeding" boiled down to different views about the relationship between love, volition, and domination, and how the slave trade closing was a turning point in such debates, see Amy Dru Stanley, "Slave Breeding and Free Love," in *Capitalism Takes Command*, ed. Michael Zakim and Gary J. Kornblith, 119–144 (Chicago: University of Chicago Press, 2012).

18. For discussions of how enslaved women were encouraged or compelled to reproduce, and for slaveholder rhetoric about enslaved women's supposedly easy childbirths, see White, *Ar'n't I A Woman?*; Gordon-Reed, *Thomas Jefferson and Sally Hemings*; Jennifer L. Morgan, *Laboring Women: Reproduction and Gender in New World Slavery* (Philadelphia: University of Pennsylvania Press, 2004); and Frances Anne Kemble, *Journal of a Residence on a Georgian Plantation in 1838–1839* (Savannah, GA: Beehive Foundation, 1992).

19. A number of scholars have written about distinct shifts in how people expressed and evaluated emotions from the eighteenth century to the turn of the nineteenth century, especially with the rise of sentimentalism as a cultural genre and a mode of articulating emotions. According to Jan Lewis, an "ideal of restraint" predominated in the eighteenth century and is evident in the way people conveyed emotions in letters, tempering ardent love or bitter anger for the sake of politeness and moderation. But Lewis argues that as the nineteenth century dawned, and the "cult of sensibility" flourished, elites increasingly believed that expressing emotions was valuable, and they did so more openly in diaries, letters, and other texts. Lewis, *Pursuit of Happiness*, 28–30, 36–38, 181, 186, 206, 214, 216–217, 222–223, 228.

20. Should people not know how to write in the sentimental mode, they could turn to etiquette guides, which stressed the importance of penning proper letters and urged readers to write descriptively about their emotions in journals. One author observed that diaries had long "consisted of the driest details," but that young people "should be encouraged to record their feelings in them; their hopes and fears . . . their joys and their sorrows." William A. Alcott, *The Young Woman's Guide to Excellence* (Boston: Charles H. Peirce, Binney and Otherman, W. J. Reynolds and Co., 1849), 119, 321–322.

21. Michael E. Woods argues that while it had much in common with Northern "domestic sentimentalism" a uniquely Southern brand of sentimentalism developed hand in hand with slavery as sectional tensions between North and South intensified, aptly observing that "mature

proslavery ideology was a dialect of American sentimentalism articulated with a southern accent." Woods, *Emotional and Sectional Conflict in the Antebellum United States*, 75. For more on emotions in proslavery propaganda, see 81–82, 84–87, 89.

22. For examples of explicit proslavery responses to *Uncle Tom's Cabin*, see Sawyer, *Southern Institutes*, 200, 222; W. Gilmore Simms, "The Morals of Slavery," in *Pro-Slavery Argument*, 175–285, 217; and Pollard, *Black Diamonds*, 21, 38.

23. Western expansion accelerated slaveholders' need for enslaved people, which led to increased abolitionist accusations of "slave breeding." In response proslavery writers were even more vocal in their paternalistic arguments, declaring that love was not contradicted by slavery, but rather that love and domination were inevitably and inextricably tied in the "domestic institution" of slavery. Stanley, "Slave Breeding and Free Love," 124.

24. Ball, *Fifty Years in Chains*, 27. Similarly, Moses Grandy recounted the story of an enslaved man who was so upset at his family being sold that "he dropped down dead; his heart was broken." Solomon Northup insinuated that an enslaved woman named Eliza died of "grief" after her children were sold. It was also believed that one could become sick from being emotionally overwrought. Moses Grandy, "Narrative of the Life of Moses Grandy, Late a Slave, in the United States of America," in *Five Slave Narratives: A Compendium*, ed. William Loren Katz 5–45 (New York: Arno Press and the *New York Times*, 1968), 36; Solomon Northup, "Twelve Years a Slave," in Osofsky, *Puttin' on Ole Massa*, 225–406, at 268, 280, 311; Jacobs, *Incidents in the Life of a Slave Girl*, 102.

25. An enslaved person who could not mask undesirable emotions like sorrow would depreciate in value, while other enslaved people fetched a higher price if they were marketed as "kind and affectionate to children." Northup, "Twelve Years a Slave," 310–311; Louisa Picquet, *The Octaroon: or Inside Views of Southern Domestic Life* (New York: No. 5 & 7 Mercer St., 1861), 36–38.

26. As the narrator of one enslaved woman's memoir observed, "Oh! . . . How much of joy, of sorrow, of misery and anguish have they hidden from their tormentors!" Dr. L. S. Thompson, *The Story of Mattie J. Jackson, a True Story, Written and Arranged by Dr. L. S. Thompson, as Given by Mattie* (Lawrence, MA.: Sentinel Office, 1866), 18. For examples of the importance for enslaved people of cloaking emotions like anger or sorrow, see Jacobs, *Incidents in the Life of a Slave Girl*, 42–43; Northup, "Twelve Years a Slave," 265; and Levi Douglass's and James Wright's words in Blassingame, *Slave Testimony*, 303–305.

27. H. N. McTyeire, "Plantation Life—Duties and Responsibilities," *DeBow's Review* 29, no. 3 (September 1860): 357; Mississippi Planter, "Management of Negroes upon Southern Estates," *DeBow's Review* 10 (June 1851): 621–627; Samuel Cartwright, "Diseases and Peculiarities of the Negro Race—Concluded," *DeBow's Review* 11 (September 1851): 331–336.

28. Kemble, *Journal of a Residence on a Georgian Plantation*, 24–25, 81.

29. Henson, *Life of Josiah Henson*, 43.

30. Douglass, *My Bondage and My Freedom*, 198–212.

31. Knowing that "unusual" emotions were viewed with "suspicion" did not always help enslaved people quell them. Douglass asserted that his plan to run away with several other men might have been disclosed because of their unguarded "joyous exclamations" and the fact that in the days before escape they "were . . . remarkably buoyant" and "singing." Douglass, *My Bondage and My Freedom*, 202–203.

32. For examples of enslaved people discussing how attentive they had to be to slaveholders' feelings and moods, see Ball, *Fifty Years in Chains*, 27, 60; and Douglass, *My Bondage and My Freedom*, 62, 65.

33. Ball, *Fifty Years in Chains*, 70, 27.

34. For more on how enslaved people exerted influence over their sale, see Johnson, *Soul by Soul*, particularly chap. 6, "Acts of Sale," 162–188.

35. Kemble, *Journal of a Residence on a Georgian Plantation*, 65.

36. The interactions between Fanny Kemble and Jack also speak volumes about how complicated the affective relationships between enslaved people and members of the planter class could be. As Nell Irvin Painter argues, "hierarchy by no means precludes attachment." While it is true that all kinds of "attachment[s]" developed between enslaved people and slaveholders for a number of reasons, the writings of former slaves also call into question the depth and authenticity of some of those affections. Nell Irvin Painter, *Soul Murder and Slavery*, Fifteenth Charles Edmondson Historical Lectures, Baylor University, April 5–6, 1993 (Waco, TX: Markham Press Fund, Baylor University Press, 1995), 25. In his slave narrative, Charles Ball argued that "there never can be any affinity of feeling between master and slave." Ball posited that any emotions approaching "affinity" that occurred between an enslaved person and their owner were always rooted in a past, present, or future negotiation, contingent on the advantages or disadvantages that could be exchanged. Ball, *Fifty Years in Chains*, 218.

37. The most notable are Reddy, *Navigation of Feeling*; Rosenwein, "Worrying About Emotions in History"; and works by Peter N. Stearns and Carol Z. Stearns, including "Emotionology," and *Anger: The Struggle for Emotional Control in America's History* (Chicago: University of Chicago Press, 1989). For more discussions of how emotions are socially constructed and historically contingent, see Lewis, *Pursuit of Happiness*; Peter N. Stearns and Timothy Haggerty, "The Role of Fear: Transitions in American Emotional Standards, 1850–1950," *American Historical Review* 96, no. 1 (February 1991): 63–94; Darrin M. McMahon, *Happiness: A History* (New York: Grove Press, 2006), 195; and Jan Plamper, "The History of Emotions: An Interview with William Reddy, Barbara Rosenwein, and Peter Stearns," *History and Theory* 49 (May 2010): 237–265.

38. In the wake of the Civil War, "Lost Cause" histories not only heaped praise on the Confederate cause, but also justified slavery with claims that enslaved people had been happy in bondage, happier than free people. See, for example, U. B. Phillips, *American Negro Slavery: A Survey of the Supply, Employment, and Control of Negro Labor, as Determined by the Plantation Regime* (New York: D. Appleton and Co., 1918). To counter myths about contented slaves, a number of psychological histories of slavery were published from the 1940s through the 1960s that attempted to diagnose nineteenth-century individuals with twentieth-century conditions, infantilizing enslaved people and ignoring their capacity for emotional resilience. This school is best exemplified by Stanley Elkins's *Slavery: A Problem in American Institutional and Intellectual Life* (Chicago: University of Chicago Press, 1976), in which Elkins argued that enslaved people were fundamentally characterized by emotional trauma, and Wilbur J. Cash's *The Mind of the South* (New York: Alfred Knopf, 1941), which stated that members of the planter class suffered from a "guilt complex."

39. See Blassingame, *Slave Community*; Gutman, *Black Family in Slavery and Freedom*; Jones, *Labor of Love, Labor of Sorrow*; and Stevenson, *Life in Black and White*. The focus on loving enslaved families was also a reaction to contemporary representations of the Black family and community. James C. Cobb and other scholars cite the 1965 report by Daniel Patrick Moynihan, titled *The Negro Family in America: The Case for National Action*, which theorized that "the problems of blacks in America's inner cities were a reflection of the deterioration of the black family 'that had begun as a result of enslavement.'" "The Negro Family: The Case for National Action," Office of Planning and Research, United States Department of Labor (March 1965), www.dol.gov

/asp/programs/history/webid-meynihan.htm. This inspired scholars such as Blassingame and Gutman to prove that enslaved people had created close-knit families and kinship networks to survive bondage. Peter Kolchin warns that this historical turn went too far in defending enslaved people's agency, that such authors have "come dangerously close to replacing a mythical world in which the slaves were objects of total control with an equally mythical world in which slaves were hardly slaves at all." Kolchin quoted in James C. Cobb, *Away Down South: A History of Southern Identity* (New York: Oxford University Press, 2007), 310, 312–313. And Kenneth Lynn stated that in focusing on loving enslaved families, these works risked perpetuating the notion of "happy-go-lucky darkies" so popular with proslavery and "Lost Cause" authors. Kenneth Lynn, "The Regressive Historians," *American Scholar* 47, no. 4 (Autumn 1978): 471–500 at 493.

40. While many nonslaveholding White Southerners were still implicated in both the slave economy and the emotional politics that upheld the institution, as overseers, slave traders, and slave patrollers, and though White Southerners of all classes expressed anxieties about how Emancipation impacted the racialized emotional hierarchies of the postwar South, nonslaveholding White Southerners are not the subject here. Given the preexisting scholarship on the emotions and relationships of White slaveholders, a similar study of the emotional history of nonslaveholding White people in the slave South would shed more light on the intersection of race, class, and the emotional politics of slavery.

41. This interpretation of sources is informed by the theories of Saidiya Hartman and of Gayatri Spivak, who posit that because there are few written accounts by the dispossessed, while sources from elites abound, scholars must read sources created by slaveowners and their political, economic, and legal allies "against the grain" in order to locate the voices of enslaved people and free people of color. Gayatri Chakravorty Spivak, "Can the Subaltern Speak?," in *Colonial Discourse and Postcolonial Theory: A Reader*, ed. Patrick Williams and Laura Chrisman, 66–111 (New York: Columbia University Press, 1994); Hartman, *Scenes of Subjection*, 10.

42. Walter Johnson argues that authors of slave narratives were not just telling their individual stories, rather they "showed the traces of prior tellings" as they "bore witness for others" who may not be able to share their personal journeys. Walter Johnson, *River of Dark Dreams: Slavery and Empire in the Cotton Kingdom* (Cambridge, MA: Belknap Press of Harvard University Press, 2013), 216.

43. Charles T. Davis and Henry Louis Gates, Jr., eds., *The Slave's Narrative* (New York: Oxford University Press, 1985), xi–xii, xiv.

44. For discussion of how enslaved children learned about the prospect of sale, see Chapter 2, "'Born and Reared in Slavery.'"

45. For more on slave narratives as works of history, memory, literature, and collaboration, see John Ernest, ed., *The Oxford Handbook of the American Slave Narrative* (New York: Oxford University Press, 2014).

46. Johnson, *Soul by Soul*, 11. For more discussion of how to critically read sources by enslaved people and slaveholding elites as both historical and consciously crafted literary texts, see 8–14.

47. For examples, see Ball, *Fifty Years in Chains*, 273, 27; James W. C. Pennington, "The Former Blacksmith" in Katz, *Five Slave Narratives*, iv–87 at viii; Northup, "Twelve Years a Slave," 364; and Jacob Stroyer, "My Life in the South," in Katz, *Five Slave Narratives*, 3–100, at 28, 72. Michael E. Woods argues that the prevalence of injunctions against disciplining enslaved people in anger underscores that far more slaveholders were ignoring these precepts rather than abiding by them. Woods, *Emotional and Sectional Conflict in the Antebellum United States*, 88.

48. J. D. B. DeBow, *The Commercial Review of the South and West, a Monthly Journal of Trade, Commerce, Commercial Polity, Agriculture, Manufacturer, Internal Improvements and General Literature*, vol. VIII, New Series vol. II (New Orleans, 1850), 70.

49. For a discussion of how letters and diaries demonstrate felt and performed emotions, see James M. McPherson, *For Cause and Comrades: Why Men Fought in the Civil War* (New York: Oxford University Press, 1997), 11–12. For more on determining the performativity of expressed emotions, see Lewis, *Pursuit of Happiness*, 17.

Chapter 1

1. Edward A. Pollard, *Black Diamonds Gathered in the Darkey Homes of the South* (New York: Negro Universities Press, 1968), 22.

2. For a discussion of how the rhetoric of paternalism informed proslavery ideology in the decade before the Civil War, see Michael E. Woods, *Emotional and Sectional Conflict in the Antebellum United States* (New York: Cambridge University Press, 2014), chap. 2, "Managed Hearts and Unmanageable Slaves," 72–95.

3. See, for example, William M. Reddy, *The Navigation of Feeling: A Framework for the History of Emotions* (New York: Cambridge University Press, 2001); Peter N. Stearns with Carol Z. Stearns, "Emotionology: Clarifying the History of Emotions and Emotional Standards," *American Historical Review* 90, no. 4 (October 1985): 813–836; Peter N. Stearns, *Jealousy: The Evolution of an Emotion in American History* (New York: New York University Press, 1989); and Rom Harré, ed., *The Social Construction of Emotions* (New York: Basil Blackwell, 1986).

4. For example, in his work on the rituals of slaveholders, Steven Stowe claims that his goal is to flesh out "a shared intellectual and emotional terrain" of the planter class. Yet Stowe does not see enslaved people as part of this "emotional terrain." Instead, he explains that he was "struck with how seldom" slaveholders "make mention of black people, even familiar, personal servants." This leads him to conclude that rather than allowing proximity to breed "intimacy" there was "an essential cultural division between the races," which meant that enslaved people in no way determined the emotional rituals and norms of slaveholders. Steven M. Stowe, *Intimacy and Power in the Old South: Ritual in the Lives of the Planters* (Baltimore: Johns Hopkins University Press, 1987), xvi–xvii.

5. Elizabeth Keckley, *Behind the Scenes in the Lincoln White House: Memoirs of an African-American Seamstress* (Mineola, NY: Dover Publications, 2006), 11.

6. Henry Bibb, "Narrative of the Life and Adventures of Henry Bibb," in *Puttin' on Ole Massa: The Slave Narratives of Henry Bibb, William Wells Brown, and Solomon Northup*, ed. Gilbert Osofsky 51–172 (New York: Harper & Row, 1969), 70–71.

7. Benjamin Palmer, "The Trust Providentially Committed to the South in Relation to the Institution of Slavery," *Southern Planter* 21 (February 1861): 116.

8. H. N. McTyeire, "Plantation Life—Duties and Responsibilities," *DeBow's Review* 29, no. 3 (September 1860): 363. Amy Dru Stanley argues that defenders of slavery depicted enslaved people as "beloved heirlooms," configuring love and domination as inextricably tied rather than contradictory, in order to rebut accusations of "slave breeding." Amy Dru Stanley, "Slave Breeding and Free Love," in *Capitalism Takes Command*, ed. Michael Zakim and Gary J. Kornblith, 119–144 (Chicago: University of Chicago Press, 2012), 126, 137–138.

9. James Henry Hammond, "Hammond's Letters on Slavery," in *The Pro-Slavery Argument: As Maintained by the Most Distinguished Writers of the Southern States, Containing the Several Essays, on the Subject, of Chancellor Harper, Governor Hammond, Dr. Simms, and Professor*

Dew, 99–174 (Charleston, SC: Walker, Richards and Co. 1852), 161. For more examples of slaveholders romanticizing lifelong bonds between slaveholders and enslaved people, see Frances Anne Kemble, *Journal of a Residence on a Georgian Plantation in 1838–1839* (Savannah: GA, Beehive Foundation, 1992), 90; and Daniel R. Hundley, *Social Relations in Our Southern States* (New York: Henry B. Price, 1860), 32–34. Booker T. Washington would even invoke nostalgia for that generational care, telling an audience of White people "you can be sure in the future, as in the past, that you and your families will be surrounded by the most patient, faithful . . . and unresentful people that the world has seen" in his famed "Atlanta Compromise" speech in 1895, promising White Southerners the restoration of that fantasy. Micki McElya, *Clinging to Mammy: The Faithful Slave in Twentieth-Century America* (Cambridge, MA: Harvard University Press, 2009), 35–36.

10. Defenders of slavery explicitly countered criticisms of slavery as a brutal or legal institution through claims of mutual affective relations. Hammond argued that though slavery was "founded on force," the institution was nevertheless able "to cultivate the tenderest and purest sentiments of the human heart" between enslaved people and their owners. Hammond, "Hammond's Letters on Slavery," 161. Richard Dana touted slavery in the pages of *Southern Planter*, reminding about "the sympathies of common home, common childhood, long and intimate relations—all those things that may ameliorate the legal relations of the master and slave." Richard H. Dana, Jr., "The Coffee and Sugar Plantations of Cuba," *Southern Planter* 19, no. 7 (July 1859): 416–419, at 417.

11. For more on the idealization of enslaved caretakers, especially the nostalgia that accrued around the romanticized mammy figure, see McElya, *Clinging to Mammy*, especially 10–12, 33, 41–42, 44–46, 48, 121.

12. *Jones v. Mason*, in Helen Tunnicliff Catterall, ed., *Judicial Cases Concerning American Slavery and the Negro: Volume I: Cases from the Courts of England, Virginia, West Virginia, and Kentucky* (New York: Negro Universities Press, 1968), 1:149–150.

13. Natchez Trace Collection Slaves and Slavery Collection, box 2.325, v48, Folder 2, Dolph Briscoe Center for American History, University of Texas at Austin. Similarly, James Gillespie gave his daughter Mary Winston two enslaved families as a token of "love and affection" on April 1, 1854. Gillespie (James A. and Family) Papers, MSS 669, Folder 1:5, Louisiana and Lower Mississippi Valley Collection, Hill Memorial Library, Louisiana State University, Baton Rouge (this archive is cited hereafter as LLMVC).

14. The gifting of enslaved people had a variety of impacts on the enslaved people involved. One 1828 case from a Virginia court pertained to a slaveholder named Talbert who bought an enslaved woman named Jenny and "made her a promise that when she should have a child for every one of his, (he then having five) he would set her free." The "promise" of freedom was intended to incentivize pregnancy, no doubt in the hopes that the gift of an enslaved child for each of the slaveholding children would keep peace and equality among the Talbert siblings. But it ultimately meant that should Jenny succeed in bearing five children she would be freed, but her children would remain in bondage. Catterall, *Judicial Cases Concerning American Slavery and the Negro*, 1:151–152. For another example of a parent working to ensure that each of his six children had their own enslaved child attendant, see Levi Douglass's and James Wright's words in *Slave Testimony: Two Centuries of Letters, Speeches, Interviews, and Autobiographies*, ed. John W. Blassingame (Baton Rouge: Louisiana State University Press, 1998), 303.

15. Slavery Manuscript Collection (collection # 503), Folder 30, Hill Memorial Library, Tulane University, New Orleans, LA.

16. For examples of enslaved people being gifted to brides or newly married couples, see Folder 32: Act of donation of slave by Mary Norton Gardner, Saint Landry Parish, to Anna Gardner, Saint Landry Parish, 1849 February 24, Rosemonde E. and Emile Kuntz Collection, 600C, Louisiana Research Collection, Tulane University, New Orleans, LA; article in *Austin Statesman,* April 1, 1931, Dolph Briscoe Center for American History, University of Texas at Austin; Charles Ball, *Fifty Years in Chains; or, The Life of an American Slave* (New York: H. Dayton Publishers, 1859), 43; Keckley, *Behind the Scenes*, 15; and James Curry in Blassingame, *Slave Testimony*, 128. See also *Applebury v. Anthony*, I Wash. Va. 287, Fall 1794; *Hopkirk v. Randolph*, 12 Fed. Cas. 513 (2 Brockenbrough 132), May 1824; *Brown v. Handley*, 7 Leigh 119, January 1836; and *Harvey v. Skipworth and others*, 16 Grattan 393, May 1863 [393], in Catterall, *Judicial Cases Concerning American Slavery and the Negro*, 1:103, 139, 180, 253.

17. William Craft, *Running a Thousand Miles for Freedom; or, The Escape of William and Ellen Craft from Slavery* (Salem, NH: Ayer Company Publishers, 1991), 2.

18. Slave Manuscript Collection 503, Folder 5, Louisiana Research Collection, Tulane University, New Orleans, LA. Members of the planter class also paid homage to deceased friends through enslaved people. When Sella Martin's owner died, the owner's friend Sherrod struck a deal with Martin to buy him, on the promise that Martin would bring him a great deal of profit if the man hired him out. When Martin was to be auctioned off, Sherrod came forward and announced, "I will have him if it cost me a farm," explaining the circumstances. The crowd was moved and supported Sherrod, encouraging others to drop out and cheering Sherrod with "deafening" "applause," for "what many felt to be a partial devotion to the memory of his friend" when he finally won. Martin observed that he "did not share so fully in this feeling as [he] might have been expected to," because he was aware that Sherrod's motives were more mercenary. Nevertheless, the White crowd believed it was an admirable way to show "devotion" to a "friend" and honor their "memory." Interestingly, Martin recalled feeling "expected" to "share" the joy and admiration of the crowd. Sella Martin, in Blassingame, *Slave Testimony*, 725–726.

19. Henry Box Brown, *Narrative of the Life of Henry Box Brown, Written by Himself*, ed. Richard Newman (New York: Oxford University Press, 2002), 29.

20. Pollard, *Black Diamonds*, 97, 98, 30, 38–39.

21. For more on the courtship practices of members of the planter class, see Catherine Clinton, *The Plantation Mistress: Woman's World in the Old South* (New York: Pantheon, 1984), 60–65; Elizabeth Fox-Genovese, *Within the Plantation Household: Black and White Women of the Old South* (Chapel Hill: University of North Carolina Press, 1988), especially the prologue and chap. 1; and Stowe, *Intimacy and Power in the Old South.* For discussions of the courtship practices of enslaved people, see Michael J. Cassity, *Legacy of Fear: American Race Relations to 1900* (Westport, CT: Greenwood Press, 1985), 79–80; Emily West, *Chains of Love: Slave Couples in Antebellum South Carolina* (Urbana: University of Illinois Press, 2004); and Rebecca J. Fraser, *Courtship and Love Among the Enslaved in North Carolina* (Jackson: University Press of Mississippi, 2007).

22. Ball, *Fifty Years in Chains*, 56, 208, 262–265.

23. Frederick Law Olmsted, *The Cotton Kingdom: A Traveler's Observations on Cotton and Slavery in the American Slave States, 1853–1861* (New York: Da Capo Press, 1996), 239.

24. Moses Grandy, "Narrative of the Life of Moses Grandy, Late a Slave, in the United States of America," in *Five Slave Narratives: A Compendium*, ed. William Loren, 5–45 (New York: Arno Press and the *New York Times*, 1968), 20.

25. Clinton, *Plantation Mistress*, 63.

26. Martin, in Blassingame, *Slave Testimony*, 703.

27. L. S. Thompson, *The Story of Mattie J. Jackson, a True Story, Written and Arranged by Dr. L. S. Thompson, as Given by Mattie* (Lawrence, MA.: Sentinel Office, 1866), 16–18.

28. Ball, *Fifty Years in Chains*, 208, 262–265.

29. James W. C. Pennington, "The Former Blacksmith," in Katz, *Five Slave Narratives*, iv–87, at 73.

30. Keckley, *Behind the Scenes*, 15.

31. Douglass and Wright, in Blassingame, *Slave Testimony*, 303.

32. April 27, 1801, Last Will and Testament of Claude Thomas Pierre Metoyer, Joe Henry Collection, Folder #8, 8–10, Cammie G. Henry Research Center, Watson Memorial Library, Northwestern State University of Louisiana.

33. Michael D. Wynne Collection (Moore, John and Family Papers) #2973, W-31, Folder 2, LLMVC. The attachment that slaveholders purported to feel for enslaved people was commonly referenced when slaveholders feared losing said enslaved people. For example, Frederick Douglass described a slave mistress's feelings for two enslaved men, named Henry and John, saying that she "was very much attached—after the southern fashion—to Henry and John," because they had "been reared from childhood in her house." Frederick Douglass, *My Bondage and My Freedom* (New York: Penguin, 1993), 214–215.

34. Frederick Douglass, *Narrative of the Life of Frederick Douglass, an American Slave* (New York: Barnes and Noble Classics, 2003), 52.

35. Pollard, *Black Diamonds*, 77–78.

36. Pennington, "Former Blacksmith," 73.

37. Stroyer observed that eventually the son came into wealth and his father pardoned him, "But poor Jim was not there to forgive him." Jacob Stroyer, "My Life in the South," in Katz, *Five Slave Narratives*, 3–100, at 51–52.

38. Batchelor (Albert A.) Papers 1855–1863, MSS 919, S:143, box 1A, Folder 2A, LLMVC.

39. Bond (Priscilla "Mittie" Munnikhuysen) Diary, Typewritten Edited Copy, Diary 1858–1865, 60–61, LLMVC.

40. Ibid., 64–65.

41. Kemble, *Journal of a Residence on a Georgian Plantation*, 62–63.

42. Solomon Northup, "Twelve Years a Slave," in Osofsky, *Puttin' on Ole Massa*, 225–406, at 351, 333.

43. For more discussion of the jealous slave mistress as real or figurative, see Deborah Gray White, *Ar'n't I a Woman? Female Slaves in the Plantation South* (New York: W. W. Norton, 1999), 39–46; Clinton, *Plantation Mistress*; Fox-Genovese, *Within the Plantation Household*; Harriet Jacobs, *Incidents in the Life of a Slave Girl* (Mineola, NY: Dover Publications, 2001); and Craft, *Running a Thousand Miles for Freedom*, 2. For more on the increasing regionalization of jealousy in the antebellum period, including the role of the jealous slave mistress figure in Northern perceptions that jealousy was elitist, antiquated, and feminine, see Woods, *Emotional and Sectional Conflict in the Antebellum United States*, chap. 3, "Jealousy and the Sectionalization of Emotional Styles."

44. C. Vann Woodward, ed., *Mary Chesnut's Civil War* (New Haven, CT: Yale University Press, 1981), 29, 31, 71–72, 168.

45. Jacobs, *Incidents in the Life of a Slave Girl*, 46. For more discussion of the complicated dynamics between enslaved women and women of the planter class, particularly the violence wielded by White female slaveholders, see Thavolia Glymph, *Out of the House of Bondage: The Transformation of the Plantation Household* (New York: Cambridge University Press, 2008).

46. Louisa Picquet, *The Octaroon: or Inside Views of Southern Domestic Life* (New York: No. 5 & 7 Mercer St., 1861), 36–38.

47. Reddy, *Navigation of Feeling*, 61.

48. Olmsted, *Cotton Kingdom*, 277–278.

49. Ball, *Fifty Years in Chains*, 55–56.

50. Walter Johnson, *Soul by Soul: Life Inside the Antebellum Slave Market* (Cambridge, MA: Harvard University Press, 1999), 103–107. For more on the related idea of Southern honor, see Bertram Wyatt-Brown, *Southern Honor: Ethics and Behavior in the Old South* (New York: Oxford University Press, 2007); and Kenneth S. Greenberg, "The Nose, the Lie, and the Duel in the Antebellum South," *American Historical Review* 95, no. 1 (1990): 57–74.

51. Hundley, *Social Relations in Our Southern States*, 185.

52. McTyeire, "Plantation Life," 358; Olmsted, *Cotton Kingdom*, 277–278. For other examples of proslavery authors discussing how shame and pride were based on one's abilities as a master, and determined in the court of public opinion, see "Cotton Planters' Convention," in *DeBow's Review of the Southern and Western States, Vol. XII*, ed. J. D. B. DeBow (New Orleans, LA: Office, Exchange Place, 1852), 278; and Hundley, *Social Relations in Our Southern States*, 186.

53. Douglass, *My Bondage and My Freedom*, 48. For more on the perceived relationship between "public opinion" and treatment of enslaved people, see Hundley, *Social Relations in Our Southern States*, 63.

54. Ball, *Fifty Years in Chains*, 27.

55. Keckley, *Behind the Scenes*, 38.

56. Jacobs, *Incidents in the Life of a Slave Girl*, 102–103.

57. Ibid., 13–14, 28, 30. For more in Jacobs on the power of gossip, see 47–48.

58. Ibid., 13–14.

59. "Crop and Supply of Cotton," *DeBow's Review* 12 (January 1852): 76–81, at 77; "Fruit Culture for the South," *DeBow's Review* 12 (May 1852): 535–539, at 536; "Chancellor Harper's Memoir on Slavery," *DeBow's Review* 10 (January 1851): 47–65, at 56.

60. "The City of Mobile," *DeBow's Review* 3 (January 1847): 88–89, at 89; "Virginia Commercial Convention," *DeBow's Review* 12 (January 1852): 30–41, at 37; "Crop and Supply of Cotton," *DeBow's Review* 12 (January 1852): 76–81, at 81.

61. "Cotton Planters' Convention," 278.

62. "Chancellor Harper's Memoir on Slavery," 56. They are also terrified of abolitionists, believing that all antislavery advocates want to not only free, but also arm, the enslaved. James Stirling, *Letters from the Slave States* (New York: Negro Universities Press, 1969), 201.

63. Ball, *Fifty Years in Chains*, 320–321.

64. William W. Hening, ed., *Laws of Virginia, Vol. 2* (Philadelphia, 1832), 481–482, 492–493.

65. Caleb Green, Jr., letter, August 29, 1835, MSS 480, Folder 1, Historic New Orleans Collection (this archive is hereafter cited as HNOC).

66. Caleb Green, Jr., letter, October 5, 1840, MSS 480, Folder 1, HNOC.

67. Olmsted, *Cotton Kingdom*, 303. Mary Chesnut expressed similar concerns after a friend was suffocated to death in her bed by slaves. Woodward, *Mary Chesnut's Civil War*, 198–199.

68. The Battiste conviction is discussed in *Withers v. Coyles*, 36 Ala. 320, June 1860, in Helen Tunnicliff Catterall, ed., *Judicial Cases Concerning American Slavery and the Negro: Volume III: Cases from the Courts of Georgia, Florida, Alabama, Mississippi and Louisiana* (New York: Negro Universities Press, 1968), 3:242. Battiste was also charged with repeated burglaries

and muggings and was even accused of being deliberately "difficult to arrest" as he "wore his clothes without buttons" in order to change quickly and avoid identification.

69. Stirling, *Letters from the Slave States*, 201, 298–299. For more of Stirling's discussions of slaveholders' fears of enslaved people, see 294, 301.

70. Molly Rogers, *Delia's Tears: Race, Science, and Photography in Nineteenth-Century America* (New Haven, CT: Yale University Press, 2010), 145.

71. T. W. Higginson, "Nat Turner's Insurrection," *Atlantic*, August 1861, https://www.theatlantic.com/magazine/archive/1861/08/nat-turners-insurrection/308736/. Interestingly, William Harper dismissed the idea that Southern society was rife with would-be Nat Turners. He claimed that visitors to the South "commonly supposed" that a great deal of time and energy was expended in the "formidable" "task of keeping down insurrection." Instead, Harper called these fears "absolutely ludicrous," mocking the notion that Southerners "have been supposed to be nightly reposing over a mine, which may at any instant explode." This hinted that some White Southerners viewed fear of enslaved people as an inappropriate feeling, or at least that one should not air such emotions publicly. "Chancellor Harper's Memoir on Slavery," 51–52.

72. See Jacobs, *Incidents in the Life of a Slave Girl*, chap. 12, "Fear of Insurrection"; Judith Kelleher Schafer, "The Immediate Impact of Nat Turner's Insurrection on New Orleans," *Louisiana History: The Journal of the Louisiana Historical Association* 21, no. 4 (1980): 361–376.

73. Jed Handelsman Shugerman, "The Louisiana Purchase and South Carolina's Reopening of the Slave Trade in 1803," *Journal of the Early Republic* 22 (Summer 2002): 263–290. For more on how fears about slave rebellions, including the Haitian Revolution, shaped policy and slaveholders' fears, see Howard A. Ohline, "Georgetown, South Carolina Racial Anxieties and Militant Behavior, 1802," *South Carolina History Magazine* 73, no. 3 (July 1972): 130–140; James H. Dormon, "The Persistent Specter: Slave Rebellion in Territorial Louisiana," *Louisiana History: The Journal of the Louisiana Historical Association* 18, no. 4 (1977): 389–404; and John Herbert Roper and Lolita G. Brockington, "Slave Revolt, Slave Debate: A Comparison," *Phylon* 45, no. 2 (1984): 98–110.

74. Map of New Orleans, 1803, HNOC.

75. Schafer, "Immediate Impact."

76. For a discussion of the economic "flush times" for slaveholders, and the factors accelerating the spread of slavery and the Cotton Kingdom in the 1820s onward, see Walter Johnson, *River of Dark Dreams: Slavery and Empire in the Cotton Kingdom* (Cambridge, MA: Harvard University Press, 2013), 5–14, 266–267.

77. See Herbert Aptheker, *American Negro Slave Revolts*, 5th ed. (New York: International Publishers, 1983); Eugene D. Genovese, *Roll, Jordan, Roll: The World the Slaves Made* (New York: Vintage, 1976), 607; and Marie Jenkins Schwartz, "Family Life in the Slave Quarters: Survival Strategies," *OAH Magazine of History* 15, no. 4, Family History (Summer 2001): 36–41.

78. Douglass, *My Bondage and My Freedom*, 236.

79. Northup, "Twelve Years a Slave," 363.

80. W. E. B. Du Bois, *The Souls of Black Folk*, ed. Henry Louis Gates, Jr., and Terri Hume Oliver (New York: W. W. Norton, 1999), 27.

Chapter 2

1. Willie Lee Rose claims that most slave narratives included a memory of the "traumatic moment of realizing the limits of being in bondage." Rose contends that this trope was more than a literary device; rather, it signaled a defining "distinct social process" for all enslaved

children as they recognized that they were enslaved. In contrast, Calvin Schermerhorn argues that enslaved children did not immediately grasp the totality of enslavement and that their "lack of awareness of the full circumstances of enslavement" fostered "childish resiliency" in the face of bondage. Willie Lee Rose, in *Slavery and Freedom*, ed. William W. Freehling, 37–48 (New York: Oxford University Press, 1982), 38; Calvin Schermerhorn, "'Left Behind but Getting Ahead': Antebellum Slavery's Orphans in the Chesapeake, 1820–60," in *Children in Slavery Through the Ages*, ed. Gwyn Campbell, Suzanne Miers, and Joseph C. Miller, 204–224(Athens: Ohio University Press, 2009), 214.

2. Harriet Jacobs, *Incidents in the Life of a Slave Girl* (Mineola, NY: Dover Publications, 2001), 9–10. Lizzie Gibson expressed similar sentiments about the emotional blow of losing her mother. Gibson recalled, "[I] spent my happiest days of slavery in my childish days" and "thought it was always to be just that way; but at the age of seven years that thought was changed, and a sorrowful change it was," when she and her siblings were "taken from [their] mother." Lizzie Gibson, in *Slave Testimony: Two Centuries of Letters, Speeches, Interviews, and Autobiographies*, ed. John W. Blassingame (Baton Rouge: Louisiana State University Press, 1998), 738–739.

3. Henry Bibb, "Narrative of the Life and Adventures of Henry Bibb, an American Slave, Written by Himself," in *Puttin' on Ole Massa: The Slave Narratives of Henry Bibb, William Wells Brown, and Solomon Northup*, ed. Gilbert Osofsky, 51– 172 (New York: Harper & Row, 1969), 64–65.

4. Lunsford Lane, "The Narrative of Lunsford Lane, formerly of Raleigh, N.C.," in *Five Slave Narratives: A Compendium*, ed. William Loren Katz, 1–54 (New York: Arno Press and the *New York Times*, 1968), 7, 8.

5. Frederick Douglass, *My Bondage and My Freedom* (New York: Penguin, 1993), 113.

6. Rose, *Slavery and Freedom*, 39. See also Nell Irvin Painter, *Soul Murder and Slavery*, Fifteenth Charles Edmondson Historical Lectures, Baylor University, April 5–6, 1993 (Waco, TX: Markham Press Fund, Baylor University Press, 1995), 10–11.

7. Enslaved children are mentioned in some monographs on plantation communities and enslaved families, but such works fail to sufficiently explore the emotional development of enslaved children, the relationships that such children forged, and how they affectively adapted to slavery. Even studies that focus more specifically on the experience of slavery for children do not sufficiently address the emotional dimensions, how affective norms were learned, and how that process related to the emotional development of children of the planter class. See Marie Jenkins Schwartz, "Family Life in the Slave Quarters: Survival Strategies," *OAH Magazine of History* 15, no. 4, Family History (Summer 2001): 36–41; John Blassingame, *The Slave Community: Plantation Life in the Antebellum South*, rev. ed. (New York: Oxford University Press, 1979); Jacqueline Jones, *Labor of Love, Labor of Sorrow: Black Women, Work, and the Family from Slavery to the Present* (New York: Vintage, 1995); Deborah Gray White, *Ar'n't I a Woman? Female Slaves in the Plantation South*, rev. ed. (New York: W. W. Norton, 1999); Catherine Clinton, *The Plantation Mistress: Woman's World in the Old South* (New York: Pantheon, 1984); and Brenda E. Stevenson, *Life in Black and White: Family and Community in the Slave South* (New York: Oxford University Press, 1997). For other works that specifically address the experience of enslaved children, see Wilma King, *Stolen Childhood: Slave Youth in Nineteenth Century America* (Bloomington: Indiana University Press, 1998); Steven Mintz, *Huck's Raft: A History of American Childhood* (Cambridge, MA: Belknap Press of Harvard University Press, 2004); and Campbell, Miers, and Miller, *Children in Slavery Through the Ages*.

8. Historian Phillip Aries claims that the concept of a distinct period of childhood "separate . . . from adulthood" gained traction among the European aristocracy in the sixteenth century,

and it reached its zenith in the nineteenth century. Philippe Aries, *Centuries of Childhood* (New York: Vintage, 1965), 128. For more on childhood as a modern construct, see Heather Montgomery, *An Introduction to Childhood: Anthropological Perspectives on Children's Lives* (Malden, MA: Wiley-Blackwell, 2009), 56; and Gwyn Campbell, Suzanne Miers, and Joseph C. Miller, "Editor's Introduction," in Campbell, Miers, and Miller, *Children in Slavery Through the Ages*, 1–18, at 3.

9. Nell Irvin Painter also warns those who embark on affective studies of slavery that one cannot expect to apply a "twentieth-century psychology . . . to the culture of eighteenth- and nineteenth-century societies." Painter *Soul Murder and Slavery*, 8; King, *Stolen Childhood,* xix.

10. King, *Stolen Childhood,* xviii; Rose, *Slavery and Freedom*, 39, xix. For more on the challenges of studying children, see Judy Dunn, "Understanding Feelings: The Early Stages," in *Making Sense: The Child's Construction of the World*, ed. Jerome Bruner and Helen Haste, 20–30 (New York: Methuen, 1987), 26.

11. Historians point out that when former slaves recorded their childhood experiences as adults years later, these recollections have been "filtered through later experiences." Campbell, Miers, and Miller, "Editor's Introduction," 1.

12. For example, see Douglass, *My Bondage and My Freedom*, 40, 60; and Henry Box Brown, *Narrative of the Life of Henry Box Brown, Written by Himself*, ed. Richard Newman (New York: Oxford University Press, 2002), 16. Many narratives also include childhood stories that the authors' parents had told them. Though the authors might not remember the events themselves, only the oft-repeated stories, the lessons embedded in their parents' tales were often revealing. See also William Wells Brown, "Narrative of William W. Brown, a Fugitive Slave, Written by Himself," in Osofsky, *Puttin' on Ole Massa*, 173–224, at 183–184, 187.

13. Historian Emily West, for example, argues that despite what might be "imperfect recall," or memories of childhood that "may have dimmed with age," later narratives like Works Progress Administration interviews "hold immense historical value." Emily West, *Chains of Love: Slave Couples in Antebellum South Carolina* (Urbana: University of Illinois Press, 2004), 7.

14. Childhood anthropologist Heather Montgomery observes that a child "is born into a complex web of social relationships" and therefore children need to understand the rules and structure of this "web" in order to "become active members" of that social order. Montgomery, *Introduction to Childhood*, 106. According to Margaret Mead, children learn the hierarchies of the society around them by learning "the essential avoidances," what is dangerous or taboo, who has power over them, and the ramifications for violating those rules. Young Samoan children, for example, were warned not to put their hands in fire, or to play with knives, but they were also cautioned against touching sacred objects or disrespecting the chief. Through "occasional cuffings" and reprimands, children quickly learned that overstepping the boundaries of social hierarchies was as dangerous as playing with fire. Margaret Mead, *Coming of Age in Samoa: A Psychological Study of Primitive Youth for Western Civilization* (New York: William Morrow, 2001), 18, 20. For more on how children learn how to relate to others by observing power dynamics between people, see Dunn, "Understanding Feelings," 30–31.

15. Douglass, *My Bondage and My Freedom*, 33–34, 36, 63.

16. Jacobs, *Incidents in the Life of a Slave Girl*, 11, 18. Harriet Jacobs suggested that these lessons were particularly difficult for her and her brother to grasp because their father had "more of the feelings of a freeman than is common among slaves." Consequently, her brother William "was a spirited boy, and being brought up under such influences, he early detested the name of master and mistress."

17. Jacob Stroyer, "My Life in the South," in Katz, *Five Slave Narratives*, 3–100, at 17–18.

18. For example, see Jacobs, *Incidents in the Life of a Slave Girl*, 115–116; Solomon Northup, "Twelve Years a Slave," in Osofsky, *Puttin' on Ole Massa*, 225–406, at 244–245, 265; and Stroyer, "My Life in the South," 20, 25.

19. As Wilma King asserts, "If childhood was a special time for enslaved children," it was due to the efforts of their parents, who worked to protect them from "slaveholders who sought to control them psychologically." King, *Stolen Childhood*, 1. For more on how the affective ties of family helped enslaved people survive and resist slavery, see Schwartz, "Family Life in the Slave Quarters."

20. I do not mean to suggest that enslaved families were free from neglect and abuse. The conditions of slavery may have made many parents yearn to protect their children, but Nell Irvin Painter notes that it could also foster sexual, emotional, and physical abuse. Painter, *Soul Murder and Slavery.*

21. Jacobs, *Incidents in the Life of a Slave Girl*, 8.

22. Douglass, *My Bondage and My Freedom*, 32–33.

23. Charles Ball, *Fifty Years in Chains; or, The Life of an American Slave* (New York: H. Dayton Publishers, 1859), 12.

24. L. S. Thompson, *The Story of Mattie J. Jackson, a True Story, Written and Arranged by Dr. L. S. Thompson, as Given by Mattie* (Lawrence, MA.: Sentinel Office, 1866), 6–7.

25. As Wilma King observes, enslaved parents had little free time "to indulge their children, yet many never stopped trying to foster positive relationships with them." King, *Stolen Childhood*, 18–19.

26. Lane, "Narrative of Lunsford Lane," 6.

27. Brown, "Narrative of William W. Brown," 187.

28. Gibson, in Blassingame, *Slave Testimony*, 738–739.

29. Lawrence Levine, *Black Culture and Black Consciousness: Afro-American Folk Thought from Slavery to Freedom* (New York: Oxford University Press, 2007), 83, 101, 121. For more discussion of trickster tales as pedagogical tools, see chap. 2, "The Meaning of Slave Tales," especially 81–135.

30. Ibid., 91–93.

31. For more on enslaved children being sold, see Susan Eva O'Donovan, "'Traded Babies': Enslaved Children in America's Domestic Migration, 1820–60," in Campbell, Miers, and Miller, *Children in Slavery Through the Ages*, 88–102, at 89–90, 98.

32. Tabb Gross and Lewis Smith, in Blassingame, *Slave Testimony*, 346–347.

33. Brown, *Narrative of the Life of Henry Box Brown*, 16. Other authors idealized the conversation about separation in verse. At the end of Lunsford Lane's 1842 narrative, a poem entitled "The Slave Mother's Address," by "J.P.B" functioned as a cautionary tale from mother to child about slave sales, saying:

> And if perchance some tender joy
> Should bloom upon thy heart,
> Another's hand may enter there,
> And tear it soon apart.
> Thou art a little joy to me,
> But soon thou may'st be sold. (55–56)

The poem implied that happiness was possible for enslaved children, but that it was always in peril due to the threat of sale. It might instill fear in a child to know that sale was always imminent, but the words also sought to provide solace, through the comfort of having known a mother's love. Of course, the poem was clear that if a child was sold it destroyed the "joy" of child and parent. The poem concluded with the mother saying she would "gladly" see her child dead and buried "beneath the sod" in order to have her child be "Unmarr'd with grief," and "free" in "spirit," if not in body. The poem thus ended with a wish for the child's death, hinting that if the mother's child ever had their own "little ones" they would understand these feelings. In this way the poem served as a collection of the different emotional lessons and challenges that enslaved people faced over the course of their life.

34. Douglass, *My Bondage and My Freedom*, 32–34, 38.

35. Lane, "Narrative of Lunsford Lane," 8. Similarly, Charles Ball recalled being sold away from his mother: "young as I was, the horrors of that day sank deeply into my heart." Ball, *Fifty Years in Chains*, 11.

36. Gibson, in Blassingame, *Slave Testimony*, 738–739. Gibson only saw her siblings again at a subsequent auction.

37. As Trudier Harris argues in her study of African American writing about the South, whether in reality or in fiction, "Black people and Black characters had to become diviners, fortune tellers who must always read any situation correctly or suffer the consequences." Trudier Harris, *The Scary Mason-Dixon Line: African American Writers and the South* (Baton Rouge: Louisiana State University Press, 2009), 12. According to historian Calvin Schermerhorn, enslaved children in particular became schooled in learning about their world "through observation," developing their "abilities to judge character and reliability" in order to identify possible allies as well as potential threats. Schermerhorn, "Left Behind but Getting Ahead," 205, 216. See also Judy Dunn on the importance of learning to identify "the feelings and wishes of other people in their world" as part of socialization. Dunn, "Understanding Feelings," 26–27.

38. In 1840 Charles Darwin began recording the behavior of his two-month-old baby. Darwin observed that his son "studies expressions of those around him" and responds accordingly. Research almost 150 years later supports this finding, showing that, when in "ambiguous" or uncertain situations, babies look to the expressions of adults to establish how to respond, and "if the adults look worried, babies are more likely to cry . . . than if adults look happy or unconcerned." This is called "social referencing." Ben S. Bradley, *Visions of Infancy: A Critical Introduction to Child Psychology* (Cambridge, MA: Polity Press with Basil Blackwell, 1989), 14–16. For more on Darwin's research into human emotional development, see Charles Darwin, *The Expression of the Emotions in Man and Animals*, ed. Paul Ekman (New York: HarperCollins, 2009).

39. Douglass, *My Bondage and My Freedom*, 39.

40. Ibid., 62–63, 65, 137.

41. Ibid., 61–62.

42. Jacobs, *Incidents in the Life of a Slave Girl*, 27.

43. Wilma King argues that "one of the most unsettling events in the lives of slaves was the early separation of mothers and children when the women returned to work." King, *Stolen Childhood*, 13. According to Henry Bibb, enslaved mothers who did field labor were not permitted to return to the quarters during the day to nurse their babies, so they were forced to "carry them to the cotton fields and tie them in the shade of a tree" so that they could tend to their babies on their lunch break. Those infants had many threats to contend with, including "scorching rays of the sun[,] . . . poisonous rattle snakes," and "large alligators," which meant that enslaved babies were "often found dead in the field and in the quarter for want of the care of their mothers." Bibb, "Narrative of the Life and Adventures of Henry Bibb," 112–118.

44. Brown, "Narrative of William W. Brown," 180–181.

45. Douglass, *My Bondage and My Freedom*, 35.

46. Because of these conditions, most enslaved children endured a great deal of uncertainty, leading many to feel what Nell Irvin Painter calls "'soul murder' which may be summed up as depression, lowered self-esteem, and anger." Painter, *Soul Murder and Slavery*, 7.

47. Douglass, *My Bondage and My Freedom*, 32–33, 100.

48. See Sarah Meer, "Autobiography, Authenticity and Nineteenth-Century Ideas of Race," in *The Uses of Autobiography*, ed. Julia Swindells, 89– 97 (Bristol, PA: Taylor and Francis 1995); and William Andrews, ed., *Critical Essays on Frederick Douglass* (Boston: G. K. Hall, 1991).

49. Moses Grandy, "Narrative of the Life of Moses Grandy, Late a Slave, in the United States of America," in Katz, *Five Slave Narratives*, 5–45, at 6.

50. According to Calvin Schermerhorn, emotions served as both the means and ends, as the "pain and loss" that enslaved people experienced were "stimulated strategies for survival." Schermerhorn claims that for enslaved children one of those "strategies" was "to recruit others who could care for them." Schermerhorn, "Left Behind but Getting Ahead," 204. Wilma King contends that older enslaved people were crucial to helping young slaves navigate slavery whether they were "related or not." King, *Stolen Childhood*, 14–15. Similarly, childhood anthropologist Heather Montgomery asserts that "children themselves take an active part in forming their families." Montgomery, *Introduction to Childhood*, 132–133.

51. Douglass, *My Bondage and My Freedom*, 42, 51, 58, 83, 97, 106. For another example of affective relationships between slaveholders and enslaved children, see Grandy, "Narrative of the Life of Moses Grandy," 6.

52. Frederick Douglass, *Narrative of the Life of Frederick Douglass, an American Slave* (New York: Barnes and Noble Classics, 2003), 36. In his second autobiography Douglass mentioned again how "Mas' Daniel" had given him "cake," but he also claimed that he "learned many things" from him. He does not say what he "learned," but it is clear that establishing an affective relationship with a slaveholder could yield a variety of advantages for an enslaved child. See more on Douglass's relationship with Daniel Lloyd in Douglass, *My Bondage and My Freedom*, 83, 97.

53. Edward A. Pollard, *Black Diamonds Gathered in the Darkey Homes of the South* (New York: Negro Universities Press, 1968), 75.

54. Child psychologist Ben Bradley explains that it is common for children to display signifiers of affection to gain basic necessities, a practice he labels "cupboard love." Bradley, *Visions of Infancy*, 105.

55. Douglass refers to Daniel Lloyd as "a friend" and also describes Lucretia Auld as someone he "regarded" as a friend. He also held no illusions about the nature of these relationships, stating that Auld "pitied" him, "if she did not love" him. Douglass, *My Bondage and My Freedom*, 59–60, 83, 97.

56. Children's psychologist Judith Rich Harris claims that children learn social norms best from other children because "in every society, acceptable behavior depends on whether you're a child or an adult." Montgomery, *Introduction to Childhood*, 126.

57. Heather Montgomery argues that for many children "the links between play, socialization, and work are extremely blurred." Ibid., 149.

58. King, *Stolen Childhood*, 14. For more on enslaved children and work, see Schwartz, "Family Life in the Slave Quarters."

59. Sella Martin hinted at this complex relationship when he recalled how he used to "play" with "the son of [his] master, and whose attendant [he] was." Martin, in Blassingame, *Slave Testimony*, 706.

60. A number of authors of slave narratives mention playing with the children who would become their owners. Henry Bibb recalled how Harriet White was his "playmate" when they were children but also "the legitimate owner" of his mother and all his mother's children. Linda Brent also became very attached to the child who legally owned her, a "Miss Flint" who "was endeared to [her] by many recollections." Slaveholding parents frequently assigned specific enslaved people to children in their wills. Grandy, "Narrative of the Life of Moses Grandy," 6; Bibb, "Narrative of the Life and Adventures of Henry Bibb," 64–65; Jacobs, *Incidents in the Life of a Slave Girl*, 76.

61. Lane, "Narrative of Lunsford Lane," 6, 49–50; Douglass, *My Bondage and My Freedom*, 59. Mattie Jackson described a similar experience: "How well I remember those happy days! Slavery had no horror then for me, as I played . . . with the same joyful freedom as the little white children." Thompson, *The Story of Mattie J. Jackson*, 13. Some proslavery authors also employed the trope of childhood as egalitarian and free of race-based prejudice. Slaveholder Edward Pollard recalled that his enslaved friends, "in all the affairs of fun and recreation, associated with [him] on terms of perfect equality." Pollard, *Black Diamonds*, 50–51.

62. Slavery Scrapbook 3L398, Dolph Briscoe Center for American History, University of Texas at Austin.

63. Childhood sociologists see the liminal quality of play as integral to maturation. Montgomery, *Introduction to Childhood*, 141.

64. James W. C. Pennington, "The Former Blacksmith," in Katz, *Five Slave Narratives*, iv–87, at 3.

65. It is also notable that Pennington chose to imagine the whip as a horse, rather than pretend that he was an overseer with a whip. Because of cases like these, Heather Montgomery cautions against "seeing children's play as simply imitative," because doing so belies "the ways that children are creative and imaginative." She brings up the example of the "role-playing" games of the Mehinaku of Amazonia and how Mehinaku children "incorporat[e] adult activities into their own world and simultaneously mock . . . them." Also, the fact that he was pretending does not mean he was *not* thinking about the larger society he occupied. Montgomery, *Introduction to Childhood*, 146–148. Judy Dunn suggests that even when engaged in make-believe, children may be working through their understanding of the "social roles and rules of their world." Dunn, "Understanding Feelings," 32.

66. Stroyer, "My Life in the South," 11–13.

67. Of course, these feelings could be suppressed only so much. Douglass suggests that even at play slavery still influenced his feelings: "in all my sports and plays, and in spite of them, there would, occasionally, come the painful foreboding that . . . I must soon be called away to the home of my master." Douglass, *My Bondage and My Freedom*, 70, 37.

68. Ibid., 39–40.

69. Frances Anne Kemble, *Journal of a Residence on a Georgian Plantation in 1838–1839* (Savannah, GA: Beehive Foundation, 1992), 4–5.

70. Thomas Jefferson, *Notes on the State of Virginia, with an Appendix* (Boston: H. Sprague, 1802), 223.

71. Tattler, "Management of Negroes," *Southern Planter* 11, no. 2 (February 1851): 39–43.

72. Frederick Law Olmsted, *The Cotton Kingdom: A Traveler's Observations on Cotton and Slavery in the American Slave States, 1853–1861* (New York: Da Capo Press, 1996), 572–573.

73. Northup, "Twelve Years a Slave," 338, 370–371.

74. Thomas Roderick Dew, "Professor Dew on Slavery," in *The Pro-Slavery Argument: As Maintained by the Most Distinguished Writers of the Southern States, Containing the Several*

Essays, on the Subject, of Chancellor Harper, Governor Hammond, Dr. Simms, and Professor Dew, 287–490 (Charleston, SC: Walker, Richards and Co., 1852), 456.

75. Daniel R. Hundley, *Social Relations in Our Southern States* (New York: Henry B. Price, 1860), 32–33.

76. James Henry Hammond, "Hammond's Letters on Slavery," in *Pro-Slavery Argument*, 99–174, at 161. See also H. N. McTyeire, "Plantation Life—Duties and Responsibilities," *DeBow's Review* 29, no. 3 (September 1860): 363.

77. Hundley, *Social Relations in Our Southern States*, 32–34. The antislavery Fanny Kemble also romanticized the long-term effect of childhood intimacy between free and enslaved children. Kemble theorized that as masters and slaves were increasingly linked for "successive generations" then over time "the relations of owner and slave" would "lose some . . . harsher features." Kemble, *Journal of a Residence on a Georgian Plantation*, 90.

78. Tattler, "Management of Negroes," 39–43.

79. Pollard, *Black Diamonds*, 48–49.

80. Douglass, *My Bondage and My Freedom*, 103.

81. Pollard, *Black Diamonds*, 41.

82. According to child studies scholar Judy Dunn, children "very frequently 'play' with pretend feelings states," engaging in games that require them "to 'take on' a feeling state other than their own." Dunn, "Understanding Feelings," 32.

83. Anya Jabour, "Albums of Affection: Female Friendship and Coming of Age in Antebellum Virginia," *Virginia Magazine of History and Biography* 107, no. 2 (Spring 1999): 125–158, at 137.

84. Jacobs, *Incidents in the Life of a Slave Girl*, 20.

85. Pollard, *Black Diamonds*, 30, 38–39.

86. Fortunately, for Henson, this kindness was repaid years later when Henson sought to buy his freedom and informed Francis of this plan. The slaveholder responded with a "sympathy which penetrates the heart of a slave, so little accustomed . . . to the exhibition of any such feeling on the part of a white man." So Henson's kindness to Francis as a child paid off, as he agreed to help Henson to freedom. Of course, far too often childhood attachments did *not* lead to greater empathy on the part of members of the planter class. Henson acknowledged that his case was anomalous when noting that enslaved people were not "accustomed" to such responses from slaveholders. Josiah Henson, *The Life of Josiah Henson: Formerly a Slave, Now an Inhabitant of Canada* (Boston: Arthur D. Phelps, 1849), 20, 32.

87. Douglass, *My Bondage and My Freedom*, 224.

88. Lane, "Narrative of Lunsford Lane," 7.

89. Painter, *Soul Murder and Slavery*, 26. See also Pollard, *Black Diamonds*, 42, where he talks about how his feelings about enslaved people changed over time.

90. Hundley, *Social Relations in Our Southern States*, 161.

91. Jefferson, *Notes on the State of Virginia*, 223.

92. Northup, "Twelve Years a Slave," 367–368.

93. Ibid., 370.

94. Brown, "Narrative of William W. Brown," 183–184.

95. Pollard further justified his actions by explaining that his enslaved "playmates" served as "conspirators," and indeed "no one enjoyed the sport more heartily" than his "sable companions." Perhaps they did enjoy watching elders they had been taught to respect be tricked and pelted with fruit, or perhaps they were unwilling accomplices in Pollard's efforts to exercise his

nascent power. Pollard, *Black Diamonds*, 50–51. Interestingly, Harriet Jacobs's brother decried the "meanness" of his "young master," in particular that the young man would trick an elderly enslaved "man who kept a fruit stand" with counterfeit coins. Jacobs, *Incidents in the Life of a Slave Girl*, 18–19.

96. Pollard, *Black Diamonds*, 76–77.

97. Ibid., 76–77. William Wells Brown also played on this very fear, warning slaveholders that "in every southern household there may be a Nat Turner. . . . The slaveholder should understand that he lives upon a volcano." William Wells Brown, *The Black Man: His Antecedents, His Genius, and His Achievements* (New York: Thomas Hamilton, 1863), 73.

98. Pollard, *Black Diamonds*, 76–77.

99. Harriet Jacobs made clear that all slaveholding children were threatened by the perversion of slavery, noting "the slaveholder's sons are, of course, vitiated, even while boys, by the unclean influences everywhere around them. Nor do the master's daughters always escape." Jacobs, *Incidents in the Life of a Slave Girl*, 46.

100. Olmsted, *Cotton Kingdom*, 574.

101. For more on displaying different "fronts" in different interactions and based on status, see Erving Goffman, *The Presentation of Self in Everyday Life* (New York: Doubleday, 1990). As Olmsted's passage suggests, young members of the planter class learned that in the plantocracy not only that they could exert control over enslaved people on their own plantation, but also that any enslaved person could be subject to their wiles. William Wells Brown described how one day, while running errands for his master, he was "attacked by several large boys, sons of slave-holders, who pelted" him with "snowballs" and "stones and sticks" until he was "overpowered." Though he did not belong to any of their families after Brown allegedly "hurt" one of his assailants, that boy's father punished Brown by beating him so severely that "it was five weeks before [he] was able to walk again." This served as a lesson for the boys as well as Brown that slaveholders could enact their desires on any enslaved bodies without retribution. Brown, "Narrative of William W. Brown," 186–187.

102. Tattler, "Management of Negroes," 39–43.

103. Montgomery, *Introduction to Childhood*, 169.

104. Pollard, *Black Diamonds*, 75–76. For more discussion of the meaning and origins of this song, see Levine, *Black Culture and Black Consciousness*, 95.

105. Pollard, *Black Diamonds*, 116–119.

106. Heather Montgomery notes that the practice of terrifying children is not atypical, that "a common method of keeping children disciplined is by the use of threats of the supernatural, nonhuman beings that will come to take them away if they misbehave." Montgomery, *Introduction to Childhood*, 169.

107. Douglass, *Narrative of the Life of Frederick Douglass*, 55. Frederick Douglass would go on to observe in his second autobiography that "it is easy to see, that, in entering upon the duties of a slaveholder, some little experience is needed." Douglass, *My Bondage and My Freedom*, 113.

108. Ibid., 55.

109. Ibid., 40, 43.

110. Douglass, *My Bondage and My Freedom*, 113.

111. Douglass, *Narrative of the Life of Frederick Douglass*, 40, 43.

112. Jacobs, *Incidents in the Life of a Slave Girl*, 24.

113. Martin, in Blassingame, *Slave Testimony*, 706–707, 728.

114. Jacobs, *Incidents in the Life of a Slave Girl*, 40.

115. Pennington, "Former Blacksmith," 73.

116. Dew, "Professor Dew on Slavery," 456.

117. Hammond, "Hammond's Letters on Slavery," 127–128.

Chapter 3

1. Abraham Lincoln, letter to Mary Speed, September 27, 1841, in *Abraham Lincoln: Speeches and Writings, 1832–1858* (New York: Library of America, 1989), 74–75. That he was writing to Mary Speed, the proslavery sister of his close friend Joshua Speed, may have shaped how Lincoln depicted people on their way to be sold.

2. Saidiya Hartman challenges the belief that activities like dancing and singing were signifiers of genuine contentment for enslaved people. According to Hartman, witnesses who accepted that idea were implying that slavery was "socially endurable" or "bearable," thereby diminishing the violence inherent to scenes of supposed enjoyment. Saidiya Hartman, *Scenes of Subjection: Terror, Slavery, and Self-Making in Nineteenth-Century America* (New York: Oxford University Press, 1997), 34–35.

3. Elizabeth Keckley, *Behind the Scenes in the Lincoln White House: Memoirs of an African-American Seamstress* (Mineola, NY: Dover Publications, 2006), 29.

4. James M. McPherson, "Who Freed the Slaves?," *Proceedings of the American Philosophical Society* 139, no. 1 (March 1995): 1–10.

5. Harriet Martineau, *Society in America*, vol. 1 (New York: Saunders & Otley, 1837), 255.

6. For a discussion of how paintings of supposedly happy and dancing enslaved people were also employed as proslavery propaganda, see Simon Gikandi, *Slavery and the Culture of Taste* (Princeton, NJ: Princeton University Press, 2011), 188–190.

7. Ibid., 36.

8. Darrin M. McMahon, *Happiness: A History* (New York: Grove Press, 2006), xi, 14, 186, 201–202, 234.

9. Mrs. Harrison Smith, "Who Is Happy?," *Lady's Book* (May 1839): 216.

10. McMahon, *Happiness*, 14, 186, 201–202, 234.

11. McMahon calls the Age of Enlightenment "an age anxious to be happy." Ibid., 195, 208–210, 236, 247.

12. Jean-Jacques Rousseau, *Reveries of a Solitary Walker* (New York: Penguin, 1979), 88–89.

13. McMahon, *Happiness*, 186.

14. Abbé Pestré, "Bonheur," in *Encyclopédie, ou Dictionnaire raisonné des sciences des arts et des métiers*, 35 vols. (1751–1780), 2:322.

15. Julian P. Boyd, "The Declaration of Independence," in *The Papers of Thomas Jefferson, Vol. 1: 1760–1776*, 413–432 (Princeton, NJ: Princeton University Press, 1950); McMahon, *Happiness*, 315. Of course, Jefferson did accept a major edit, excising a paragraph condemning the slave trade, which Jefferson claimed "violat[ed]" "human nature's . . . most sacred rights of life and liberty . . . of a distant people . . . carrying them into slavery . . . to incur miserable death." So he was concerned about the rights of enslaved Africans to "life and liberty," but not so concerned that it made the final draft. Nor did he mention *their* natural right to the pursuit of happiness. McMahon, *Happiness*, 332.

16. McMahon, *Happiness*, 317–319.

17. Thomas Paine, *Common Sense* (New York: Penguin, 1986), 20, 97.

18. François Jean, Marquis de Chastellux, *De la Félicité publique, ou Considérations sur le sort des hommes dans les différentes époques de l'histoire*, 2 vols. (Amsterdam, 1772), 1:9.

19. See Benjamin Franklin, *Autobiography* (New York: W. W. Norton, 1986), 108; J. A. Leo Lemay, *The Life of Benjamin Franklin, Volume Two, Printer and Publisher, 1730–1747* (Philadelphia: University of Pennsylvania Press, 2006), 205.

20. See Alexis de Tocqueville, *Democracy in America*, 2 vols. (New York: Harper Perennial, 1988), 1:243.

21. "Are We a Happy People?," *Harper's New Monthly Magazine* 14, no. 80 (January 1857): 207–209.

22. Mrs. Harrison Smith, "Who Is Happy?," *Lady's Book* (April 1839): 97.

23. Mrs. Harrison Smith, "Who Is Happy?," *Lady's Book* (May 1839): 214–216.

24. "Are We a Happy People?," 207–209.

25. "From George Washington to Robert Morris, 12 April 1786," in *The Papers of George Washington*, Confederation Series, vol. 4, *2 April 1786–31 January 1787*, ed. W. W. Abbot, 14–17 (Charlottesville: University Press of Virginia, 1995), 15–17.

26. "Editorial—Literary—Miscellaneous, Etc.," *DeBow's Review* 14, no. 1 (January 1853): 90.

27. For more references to enslaved people being "happy," see William Harper, "Harper's Memoir on Slavery," in *Pro-Slavery Argument*, 1–98, at 11, 14, 16; George Fitzhugh, *Cannibals All!* (Richmond, VA: A. Morris, 1857), 47; "The Two Great Evils of Virginia and Their One Common Remedy," *Southern Planter* 19, no. 10 (October 1859): 644; and Edward A. Pollard, *Black Diamonds Gathered in the Darkey Homes of the South* (New York: Negro Universities Press, 1968), 21–22, 25.

28. Samuel Cartwright, "Diseases and Peculiarities of the Negro Race," *DeBow's Review* 11, no. 1 (July 1851): 64–69, at 65, 69.

29. W. Gilmore Simms, "The Morals of Slavery," in *Pro-Slavery Argument*, 175–285, at 217.

30. Pollard described one enslaved man in particular as being a "better-dispositioned and happier old boy" than he had ever met. Pollard, *Black Diamonds*, 58; Martineau, *Society in America*, 1:255.

31. Thomas Roderick Dew, "Professor Dew on Slavery," in *Pro-Slavery Argument*, 287–490, at 442, 459, 460.

32. "Governor Hammond's Letters on Slavery, No. 3," *DeBow's Review* 8 (February 1850): 123.

33. Frederick Law Olmsted, *The Cotton Kingdom: A Traveler's Observations on Cotton and Slavery in the American Slave States, 1853–1861* (New York: Da Capo Press, 1996), 614.

34. Of course, many proslavery authors believed that happiness was rooted in race. As Sterling Neblett wrote, "The white man has more individuality and care, the black man more faith and contentment." Sterling Neblett, "For *Southern Planter* from the Nottoway Club, Brickland, Va.," *Southern Planter* 20, no. 6 (June 1860): 359–360.

35. Harper, "Harper's Memoir on Slavery," 61. For claims about enslaved people being happier than free Black people, see Dew, "Professor Dew on Slavery," 426, 427–428; Fitzhugh, *Cannibals All!*, 296; and Harper, "Harper's Memoir on Slavery," 15–16. For more assertions that enslaved people were happier than Africans, see William R. Smith, *The History and Debates of the Convention of the People of Alabama, Begun and Held in the City of Montgomery, on the Seventh Day of January, 1861, in Which Is Preserved the Speeches of the Secret Sessions, and Many Valuable State Papers* (Montgomery, AL: White, Pfister & Co., 1861), 201; and Martineau, *Society in America*, 1:255.

36. For discussions of how slave labor was cheaper or more efficient, see "Improvement," *Southern Planter* 2, no. 12 (December 1842): 278; Calx, "Estimated Costs of Free and Slave Labor," *Southern Planter* 12, no. 3 (March 1852): 71–73; and Edmund Ruffin, "Address of Mr. Ruffin," *Southern Planter* 13, no. 12 (December 1853): 8–16. A comparison of slavery and free labor

in an article from *Southern Planter* entitled "On Lime—as Used in Pennsylvania" demonstrates how seemingly any discussion in the slaveholders' journal could devolve into a discussion of the merits of free labor versus enslaved labor. Letters to Editor, *Southern Planter*, 4, no. 12 (December 1844): 265, 268.

37. For more examples of proslavery arguments that enslaved people are happier than free laborers, see "Song of the Cane Fields," *DeBow's Review* 8 (1850): 68; Harper, "Harper's Memoir on Slavery," 24; "Misery and Degradation of British Workmen-Slave Laws," *DeBow's Review* 14, no. 1 (January 1853): 271; and "An Address Delivered Before the Virginia State Agricultural Society, by Franklin Minor of Ridgeway, Albemarle," *Southern Planter* 15, no. 12 (December 1855): 378. For an excellent discussion about how different definitions of emotions, especially happiness, reflected and contributed to increasing sectional tensions over free labor versus enslaved labor, see Michael E. Woods, *Emotional and Sectional Conflict in the Antebellum United States* (New York: Cambridge University Press, 2014), chap. 1, "Free Labor, Slave Labor, and the Political Economy of Happiness," 35–71.

38. "The Two Great Evils of Virginia and Their One Common Remedy—Continued," *Southern Planter* 19, no. 11 (November 1859): 671.

39. Edmund Ruffin, "Slavery and Free Labor Compared," in *American Colonization Unveiled*, ed. Edmund Ruffin, 1–28 (Washington: L. Towers, 1859), 2, 3.

40. Pollard, *Black Diamonds*, 48.

41. Fitzhugh, *Cannibals All!*, 276, 321. For more of Fitzhugh comparing the "happiness" of enslaved people and free laborers, see 30, 47, 59, 61, 232, 234, 246, 273, 302, 317, 339.

42. James Henry Hammond, "Hammond's Letters on Slavery," in *Pro-Slavery Argument*, 99–174, at 162.

43. William Harper remarked that if one contrasted the emotions "of the most happy, and the most miserable of man [one] should perhaps be startled to find the difference so much less than . . . previous impressions" could lead one to think. Harper, "Harper's Memoir on Slavery," 24–25.

44. Mississippi Planter, "Management of Negroes upon Southern Estates," *DeBow's Review* 10 (June 1851): 625. For more on the supposedly mutual contentment of slaveholders and enslaved people, see Olmsted, *Cotton Kingdom*, 615; and Pollard, *Black Diamonds*, 57–58.

45. CTB, "Letters from Senior Editor," *Southern Planter* 2, no. 11 (November 1842): 245–246.

46. Fitzhugh, *Cannibals All!*, 302.

47. Dew, "Professor Dew on Slavery," 460.

48. Pollard, *Black Diamonds*, 25, 42; Smith, *History and Debates*, 201. For more of Pollard's ruminations on happiness, see 40, 42, 50–51.

49. Pollard, *Black Diamonds*, 42.

50. Harper, "Harper's Memoir on Slavery," 5, 243.

51. Dew, "Professor Dew on Slavery," 460. Dew also warned that ending slavery would cut off an enslaved person's "very sources of . . . happiness." Ibid., 293.

52. "Address of Hon. A. H. H. Stuart Before the Central Agricultural Society of Virginia, at Richmond, Oct. 28th, 1859," *Southern Planter* 20, no. 6 (June 1860): 334.

53. Smith, *History and Debates*, 201.

54. Pollard, *Black Diamonds*, 40, 42.

55. Ibid., 51. Elsewhere Pollard expressed a similar sentiment, that "God gives happiness to men, without reference to the circumstances that surround them: he gives it to the beggar as well as the lord; to the slave as well as the master." Ibid., 40.

56. Simms, "Morals of Slavery," 259.

57. Harper, "Harper's Memoir on Slavery," 6–7, 10–11, 13–14.

58. William Wells Brown, "Narrative of William W. Brown, a Fugitive Slave, Written by Himself," in *Puttin' on Ole Massa: The Slave Narratives of Henry Bibb, William Wells Brown, and Solomon Northup*, ed. Gilbert Osofsky, 173–224 (New York: Harper & Row, 1969), 194. For more on how enslaved people "in the pens were instructed to appear happy" as to "enhance" their "value," see Walter Johnson, *Soul by Soul: Life Inside the Antebellum Slave Market* (Cambridge, MA: Harvard University Press, 2001), 130; and Hartman, *Scenes of Subjection*, 37.

59. Northup, "Twelve Years a Slave," 264–265, 268, 280, 311.

60. For examples of enslaved people being sold at reduced prices after being labeled "disaffected" or discontented, see James W. C. Pennington, "The Former Blacksmith," in *Five Slave Narratives: A Compendium*, ed. William Loren Katz, iv–87 (New York: Arno Press and the *New York Times*, 1968), 58; Sella Martin, in *Slave Testimony: Two Centuries of Letters, Speeches, Interviews, and Autobiographies*, ed. John W. Blassingame (Baton Rouge: Louisiana State University Press, 1998), 728; Frederick Douglass, *My Bondage and My Freedom* (New York: Penguin, 1993), 88; and Johnson, *Soul by Soul*, 28.

61. Douglass, *My Bondage and My Freedom*, 119.

62. Ibid., 88. In his first narrative Douglass uses almost identical wording, stating that this is why the enslaved "almost universally say they are contented." Frederick Douglass, *Narrative of the Life of Frederick Douglass, an American Slave* (New York: Barnes and Noble Classics, 2003), 30.

63. Fitzhugh, *Cannibals All!*, 126.

64. "The Two Great Evils of Virginia and Their One Common Remedy," 644. William Harper also wrote that enslaved people "should be made to labor," as this was vital to both their "happiness" and their "usefulness." Harper, "Harper's Memoir on Slavery," 65.

65. Cartwright, "Diseases and Peculiarities of the Negro Race," 69. See also Samuel Cartwright, "How to Save the Republic, and the Position of the South in the Union," *DeBow's Review* 11, no. 2 (August 1851): 188–189.

66. Harper, "Harper's Memoir on Slavery," 65.

67. Dew, "Professor Dew on Slavery," 336.

68. "All About Overseers," *Southern Planter* 18, no. 7 (July 1858): 411–413, at 411, 412.

69. Tattler, "Management of Negroes," *Southern Planter* 11, no. 2 (February 1851): 39–43.

70. Simms, "Morals of Slavery," 261.

71. Douglass discussed how one of his owners told him that knowledge would not make him happy. Douglass repeated this belief throughout his narratives, observing in his second memoir, "I almost envied my fellow slaves their stupid contentment" and "To make a contented slave, you must make a thoughtless one." Douglass, *Narrative of the Life of Frederick Douglass*, 90; Douglass, *My Bondage and My Freedom*, 118–119, 233.

72. "How the South Is Affected by Her Slave Institutions," *DeBow's Review* 11, no. 4 (October 1851): 358.

73. Pollard, *Black Diamonds*, 48, 116.

74. Douglass, *Narrative of the Life of Frederick Douglass*, 90.

75. Professor Holcombe, "Speech to the Annual Meeting of the Agricultural Society," *Southern Planter* 20, no. 1 (January 1859): 29. Later in the speech Holcombe refers to other building blocks of enslaved happiness, including "food, clothing[, and] . . . holydays." Ibid., 39.

76. Fitzhugh, *Cannibals All!*, 317, 126.

77. "Governor Hammond's Letters on Slavery," 123.

78. Timothy Flint, *Recollections of the Last Ten Years* (Boston: Cummings, Hilliard, and Company, 1826), 139–140.

79. Mississippi Planter, "Management of Negroes upon Southern Estates," 625.

80. Holcombe, "Speech to the Annual Meeting of the Agricultural Society," 29, 39.

81. Flint, *Recollections of the Last Ten Years*, 140.

82. A Planter, "Cornshucking," *Southern Planter* 18, no. 11 (November 1858): 666–667.

83. How some slaveholders viewed holidays is evident in a parody slave pass written in verse by a South Carolina slaveholder:

> Permit me friends poor sable Dick
> Who scarce can walk without the stick
> To pass to Mr. B_____'s plantation,
> To see the people of his nation.
> This poor old man has lost his wife,
> It touches hard upon his life.
> Then pray permit him to depart,
> And seek a wife to mend his heart.
> Christmas comes but once a year,
> To give poor nigger happy cheer . . .

Major Hugh Lide, Copy of a Slave Pass Written in Verse, Slavery Papers, Series 2092.2, Southern Historical Collection, Louis Round Wilson Special Collections Library, University of North Carolina at Chapel Hill (this archive is hereafter cited as SHC).

84. Northup, "Twelve Years a Slave," 342, 347, 345, 383.

85. Douglass, *Narrative of the Life of Frederick Douglass*, 70–71; Douglass, *My Bondage and My Freedom*, 186–187.

86. Bayside Plantation Journal, vol. 1, 1846–1852, Folder 1, Bayside Plantation Records, SHC.

87. Pierre Prudhomme Plantation Record Books, 1857 and 1860, Folders 272 and 274, Prudhomme Family Papers #613, Series 3.1.5, SHC.

88. Bayside Plantation Journals, vol. 1, 1846–1852, and vol. 3, 1860–25 Oct. 1862, Folder 1, SHC.

89. A Planter, "Cornshucking," 666–667.

90. Pierre Prudhomme Plantation Record Books, 1857 and 1860, Folders 272 and 274, SHC.

91. SSV, "For the Southern Planter, the Agricultural Year," *Southern Planter* 3, no. 10 (October 1843): 240.

92. Tattler, "Management of Negroes," 39–43.

93. Bayside Plantation Journal, vol. 3, 1860–25 Oct. 1862, Folder 1, SHC.

94. Northup, "Twelve Years a Slave," 342, 347, 345, 383.

95. Douglass, *Narrative of the Life of Frederick Douglass*, 70–71

96. Douglass, *My Bondage and My Freedom*, 186–187.

97. Ibid., 186–187. Douglass, *Narrative of the Life of Frederick Douglass*, 78. Of course, here Douglass glosses over the fact that some enslaved people took advantage of holidays to run away. William and Ellen Craft used the extended break of Christmas to escape, while one of Douglass's runaway attempts involved using a counterfeit slave pass to travel for "the Easter holidays." William Craft, *Running a Thousand Miles for Freedom; or, The Escape of William and Ellen Craft from Slavery* (Salem, NH: Ayer Company Publishers, 1991), 31, 68, 80.

98. Pollard, *Black Diamonds*, 25, 40.

99. Dew, "Professor Dew on Slavery," 459–460. Dew repeatedly conflated freedom, knowledge, and misery when comparing abolitionists to "the serpent in the garden of Eden," swearing that telling enslaved people their "situation is degrading" was what made enslaved people miserable. Ibid., 459–460.

100. Harper, "Harper's Memoir on Slavery," 94.

101. Frances Anne Kemble, *Journal of a Residence on a Georgian Plantation in 1838–1839* (Savannah, GA: Beehive Foundation, 1992), 49–50.

102. Martineau, *Society in America*, 1:150; James Stirling, *Letters from the Slave States* (New York: Negro Universities Press, 1969), 49. For more of Stirling challenging proslavery claims that enslaved people are happy, see Stirling, *Letters from the Slave States*, 47–49, 201, 292.

103. Elizabeth Clark, "'The Sacred Rights of the Weak': Pain, Sympathy, and the Culture of Individual Rights in Antebellum America," *Journal of American History* 82, no. 2 (September 1995): 463–493, at 464–468.

104. James Bradley, in Blassingame, *Slave Testimony*, 689.

105. Douglass, *My Bondage and My Freedom*, 192.

106. Henry Bibb, "Narrative of the Life and Adventures of Henry Bibb, an American Slave, Written by Himself," in Osofsky, *Puttin' on Ole Massa*, 51–172, at 67.

107. Douglass, *My Bondage and My Freedom*, 76.

108. Northup, "Twelve Years a Slave," 288.

109. Douglass, *My Bondage and My Freedom*, 151.

110. Douglass, *Narrative of the Life of Frederick Douglass*, 26–27.

111. Douglass, *My Bondage and My Freedom*, 75–76.

112. Rather than depicting happiness, formerly enslaved authors sometimes called attention to enslaved unhappiness by comparing their misery with the joy of others. See, for example, Douglass, *Narrative of the Life of Frederick Douglass*, 63–64. Often this contrast between sorrow and external joy was highlighted through depictions of nature as "happy" or beautiful. See Northup, "Twelve Years a Slave," 250, 368; and Bibb, "Narrative of the Life and Adventures of Henry Bibb," 121.

113. Keckley, *Behind the Scenes*, 30.

114. Moses Grandy, "Narrative of the Life of Moses Grandy," in Katz, *Five Slave Narratives*, 5–45, at 6.

115. As historian Terri Snyder observes, suicide can be "an anguished act of personhood" and resistance even when "suicide was not . . . [an] intentional act." In some African cultures suicide was taboo, but in others it was viewed as "a praiseworthy and honorable response to peril." Terri L. Snyder, *The Power to Die: Slavery and Suicide in British North America* (Chicago: University of Chicago Press, 2015), 4, 9.

116. Dr. L. S. Thompson, *The Story of Mattie J. Jackson, a True Story, Written and Arranged by Dr. L. S. Thompson, as Given by Mattie* (Lawrence, MA.: Sentinel Office, 1866), 6.

117. The trope of the happy childhood found in so many slave narratives was no doubt also intended to garner sympathy from mid-nineteenth-century readers who placed increasing value on childhood as a special and protected time. Philippe Aries, *Centuries of Childhood* (New York: Vintage, 1965), 128; Heather Montgomery, *An Introduction to Childhood: Anthropological Perspectives on Children's Lives* (Malden, MA: Wiley-Blackwell, 2009).

118. Thompson, *Story of Mattie L. Jackson*, 13; Harriet Jacobs, *Incidents in the Life of a Slave Girl* (Mineola, NY: Dover Publications, 2001), 8–10; Gibson, in Blassingame, *Slave Testimony*, 738–739.

119. Douglass, *My Bondage and My Freedom*, 35. Both Douglass and Harriet Jacobs compared the brief sorrows of children to weather, with Jacobs stating that "childhood is like a day in spring, alternately shower and sunshine," while Douglass opined that the tears of a child were like "the dew-drop on the rose" that dries quickly in "the summer breeze." Jacobs, *Incidents in the Life of a Slave Girl*, 102; Douglass, *My Bondage and My Freedom*, 34.

120. Thompson, *Story of Mattie L. Jackson*, 13; Jacobs, *Incidents in the Life of a Slave Girl*, 10.

121. Douglass, *My Bondage and My Freedom*, 34.

122. Gibson, in Blassingame, *Slave Testimony*, 738–739; Bibb, "Narrative of the Life and Adventures of Henry Bibb," 64–65.

123. Jacobs, *Incidents in the Life of a Slave Girl*, 10.

124. Thompson, *Story of Mattie L. Jackson*, 6.

125. Northup, "Twelve Years a Slave," 278; Martin, in Blassingame, *Slave Community*, 706.

126. Douglass, *My Bondage and My Freedom*, 196–197, 200.

127. Douglass, *Narrative of the Life of Frederick Douglass*, 25–27.

128. Ibid., 25–27.

129. Jacobs, *Incidents in the Life of a Slave Girl*, 16.

130. Bibb, "Narrative of the Life and Adventures of Henry Bibb," 75, 76–77.

131. Douglass, *Narrative of the Life of Frederick Douglass*, 92.

132. Jacobs, *Incidents in the Life of a Slave Girl*, 33, 35.

133. Enslaved authors repeatedly depicted the mixed feelings they had about love and romantic relationships. Jacobs questioned the point of falling in love but also admitted that her love for a free man "had been [her] support through many trials." Jacobs, *Incidents in the Life of a Slave Girl*, 33, 35. Frederick Douglass claimed that love could bind one to slavery but also that "love" could not "be annihilated by . . . anyone." Douglass, *My Bondage and My Freedom*, 65–67. Meanwhile Henry Bibb may have hated the idea of giving his heart to an enslaved woman but he confessed to seeking the aid of a "conjurer" for a potion "to make any girl love" him. On one page he described "the time and place of [his] marriage" as one of the most trying" of his life, and on the next he described the early days of marriage as "one of the most happy seasons" of his life. In bondage, joy and sorrow went hand in hand, and the "sweet[est]" memories were seemingly both tainted and intensified by enslavement. Bibb, "Narrative of the Life and Adventures of Henry Bibb," 73, 75, 78, 79.

134. Keckley, *Behind the Scenes*, 46.

135. Jacobs, *Incidents in the Life of a Slave Girl*, 49, 54.

136. Bibb, "Narrative of the Life and Adventures of Henry Bibb," 75, 81.

137. For more on how ideas about parenthood and children were evolving in the nineteenth century, see Aries, *Centuries of Childhood*, 128; Montgomery, *Introduction to Childhood*, 56; and Gwyn Campbell, Suzanne Miers, and Joseph C. Miller, eds., *Children in Slavery Through the Ages* (Athens: Ohio University Press, 2009), 3.

138. Bibb, "Narrative of the Life and Adventures of Henry Bibb," 88.

139. Leonard Black, *The Life and Sufferings of Leonard Black, a Fugitive from Slavery, Written by Himself* (New Bedford, MA: Press of Benjamin Lindsey, 1847), 14, 15.

140. Thompson, *Story of Mattie J. Jackson*, 18–19, 7–8.

141. Jacobs, *Incidents in the Life of a Slave Girl*, 53, 54.

142. Northup, "Twelve Years a Slave," 369, 296.

143. Ibid., 338.

144. Stirling, *Letters from the Slave States*, 47–48.

145. Saidiya Hartman argues "plantation nostalgia" proliferated after the war, manifesting itself in "happy scenes of the plantation." Hartman, *Scenes of Subjection*, 29.

146. David Blight, *Race and Reunion: The Civil War in American Memory* (Cambridge, MA: Harvard University Press, 2001), 262. This was at odds with how post-Emancipation abolitionists continued to argue that to be free was to be able to experience joy, and thus slavery and happiness were incommensurate. For example, in 1872 Senator Charles Sumner referred to slavery as "those unhappy days before the war." Amy Dru Stanley, "Revolutionizing Human Rights," in *The World the Civil War Made*, ed. Gregory P. Downs and Kate Masur, 269–302 (Chapel Hill: University of North Carolina Press, 2015), 280.

147. Examples of Lost Cause literature include Joel Chandler Harris's *Uncle Remus* series; Thomas Nelson Page's *In Ole Virginia* (1887) and *Red Rock* (1898); Thomas F. Dixon, Jr.'s novels, including *The Leopard's Spots* (1902) and *The Clansman* (1905), which was later adapted into the 1915 Lost Cause film *Birth of a Nation*; Mary Johnston's *Cease Firing* (1912); and Margaret Mitchell's *Gone with the Wind* (1936). For more on the Lost Cause apologist genre, see Blight, *Race and Reunion*, 5, 111, 222–223, 225, 226, 251, 262–263, 284, 393–394; and William Garrett Piston, *Lee's Tarnished Lieutenant: James Longstreet and His Place in Southern History* (Athens: University of Georgia Press, 1987), 157–158.

148. Charlie Moses, in Federal Writers' Project, *Slave Narratives: A Folk History of Slavery in the United States from Interviews with Former Slaves, 1936–1938*, vol. 9, Mississippi Narratives (Washington, DC: Library of Congress, 1941), 1.

149. Richard Wright, *Black Boy* (New York: Harper Perennial Modern Classics, 2006), 178, 182.

150. Ibid., 195–196.

151. Zora Neale Hurston, *Mules and Men* (New York: Harper Perennial, 1975), 1–3.

152. Wright exhibited this in his memoir, where only once he was around other young Black men was he "happy," able to freely "talk, joke, sing" without the anxiety of performing for White people. Wright, *Black Boy*, 195–196.

153. U. B. Phillips, "Chapter I: The Discovery and Exploitation of Guinea," in *American Negro Slavery: A Survey of the Supply, Employment, and Control of Negro Labor, as Determined by the Plantation Regime* (1918), 8. According to historian Kenneth Lynn, "In *American Negro Slavery* (1918), Phillips portrayed slavery primarily as a system of social relationships between patriarchal White masters and happy-go-lucky-darkies." Lynn theorized that Phillips's historiographical claim that the enslaved had been happy furthered the Lost Cause narrative while functioning as "implicit" support for segregation for Southern and Northern readers. Kenneth Lynn, "The Regressive Historians," *American Scholar* 47, no. 4 (Autumn 1978): 471–500, at 493.

154. W. J. Cash, *The Mind of the South—with a New Introduction by Bertram Wyatt-Brown* (New York: Vintage, 1991), 49. For more on how historians perpetuated the notion of "black satisfaction" at the turn of the twentieth century, see C. Vann Woodward, *Thinking Back: The Perils of Writing History* (Baton Rouge: Louisiana State University Press, 1986), 74.

155. A subsequent wave of authors argued against the historiography of the happy slave by asserting that the trauma of enslavement dictated emotions for enslaved people. For example, Stanley Elkins famously called Phillips's thesis into question in his 1959 history, rejecting Phillips's depiction of enslaved people as contented "Sambos," but Elkins's affective portrayal of the enslaved was still simplistic and rooted in stereotypes. Elkins argued that slavery was marked by totalizing trauma, and enslaved people's emotions were wholly determined by their infantilizing owners, observing that "the Negro was to be a child forever . . . a happy child." Stanley

Elkins, *Slavery: A Problem in American Institutional and Intellectual Life* (Chicago: University of Chicago Press, 1976), 82, 132. Throughout the twentieth century the historiographical pendulum swung back and forth, in turns focusing on the misery or contentment of enslaved people. In response to Elkins's characterization of enslaved people as emotionally ravaged and childlike, a number of historians challenged his theories by shifting their scholarly focus from the slaveholder's perspective to that of enslaved people. Using slave narratives as their primary sources, these authors argued that enslaved people were not emotionally effaced by bondage, or indoctrinated by slaveholders; rather, they fought to create close-knit families and communities to survive and resist slavery. For examples, see John Blassingame, *The Slave Community: Plantation Life in the Antebellum South* (New York: Oxford University Press, 1972); Herbert Gutman, *The Black Family in Slavery and Freedom, 1750–1925* (New York: Vintage, 1977); Jacqueline Jones, *Labor of Love, Labor of Sorrow: Black Women, Work, and the Family from Slavery to the Present* (New York: Vintage, 1995); Brenda E. Stevenson, *Life in Black and White: Family and Community in the Slave South* (New York: Oxford University Press, 1997); and Marie Jenkins Schwartz, "Family Life in the Slave Quarters: Survival Strategies," *OAH Magazine of History* 15, no. 4, Family History (Summer 2001): 36–41. However, some scholars countered that this historical turn went too far in touting the emotional agency of enslaved people, and the role of the family in creating stability and sheltered contentment, and thus risked perpetuating the "mythical world" of "happy-go-lucky darkies" so popular with proslavery and Lost Cause authors. Historian Peter Kolchin observed that in trying to create a view from the slave quarters, such authors had "come dangerously close to replacing a mythical world in which the slaves were objects of total control with an equally mythical world in which slaves were hardly slaves at all." Peter Kolchin, *American Slavery, 1619–1877* (New York: Hill and Wang, 1993), 148–149; Lynn, "Regressive Historians," 493. In an effort to avoid simplistic affective portrayals, or speculation about felt emotions, more recent scholars have written about the performative nature of enslaved people's supposed happiness and the inherent violence of slaveholders requiring that enslaved people appear contented. For examples, see Hartman, *Scenes of Subjection*; and Johnson, *Soul by Soul.*

Chapter 4

1. Frances Anne Kemble, *Journal of a Residence on a Georgian Plantation in 1838–1839* (Savannah, GA: Beehive Foundation, 1992), 24–25. Kemble explained that the enslaved people at that plantation "once were, but no longer are, permitted to keep pigs." Ibid., 25.

2. Trudy Govier, *Social Trust and Human Communities* (Montreal: McGill-Queen's University Press, 1997), 26.

3. Ibid., 4–6, 16, 25. For more discussion of when trust succeeds, and when it breaks down, see Anne Warfield Rawls and Gary David, "Accountably Other: Trust, Reciprocity, and Exclusion in a Context of Situated Practice," *Human Studies* 28, no. 4 (October 2005): 469–497; and Erving Goffman, *The Presentation of Self in Everyday Life* (New York: Doubleday, 1990).

4. Dr. D. McCauley, "Humbugiana," *DeBow's Review* 1, no. 5 (May 1846): 444–449.

5. Karen Halttunen, *Confidence Men and Painted Women: A Study of Middle-Class Culture in America, 1830–1870* (New Haven, CT: Yale University Press, 1982), xiii, xiv, xv, 35, 51.

6. "The Duties of an Overseer," *Southern Planter* 17, no. 7 (July 1857): 415.

7. Kemble, *Journal of a Residence on a Georgian Plantation*, 154, 60, 25. For another discussion of the Irish as liars, see C. Vann Woodward, ed., *Mary Chesnut's Civil War* (New Haven,

CT: Yale University Press, 1981), 56. For more on stereotypes of enslaved people as liars, see Kenneth M. Stampp, *Peculiar Institution: Slavery in the Antebellum South* (New York: Vintage, 1989), chap. 3; Lawrence Levine, *Black Culture and Black Consciousness: Afro-American Folk Thought from Slavery to Freedom* (New York: Oxford University Press, 2007), 102–132; and Thomas D. Morris, *Southern Slavery and the Law, 1619–1860* (Chapel Hill: University of North Carolina Press, 1996), chap. 12.

8. H. N. McTyeire, "Plantation Life—Duties and Responsibilities," *DeBow's Review* 29, no. 3 (September 1860): 363.

9. Henry Bibb, "Narrative of the Life and Adventures of Henry Bibb, an American Slave, Written by Himself," in in *Puttin' on Ole Massa: The Slave Narratives of Henry Bibb, William Wells Brown, and Solomon Northup*, ed. Gilbert Osofsky, 51–172 (New York: Harper & Row, 1969), 122. The subject of enslaved people feigning health or illness also led to a number of legal battles. Slaveowners filed suits claiming they had been sold enslaved people who appeared "sound" of body and mind, only to have them grow ill or die. Some plaintiffs blamed slave traders or dishonest doctors. In the 1833 case of *Shellman v. Scott*, a Georgia court determined that several enslaved people had "feigned" "derangement," which "greatly reduce[d] their value." *Shellman v. Scott*, R.M.C. 380, May 1833 (Georgia), in Helen Tunnicliff Catterall, ed., *Judicial Cases Concerning American Slavery and the Negro: Volume III: Cases from the Courts of Georgia, Florida, Alabama, Mississippi and Louisiana* (New York: Negro Universities Press, 1968), 3:14. For another case in which enslaved people were accused of faking illness, see *State v. Abram, (a slave)*, 10 Ala. 928. January 1847, in ibid., 3:162.

10. Kemble, *Journal of a Residence on a Georgian Plantation*, 72.

11. For other examples of enslaved people being accused of "playing possum" or "possuming," see William Wells Brown, "Narrative of William W. Brown, a Fugitive Slave, Written by Himself," in Osofsky, *Puttin' on Ole Massa*, 173–224, at 200–201; and *Jordan v. State*, in Catterall, *Judicial Cases Concerning American Slavery and the Negro*, 3:55–56.

12. Martin, in *Slave Testimony: Two Centuries of Letters, Speeches, Interviews, and Autobiographies*, ed. John W. Blassingame (Baton Rouge: Louisiana State University Press, 1998), 717–718.

13. Morris, *Southern Slavery and the Law*, 269–270. For more on enslaved people being unable to testify in court, see Frederick Douglass, *Narrative of the Life of Frederick Douglass, an American Slave* (New York: Barnes and Noble Classics, 2003), 34.

14. Moses Grandy, "Narrative of the Life of Moses Grandy, Late a Slave, in the United States of America," in *Five Slave Narratives: A Compendium*, ed. William Loren Katz, 5–45 (New York: Arno Press and the *New York Times*, 1968), 37.

15. Jacob Stroyer, "My Life in the South," in Katz, *Five Slave Narratives*, 3–100, at 72–75.

16. "Query to Subscribers Far South," *Southern Planter* 17, no. 8 (August 1857): 461. For more references to perceptions that enslaved people were prone to theft, see Tattler, "Management of Negroes," *Southern Planter* 11, no. 2 (February 1851): 39–43; J.B.M'C, "The Law of Enclosures," *Southern Planter* 12, no. 7 (July 1852): 200–201; Eugene D. Genovese, *Roll, Jordan, Roll: The World the Slaves Made* (New York: Vintage, 1976), 599–600, 603; and Gwendolyn Midlo Hall, *Social Control in Slave Plantation Societies: A Comparison of St. Domingue and Cuba* (Baltimore: Johns Hopkins University Press, 1971).

17. Stroyer, "My Life in the South," 26.

18. James Pennington recalled that his former owner often "saw fit to entrust [Pennington] with considerable money[,] . . . not a cent" of which "was ever coveted or kept." James W. C.

Pennington, "The Former Blacksmith," in Katz, *Five Slave Narratives*, iv–87, at 79–80. See also Josiah Henson, *The Life of Josiah Henson: Formerly a Slave, Now an Inhabitant of Canada* (Boston: Arthur D. Phelps, 1849), 21; Woodward, *Mary Chesnut's Civil War*, 332; and Thomas Hughes, in Blassingame, *Slave Testimony*, 209–212.

19. Kemble, *Journal of a Residence on a Georgian Plantation*, 60, 143, 81, 124–125.

20. Thomas Roderick Dew, "Professor Dew on Slavery," in *The Pro-Slavery Argument: As Maintained by the Most Distinguished Writers of the Southern States, Containing the Several Essays, on the Subject, of Chancellor Harper, Governor Hammond, Dr. Simms, and Professor Dew*, 287–490 (Charleston, SC: Walker, Richards and Co., 1852), 458.

21. William Harper, "Harper's Memoir on Slavery," in *Pro-Slavery Argument*, 1–98, at 39–40, 94.

22. Ibid., 81.

23. James Henry Hammond, "Hammond's Letters on Slavery," in *Pro-Slavery Argument*, 99–174, at 161.

24. George S. Sawyer, *Southern Institutes* (Philadelphia: J. B. Lippincott & Co., 1858), 225–226, 197. Sawyer also claimed that enslaved people were "generally extremely credulous . . . and easily duped." In his view enslaved people were not only trust*worthy* they were *trusting*. Ibid., 199.

25. The idea was prevalent enough for one Alabama judge to reference "the known disposition of at least a portion of abolitionists . . . to delude" slaves into "escaping." *Mangham v. Cox and Waring*, 29 Ala. 81, June 1856, in Catterall, *Judicial Cases Concerning American Slavery and the Negro*, 3:211–212.

26. Harriet Jacobs, *Incidents in the Life of a Slave Girl* (Mineola, NY: Dover Publications, 2001), 110–112.

27. Daniel R. Hundley, *Social Relations in Our Southern States* (New York: Henry B. Price, 1860), 231.

28. Edward A. Pollard, *Black Diamonds Gathered in the Darkey Homes of the South* (New York: Negro Universities Press, 1968), 19, 31–32.

29. Jacobs, *Incidents in the Life of a Slave Girl*, 39. For more on former slaves who describe their owners as hypocrites, see Bibb, "Narrative of the Life and Adventures of Henry Bibb," 69, 118; and Henry Box Brown, *Narrative of the Life of Henry Box Brown, Written by Himself*, ed. Richard Newman (New York: Oxford University Press, 2002), 37–41.

30. Douglass, *Narrative of the Life of Frederick Douglass*, 47. William Craft was given similar council when traveling north with his wife, who was dressed as a White male slaveholder. A White guard on the train told William, "When you get to Philadelphia, run away . . . and have your liberty." Afraid that it might be a trap, William replied that he would "never run away from such a good master." This skepticism dissipated when William encountered a free Black man on the train, who told him about a local abolitionist who harbored runaways, and William "thanked him kindly." Notably, when a Black man broached the subject, William thanked the man, implying that he might want to run or at least was not opposed to the idea. William Craft, *Running a Thousand Miles for Freedom; or, The Escape of William and Ellen Craft from Slavery* (Salem, NH: Ayer Company Publishers, 1991), 77–78. For more on distrusting White people who profess their opposition to slavery, see Bibb, "Narrative of the Life and Adventures of Henry Bibb," 85.

31. For other examples of enslaved people learning that they cannot trust poor White people in particular, see Douglass, *Narrative of the Life of Frederick Douglass*, 47; Stroyer, "My Life in the South," 26; Pennington, "Former Blacksmith," 58–59; and Dr. L. S. Thompson, *The*

Story of Mattie J. Jackson, a True Story, Written and Arranged by Dr. L. S. Thompson, as Given by Mattie (Lawrence, MA.: Sentinel Office, 1866), 5–6.

32. Jacobs, *Incidents in the Life of a Slave Girl*, 131.

33. Brown, *Narrative of the Life of Henry Box Brown*, 42–43.

34. Grandy, "Narrative of the Life of Moses Grandy," 5–6, 11–12, 46.

35. Brown, *Narrative of the Life of Henry Box Brown*, 27–28.

36. Jacobs, *Incidents in the Life of a Slave Girl*, 111, 112.

37. Martin, in Blassingame, *Slave Testimony*, 712–713.

38. Jacobs, *Incidents in the Life of a Slave Girl*, 14–15, 117. Jacobs was equally wary of the vows made by her mistress, who "promised to protect" Jacobs from her husband's sexual abuses. Jacobs said that she "should have been comforted by this": "My experiences in slavery had filled me with distrust. . . . I knew I could not expect kindness or confidence from her." Ibid., 31.

39. For example, Mattie Jackson was told that her grandfather was emancipated then kidnapped, robbed of his free papers, and sold into slavery by his White male business partner, a "Judas-like friend, who had received the bounty." The moral of the story was twofold: that freedom was vulnerable and that White people could not be trusted. Thompson, *Story of Mattie L. Jackson*, 5–6. Similarly, a White man who worked for years beside James W. C. Pennington's father and "professed a warm friendship to [their] family" betrayed the Penningtons by giving a letter from James intended for James's father to their master. Suspecting that they had helped James run away, the Pennington "family was divided" and sold South. Interestingly, the family was eventually reunited and sent "back to Virginia," which James attributed to the fact that his father was in a "situation of considerable trust," which enabled him to prove his loyalty and trustworthiness. Pennington, "Former Blacksmith," 58–59.

40. Douglass, *Narrative of the Life of Frederick Douglass*, 30–31.

41. Ibid., 30–31.Douglass recounted this same anecdote almost verbatim in his second narrative. Frederick Douglass, *My Bondage and My Freedom* (New York: Penguin, 1993), 88–89.

42. Brown, *Narrative of the Life of Henry Box Brown*, 45.

43. Ibid., 48.

44. Jacobs, *Incidents in the Life of a Slave Girl*, 108.

45. Bibb, "Narrative of the Life and Adventures of Henry Bibb," 122.

46. Douglass, *Narrative of the Life of Frederick Douglass*, 61.

47. Trudy Govier explains that "trust is the glue of social life," critical to the success of all "complex societies." Govier, *Social Trust and Human Communities*, 26.

48. Douglass, *My Bondage and My Freedom*, 203.

49. Harper, "Harper's Memoir on Slavery," 81; Jacobs, *Incidents in the Life of a Slave Girl*, 110.

50. Craft, *Running a Thousand Miles for Freedom*, 59.

51. McTyeire, "Plantation Life," 363.

52. Legal records reveal that some slaveholders spoke in their wills of leaving "faithful" enslaved people to be cared for by their heirs: for example, *Tooke v. Hardeman*, 7 Ga. 20, June 1849; *Walker v. Jones*, 23 Ala. 448, June 1853; *Harden v. Mangham*, 18 Ga. 563, August 1855; *Pace v. Mealing*, 21 Ga. 28, March 1857; *Sheftall v. Roberts*, 30 Ga. 453, January 1860; and *Cobb v. Battle*, 34 Ga. 458, June 1866. This was sometimes done after states like Georgia limited the ability of slaveholders to fully manumit enslaved people. For other examples of slaveholders freeing "trusty" and "faithful" enslaved people, see *Carroll v. Brumby*, 13 Ala. 102, January 1848; *Cleland v. Waters*, 16 Ga. 496, October 1854; *Hughes v. Allen*, 31 Ga. 483, November 1860. See Catterall, *Judicial Cases Concerning American Slavery and the Negro*, 3:23, 190, 44, 54, 74, 92, 166, 38–39, 80.

53. *Scranton v. Rose Demere and John Demere, by prochein ami*, Ga. 92, January 1849 [93]. Ibid., 3:21–22.

54. All too often even an owner's intentions to manumit a person did not suffice; many court cases reveal that the state could ignore the requests made in wills to manumit slaves. Examples include *Spencer v. Negroes Amy and Thomas*, R.M.C. 178, May 1822 (Georgia); *American Colonization Society v. Bass*, 18 Ga. 127, May 1855; *Word v. Mitchell*, 32 Ga. 623, May 1861; *Harrison v. Harrison*, 9 Ala. 470, January 1846; and *Hooper v. Hooper*, 32 Ala. 669, June 1858, Ibid., 3:9, 42–43, 84, 159, 226–227. The state was not the only obstacle. Some records indicate that a slaveowner promised manumission to enslaved people, only to have their heirs renege the offer. David Holmes, in Blassingame, *Slave Testimony*, 297.

55. Brown, *Narrative of the Life of Henry Box Brown*, 26–28.

56. Douglass, *My Bondage and My Freedom*, 220–221.

57. Jacobs, *Incidents in the Life of a Slave Girl*, 26.

58. James Hope, in Blassingame, *Slave Testimony*, 12–13. Enslaved people were known to make similar promises to would-be buyers. Solomon Northup recalled that when a man tried to buy only one of Eliza's children, she begged him to buy her daughter and herself as well and "promised . . . to be the most faithful slave that ever lived." In this way Eliza was attaching her loyalty to the combined value of her daughter and herself, offering future fidelity in exchange for not losing her daughter. Solomon Northup, "Twelve Years a Slave," in Osofsky, *Puttin' on Ole Massa*, 225–406, at 264–265.

59. Henson, *Life of Josiah Henson*, 47, 32–33.

60. Ibid., 47.

61. Elizabeth Keckley, *Behind the Scenes in the Lincoln White House: Memoirs of an African-American Seamstress* (Mineola, NY: Dover Publications, 2006), 48, 18–19.

62. Bibb, "Narrative of the Life and Adventures of Henry Bibb," 169–170. As the Bibb passages show, describing an enslaved person as "Christian" was intended to signal their honesty and integrity. According to William Wells Brown, an enslaved person might be described by an auctioneer as "a good cook, good washer, a good obedient servant. She has got religion!" to express to would-be buyers that an enslaved person would be loyal and docile, as they found "religion very profitable to them." Brown, "Narrative of William Wells Brown," 211.

63. For more on how distrustful enslaved people were valued, see Eugene Genovese's chapter on theft by enslaved people in *Roll, Jordan, Roll*, 607. Court cases also reveal how often masters lied about the veracity and criminal history of enslaved people. See *Cozzins v. Whitaker*, 3 Stew. And P. 322, January 1833 [323]; and *Bell v. Troy*, 35, Ala. 184, June 1859 [186], in Catterall, *Judicial Cases Concerning American Slavery and the Negro*, 3:137, 235.

64. Bibb, "Narrative of the Life and Adventures of Henry Bibb," 114.

65. Brown, *Narrative of the Life of Henry Box Brown*, 37–38.

66. Bibb, "Narrative of the Life and Adventures of Henry Bibb," 118.

67. Brown, *Narrative of the Life of Henry Box Brown*, 37–39, 41. Henry Bibb and Solomon Northup concurred that enslaved people's religious instruction from their owners solely focused on the precept of "obey thy master." Bibb, "Narrative of the Life and Adventures of Henry Bibb," 69; Northup, "Twelve Years a Slave," 292.

68. Douglass, *My Bondage and My Freedom*, 143. For another example of former slaves' thoughts on the hypocrisy of religious slaveholders, see Charles Ball, *Fifty Years in Chains; or, The Life of an American Slave* (New York: H. Dayton Publishers, 1859), 15.

69. For example, when his owner sent him down the Mississippi, Henson decided to kill the slave traders, steal their money, and flee. He went into minute detail describing how he was about to slay a man with an axe when "suddenly the thought came to [him], 'What! Commit *murder*! and you a Christian?'" and he grew ashamed of his homicidal intentions. Henson may have laid out these hypothetical plots to build suspense, but by first explaining how he was justified in murdering slave traders, then articulating why he did not, he emphasized his personal integrity. Henson, *Life of Josiah Henson*, 41–43.

70. Ibid., 23–25.

71. Noted sociologist Erving Goffman argued that in social scenarios where deceit is not expected it is much easier to enact, but once someone believes that another person is untrustworthy then they are on guard for dishonesty, forcing any "con-man" to work doubly hard to assuage concerns that they should not be trusted. Goffman, *Presentation of Self in Everyday Life*, 8, 225.

72. Bibb, "Narrative of the Life and Adventures of Henry Bibb," 118.

73. Martin, in Blassingame, *Slave Testimony*, 702, 709–712.

74. Northup, "Twelve Years a Slave," 352–354. This defense did not work when Epps accused the enslaved Patsey of having sexual relations with a White neighbor. Though Patsey swore she had only gone to their house to borrow soap, Epps claimed she had gone there to indulge a "baser passion." When she denied this he declared that she was lying, to which she responded, "I *don't* lie, massa. If you kill me, I'll stick to that." Knowing that Epps would beat her regardless of whether she was telling the truth, she sought to defend her honesty by staking her life on it. In this way she emphasized that she was telling the truth, while perhaps subtly reminding him that brutally beating her would not incite her to reverse her statement. This suggests that enslaved women may have had a more difficult time proving their trustworthiness, or at least defending their innocence, to slaveholders. Ibid., 367.

75. Bibb, "Narrative of the Life and Adventures of Henry Bibb," 132.

76. Eugene Genovese argued that though theft among the enslaved was rare, "one or two thieves would keep an entire plantation agitated and foster mutual suspicion." Genovese, *Roll, Jordan, Roll*, 607.

77. Stroyer, "My Life in the South," 63–64.

78. According to sociologist Niklas Luhmann, people learn how to trust from a young age, typically from family members. Govier, *Social Trust and Human Communities*, 26.

79. Brown, *Narrative of the Life of Henry Box Brown*, 17, 37–38; Pennington, "Former Blacksmith," 30.

80. Stroyer, "My Life in the South," 58.

81. According to Lawrence Levine, given the starvation rations enslaved people were given it is little wonder that obtaining food was the focus in so many trickster tales, especially "through guile from some stronger animal." He also observes that such stories are teaching the double standard of honesty, because "only rarely do these stories picture slaves stealing from one another." Levine, *Black Culture and Black Consciousness*, 108, 128, 131. For more discussion of the meaning and uses of trickster tales, see chap. 2, "The Meaning of Slave Tales," 81–135.

82. Marie Jenkins Schwartz explains that parents turned a blind eye to the origins of the food their children brought them, "in part because they reasoned that slaves were not committing theft when they took from their owners," because "owners were the real thieves." Marie Jenkins Schwartz, "Family Life in the Slave Quarters: Survival Strategies," *OAH Magazine of History* 15,

no. 4, Family History (Summer 2001): 36–41, at 37, 39. Throughout the South many historic plantation home tours refer to the paths between external kitchens and plantation homes as a "whistle walk," claiming that the name comes from the supposedly antebellum practice of slave mistresses insisting that the enslaved people, often children, tasked with bringing food from kitchen to table must whistle as they did so. This was based on the idea that one could not whistle and chew stolen food at the same time. Scholar of sound Mark M. Smith argues that while "forms of aural control were real," and while many "southern historic house museums" relate stories of their "whistle walks," "little evidence exists to support such claims" that this method of surveillance was employed in the antebellum period. This suggests that this story, which I have heard from a docent at Melrose Plantation in Melrose, Louisiana, was a post-Emancipation construct intended to perpetuate the White supremacist idea that enslaved people were innately deceitful. Mark M. Smith, *Listening to Nineteenth Century America* (Chapel Hill: University of North Carolina Press, 2001), 76.

83. Calvin Schermerhorn points out that enslaved children "learned survival behavior in an environment that rewarded deception." Calvin Schermerhorn, "'Left Behind but Getting Ahead': Antebellum Slavery's Orphans in the Chesapeake, 1820–60," in *Children in Slavery Through the Ages*, ed. Gwyn Campbell, Suzanne Miers, and Joseph C. Miller, 204– 224 (Athens: Ohio University Press, 2009), 217–218. For more on children and trust, see Goffman, *Presentation of Self in Everyday Life*, 91.

84. Schwartz, "Family Life in the Slave Quarters," 39.

85. Jacobs, *Incidents in the Life of a Slave Girl*, 115, 116.

86. Ibid., 123, 128.

87. Ibid., 146.

88. Stroyer, "My Life in the South," 42–43, 57–59. Stroyer notes that "these customs" were only used "among the negroes . . . for they did not consider it stealing when they took anything from their master." Ibid., 59.

89. Douglass, *My Bondage and My Freedom*, 196–197.

90. Ibid., 173, 217. For another example of a would-be fugitive being "betrayed" by a trusted, fellow enslaved person, see Leonard Black, *The Life and Sufferings of Leonard Black, a Fugitive From Slavery, Written by Himself* (New Bedford, MA: Press of Benjamin Lindsey, 1847), 22.

91. Northup, "Twelve Years a Slave," 353, 374–377.

92. Erving Goffman contends that time is crucial to forging trust. Goffman, *Presentation of Self in Everyday Life*, 16.

93. Martin, in Blassingame, *Slave Testimony*, 715–716.

94. Stroyer, "My Life in the South," 63–64.

95. Bibb, "Narrative of the Life and Adventures of Henry Bibb," 93–94.

96. For a discussion of the relationship between space, mobility, resistance, and gender in the antebellum South, see Stephanie Camp, *Closer to Freedom: Enslaved Women and Everyday Resistance in the Plantation South* (Chapel Hill: University of North Carolina Press, 2004).

97. Martin, in Blassingame, *Slave Testimony*, 712–713.

98. William later told his sister that he refused his owner's money because he would not "tak[e] any money from his master on false pretences." Though he planned to run away, he wanted to emphasize that he was not a thief. Jacobs, *Incidents in the Life of a Slave Girl*, 110–112.

99. Douglass, *My Bondage and My Freedom*, 237–238, 242. Josiah Henson had earned the reputation of being a "trust-worthy slave" over the years, so he was able to do exactly what

Douglass described. With the confidence of his owner, Henson was permitted to travel as a preacher, gaining the money to buy his freedom. Henson, *Life of Josiah Henson*, 28–30.

100. As Karen Halttunnen argues, in the "treacherous city . . . character had to be assessed quickly within relatively fleeting relationships." Halttunen, *Confidence Men and Painted Women*, 51.

101. For example, see Frederick Law Olmsted, *The Cotton Kingdom: A Traveler's Observations on Cotton and Slavery in the American Slave States, 1853–1861* (New York: Da Capo Press, 1996), 574; Douglass, *Narrative of the Life of Frederick Douglass*, 30.

102. Pennington, "Former Blacksmith," 22.

103. Ibid., 23.

104. Martin, in Blassingame, *Slave Testimony*, 733–734.

105. Brown, "Narrative of William Wells Brown," 218–219. James W. C. Pennington also experienced the moment of judgment when he had to decide whether to trust a Quaker man that a neighbor had directed him to go see. Though in the free state of Pennsylvania, he remained wary of strangers until the man offered him food and shelter and Pennington's "fear subsided." As a result, the Quaker won Pennington's "confidence," and he felt that he "might confide to him a fact which [he] had, as yet, confided to no one"—the fact that he was a fugitive. Pennington, "Former Blacksmith," 41.

106. Douglass, *Narrative of the Life of Frederick Douglass*, 93. For other examples of skepticism of White people by fugitive slaves, see Jacobs, *Incidents in the Life of a Slave Girl*, 131, 138–139.

107. Craft, *Running a Thousand Miles for Freedom*, 83–85.

108. See, for example, Brown, "Narrative of William Wells Brown," 207; Grandy, "Narrative of the Life of Moses Grandy," 34; Northup, "Twelve Years a Slave," 280, 282; Henson, *Life of Josiah Henson*, 5, 19; Pennington, "Former Blacksmith," 8; and Jacobs, *Incidents in the Life of a Slave Girl*, 110–112.

109. Henry McMillan, in Blassingame, *Slave Testimony*, 379–381.

110. Bibb, "Narrative of the Life and Adventures of Henry Bibb," 66, 95; Jacobs, *Incidents in the Life of a Slave Girl*, 85. Bibb explained that "the only weapon of self-defense that [he] could use successfully was that of deception," which he referred to as "the most effective defense a slave can use," while Jacobs claimed that "cunning" was "the only weapon of the weak and oppressed against the strength of tyrants."

111. Jacobs, *Incidents in the Life of a Slave Girl*, 137.

112. That is to say that the least of formerly enslaved people's concerns was atoning for any past lies. Laurence Levine argues that while trickster tales might "have served as a convenient channel for whatever guilt slaves felt" about stealing or lying, "but on the whole the evidence indicates that the slaves' strong convictions regarding the injustice they suffered at the hands of whites, who themselves were guilty of hypocrisy and gross immorality, were sufficient to allow them to relax or neutralize their normal standards and mores in certain situations." Levine, *Black Culture and Black Consciousness*, 124.

113. Northup, "Twelve Years a Slave," 227, 388. In the same vein, Harriet Jacobs commenced the preface to her autobiography with the aside "Reader, be assured this narrative is no fiction." Jacobs, *Incidents in the Life of a Slave Girl*, 2.

114. See, for example, Bibb, "Narrative of the Life and Adventures of Henry Bibb," 153.

115. Grandy, "Narrative of the Life of Moses Grandy," iii–iv.

116. Joanne M. Braxton, "Harriet Jacobs' 'Incidents in the Life of a Slave Girl': The Re-Definition of the Slave Narrative Genre," *Massachusetts Review* 27, no. 2 (Summer 1986): 379–387, at 383.

117. Lunsford Lane, "The Narrative of Lunsford Lane, formerly of Raleigh, N.C.," in Katz, *Five Slave Narratives*, 1–54, at 27, 29–30.

Chapter 5

1. Frederick Douglass, *My Bondage and My Freedom* (New York: Penguin, 1993), 219. Frederick Douglass frequently differentiated between physical and emotional or mental abuse, arguing that the latter was far more brutal, and that his "troubles from the beginning, have been less physical than mental." Ibid., 237. See also 107, 161–162.

2. See, for example, William Harper, "Harper's Memoir on Slavery," in *The Pro-Slavery Argument: As Maintained by the Most Distinguished Writers of the Southern States, Containing the Several Essays, on the Subject, of Chancellor Harper, Governor Hammond, Dr. Simms, and Professor Dew*, 287–490 (Charleston, SC: Walker, Richards and Co., 1852), 17, 56–59; Thomas Jefferson, *Notes on the State of Virginia, with an Appendix* (Boston: H. Sprague, 1802), 190–195; Timothy Flint, *Recollections of the Last Ten Years* (Boston: Cummings, Hilliard, and Company, 1826), 137; and Edward A. Pollard, *Black Diamonds Gathered in the Darkey Homes of the South* (New York: Negro Universities Press, 1968), 38–39.

3. A noted exception is Saidiya Hartman's *Scenes of Subjection*, in which she argues that attention to spectacularized violence desensitizes audiences to that violence while reinforcing the idiom of "black suffering," and it ignores the variety of ways that slavery's violence was manifested in the mundane, including through commodification and forced performances like minstrel shows. Saidiya Hartman, *Scenes of Subjection: Terror, Slavery, and Self-Making in Nineteenth-Century America* (New York: Oxford University Press, 1997), 19–28.

4. Lawrence Meir Friedman, *Crime and Punishment in American History* (New York: Basic Books, 1993), 85.

5. Some authors speak of there being a "variety of measures used to keep slaves in line" other than whipping, yet only go on to discuss physical forms of correction, listing branding, stocks, and execution as other possible punishments. See, for example, Daniel E. Walker, *No More, No More: Slavery and Cultural Resistance in Havana and New Orleans* (Minneapolis: University of Minnesota Press, 2004); Elizabeth Dale, *Criminal Justice in the United States, 1789–1939* (Cambridge: Cambridge University Press, 2011); Edward L. Ayers, *Vengeance and Justice: Crime and Punishment in the 19th-Century American South* (New York: Oxford University Press, 1984); and Eugene D. Genovese, *Roll, Jordan, Roll: The World the Slaves Made* (New York: Vintage, 1976), 63–64.

6. Vernetta D. Young and Zoe Spencer assert that "the punishment of slaves was usually corporeal" and that "noncorporeal punishments typically were not used" to punish slaves, arguing that it would be "futile and counterproductive" to try to provoke feelings, in particular humiliation, in enslaved people, who were already thoroughly inculcated with "stereotypes about their inferiority." Vernetta D. Young and Zoe Spencer, "Multiple Jeopardy: The Impact of Race, Gender, and Slavery on the Punishment of Women in Antebellum America," in *Race, Gender and Punishment*, ed. Mary Bosworth and Jeanne Flavin, 65– 76 (Piscataway, NJ: Rutgers University Press, 2006), 71–72.

7. Samuel Cartwright, "Diseases and Peculiarities of the Negro Race," *DeBow's Review* 11, no. 1 (July 1851): 65–69.

8. Friedman, *Crime and Punishment in American History*, 88.

9. Henry Box Brown, *Narrative of the Life of Henry Box Brown, Written by Himself*, ed. Richard Newman (New York: Oxford University Press, 2002), 3, 4, 28.

10. Lunsford Lane, "The Narrative of Lunsford Lane, formerly of Raleigh, N.C.," in *Five Slave Narratives: A Compendium*, ed. William Loren Katz, 1–54 (New York: Arno Press and the *New York Times*, 1968), 52.

11. Articles about overseers and advertisements in agricultural journals like *Southern Planter* and *DeBow's Review* reveal the extent to which planters were concerned about managing their slaves. For example, one plantation account book by J. W. Randolph of Richmond, Virginia, advertised in *Southern Planter* and *DeBow's Review*, touted its chapter on the "Rules for the Government and Discipline of the Negroes." "Plantation Book," *Southern Planter* 12, no. 8 (August 1852): 255; *DeBow's Review* 14, no. 1 (January 1853): 92. For more on disciplining the enslaved, see Tattler, "Management of Negroes," *Southern Planter* 11, no. 2 (February 1851): 39–43.

12. Jacob Stroyer, "My Life in the South," in Katz, *Five Slave Narratives*, 3–100, at 74–75.

13. In his history of punishment in the nineteenth-century South, Edward Ayers points out that the majority of "white Southerners simply did not perceive whipping to be particularly cruel or even harsh punishment for blacks." Ayers, *Vengeance and Justice*, 101–102.

14. "Misery and Degradation of British Workmen-Slave Laws," *DeBow's Review* 14, no. 1 (January 1853): 271.

15. Genovese, *Roll, Jordan, Roll*, 63.

16. Harper, "Harper's Memoir on Slavery," 34.

17. "Misery and Degradation," 271.

18. "Song of the Cane Fields," *DeBow's Review* 8 (1850): 68.

19. Harper, "Harper's Memoir on Slavery," 34.

20. Eugene Genovese notes that some used a "Cowhide paddle," believing that it "left no scars while inflicting terrible pain." Genovese, *Roll, Jordan, Roll*, 65. Similarly, Gwendolyn Midlo Hall observes that some slaveholders in St. Domingue viewed the punishment of cutting the hamstrings of frequent runaways with "great repugnance" in part because it would "diminish" a slave's "value." Gwendolyn Midlo Hall, *Social Control in Slave Plantation Societies: A Comparison of St. Domingue and Cuba* (Baltimore: Johns Hopkins University Press, 1971), 75.

21. *Whitney vs. Whitney*, Mississippi, 7S. and M. 740, November 1846 [750], in Helen Tunnicliff Catterall, ed., *Judicial Cases Concerning American Slavery and the Negro: Volume III: Cases from the Courts of Georgia, Florida, Alabama, Mississippi and Louisiana* (New York: Negro Universities Press, 1968), 3:310.

22. Tattler, "Management of Negroes," 41.

23. Of course, Cartwright undermined this point by conceding that a "frightened" enslaved person would not run away. Though Cartwright called for "kind" and "gracious" attitudes to enslaved people, he acknowledged that coercing an enslaved person to feel fear would likely get the same result: an enslaved person who was not inclined to run away. Either way, the goal was to maintain affective control. Cartwright, "Diseases and Peculiarities."

24. Mississippi Planter, "Management of Negroes upon Southern Estates," *DeBow's Review* 10 (June 1851): 625. Similarly, W. W. Gilmer observed in "Management of Servants" that "a great deal of whipping is not necessary. . . . The hope of reward and fear of punishment induce human action in master and servant." W. W. Gilmer, "Management of Servants," *Southern Planter* 12, no. 4 (April 1852): 106–107.

25. See, for example, "Harvest," *Southern Planter* 12, no. 6 (June 1852): 177–179; and "Overseers," *Southern Planter* 16, no. 5 (May 1856): 147–148.

26. For more on White Southern men of the planter class's desire to dominate kin, peers, subordinates, and enslaved people, see Stephanie McCurry, *Masters of Small Worlds: Yeoman Households, Gender Relations, and the Political Culture of the Antebellum South Carolina Low Country* (New York: Oxford University Press, 1995); and Kenneth S. Greenberg, "The Nose, the Lie, and the Duel in the Antebellum South," *American Historical Review* 95, no. 1 (February 1990): 57–74.

27. From an 1848 letter to William Gilmore Simms, quoted in Drew Gilpin Faust, *James Henry Hammond and the Old South: A Design for Mastery* (Baton Rouge: Louisiana State University Press, 1982), 4. According to Faust, Hammond was inculcated with the drive for absolute discipline from a young age by his father, who advised the then-teenaged Hammond in an 1826 letter that the "greatest contests that the greatest men have ever had . . . were with their passions to subdue and over come them." Faust, *James Henry Hammond and the Old South*, 9. For more on Hammond's battle to master his body, face, speech, and "passions," see ibid., 225.

28. Ibid., 307.

29. For examples of injunctions against disciplining the enslaved in anger, see "Overseers," *Southern Planter* 16, no. 5 (May 1856): 147–148; "The Duties of an Overseer," *Southern Planter* 17, no. 7 (July 1857): 415; and "From Affleck's Cotton Plantation Record and Account Book—the Duties of an Overseer," *American Cotton Planter* 2, no. 12 (December 1854): 333–355.

30. H. N. McTyeire, "Plantation Life—Duties and Responsibilities," *DeBow's Review* 29, no. 3 (September 1860): 361.

31. Tattler, "Management of Negroes," 42.

32. Jefferson, *Notes on the State of Virginia*, 223.

33. Charles Ball, *Fifty Years in Chains; or, The Life of an American Slave* (New York: H. Dayton Publishers, 1859), 273, 27.

34. Stroyer, "My Life in the South," 72.

35. Solomon Northup, "Twelve Years a Slave," in in *Puttin' on Ole Massa: The Slave Narratives of Henry Bibb, William Wells Brown, and Solomon Northup*, ed. Gilbert Osofsky, 225–406 (New York: Harper & Row, 1969), 364.

36. James W. C. Pennington, "The Former Blacksmith," in Katz, *Five Slave Narratives*, iv–87, at viii.

37. Stroyer, "My Life in the South," 28.

38. Douglass, *My Bondage and My Freedom*, 65. Emphasizing this point, he contrasted the "delight" his master Lloyd took in whipping an enslaved woman with the demeanor of the overseer, Mr. Sevier, who was perceived to "take no especial pleasure" in whipping slaves. Ibid., 67, 73.

39. According to Genovese, "a master who used his whip too often or with too much vigor risked . . . hatred" from those they enslaved. Genovese, *Roll, Jordan, Roll*, 124–125.

40. "Hiring Negroes," *Southern Planter* 12, no. 12 (December 1852): 376–379.

41. Douglass, *Narrative of the Life of Frederick Douglass*, 42.

42. *Commonwealth v. Turner*, VA, 5 Randolph 678, November 1827, in Helen Tunnicliff Catterall, ed., *Judicial Cases Concerning American Slavery and the Negro: Volume I: Cases from the Courts of England, Virginia, West Virginia, and Kentucky* (New York: Negro Universities

Press, 1968), 1:150. In the case, a slaveholder was sued "for cruelly beating his own slave." The court upheld a lower court's decision to indict. Ibid., 150.

43. Harriet Jacobs, *Incidents in the Life of a Slave Girl* (Mineola, NY: Dover Publications, 2001), 30–32.

44. J. D. B. DeBow, *The Commercial Review of the South and West, a Monthly Journal of Trade, Commerce, Commercial Polity, Agriculture, Manufacturer, Internal Improvements and General* Literature, vol. VIII, New Series vol. II (New Orleans, 1850), 70.

45. Henry Bibb, "Narrative of the Life and Adventures of Henry Bibb, an American Slave, Written by Himself," in Osofsky, *Puttin' on Ole Massa*, 51–172, at 115.

46. Sally Hadden argues that Southern slave patrols were known to "toy . . . with a slave, threatening a whipping." Sally E. Hadden, *Slave Patrols: Law and Violence in Virginia and the Carolinas* (Cambridge, MA: Harvard University Press, 2001), 118.

47. Douglass, *Narrative of the Life of Frederick Douglass*, 55.

48. Jacobs, *Incidents in the Life of a Slave Girl*, 72.

49. Ibid., 26.

50. Grandy, "Narrative of the Life of Moses Grandy," 36.

51. Madison Jefferson, in *Slave Testimony: Two Centuries of Letters, Speeches, Interviews, and Autobiographies*, ed. John W. Blassingame (Baton Rouge: Louisiana State University Press, 1998), 217, 218, 221.

52. Jacobs, *Incidents in the Life of a Slave Girl*, 42–43, 88; Ball, *Fifty Years in Chains*, 10–11, 70; Northup, "Twelve Years a Slave," 264–265, 268, 280, 311; William J. Anderson, *Life and Narrative of William J. Anderson, Twenty-Four Years a Slave* (Chicago: Daily Tribune Book and Job Printing Office, 1857), 14, 15.

53. Douglass, *My Bondage and My Freedom*, 192. Daniel Walker identifies a similar practice in Havana, where some slaveholders would pay to have one or two enslaved people whipped each month, not for a specific crime but to keep the other enslaved people from becoming "unmanageable." Walker, *No More, No More*, 28.

54. For more on the punitive use of spectacle, in particular public executions, see Michel Foucault, *Discipline and Punish: The Birth of the Prison* (New York: Vintage, 1995); Michael S. Hindus, *Prisons and Plantations: Crime, Justice and Authority in Massachusetts and South Carolina, 1767–1878* (Chapel Hill: University of North Carolina Press, 1980); and Friedman, *Crime and Punishment in American History*.

55. Olmsted, *Cotton Kingdom*, 572–573.

56. Douglass, *Narrative of the Life of Frederick Douglass*, 33–34; Douglass, *My Bondage and My Freedom*, 93.

57. Grandy, "Narrative of the Life of Moses Grandy," 36.

58. Douglass, *Narrative of the Life of Frederick Douglass*, 32.

59. For more on the use of shaming punishments in the North and South, see Friedman, *Crime and Punishment in American History*; and Hindus, *Prisons and Plantations*.

60. For the mention of inciting anxiety to control enslaved people, see Bibb, "Narrative of the Life and Adventures of Henry Bibb," 115. For reference to appealing to "pride" to control enslaved people, see "Harvest."

61. "All About Overseers," *Southern Planter* 18, no. 7 (July 1858): 413. For more on invoking fear to punish the enslaved, see Gilmer, "Management of Servants," 106–107.

62. "Duties of an Overseer," 415.

63. Z. Kingsley, *A Treatise on the Patriarchal System of Society as It Exists . . . Under the Name of Slavery. By an Inhabitant of Florida* (1833), 21–22.

64. Douglass, *My Bondage and My Freedom*, 129.

65. For more on enslaved people's fears of being sold away from family, see Amy Murrell Taylor, *The Divided Family in Civil War America* (Chapel Hill: University of North Carolina Press, 2005), 192.

66. George S. Sawyer, *Southern Institutes* (Philadelphia: J. B. Lippincott & Co., 1858), 222; Lewis Hayden, quoted in Blassingame, *Slave Testimony*, 697. For more examples of arguments that enslaved people or people of African descent were emotionally different or limited, see Drew Gilpin Faust, ed., *The Ideology of Slavery: Proslavery Thought in the Antebellum South, 1830–1860* (Baton Rouge: Louisiana State University Press, 1981), 79; Harper, "Harper's Memoir on Slavery," 17, 56–59; Jefferson, *Notes on the State of Virginia*, 190–195; Flint, *Recollections of the Last Ten Years*, 139–140; Pollard, *Black Diamonds*, 38–39; and Ezra Tawil, *The Making of Racial Sentiment: Slavery and the Birth of the Frontier Romance* (New York: Cambridge University Press, 2006). For more examples of members of the planter class comparing the family bonds of enslaved people to those of animals, see Jacobs, *Incidents in the Life of a Slave Girl*, 86–87; and Frances Anne Kemble, *Journal of a Residence on a Georgian Plantation in 1838–1839* (Savannah, GA: Beehive Foundation, 1992), 60.

67. Bibb, "Narrative of the Life and Adventures of Henry Bibb," 113, 116.

68. Pennington, "Former Blacksmith," 12–13, 58.

69. See, for example, Hayden, in Blassingame, *Slave Testimony*, 695–696; and Jefferson, in Blassingame, *Slave Testimony*, 217, 218, 221.

70. Kemble, *Journal of a Residence on a Georgian Plantation*, 108.

71. Butler Family Papers, June–Dec 1860, MSS 1026, Box 5 of 18, Lower Mississippi Valley Collection, Louisiana State University, Baton Rouge.

72. Ibid.

73. Ibid.

74. Ibid.

75. Jacobs, *Incidents in the Life of a Slave Girl*, 58–66.

76. Douglass, *My Bondage and My Freedom*, 65–67.

77. A number of historians have written about how enslaved people survived and resisted slavery through affective ties, and by fighting attempts to sever those bonds, most notably John Blassingame, *The Slave Community: Plantation Life in the Antebellum South* (New York: Oxford University Press, 1972); Herbert Gutman, *The Black Family in Slavery and Freedom, 1750–1925* (New York: Vintage, 1977); Jacqueline Jones, *Labor of Love, Labor of Sorrow: Black Women, Work, and the Family from Slavery to the Present* (New York: Vintage, 1985); and Marie Jenkins Schwartz, "Family Life in the Slave Quarters: Survival Strategies," *OAH Magazine of History* 15, no. 4, Family History (Summer 2001): 36–41.

78. Northup, "Twelve Years a Slave," 264–265.

79. Ibid., 268, 280, 311. For another example of an enslaved mother being punished for refusing to suppress grief over being separated from her children, see Ball, *Fifty Years in Chains*, 10–11.

80. Stephanie Camp argues that joy and pleasure specifically functioned as a form of resistance in an institution in which the enslaved body was so often objectified and reduces to a "site . . . of suffering." Stephanie Camp, *Closer to Freedom: Enslaved Women and Everyday Resistance in the Plantation South* (Chapel Hill: University of North Carolina Press, 2004), 62–64, 68.

81. Jacobs, *Incidents in the Life of a Slave Girl*, 22–23.
82. Ibid., 36–37.
83. Martin, in Blassingame, *Slave Testimony*, 728.

Chapter 6

1. Solomon Northup, "Twelve Years a Slave," in *Puttin' on Ole Massa: The Slave Narratives of Henry Bibb, William Wells Brown, and Solomon Northup*, ed. Gilbert Osofsky, 225–406 (New York: Harper & Row, 1969), 348.

2. Some proslavery advocates challenged the precepts of the Founding Fathers, and the idea that the preamble to the Declaration of Independence promised equality and liberty for all, including enslaved people. In a proslavery essay, William Harper posited that "no man was ever born free . . . that no two men were ever born equal," and that people, including children and prisoners, were regularly denied their freedom. William Harper, "Harper's Memoir on Slavery," in *The Pro-Slavery Argument: As Maintained by the Most Distinguished Writers of the Southern States, Containing the Several Essays, on the Subject, of Chancellor Harper, Governor Hammond, Dr. Simms, and Professor Dew*, 287–490 (Charleston, SC: Walker, Richards and Co., 1852), 5–7. Meanwhile, William Gilmore Simms contended that the Declaration was written in "angry" times, by "angry" forefathers, and "what they alleged to be self-evident *then*, is at this time, when we are comparatively cool, a source of very great doubt and disputation." William Gilmore Simms, "The Morals of Slavery," in *Pro-Slavery Argument*, 175–285, at 250–251.

3. Northup, "Twelve Years a Slave," 338. Many authors of slave narratives discussed how long they had dreamed of becoming free. For example, James L. Bradley recalled, "From the time I was fourteen years old, I used to think a great deal about freedom. It was my heart's desire. . . . My heart ached to feel within me the life of liberty." Bradley claimed that for enslaved people freedom was "the great thought and feeling that fills the mind full all the time." James L. Bradley, in *Slave Testimony: Two Centuries of Letters, Speeches, Interviews, and Autobiographies*, ed. John W. Blassingame (Baton Rouge: Louisiana State University Press, 1998), 688, 690. See also Jacob Stroyer, "My Life in the South," in *Five Slave Narratives: A Compendium*, ed. William Loren Katz, 3–100 (New York: Arno Press and the *New York Times*, 1968), 21.

4. Northup, "Twelve Years a Slave," 370.

5. Tera W. Hunter, *To 'Joy My Freedom: Southern Black Women's Lives and Labors After the Civil War* (Cambridge, MA: Harvard University Press, 1997), 1–2.

6. For example, see Stroyer, "My Life in the South," 35; Northup, "Twelve Years a Slave," 227; James Madison, in Blassingame, *Slave Testimony*, 267; Charles Ball, *Fifty Years in Chains; or, The Life of an American Slave* (New York: H. Dayton Publishers, 1859), 298–299; Leonard Black, *The Life and Sufferings of Leonard Black, A Fugitive from Slavery, Written by Himself* (New Bedford, MA: Press of Benjamin Lindsey, 1847), 22; and Ira Berlin, Barbara J. Fields, Steven F. Miller, Joseph P. Reidy, and Leslie S. Rowland, eds., *Free at Last: A Documentary History of Slavery, Freedom, and the Civil War* (New York: New Press, 1992), 185–186, 193.

7. Henry Bibb, "Narrative of the Life and Adventures of Henry Bibb, an American Slave, Written by Himself," in Osofsky, *Puttin' on Ole Massa*, 225–406, at 94; Stroyer, "My Life in the South," 61.

8. Jean Baptiste Meuillon Papers, 713, Louisiana Research Collection, Tulane University, New Orleans, LA.

9. *Trudeau's Executive v. Robinette*, 4 Mart. La. 577, January 1817. For more reference to the language of "enjoying" freedom, or freedom to be "enjoyed" in court cases, see *Bazzi v.*

Rose and Her Child, 8 Mart. La. 149, May 1820; *Catin v. D'Orgenoy's Heirs*, 8 Mart. La. 218, June 1820; and *Julien v. Langlish*, 9 Mart. La. 205, January 1821, in Helen Tunnicliff Catterall, ed., *Judicial Cases Concerning American Slavery and the Negro: Volume III: Cases from the Courts of Georgia, Florida, Alabama, Mississippi and Louisiana* (New York: Negro Universities Press, 1968), 3:463–467.

10. William M. Reddy, *The Navigation of Feeling: A Framework for the History of Emotions* (New York: Cambridge University Press, 2001), 129. For more, see chap. 4, "Emotional Liberty," in particular.

11. Thomas Roderick Dew, "Professor Dew on Slavery," in *Pro-Slavery Argument*, 287–490, at 293, 437.

12. "The Two Great Evils of Virginia and Their One Common Remedy," *Southern Planter* 19, no. 10 (October 1859): 644.

13. William Craft, *Running a Thousand Miles for Freedom; or, The Escape of William and Ellen Craft from Slavery* (Salem, NH: Ayer Company Publishers, 1991), 37.

14. Jacobs, *Incidents in the Life of a Slave Girl*, 72.

15. *Roger, next friend of negro woman Antoinette, her two children, and negro man Jack, v. Marlow*, R.M.C. 542, May 1837, in Catterall, *Judicial Cases Concerning American Slavery and the Negro*, 3:14–15.

16. It is notable that Phillip Moore said that manumitting Henrietta was "the dying wish of his late mother." Judging by how many slaveholders employed such language in court, it suggests that they believed that affective claims could compete with legal claims. Slave Manuscript Collection 503, Folder 5, Louisiana Research Collection, Tulane University, New Orleans, LA.

17. Jean Baptiste Meuillon Papers, 713, Louisiana Research Collection, Tulane University, New Orleans, LA.

18. Lunsford Lane, "The Narrative of Lunsford Lane, Formerly of Raleigh, N.C.," in Katz, *Five Slave Narratives*, 1–54, at 17.

19. American Convention for Promoting the Abolition of Slavery, *Minutes of the Proceedings of the Third Convention of Delegates from the Abolition Societies Established in Different Parts of the United States Assembled at Philadelphia, on the First Day of January, One Thousand Seven Hundred and Ninety-Six, and Continued, by Adjournments, Until the Seventh Day of the Same Month, Inclusive* (Philadelphia: Zachariah Poulson, 1796), 12–15.

Proslavery advocates also argued that enslaved people were emotionally unfit for freedom. William Harper cautioned that unless the enslaved population was "prepared for its enjoyment," freedom would be "fatal to himself and others" and former slaves would be "miserable." Harper, "Harper's Memoir on Slavery," 48–49, 73.

20. C. Vann Woodward, ed., *Mary Chesnut's Civil War* (New Haven, CT: Yale University Press, 1981), 78.

21. Ibid., 407, 467, 535, 159, 375, 220.

22. A December 23, 1861, report from Hilton Head, SC, via the *New York Tribune*, in Blassingame, *Slave Testimony*, 360–363.

23. Letter from William Birney, January 28, 1964, in Berlin et al., *Free at Last*, 346–348.

24. Dew, "Professor Dew on Slavery," 439; Harper, "Harper's Memoir on Slavery," 48–49, 73. For more on White fears about slave rebellion during the war, see Hunter, *To 'Joy My Freedom*, 20; and Berlin et al., *Free at Last*, 4, 5, 131, 133.

25. For examples of Union officers remarking on how formerly enslaved people choose not to resort to revenge when interacting with former slaveholders or Confederates, see Berlin et al., *Free at Last*, 115–116, 491.

26. Woodward, *Mary Chesnut's Civil War*, 198–199. Chesnut mentioned more incidents of slaveholders killing enslaved people during the war. Ibid., 235.

27. Ibid., 233, 234, 415.

28. Alonzo Jackson testimony, March 17, 1873, in Berlin et al., *Free at Last*, 154–155, 160–161.

29. Woodward, *Mary Chesnut's Civil War*, 235, 794, 699, 704. Chesnut described one incident of how enslaved people were "mask[ing]" their feelings after she gave some of her diamonds to an enslaved woman to hide from Union soldiers. Though Chesnut trusted the woman enough to hand over her precious jewels, she was upset that the woman showed no emotional response. Rather, the enslaved woman viewed the gems "with as little apparent interest . . . as if they were garden peas." The scene highlights that Chesnut was growing increasingly concerned about enslaved people's lack of affect, and it suggests she was perhaps testing the woman by asking her to harbor the stones. Ibid., 794.

30. William Wells Brown, "Narrative of William W. Brown, a Fugitive Slave, Written by Himself," in Osofsky, *Puttin' on Ole Massa*, 173–224, at 205. On the following page Brown repeated this sentiment, claiming "the thought that I should one day be free . . . made my heart leap for joy." Ibid., 206.

31. Bibb, "Narrative of the Life and Adventures of Henry Bibb," 151. For more examples of the trope of affective transformation, see Northup, "Twelve Years a Slave," 400; and Dr. L. S. Thompson, *The Story of Mattie J. Jackson, a True Story, Written and Arranged by Dr. L. S. Thompson, as Given by Mattie* (Lawrence, MA.: Sentinel Office, 1866), 28.

32. Elizabeth Keckley, *Behind the Scenes in the Lincoln White House: Memoirs of an African-American Seamstress* (Mineola, NY: Dover Publications, 2006), 21.

33. Lane, "Narrative of Lunsford Lane," 17.

34. Similarly, William Wells Brown described how becoming free made him feel differently. He observed that "the fact" that he "was a freeman" made him feel that he was not himself. Brown, "Narrative of William W. Brown," 220.

35. Moses Grandy, "Narrative of the Life of Moses Grandy, Late a Slave, in the United States of America," in Katz, *Five Slave Narratives*, 5–45, at 11–16, 19–22, 25. Of course, having one's freedom bought could also be a complicated emotional experience. When the family Harriet Jacobs worked for in New York bought her freedom she was "deeply grateful," but she loathed her former master and resented reimbursing him for something she believed had "never rightfully belonged to him." Regardless, Jacobs noted that in spite of her opposition to Flint being paid, she had a visceral emotional reaction to being free, that "when it was done [she] felt as if a heavy load had been lifted from [her] weary shoulders." Jacobs, *Incidents in the Life of a Slave Girl*, 163.

36. The trope of Emancipation from slavery as emotional transformation influenced later literature. Toni Morrison recollected that after quitting a job in publishing to pursue writing, she felt an affective metamorphosis that was initially difficult to describe, writing that she "knew what fear felt like; this was different": "Then it slapped me: I was happy; free in a way I had never been, ever. It was the oddest sensation. Not ecstasy, not satisfaction. . . . It was a purer delight, a rogue anticipation with certainty." This feeling, which she eventually identified as "the shock of liberation," led her to think about what freedom would have meant to women who had been enslaved. She remembered reading a history of an enslaved woman, Margaret Garner, and from there she began to develop the book that became the acclaimed *Beloved*. Acquainted with slave narratives, Toni Morrison felt an emotional revolution and thought of freedom from enslavement. Toni Morrison, *Beloved* (New York: Vintage, 2004), xv–xvii.

37. Frederick Douglass, *Narrative of the Life of Frederick Douglass, an American Slave* (New York: Barnes and Noble Classics, 2003), 93.

38. Brown, "Narrative of William W. Brown," 219–220.

39. Douglass, *Narrative of the Life of Frederick Douglass*, 93.

40. Jacobs, *Incidents in the Life of a Slave Girl*, 157. Frederick Douglass had similar feelings, detailing in his second narrative how "a sense of . . . loneliness and helplessness crept over" him, covering him "with something bordering on despair." Being in a city only magnified that "loneliness," as he was "in the midst of thousands of my fellow-men . . . yet a perfect stranger!" Frederick Douglass, *My Bondage and My Freedom* (New York: Penguin, 1993), 249.

41. Jacobs, *Incidents in the Life of a Slave Girl*, 139, 133–134. According to Jacobs, part of how she came to trust White people was through her interactions with the New York family she worked for as a nurse. Jacobs began the job "with the distrustful feelings" she had brought with her "out of slavery," but after several months the family's kindness was "thawing" her "chilled heart" and she "gradually became . . . more cheerful." Ibid., 138–139.

42. Peter Smith, in Blassingame, *Slave Testimony*, 245.

43. David Barrett, in Blassingame, *Slave Testimony*, 189, 198.

44. Levi Douglass, in Blassingame, *Slave Testimony*, 304. For another example of an emotional transformation upon reaching Canada, see Josiah Henson, *The Life of Josiah Henson: Formerly a Slave, Now an Inhabitant of Canada* (Boston: Arthur D. Phelps, 1849), 58–59.

45. Jacobs, *Incidents in the Life of a Slave Girl*, 148–149, 153.

46. Edinbur Randall, in Blassingame, *Slave Testimony*, 320.

47. Jacobs, *Incidents in the Life of a Slave Girl*, 155–159.

48. District of Columbia, January–June 1863, 15915, AMA Collection Box 20, Amistad Research Center at Tulane University, New Orleans, LA.

49. South Carolina, Jan.–March 1863, H5170, AMA Collection Box 156, Amistad Research Center at Tulane University, New Orleans, LA. While on furlough in Washington, DC, Emma Edmonds also saw a "contraband camp." She declared that "all were happy, because they were free—and there seemed to be no room for anything like gloom or despondency in their hearts." Emma E. Edmonds, *Nurse and Spy in the Union Army, Comprising the Adventures and Experiences of a Woman in Hospitals, Camps, and Battle-Fields* (Chicago: J. A. Stoddard & Co., 1865), 238–241.

50. Lizzie Gibson, in Blassingame, *Slave Testimony*, 738–739. Jacob Stroyer used similar language to explain the feeling of the war's end, exclaiming that "at last came freedom. And what joy it brought!" Stroyer, "My Life in the South," 99.

51. Stroyer, "My Life in the South," 99. Histories of Emancipation often depict the end of the Civil War as a collective affective transformation. W. E. B. Du Bois observed that it was "difficult to write of this period calmly, so intense was the feeling." W. E. B. Du Bois, *The Souls of Black Folk*, ed. Henry Louis Gates, Jr., and Terri Hume Oliver (New York: W. W. Norton, 1999), 27, 21.

52. Du Bois, *Souls of Black Folk*, 27.

53. John David Smith, *An Old Creed for the New South: Proslavery Ideology and Historiography, 1865–1918* (Carbondale: Southern Illinois University Press, 2008), 17–18.

54. Shawn Leigh Alexander, ed., *Reconstruction Violence and the Ku Klux Klan Hearings* (Boston: Bedford / St. Martin's, 2015), 102.

55. In October 1865 a former Mississippi slaveholder wrote to state legislators that "the whole south is resting upon a volcano," and Elizabeth Botume of South Carolina wrote in 1868 that they all "seemed to be living over a volcano." E. G. Baker, letter, October 22, 1865, in Berlin et al., *Free at Last*, 519–521; Elizabeth Hyde Botume, *First Days Amongst the Contrabands* (Boston, Lee and Shepard, 1893), 267–289.

56. John Hope Franklin argued that White Southerners' "wild, nightmarish fear" of slave rebellions increased after the war's end, and stemmed from their own "sense of guilt and despair." John Hope Franklin, *Reconstruction After the Civil War* (Chicago: University of Chicago Press, 1994), 3, 6, 93–97. For more on fears of uprisings by free Black people, see Eric Foner, *Reconstruction: America's Unfinished Revolution, 1863–1877* (New York: Harper & Row, 1988), 121–122.

57. Smith, *Old Creed for the New South*, 18–19, 25, 26, 52.

58. Michael J. Cassity, *Legacy of Fear: American Race Relations to 1900* (Westport, CT: Greenwood Press, 1985), 130–131.

59. Drew Gilpin Faust, *James Henry Hammond and the Old South: A Design for Mastery* (Baton Rouge: Louisiana State University, 1982), 104.

60. Susan Bradford Eppes, *Through Some Eventful Years* (Macon, GA: J. W. Burke, 1926), 283.

61. Joseph Holmes to Nickels Holmes, November 24, 1867, Nickels Holmes Papers, Duke University, Durham, NC.

62. As early as 1863 slaveholders in Occupied Louisiana complained about adopting free labor practices, arguing that if they could not exercise "unlimited control of their slaves" and "punish them as they please," they would be financially "*ruined*." They contended that even an occupying army and the Emancipation Proclamation should not prevent them from "inflict[ing] corporal punishment, and, as they say, make the slave *fear* them." Lieutenant Enoch Foster, Jr., letter, June 8, 1863, in *Freedom: A Documentary History of Emancipation, 1861–1867, Selected from the Holdings of the National Archives of the United States*, Series I, vol. 3, ed. Ira Berlin, Thavolia Glymph, Steven F. Miller, Joseph P. Reidy, Leslie S. Rowland, and Julie Saville (New York: Cambridge University Press, 1991), 428–429.

63. David Schenck Diary, Southern Historical Collection, University of North Carolina at Chapel Hill, Chapel Hill, NC.

64. William Elliott letter, March 25, 1866, Elliott-Gonzalez Papers, 1009, Southern Historical Collection, University of North Carolina at Chapel Hill, Chapel Hill, NC.

65. Cassity, *Legacy of Fear*, 147–148.

66. Burd quoted in Scott Reynolds Nelson, *Steel Drivin' Man: John Henry, the Untold Story of an American Legend* (New York: Oxford University Press, 2008), 50.

67. General John M. Palmer, letter, August 22, 1865, in Berlin et al., *Free at Last*, 418–422.

68. *Report of the Joint Committee on Reconstruction*, 39th Congress, First Session (Washington, DC, 1866), part III, 101–102.

69. Stephen Tomlinson, *Head Masters: Phrenology, Secular Education, and Nineteenth-Century Social Thought* (Tuscaloosa: University of Alabama Press, 2005), 359, 348.

70. Robert Dale Owen, *The Wrong of Slavery: The Right of Emancipation and the Future of the African Race in the United States* (Philadelphia: J. B. Lippincott and Co., 1864), 220; Tomlinson, *Head Masters*, 350. Like Howe, Owen infantilized Black people's emotions, stating that "their cheerfulness and love of mirth overflow with the exuberance of childhood." Ibid., 220.

71. James Madison, in Blassingame, *Slave Testimony*, 267.

72. Granville Bibb, John Bibb, and Lewis Bibb, in Blassingame, *Slave Testimony*, 286.

73. Brown, "Narrative of William W. Brown," 220.

74. Woodward, *Mary Chesnut's Civil War*, 827.

75. Jourdan Anderson to Colonel P. H. Anderson, August 7, 1865, in Lydia Maria Child, *The Freedmen's Book* (Boston: Ticknor and Fields, 1866), 265.

76. Ibid., 265. Jourdan Anderson emphasized how little he trusted the colonel in his closing remarks, asking the colonel to thank a man named George Carter for "taking the pistol from"

the colonel when the colonel was "shooting" at him. In this way Jourdan Anderson reminded his master that he had much to "forgive." Ibid., 265.

77. C. Graham, letter, July 24, 1865, in Berlin et al., *Free at Last,* 408, 413–414.

78. William H. Robinson, *From Log Cabin to the Pulpit, or, Fifteen Years in Slavery* (Eau Claire, WI: James H. Tifft, 1913), 16–17, 25, 105, 108, 117–119.

79. DeForest quoted in Heather Andrea Williams, *Help Me to Find My People: The African American Search for Family Lost in Slavery* (Chapel Hill: University of North Carolina Press, 2012), 146. For more on former slaves' efforts to reunite with loved ones, see Foner, *Reconstruction,* 78, 82–84; and Hunter, *To 'Joy My Freedom,* 1, 3, 20.

80. John Q. A. Dennis, letter, July 26, 1864, in Berlin et al., *Free at Last,* 120–121.

81. Ibid., 373–374.

82. For more discussion of how formerly enslaved people believed that freedom was inextricably tied to being able to love freely, and to protect one's family, see Kidada E. Williams, *They Left Great Marks on Me: African American Testimonials of Racial Violence from Emancipation to World War I* (New York: New York University Press, 2012), 22–26; and Amy Dru Stanley, "Slave Breeding and Free Love," in *Capitalism Takes Command,* ed. Michael Zakim and Gary J. Kornblith, 119–144 (Chicago: University of Chicago Press, 2012), 136–142.

83. Some were much more concise. Alexander Buford's 1909 ad in an Alabama paper read simply "wants to find his folks." "Mr. Alexander Buford is searching for his folks," Information Wanted Ad, *Huntsville Journal* (Huntsville, AL), March 4, 1909, "Last Seen: Finding Family After Slavery," accessed May 9, 2019, http://informationwanted.org/items/show/3402.

84. "Susan Cheek searching for Anthony Newby," Information Wanted Ad, *Appeal* (St. Paul and Minneapolis, MN), November 27, 1897, "Last Seen: Finding Family After Slavery," accessed May 9, 2019, http://informationwanted.org/items/show/2176.

85. "Eliza Montgomery searching for her brother, Dick Bush," Information Wanted Ad, *Baptist Times* (Garnett, KS), March 1892 [published in a monthly newspaper], "Last Seen: Finding Family After Slavery," accessed May 9, 2019, http://informationwanted.org/items/show/3433.

86. An accomplishment that she or the paper's editor acknowledged in their use of italics for emphasis in her ad. "Jane Bell is searching for five of her children: Polly Bell, Grafton Bell, Jeremiah Bell, Lorenzo Bell, and Fanny Bell," Other: Information Wanted Letter to the Editor, *Republican Banner* (Nashville, TN), May 13, 1871, "Last Seen: Finding Family After Slavery," accessed May 9, 2019, http://informationwanted.org/items/show/3431.

87. "John and Barbara Brooks seek brother Wesley," Information Wanted Ad, *Anglo-African* (New York City), August 12, 1865, "Last Seen: Finding Family After Slavery," accessed May 9, 2019, http://informationwanted.org/items/show/3469. For more on how African Americans wrote or testified about their pain in the postwar era both as a claim for citizenship rights and as a form of resistance against White supremacist violence, see Williams, *They Left Great Marks on Me,* chaps. 1 and 2.

88. Although it is impossible to know how many enslaved families were found, the digital collection "Last Seen: Finding Family After Slavery" insinuates that it was exceedingly rare, especially as time went on. As of May 2019 of the thousands of missing family ads on the site, only about a dozen shared stories of loved ones being reunited. "Last Seen: Finding Family After Slavery," accessed May 9, 2019, http://informationwanted.org/items/browse?tags=reunited. For more on this incredible database of sources, see Ari Shapiro and Maureen Pao, "After Slavery Searching for Loved Ones in Wanted Ads," National Public Radio, February 22, 2017, https://

www.npr.org/sections/codeswitch/2017/02/22/516651689/after-slavery-searching-for-loved-ones-in-wanted-ads.

89. Nettie Henry, in Federal Writers' Project, ed., *Slave Narratives: A Folk History of Slavery in the United States from Interviews with Former Slaves, 1936–1938*, vol. 9, Mississippi Narratives (Washington, DC: Library of Congress, 1941), https://www.gutenberg.org/files/12055/12055-h/12055-h.htm. See also Reverend James Singleton of Simpson, Mississippi, who was only nine when the war ended but remembered that "after the war . . . pappy came an got" him after traveling from South Carolina. A Northern journalist reporting in the postwar South encountered a similarly dedicated father. In North Carolina the reporter met a weary man who had walked over six hundred miles from a plantation in western Georgia in the hopes of finding his wife and children. John Richard Dennett, *The South as It Is: 1865–1866* (New York: Viking, 2010), 130–131. For examples of children trying to track down their father or mother after the war, see Anonymous, "Mrs. Thomas L. Johnson seeks family," Information Wanted Ad, *Anglo-African* (New York City), August 12, 1865, "Last Seen: Finding Family After Slavery," accessed May 9, 2019, http://informationwanted.org/items/show/3454; and "Mrs. Ann Hampton searching for her mother, Nellie Beecham," Information Wanted Ad, *Twice-a-Week Independent* (Coffeyville, KS), March 20, 1896, "Last Seen: Finding Family After Slavery," accessed May 9, 2019, http://informationwanted.org/items/show/3422.

90. Anna Baker in *Slave Narratives: A Folk History of Slavery in the United States from Interviews with Former Slaves, 1936–1938*, vol. 9, Mississippi Narratives (Washington, DC: Library of Congress, 1941), https://www.gutenberg.org/files/12055/12055-h/12055-h.htm#BakerAnna.

91. Berlin et al., *Free at Last*, 220–222, 507–509.

92. According to Amy Dru Stanley, the idea that free people had a government-protected right to experience joy was a totally "unprecedented conception that being human included the inherent right to pursue amusement in public." Amy Dru Stanley, "Revolutionizing Human Rights," in *The World the Civil War Made*, ed. Gregory P. Downs and Kate Masur, 269–302 (Chapel Hill: University of North Carolina Press, 2015), 269–271. For more discussion of how freedom entailed "volition" in work and romance, and "the emancipation of feelings and inclinations," see Stanley, "Slave Breeding and Free Love," 136–143.

93. See, for example, Berlin et al., *Free at Last*, 98, 520–521.

94. Shane White and Graham White, *Stylin': African American Expressive Culture from Its Beginnings to the Zoot Suit* (Ithaca, NY: Cornell University Press, 1998), 127, 129.

95. Nelson, *Steel Drivin' Man*, 44, 52.

96. Botume, *First Days Amongst the Contrabands*, 267–289.

97. For a discussion of the pride and pleasure that enslaved women in particular derived from making and wearing fancy clothing to illicit parties, and how that enjoyment was a form of resistance against the objectification, physical violence, and material scarcity of slavery, see Stephanie Camp, *Closer to Freedom: Enslaved Women and Everyday Resistance in the Plantation South* (Chapel Hill: University of North Carolina Press, 2004), 68, 78–86.

98. Sidney Andrews, *South Since the War* (Boston: Ticknor and Fields, 1866), 186–187.

99. For a discussion of clothing and mourning practices during the Civil War, see Drew Gilpin Faust, *This Republic of Suffering: Death and the American Civil War* (New York: Vintage Civil War Library, 2009), 146–149.

100. For examples of White Southerners responding to Black veterans in Union uniforms with resentment and violence, see *Daily Index* (Petersburg, FL), March 1, 1866; Nelson, *Steel Drivin' Man*, 44, 52; White and White, *Stylin'*, 127–131; and Berlin et al., *Free at Last*, 514–515.

101. Hunter, *To 'Joy My Freedom*, 2–3.

102. White and White, *Stylin'*, 127–128.

103. "Affairs at Charleston," *New York Times*, March 30, 1865, 3.

104. White and White, *Stylin'*, 128, 132, 134–135.

105. "Affairs at Charleston," 3.

106. White and White, *Stylin'*, 136.

107. Harriet Prescott Spofford, "The Streets of Washington," *Harper's New Monthly Magazine* 37, no. 21 (August 1868): 414.

108. Mitch Kachun, *Festivals of Freedom: Memory and Meaning in African American Emancipation Celebrations, 1808–1915* (Amherst: University of Massachusetts Press, 2006), 118.

109. Frederick Douglass, "January First 1863," *Douglass' Monthly* (January 1863): 769–770.

110. Henry McNeal Turner, "On the Anniversary of Emancipation" (1866), in *Respect Black: The Writings and Speeches of Henry McNeal Turner*, ed. Edwin S. Redkey, 5–7 (New York: Arno Press, 1971), 5–6.

111. Kachun, *Festivals of Freedom*, 118, 179–180. See 254 and 260 for more discussion of Juneteenth. Kathleen Ann Clark, *Defining Moments: African American Commemoration and Political Culture in the South, 1863–1913* (Chapel Hill: University of North Carolina Press, 2005), 54. For another example of newly freed people preemptively stating that their post-Emancipation actions were not rooted in revenge or a "feeling of resentment toward . . . former owners," see "Resolutions of Petersburg Negroes," June 9, 1865, in *Documentary History of the Negro People in the United States, Volume 2: From the Reconstruction to the Founding of the NAACP*, ed. Herbert Aptheker (New York: Citadel, 1992), 538.

112. "Slave and Slaveocracy," *Nation* 1 (August 17, 1865): 202. For more examples of White people's reluctance to part with slavery, see Woodward, *Mary Chesnut's Civil War*, 829; Tomlinson, *Head Masters*, 347; and Smith, *Old Creed for the New South*, 27, 8.

113. Though in Atlanta former slaves had more latitude, Tera Hunter notes that "in rural areas of Georgia, residents were isolated, and thus more vulnerable to elements intent on depriving them of life, liberty and happiness." Hunter, *To 'Joy My Freedom*, 2–3.

114. Mollie Williams, in *Slave Narratives: A Folk History of Slavery in the United States from Interviews with Former Slaves, 1936–1938*, vol. 9, Mississippi Narratives (Washington, DC: Library of Congress, 1941), https://www.gutenberg.org/files/12055/12055-h/12055-h.htm. For more examples of White supremacist terrorist violence during Reconstruction, see Foner, *Reconstruction*, 119–120; James Lucas and Isaac Stier, both in in *Slave Narratives: A Folk History of Slavery in the United States from Interviews with Former Slaves, 1936–1938*, vol. 9, Mississippi Narratives (Washington, DC: Library of Congress, 1941), https://www.gutenberg.org/files/12055/12055-h/12055-h.htm.

115. Alexander, *Reconstruction Violence and the Ku Klux Klan Hearings*, 45–52.

116. Ibid., 61–66, 79–83, 56–60, 87–92.

117. *Report of the Select Committee to Inquire into the Mississippi Election of 1875 with the Testimony and Documentary Evidence*, vol. 2, 44th Congress, Second Session, Senate Report 527 (Washington, DC, 1876), part II, 103–107.

118. Alexander, *Reconstruction Violence and the Ku Klux Klan Hearings*, 35–38.

119. Sam McAllum, in *Slave Narratives: A Folk History of Slavery in the United States from Interviews with Former Slaves, 1936–1938*, vol. 9, Mississippi Narratives (Washington, DC: Library of Congress, 1941), https://www.gutenberg.org/files/12055/12055-h/12055-h.htm.

120. Foner, *Reconstruction*, 79, 120. For more on White concerns about "surrendering the etiquette of slavery," see Smith, *Old Creed for the New South*, 7; and White and White, *Stylin'*, 127–129.

121. "Laws of Mississippi, 1865," in Walter Lynwood Fleming, *Documentary History of Reconstruction*, 281– 290 (Cleveland, A. H. Clark, 1906), 290.

122. Daniel A. Novak, *The Wheel of Servitude: Black Forced Labor After Slavery* (Lexington, KY: University Press of Kentucky, 1978), 6; "Laws of Mississippi, 1865," 290.

123. Alonzo T. and Millard Mial Papers, North Carolina Division of Archives and History, quoted in Roger L. Ransom and Richard Sutch, *One Kind of Freedom* (New York: Cambridge University Press, 1977), 91.

124. Charles C. Jones, Jr., *Negro Myths from the Georgia Coast, Told in the Vernacular* (Detroit, MI: Singing Tree Press, Book Tower, 1969). For more examples of Lost Cause literature, see Joel Chandler Harris's *Uncle Remus* series; Thomas Nelson Page's novels, including *In Ole Virginia: Or Marse Chan and Other Stories* (1887) and *Red Rock* (1898); and Thomas F. Dixon, Jr.'s novels, including *The Leopard's Spots* (1902) and *The Clansman* (1905). For more on the Lost Cause apologist genre that David Blight has labeled "the Plantation School," see David W. Blight, *Race and Reunion: The Civil War in American Memory* (Cambridge, MA: Harvard University Press, 2001).

125. Micki McElya argues that post-Emancipation nostalgia accrued heavily around the cultural totem that was the mammy figure. She asserts that the nationwide popularity of this genre of literature demonstrates that "Sentimental evocations of plantation abundance and benign slavery held increasing allure for non-southern whites as well, as it appealed to their own racism, fears, and post-war concerns," and the perpetuation of "the image of the faithful slave . . . contributed to the dismantling of Reconstruction." Micki McElya, *Clinging to Mammy: The Faithful Slave in Twentieth-Century America* (Cambridge, MA: Harvard University Press, 2009), 10–12. For more of McElya's discussion of "white supremacist nostalgia for antebellum paternalism," see 10–12, 33, 35–36, 39–42, 44–46, 48, 121. For a discussion of how White Southerners used music to express and exorcise their nostalgia for slavery and its emotional power dynamics, see Gavin James Campbell, *Music and the Making of a New South* (Chapel Hill: University of North Carolina Press, 2004), 69, 76–78, 94. For more on cultural nostalgia for slavery, see Tara McPherson, *Reconstructing Dixie: Race, Gender, and Nostalgia in the Imagined South* (Durham, NC: Duke University Press, 2004).

126. July 7, 1885, Paul Hayne Papers, Duke University, Durham, NC.

127. Du Bois, *Souls of Black Folk*, 27–28, 45. For more on Black disillusionment at the end of Reconstruction, see Franklin, *Reconstruction After the Civil War*, 215–217; Kachun, *Festivals of Freedom*, 197; and Peter Kolchin, "The Tragic Era? Interpreting Southern Reconstruction in Comparative Perspective," in *The Meaning of Freedom: Economics, Politics, and Culture After Slavery*, ed. F. McGlynn and S. Drescher, 291– 309 (Pittsburgh: University of Pittsburgh Press, 1992), 292, 293.

Epilogue

1. Frederick Douglass, *Why Is the Negro Lynched?* (Bridgwater, UK: John Whitby and Sons, 1895), 15, 7.

2. Ibid., 2.

3. W. E. B. Du Bois, *The Souls of Black Folk*, ed. Henry Louis Gates, Jr., and Terri Hume Oliver (New York: W. W. Norton, 1999), 33.

4. Peter Stearns and Timothy Haggerty argue that fear has biological components but is also learned, and that what fears are considered appropriate in a given time and culture are based on myriad factors, including a person's age, gender, and profession. Peter N. Stearns and Timothy Haggerty, "The Role of Fear: Transitions in American Emotional Standards, 1850–1950," *American Historical Review* 96, no. 1 (February 1991): 63–94, at 63, 64.

5. Richard Wright, *Black Boy* (New York: Harper Perennial Modern Classics, 2006), 302. As Michael Cassity observed in his anthology about American race relations, many Americans have long "feared that greater freedom for others necessarily implies a loss for themselves." Michael J. Cassity, *Legacy of Fear: American Race Relations to 1900* (Westport, CT: Greenwood Press, 1985), 1.

6. Black fear in the Jim Crow South was so prevalent that it infused literature from and about the region throughout the twentieth century, becoming a prominent-enough trope to elicit literary commentary. In her work on how Black authors write about the South, Trudier Harris argues that the "pronounced fear of the South" and "general fear of southern white people" that Black authors documented bore many similarities to the terror described in slave narratives. Trudier Harris, *The Scary Mason-Dixon Line: African American Writers and the South* (Baton Rouge: Louisiana State University Press, 2009), 1–18.

7. A number of scholars have argued that White fears about Black people drove policy makers to legally restrict Black Southerners. See Howard W. Odum, *Race and Rumors of Race: The American South in the Early Forties* (Baltimore: Johns Hopkins University Press, 1997), 57–58, 64, 97–103; and Danielle L. McGuire, *At the Dark End of the Street: Black Women, Rape, and Resistance—a New History of the Civil Rights Movement from Rosa Parks to the Rise of Black Power* (New York: Vintage, 2010), 25, 28.

8. Micki McElya, *Clinging to Mammy: The Faithful Slave in Twentieth-Century America* (Cambridge, MA: Harvard University Press, 2009), 116.

9. Ray Stannard Baker, *Following the Color Line: An Account of Negro Citizenship in the American Democracy* (New York: Doubleday, Page & Co., 1908), 44.

10. McElya, *Clinging to Mammy*, 45.

11. Allison Davis, Burleigh B. Gardner, and Mary R. Gardner, *Deep South: A Social Anthropological Study of Caste and Class* (Chicago: University of Chicago Press, 1941); Shane White and Graham White, *Stylin': African American Expressive Culture from Its Beginnings to the Zoot Suit* (Ithaca, NY: Cornell University Press, 1998), 155.

12. Quoted in McGuire, *At the Dark End of the Street*, 72.

13. Wright, *Black Boy*, 66. For further discussion of Wright experiencing fear and distrust of White people, see 23, 179, 185, 192, 200, 231, 232, 234–235, 238, 239, 245, 253, 255, 257, 300.

14. Benjamin Mays, *Born to Rebel: An Autobiography* (New York: Scribner, 1971), 25.

15. Wright, *Black Boy*, 227.

16. Ibid., 229, 234, 227, 233, 200. For more on Black Southerners masking and performing emotions during Jim Crow, see 175, 195, 227–230, 245, 256, 277.

17. McGuire, *At the Dark End of the Street*, 68.

18. For this very reason, Wright noted in his memoir his "admiration" for "the ideology of Garveyism" not necessarily because of the Black nationalism involved, or the philosophy of economic sustainability, but because of the "emotional dynamics of its adherents" and the pride and "dignity" that their involvement in the movement inspired. Wright, *Black Boy*, 231, 286.

19. Quoted in McGuire, *At the Dark End of the Street*, 10.

20. Wright, *Black Boy*, 145–146, 182.

21. Mays, *Born to Rebel*, 25.

22. Wright, *Black Boy*, 175, 194, 195, 251.

23. Ibid., 224, 253, 250, 344.

24. Ibid., 261, 273, 278–279. For more of Wright's insights into the racialized emotional dynamics of the North, see 262–266, 282–283. For more on the emotional politics of Jim Crow, see 182, 185, 194, 200–201, 242–245, 249, 252–255, 269, 300, 318, 338, 365, 369, 372, 373.

25. Danielle McGuire argues that this shift accelerated during the Montgomery bus boycott, that "the fear that had immobilized African Americans for so long seemed to disappear as the boycott continued," replaced by a "new sense of pride and power." McGuire, *At the Dark End of the Street*, 114, 121, 126.

26. Jacquelyn Dowd Hall, "The Long Civil Rights Movement and the Political Uses of the Past," *Journal of American History* 91, no. 4 (March 2005): 1233–1263.

27. McGuire, *At the Dark End of the Street*, 53. For more on how the Civil Rights Movement's successful campaigns were helping African Americans dispel fears of White supremacist terror, while White fears were increasing, see Belinda Robnett, *How Long? How Long? African American Women in the Struggle for Civil Rights* (New York: Oxford University Press, 1997), 151.

28. McGuire, *At the Dark End of the Street*, 148, 170, 207. For more on fear of Black men and Black sexuality more generally, see Peter N. Stearns, "Fear and Contemporary History: A Review Essay," *Journal of Social History* 40, no. 2 (Winter 2006): 477–484, at 479; and Corey Robin, "Reflections on Fear: Montesquieu in Retrieval," *American Political Science Review* 94, no. 2 (June 2000): 347–360, at 351.

29. More than sixty years after Till's murder, the White woman in the grocery store (and ex-wife of one of Till's confessed killers) admitted that Till had not touched her at all and she "doesn't remember exactly what did happen." Richard Pérez-Peña, "Woman Linked to Emmett Till Murder Tells Historians Her Claims Were False," *New York Times*, January 27, 2017, https://www.nytimes.com/2017/01/27/us/emmett-till-lynching-carolyn-bryant-donham.html; McGuire, *At the Dark End of the Street*, 121.

30. William Faulkner, "On Fear," *Harper's Magazine* (June 1956): 31–34, at 31–32.

31. Robin, "Reflections on Fear"; William M. Reddy, *The Navigation of Feeling: A Framework for the History of Emotions* (New York: Cambridge University Press, 2001).

32. Faulkner, "On Fear," 32, 34.

33. That so many young Black people had imagined and feared a similar fate is another reason why the Emmett Till story reverberated so widely and then radicalized some future members of the Civil Rights Movement. See Anne Moody, *Coming of Age in Mississippi* (New York: Dell, 1992), 127–135.

34. Corey Robin argues that in highly stratified societies fear is not experienced in the same way for people with differing amounts of power because they have more or less to lose based on their rung on the social ladder. Robin, "Reflections on Fear," 358–359.

35. This had essentially been true since slave colonies started passing laws like the Virginia slave act of 1669, which stated that if an owner or overseer was punishing an enslaved person "and by the extremity of the correction should chance to die, that his death shall not be accounted a felony, but the master . . . be acquitted . . . since it cannot be presumed that premeditated malice (which alone makes murder a felony) should induce any man to destroy his own estate." William Waller Hening, *Statutes at Large; Being a Collection of All the Laws of Virginia*, vol. 11 (Richmond, VA, 1809–1823), 270. See also an 1821 South Carolina law that averred that it was a felony to murder an enslaved person but that "killing" an enslaved person "in sudden heat and passion is the same as manslaughter." J. D. B. DeBow, *The Commercial Review of the South and West*,

a Monthly Journal of Trade, Commerce, Commercial Polity, Agriculture, Manufacturer, Internal Improvements and General, Literature, vol. VIII, New Series vol. II (New Orleans, 1850), 70.

36. Robin D. G. Kelley, "Confessions of a Nice Negro, or Why I Shaved My Head," in *Speak My Name: Black Men on Masculinity and the American Dream*, ed. Don Belton, 12–22 (Boston: Beacon Press, 1995), 13.

37. Examples of this abound, from Kanye West's condemnation of President George W. Bush's response to Hurricane Katrina being "George Bush doesn't care about black people," to the invocation of "Black friends" to "shield" White people who are accused of racism. "Bush Doesn't Care About Black People," *YouTube*, April 16, 2006, https://www.youtube.com/watch?v=zIUzLpO1kxI; Ta-Nehisi Coates, "Fear of a Black President," *Atlantic*, September 2012, https://www.theatlantic.com/magazine/archive/2012/09/fear-of-a-black-president/309064/. See also Braden Goyette, "'I'm Not a Racist but...' and Other Stupid Excuses for Being Horrible," *Huffington Post*, June 6, 2014, https://www.huffingtonpost.com/2014/06/06/im-not-a-racist_n_5454615.html.

38. For more on stereotypes about Black mothers and Black women and hypersexuality, see Mary Bosworth and Jeanne Flavin, eds., *Race, Gender and Punishment: From Colonialism to This War on Terror* (New Brunswick, NJ: Rutgers University Press, 2007), 4–5.

39. See, for example, Adam Nagourney, "A Defiant Rancher Savors the Audience That Rallied to His Side," *New York Times*, April 23, 2014, https://www.nytimes.com/2014/04/24/us/politics/rancher-proudly-breaks-the-law-becoming-a-hero-in-the-west.html; and Daniel Victor, "Bill O'Reilly Defends Comments About 'Well Fed' Slaves," *New York Times*, July 27, 2016, https://www.nytimes.com/2016/07/28/business/media/bill-oreilly-says-slaves-who-helped-build-white-house-were-well-fed.html.

40. Drew Magary, "What the Duck?," *GQ*, December 17, 2013, https://www.gq.com/story/duck-dynasty-phil-robertson.

41. Erin Mosbaugh, "Recent Ad for Paula Deen Restaurant Uses Southern Slave Motif," *FirstWeFeast.Com*, October 23, 2014, https://firstwefeast.com/eat/2014/10/ad-for-paula-deen-restaurant-uses-southern-slave-motif.

42. Yanan Wang, "Scholastic Pulls Children's Book Starring George Washington's Happy Slaves," *Washington Post*, January 19, 2016; Demetria Lucas D'Oyley, "After Outrage, Publisher Pulls Happy-Slaves Children's Book," *Root*, January 17, 2016. For more on outrage over the book, see Liam Stack, "Scholastic Halts Distribution of 'A Birthday Cake for George Washington,'" *New York Times*, January 17, 2016; and Michael Schaub, "Children's Book 'A Birthday Cake for George Washington' Pulled over Depiction of Happy Slaves," *Los Angeles Times*, January 18, 2016.

43. Associated Press, "Kids Book About George Washington's Happy Slaves Is Pulled from Shelves," *New York Post*, January 18, 2016.

44. "From George Washington to Robert Morris, 12 April 1786," in *The Papers of George Washington*, Confederation Series, vol. 4, *2 April 1786–31 January 1787*, ed. W. W. Abbot (Charlottesville: University Press of Virginia, 1995), 15–17.

45. Melissa V. Harris-Perry, *Sister Citizen: Shame, Stereotypes, and Black Women in America* (New Haven, CT: Yale University Press, 2011), 34, 86–96, 274–277. For more on how the Obamas are perceived as angry or as going out of their way to mute any anger, see Roxane Gay, "The Media's Michelle Obama Problem: What a Selfie Says About Our Biases," *Salon*, December 10, 2013, https://www.salon.com/2013/12/10/the_medias_michelle_obama_problem_what_a_selfie_says_about_our_biases/.

46. See Coates, "Fear of a Black President." After the 2010 BP oil spill in the Gulf of Mexico, filmmaker Spike Lee exhorted the president to let loose his anger, advising Obama "one time,

go off!" Kristi Keck, "Charge to Obama: 'Go Off!,'" *CNN*, June 3, 2010, http://www.cnn.com/2010/POLITICS/06/02/obama.oil.spill.tone/index.html. Meanwhile, in 2016 the then-Republican presidential nominee Donald Trump also critiqued President Obama for failing to blame "radical Islamic terrorism" for a mass shooting at Pulse nightclub in Orlando, observing that during Obama's press conference "there was certainly not a lot of anger." Andrew Kaczynski, "Trump: People Can Figure Out What I Meant by My Comments on Obama and Radical Islam," *Buzzfeed*, June 13, 2016, https://www.buzzfeed.com/andrewkaczynski/trump-people-can-figure-what-i-meant-by-my-comments-on-obama?utm_term=.qwjP73B0R#.wvLyObWMK.

47. "Luther" is introduced in the series premiere of *Key and Peele*, which aired on Comedy Central on January 31, 2012, and the character reappeared in several episodes in later seasons. President Obama himself embraced the Luther character, inviting Keegan-Michael Key to perform in character with Obama, "translating" for him at the 2015 White House Correspondents Dinner.

48. For examples of assaults or murders of Black people being justified on the basis of White fear, see Kelley, "Confessions of a Nice Negro," 15. For multiple essays that address racial bias and presumptions of fear and danger in the Trayvon Martin shooting in particular, see Devon Johnson, Patricia Y. Warren, and Amy Farrell, eds., *Deadly Injustice: Trayvon Martin, Race, and the Criminal Justice System* (New York: New York University Press, 2015).

49. 2011 Florida Statute, Title XLVI, Chapter 776.012, 776.013. For an in-depth analysis of "reasonable fear" in the law, see Katheryn Russell-Brown, "Go Ahead and Shoot—the Law Might Have Your Back: History, Race, Implicit Bias, and Justice in Florida's Stand Your Ground Law," in Johnson, Warren, and Farrell, *Deadly Injustice*, 115–145, at 118–119, 121–123.

50. Kenneth Nunn, "Racism Is the Problem Here," *New York Times*, March 21, 2012, https://www.nytimes.com/roomfordebate/2012/03/21/do-stand-your-ground-laws-encourage-vigilantes/racism-is-the-problem-not-the-stand-your-ground-laws. See also Elie Mystal, "Are 'Stand Your Ground' and 'Defense of Home' Laws Racist?," *Above the Law*, March 20, 2012, https://abovethelaw.com/2012/03/are-stand-your-ground-and-defense-of-home-laws-racist/. For more on racial bias and gender bias in presumptions of fear and perceptions of danger, see Kevin M. Drakulich and Laura Siller, "Presumed Danger: Race, Bias, Stigma, and Perceptions of Crime and Criminals," in Johnson, Warren, and Farrell, *Deadly Injustice*, 23–58, at 23–27, 47, 48; and Toya Like, Lori Sexton, and Savannah Porter, "Threat, Danger, and Vulnerability: Trayvon Martin and Gwen Araujo," in Johnson, Warren, and Farrell, *Deadly Injustice*, 81–112, at 81, 85–89.

51. Cord Jefferson, "The Zimmerman Jury Told Young Black Men What We Already Knew," *Gawker*, July 14, 2013, http://gawker.com/the-zimmerman-jury-told-young-black-men-what-we-already-770650992. For musician ?uestlove's editorial about the insidious effects of internalizing racialized emotional expectations for Black men, including the assumption that Black men "don't have feelings," see ?uestlove, "That Doesn't Mean It Doesn't Sting Any Less," *Huffington Post*, July 15, 2013, https://www.huffingtonpost.com/questlove/trayvon-martin-case-verdict_b_3601148.html. For more on the impact of internalizing affective stereotypes about Black men, see Trey Ellis, "How Does It Feel to Be a Problem?," in Belton, *Speak My Name*, 9–11. For discussion of the effects of internalizing racial stereotypes on Black women, see Harris-Perry, *Sister Citizen*.

52. Opal Tometi, "#BlackLivesMatter Stands with Baltimore," *Ebony.com*, April 29, 2015.

SELECTED BIBLIOGRAPHY

Archives

Amistad Research Center at Tulane University. New Orleans, Louisiana

Dolph Briscoe Center for American History, the University of Texas at Austin. Austin, Texas

Historic New Orleans Collection. New Orleans, Louisiana

Louisiana and Special Collections, Earl K. Long Library, University of New Orleans. New Orleans, Louisiana

Louisiana Research Collection, Tulane University. New Orleans, Louisiana

Louisiana State University, Louisiana and Lower Mississippi Valley Collection, Hill Memorial Library. Baton Rouge, Louisiana

Northwestern State University of Louisiana, Cammie G. Henry Research Center. Natchitoches, Louisiana

Southern Historical Collection, Louis Round Wilson Special Collections Library, University of North Carolina at Chapel Hill. Chapel Hill, North Carolina

Newspapers and Journals

American Cotton Planter

Atlantic

DeBow's Review

Douglass' Monthly

Ebony

Harper's New Monthly Magazine

Lady's Book

Nation

New York Times

Southern Planter

Washington Post

Published Primary Sources

Alcott, William A. *The Young Woman's Guide to Excellence.* Boston: Charles H. Peirce, Binney and Otherman, W. J. Reynolds and Co., 1849.

American Convention for Promoting the Abolition of Slavery, *Minutes of the Proceedings of the Third Convention of Delegates from the Abolition Societies Established in Different Parts of the United States Assembled at Philadelphia, on the First Day of January, One Thousand Seven Hundred and Ninety-Six, and Continued, by Adjournments, Until the Seventh Day of the Same Month, Inclusive.* Philadelphia: Printed by Zachariah Poulson, 1796.

Anderson, William J. *Life and Narrative of William J. Anderson, Twenty-Four Years a Slave*. Chicago: Daily Tribune Book and Job Printing Office, 1857.

Andrews, William L., ed. *Six Women's Slave Narratives*. New York: Oxford University Press, 1988.

Aptheker, Herbert. *Documentary History of the Negro People in the United States, Volume 2: From the Reconstruction to the Founding of the NAACP.* New York: Citadel, 1992.

Baker, Ray Stannard. *Following the Color Line: An Account of Negro Citizenship in the American Democracy*. New York: Doubleday, Page, 1908.

Ball, Charles. *Fifty Years in Chains; or, The Life of an American Slave*. New York: H. Dayton Publishers, 1859.

Bell, Charles. *The Anatomy and Philosophy of Expression as Connected with the Fine Arts*. London: Henry G. Hohn, York Street, Coventry Garden, 1865.

Berlin, I., B. J. Fields, S. F. Miller, J. P. Reidy, and L. S. Rowland, eds. *Free at Last: A Documentary History of Slavery, Freedom, and the Civil War.* New York: New Press, 1992.

Berlin, I., T. Glymph, S. T. Miller, J. P. Reidy, L. S. Rowland, and J. Saville, eds. *Freedom: A Documentary History of Emancipation, 1861–1867, Selected from the Holdings of the National Archives of the United States*, series I, vol. III. New York: Cambridge University Press, 1991.

Berquin-Devallon, Pierre-Louis. *Travels in Louisiana and the Floridas in the Year 1802*. New York, I. Riley, 1806.

Black, Leonard. *The Life and Sufferings of Leonard Black, a Fugitive from Slavery, Written by Himself.* New Bedford, MA: Press of Benjamin Lindsey, 1847.

Blassingame, John, ed. *Slave Testimony: Two Centuries of Letters, Speeches, Interviews, and Autobiographies*. Baton Rouge: Louisiana State University Press, 1998.

Botume, Elizabeth Hyde. *First Days Amongst the Contrabands*. Boston: Lee and Shepard, 1893.

Brown, Henry Box. *Narrative of the Life of Henry Box Brown*. Edited by Richard Newman, with a foreword by Henry Louis Gates, Jr. New York: Oxford University Press, 2002.

Burgess, Thomas Henry. *The Physiology or Mechanisms of Blushing*. London: John Scott, 1839.

Catterall, Helen Tunnicliff, ed. *Judicial Cases Concerning American Slavery and the Negro: Volume I: Cases from the Courts of England, Virginia, West Virginia, and Kentucky*. New York: Negro Universities Press, 1968.

———. *Judicial Cases Concerning American Slavery and the Negro: Volume III: Cases from the Courts of Georgia, Florida, Alabama, Mississippi and Louisiana*. New York: Negro Universities Press, 1968.

Chastellux, François-Jean. *De la Félicité publique, ou Considérations sur le sort des hommes dans les différentes époques de l'histoire*. 2 vols. Amsterdam, 1772.

Child, Lydia Maria. *The Freedmen's Book*. Boston: Ticknor and Fields, 1866.

Craft, William. *Running a Thousand Miles for Freedom; or, The Escape of William and Ellen Craft from Slavery.* Salem, NH: Ayer Company Publishers, 1991.

Darwin, Charles. *The Expression of the Emotions in Man and Animals*. Edited by Paul Ekman. New York: HarperCollins, 2009.

DeBow, J. D. B. *The Commercial Review of the South and West, a Monthly Journal of Trade, Commerce, Commercial Polity, Agriculture, Manufacturer, Internal Improvements and General Literature*. Vol. VIII, New Series vol. II. New Orleans, 1850.

Douglass, Frederick. *My Bondage and My Freedom*. New York: Penguin, 1993.

———. *Narrative of the Life of Frederick Douglass, an American Slave*. New York: Barnes and Noble Classics, 2003.

———. *Why Is the Negro Lynched?* Bridgwater, UK: John Whitby and Sons, 1895.

Edmonds, Emma E. *Nurse and Spy in the Union Army, Comprising the Adventures and Experiences of a Woman in Hospitals, Camps, and Battle-Fields.* Chicago: J. A. Stoddard & Co., 1865.

Eppes, Susan Bradford. *Through Some Eventful Years.* Macon, GA: J. W. Burke, 1926.

Federal Writers' Project. *Slave Narratives: A Folk History of Slavery in the United States from Interviews with Former Slaves, 1936–1938.* Volume 9, Mississippi Narratives. Washington, DC: Library of Congress, 1941.

Fitzhugh, George. *Cannibals All!* Richmond, VA: A. Morris, 1857.

Fleming, Walter Lynwood. *Documentary History of Reconstruction.* Cleveland, A. H. Clark, 1906.

Flint, Timothy. *Recollections of the Last Ten Years, Passed in Occasional Residences and Journeyings in the Valley of the Mississippi, from Pittsburg and the Missouri to the Gulf of Mexico, and from Florida to the Spanish Frontier; in a Series of Letters to the Rev. James Flint of Salem, Massachusetts.* Boston: Cummings, Hilliard, and Company, 1826.

Franklin, Benjamin. *Autobiography.* New York: W. W. Norton, 1986.

Hening, William W., ed. *Laws of Virginia, Vol. 2.* Philadelphia, 1832.

Henson, Josiah. *The Life of Josiah Henson: Formerly a Slave, Now an Inhabitant of Canada.* Boston: Arthur D. Phelps, 1849.

Hundley, Daniel R. *Social Relations in Our Southern States.* New York: Henry B. Price, 1860.

Hurston, Zora Neale. *Mules and Men.* New York: HarperPerennial, 1975.

Jacobs, Harriet. *Incidents in the Life of a Slave Girl.* Mineola, NY: Dover Publications, 2001.

Jefferson, Thomas. *Notes on the State of Virginia, with an Appendix.* Boston: H. S. Sprague, 1802.

———. *The Papers of Thomas Jefferson, Vol. 1, 1760–1776.* Edited by Julian P. Boyd. Princeton, NJ: Princeton University Press, 1950.

Katz, William L., ed. *Five Slave Narratives: A Compendium.* New York: Arno Press and the *New York Times*, 1968.

Keckley, Elizabeth. *Behind the Scenes in the Lincoln White House: Memoirs of an African-American Seamstress.* Mineola, NY: Dover Publications, 2006.

Kemble, Frances Anne. *Journal of a Residence on a Georgian Plantation in 1838–1839.* Savannah, GA: Beehive Foundation, 1992.

Kingsley, Z. *A Treatise on the Patriarchal System of Society as It Exists . . . Under the Name of Slavery. By an Inhabitant of Florida.* 1833.

Lincoln, Abraham. *Abraham Lincoln: Speeches and Writings, 1832–1858.* New York: Library of America, 1989.

Martineau, Harriet. *Society in America.* Vol. I. New York: Saunders & Otley, 1837.

Mays, Benjamin. *Born to Rebel: An Autobiography.* New York: Scribner, 1971.

Moody, Anne. *Coming of Age in Mississippi.* New York: Dell, 1992.

Nott, Josiah C. *The Negro Race: Its Ethnology and History.* Mobile, AL: Mobile Daily Times, 1866.

Olmsted, Frederick Law. *The Cotton Kingdom: A Traveler's Observations on Cotton and Slavery in the American Slave States, 1853–1861.* New York: Da Capo Press, 1996.

Osofsky, Gilbert, ed. *Puttin' on Ole Massa: The Slave Narratives of Henry Bibb, William Wells Brown, and Solomon Northup.* New York: Harper & Row, 1969.

Owen, Robert Dale. *The Wrong of Slavery: The Right of Emancipation and the Future of the African Race in the United States.* Philadelphia: J. B. Lippincott and Co., 1864.

Paine, Thomas. *Common Sense.* New York: Penguin, 1986.

Pestré, Jean. "Bonheur." In *Encyclopédie, ou Dictionnaire raisonné des sciences des arts et des métiers.* 35 vols. Lucca, Italy: Vincenzo Giuntini, 1751–1780.

Picquet, Louisa. *The Octaroon: or Inside Views of Southern Domestic Life*. New York: No. 5 & 7 Mercer St., 1861.

Pollard, Edward A. *Black Diamonds Gathered in the Darkey Homes of the South*. New York: Negro Universities Press, 1968.

The Pro-Slavery Argument: As Maintained by the Most Distinguished Writers of the Southern States, Containing the Several Essays, on the Subject, of Chancellor Harper, Governor Hammond, Dr. Simms, and Professor Dew. Charleston, SC: Walker, Richards and Co. 1852.

Redkey, Edwin S., ed. *Respect Black: The Writings and Speeches of Henry McNeal Turner*. New York: Arno Press, 1971.

Report of the Joint Committee on Reconstruction. 39th Congress, First Session, part III. Washington, DC, 1866.

Report of the Select Committee to Inquire into the Mississippi Election of 1875 with the Testimony and Documentary Evidence. Vol. 2, 44th Congress, Second Session, Senate Report 527, part II. Washington, DC, 1876.

Robinson, William H. *From Log Cabin to the Pulpit, or, Fifteen Years in Slavery*. Eau Claire, WI: James H. Tifft, 1913.

Rousseau, Jean-Jacques. *Reveries of a Solitary Walker*. New York: Penguin, 1979.

Sawyer, George S. *Southern Institutes*. Philadelphia: J. B. Lippincott & Co., 1858.

Smith, L. M. *The Great American Crisis: Or Cause and Cure of the Rebellion*. Cincinnati, OH: Johnson, Stephens and Co., Steam Printers, 1862.

Smith, William R. *The History and Debates of the Convention of the People of Alabama, Begun and Held in the City of Montgomery, on the Seventh Day of January, 1861, in Which Is Preserved the Speeches of the Secret Sessions, and Many Valuable State Papers*. Montgomery, AL: White, Pfister & Co., 1861.

Stirling, James. *Letters from the Slave States*. New York: Negro Universities Press, 1969.

Thompson, L. S., Dr. *The Story of Mattie J. Jackson, a True Story, Written and Arranged by Dr. L. S. Thompson, as Given by Mattie*. Lawrence, MA: Sentinel Office, 1866.

Tocqueville, Alexis. *Democracy in America*. 2 vols. New York: HarperPerennial, 1988.

von Humboldt, Alexander. *Personal Narrative of Travel to the Equinoctial Regions of the New Continent, Vol. III*. London, 1818.

Washington, George. *The Papers of George Washington*. Edited by W. W. Abbot. Confederation Series, vol. 4, *2 April 1786–31 January 1787*. Charlottesville: University Press of Virginia, 1995.

Woodward, C. Vann, ed. *Mary Chesnut's Civil War*. New Haven, CT: Yale University Press, 1981.

Wright, Richard. *Black Boy*. New York: Harper Perennial Modern Classics, 2006

The Young Man's Own Book: A Manual of Politeness, Intellectual Improvement, and Moral Deportment. Philadelphia: John Locken, 1842.

INDEX

ACKNOWLEDGMENTS

Writing a book is simultaneously a lonely endeavor and a collaborative process, so while there have been tears along the way, this book is, more than anything, the product of the love and generosity of colleagues, mentors, friends, relatives, and perfect strangers. This book began as my dissertation at Harvard University, so first and foremost I am forever indebted to my advisors for their feedback and outside-of-the-box suggestions that led me to this project. This book would not exist if Vincent Brown had not insisted that I read William Reddy's *Navigation of Feeling*, though on the face Reddy's text on the French Revolution had little to do with my nascent project on slavery and relationships. Or if Walter Johnson had not suggested that reading fiction was invaluable to thinking through the emotionally fraught dynamics of slaveholding households, recommending Octavia Butler's *Kindred* and Valerie Martin's *Property*. I am grateful to Annette Gordon-Reed, for her work on how power operates in intimate spaces and relationships, for her encouragement, and for letting me bounce ideas off of her in her office or on the subway. All three of these brilliant scholars and educators challenged me to think in truly interdisciplinary ways, and this book is better for it.

During my time at Harvard many people gave me feedback, asking the thought-provoking questions that forged this project, including Amy Dru Stanley, Sven Beckert, Robin Bernstein, Stephen Berry, Nancy Cott, Henry Louis Gates, Jr., Jill Lepore, Darrin McMahon, Susan E. O'Donovan, John Stauffer, and Rachel St. John. I am grateful for all the help provided over the years by Am Civ's own miracle worker, Arthur Patton-Hock. I am also incredibly fortunate to have been surrounded by a dynamic cohort of graduate students, in Am Civ, History, and Studies of Women, Gender, and Sexuality. Thanks to George Blaustein, Sarah Carter, Emily Conroy-Krutz, Eli Cook, Maggie Gates, Sara Gebhardt, Jack Hamilton, Brian Hochman, Jamie Jones, Noam Maggor, Brian McCammack, Tim McGrath, Caitlin Rosenthal, Stephen Vider, Clinton Williams, and more for all the conversations in classrooms, in the Am Civ lounge, or the informal Am Civ lounge (the Cellar), which shaped this book in fundamental ways. I am grateful to everyone from the Nineteenth Century Colloquium group who read early drafts. Sally Mann's Massey Lectures at Harvard were the three most enriching days I had in grad school, and I am grateful to all who helped make that lecture series possible. I have turned to *Stand Still* through many a writer's block; Mann's use of language and her willingness to be open, whether at lunch with graduate students and or on the page, floor me.

I am lucky that my project got to grow and develop during my time at Tulane, where I had access to more archives and got to pick the brains of brilliant folks like Rosanne Adderley, Emily Clark, Liz McMahon, Linda Pollock, Randy Sparks, and Rebecca Tuuri. In New Orleans I found an intellectual community and an incomparable support system, in Corinna, Dev-ven, Lelia, Max, and everyone in Krewe Des Cartes. I have had continued support at Oakland University, helping me see this project through the final editing stages. I am grateful for Courtney Brannon Donoghue (always be hustling), Dan Clark, Joanie Lipson Freed, Rebecca Mercado Jones, Erin Meyers, James Naus, Allison Powell, and Liz Shesko. You have all been encouraging friends and dedicated colleagues. It has been a pleasure to be together through the births of so many books and babies.

I also want to thank the team at Penn Press, especially Lily Palladino and Robert Lockhart, their thoughtful suggestions have made me a better writer. Bob understands the project better than anyone and because of that insight, patience, and understanding, I have trusted him since the beginning.

I benefited enormously from being able to share my work with others at conferences, so I am grateful to conference organizers, audience members, and my fellow panelists who offered suggestions and encouragement, especially Mads Anders Baggesgaard, Mandy Cooper, Madeleine Dobie, Cassandra Good, Sarah Hand Meacham, Jennifer Palmer, Sasha Turner, and Michael E. Woods.

I owe a great deal to the many knowledgeable and dedicated archivists who helped me in the course of my research, especially Sean Benjamin, Leon Miller, and Eira Tansey at the Howard-Tilton Memorial Library at Tulane; Christopher Harter at the Amistad collection; and all the helpful staff at the Cammie G. Henry Research Center at Northwestern State University, the Dolph Briscoe Center at the University of Texas at Austin, the Earl K. Long Library's Louisiana and Special Collections at the University of New Orleans, the Historic New Orleans Collection, Houghton Library at Harvard University, and the Southern Historical Collection at the University of North Carolina at Chapel Hill. Special thanks to archivists and staff from the Lower

Mississippi Valley Collection at Louisiana State University who did more than point me toward useful collections: they also provided rides to hotels and bus stations when a Baton Rouge summer storm left the roads impassably flooded.

I am deeply thankful for the friends who have been with me through so much of this project, reading drafts of chapters and book proposals, and even giving me advice on writing acknowledgments. Katherine "The Captain" Stevens and I were in the trenches together, in Cambridge and in the archives. You will always be a wizard to me! The incomparable Laura Murphy has guided me through each step of the dissertation becoming a book, across years and continents, with Rian Thum on hand offering wisdom, wry comments, and dry cocktails. Ashley Howard has provided both life advice and some of the most useful writing suggestions that I use to this day as an author and as a teacher.

I would be remiss if I did not acknowledge the other incredible educators who shaped me, and led me on a path to history, at Caddo Magnet High School in Shreveport and at Tufts University, in particular Helaine Braunig, Sharon Buford, Thaddeus Pardue, Elizabeth Remick, Cathy Sledge, and Reed Ueda. I wish I could share this book with Gerald Gill, to show him how much he inspired me as a professor and as a scholar.

So many of the sources I read over the course of this project extolled the strength and revolutionary possibility of love, and I am grateful to have known such love. Thank you to my parents, Leslie and Donard Dwyer. Mom, you took us on a tour of Civil Rights Movement sites during one spring vacation in middle school: how could I have become anything other than a historian? Dad, you have been my unofficial academic advisor and my biggest cheerleader. Thank you both for all your love, patience, wisdom, advice, and humor. Lee Dwyer is the best brother a person could ask for, and he is a born editor. Thank you for always being a text or call away and for making me realize that I use punctuation like I am being paid by the comma. I am fortunate to have such supportive parent outlaws as well, in Linda and Bo Winn. A special thanks to Bo for braving Thanksgiving traffic so I could spend more time in the UNC collections. Thank you all for letting me turn so many family weddings and vacations into a chance to sneak off to another archive or historical site.

Writing about emotions is emotional work, and Roger Winn has been beside me for every step of the way. That journey has taken us from Boston, to New Orleans, to Detroit (with layovers in France, Denmark, England, and Scotland). Through the struggles and the victories, all of the adventures and all of the drafts, through quarantine and revolution, you have comforted me when I cried, made me laugh till I wept, and cheered me on. I cannot possibly count how many of the ideas contained in this volume were run by you, so thank you for being a sounding board. You have been a true partner, and for that and more I cherish you so much. I am grateful and humbled that along the way we have been joined by Beatrice Dwyer-Winn. I had only written about children in the abstract, so it is a marvel to see you already love so fiercely, facing the world with such courage, kindness, and curiosity. Above all else, you two have given me so much perspective on this thing called life.